# ETHICS AND DECISION MAKING IN COUNSELING AND PSYCHOTHERAPY

**Robert Rocco Cottone, PhD**, is a professor of counseling and family therapy at the University of Missouri–St. Louis in the Department of Counseling and Family Therapy. He earned his BA and MEd degrees at the University of Missouri–Columbia and his PhD degree at Saint Louis University. He has served on the American Counseling Association (ACA) Ethics Task Force that produced the 2005 revision of the Association's ethics code. He chaired the American Rehabilitation Counseling Association's and the Commission on Rehabilitation Counselor Certification's (CRCC's) collaborative *Code of Professional Ethics for Rehabilitation Counselors* task force for revision of the code in 2000. Dr. Cottone is a licensed professional counselor in Missouri and a licensed psychologist in Missouri and Arizona. He is a Certified Family Therapist (NCACFT). He is the author of several books, including *Paradigms of Counseling and Psychotherapy* (2012), *Toward a Positive Psychology of Religion: Belief Science in the Postmodern Era* (2010), and an earlier edition of this text, *Counseling Ethics and Decision Making* (2007). He has published extensively on matters of professional ethics and ethical decision making in counseling and psychology. He has also written extensively on advanced philosophical and theoretical issues in counseling and psychotherapy.

**Vilia Tarvydas, PhD, LMHC, CRC**, is professor emeritus and former chair of the Rehabilitation and Counselor Education Department at the University of Iowa. She was the founding director of the Institute on Disability and Rehabilitation Ethics (I-DARE), and continues her active scholarship with I-DARE. Dr. Tarvydas previously served as the president of the National Council on Rehabilitation Education, the American Rehabilitation Counseling Association, and the American Association of State Counseling Boards (AASCB). In the latter capacity, she was a member of the ACA/AASCB 20/20 Initiative Oversight Committee and developed the Delphi methodology that has guided that process in its last several years.

Dr. Tarvydas has extensive experience in ethics governance and leadership and has chaired the Iowa Board of Behavioral Science and its Disciplinary Committee, as well as the ACA and CRCC ethics committees. She also chaired the CRCC Code Revision Task Force that wrote the 2010 CRCC *Code of Professional Ethics*, and was a member of the ACA Code Revision Task Force that wrote the 2005 ACA *Code of Ethics*. Currently, she is a member of the ACA Ethics Appeals Committee. For the last 6 years, she has produced and provided an annual ethics webinar continuing education series that was jointly produced by I-DARE and CRCC, and is series editor for ethics for CRCC's new continuing education online learning initiative. She was the senior coeditor of a special 2010 joint edition of the new code for three professional journals in rehabilitation counseling: *Journal of Applied Rehabilitation Counseling, Rehabilitation Counseling Bulletin,* and *The Rehabilitation Professional.* Dr. Tarvydas has published and presented extensively on ethics, ethical decision making, and professional governance and standards. Her most recent textbooks are *Counseling Ethics and Decision Making* and *The Professional Practice of Rehabilitation Counseling.*

# ETHICS AND DECISION MAKING IN COUNSELING AND PSYCHOTHERAPY

## FOURTH EDITION

*Robert Rocco Cottone, PhD*
*Vilia Tarvydas, PhD, LMHC, CRC*

SPRINGER PUBLISHING COMPANY
NEW YORK

Springer Publishing Company, LLC
11 West 42nd Street
New York, NY 10036
www.springerpub.com

*Acquisitions Editor:* Sheri W. Sussman
*Composition:* Exeter Premedia Services Private Ltd

*ISBN:* 978-0-8261-7171-9
*e-book ISBN:* 978-0-8261-7172-6
*Instructor's Manual ISBN:* 978-0-8261-7205-1
*Test Bank ISBN:* 978-0-8261-7206-8
*PowerPoints ISBN:* 978-0-8261-7207-5

**Instructor's Materials: Qualified instructors may request supplements by e-mailing textbook@springerpub.com**

16 17 18 19 20 / 5 4 3 2 1

The author and the publisher of this Work have made every effort to use sources believed to be reliable to provide information that is accurate and compatible with the standards generally accepted at the time of publication. The author and publisher shall not be liable for any special, consequential, or exemplary damages resulting, in whole or in part, from the readers' use of, or reliance on, the information contained in this book. The publisher has no responsibility for the persistence or accuracy of URLs for external or third-party Internet websites referred to in this publication and does not guarantee that any content on such websites is, or will remain, accurate or appropriate.

**Library of Congress Cataloging-in-Publication Data**

Names: Cottone, R. Rocco, author. | Tarvydas, Vilia M., author.
Title: Ethics and decision making in counseling and psychotherapy / Robert
    Rocco Cottone and Vilia Tarvydas.
Description: Fourth edition. | New York, NY : Springer Publishing Company,
    LLC, [2016] | Preceded by Counseling ethics and decision making / R. Rocco
    Cottone, Vilia M. Tarvydas. 3rd ed. Upper Saddle River, N.J. :
    Pearson/Merrill Prentice Hall, ©2007. | Includes bibliographical
    references and index.
Identifiers: LCCN 2015043821| ISBN 9780826171719 | ISBN 9780826171726 (e-book)
Subjects: | MESH: Counseling—ethics. | Psychotherapy—ethics. | Decision
    Making—ethics. | Mental Health Services—ethics.
Classification: LCC BF637.C6 | NLM WM 21 | DDC 174/.91583—dc23
LC record available at http://lccn.loc.gov/2015043821

Printed in the United States of America by Bradford & Bigelow.

# CONTENTS

# CONTRIBUTOR

**David B. Peterson, PhD, CRC,** Licensed Clinical Psychologist, Professor, California State University, Los Angeles, California

# PREFACE

We welcome you to the new edition of *Ethics and Decision Making in Counseling and Psychotherapy*. This text is a major revision of a prior book, *Counseling Ethics and Decision Making*, providing continuity to faculty who have used the book in teaching courses on ethics in counseling. The new text is broader, providing a larger mental health professional perspective, including the professions of psychology, social work, and marriage and family therapy. The new book definitely has a focus on counseling as a profession, but the material is more widely directed at all mental health professions. We believe the new book enhances the strengths of the prior edition but addresses more broadly the mental health enterprise as practiced across professions.

The format of the book has been changed slightly. Many of the early chapters are updated versions of what appeared in earlier versions. For example, we retained chapters addressing the mental health professions, values in counseling, decision making, ethical principles, ethical standards, technology, ethical climate, and office/administrative practices. However, the chapters on specialty practice have been revised substantially. In the past, each specialty had its own chapter (e.g., mental health counseling, school counseling, rehabilitation, and addictions) and all ethical standards were addressed in the chapter with a specialty heading. In contrast, this revised edition addresses the standards within ethical topical chapter headings (e.g., confidentiality and privacy, informed consent, roles and relationships), and each specialty is addressed in a subsection within the chapter. In this way, the ethical standards are the focus, and each specialty's nuanced practices and ethical specifications are clearly outlined under the topic of the chapter. This format allows for easy comparison of an ethical standard across specialties, as for example, informed consent will be analyzed across all of the specialties and settings. We hope that it will enhance each reader's understanding of the standards and the different application of standards across different specialty practices. Also, qualified instructors are alerted to the very fine ancillaries to this book, including PowerPoint slides, a test bank, and an instructor's manual. **Requests for these ancillaries can be made by e-mail: textbook@springerpub.com.**

# ACKNOWLEDGMENTS

We are very appreciative of Springer Publishing Company and our editor, Sheri W. Sussman, for the support and encouragement we received throughout the process of producing *Ethics and Decision Making in Counseling and Psychotherapy*. This book represents a new relationship with Springer Publishing, and we are very happy and proud to be associated with the team at Springer.

We owe special thanks to the contributors to the earlier edition of this work, as their contributions have made a lasting impression on the current version. Special thanks go to Janine M. Bernard, Ronald E. Claus, Julie Hautamaki, Donna A. Henderson, Dennis Maki, Susan McGuire Breth, Barbara Wolf O'Rourke, Mark Pope, Christine Urish, and Jessica Walton. We also thank David B. Peterson for helping again with the technology chapter, as his contribution to that chapter is comprehensive. Also, a special thanks goes to Brittany Gilje Murphy, as she was assigned to assist in the development and production of this book at the University of Missouri–St. Louis. Her work was invaluable and highly appreciated. Ryan Neace also stepped in to help at the end of the production process, and his help was timely and valuable. Similarly, George Rashid at the University of Iowa made substantial editorial contributions to this text through his painstaking work, ensuring the accuracy and currency of the book. His contributions of time and talent were generous and expert.

We have learned over the years that relationships (professional, social, familial) are very important to everything that we do. This book is no exception. We are highly fortunate to be affiliated with universities that afforded us the time and resources to complete this work. At the University of Missouri–St. Louis, special thanks go to the Department of Counseling and Family Therapy (headed by Dr. Mark Pope, and including Drs. Susan Kashubeck-West, Angela Coker, Brian Hutchison, Holly Wagner, Mary Lee Nelson, and Emily Oliveira). Also, to the Cottone family, special thanks go to Rocco's wife, Molly, and to his children (Christopher, Kristina, Maria, Torre, and Cristiana) for their love, support, and patience through the process. Also, we thank the students at the University of Missouri–St. Louis who have been supportive and helpful in providing feedback and constructive criticism of the prior editions, which we embraced as we revised this version of the text.

At the University of Iowa, special appreciation is extended to faculty and colleagues in the Department of Rehabilitation and Counselor Education, in particular, our dean Nick Colangelo who has supported the ambitions and good projects of his faculty as well as modeling ethics in leadership. The special collaborative structure, scholarship, and energy of the talented ethics scholars and doctoral students affiliated with the University of Iowa Institute on Disability and Rehabilitation Ethics (I-DARE) have deepened the quality and relevance of this work. Gratitude is extended to the Tarvydas-Sauerberg family members who have been patient and loving, and have supported continued work on the scholarship in ethics despite distractions from their needs and concerns.

Finally, we the authors wish to express how grateful we are for the durable, intellectually stimulating, generous, patient, encouraging, and understanding long-term professional relationship and friendship that we have shared over the years. It has nurtured important personal and intellectual development contributing to good work, good life, and good ethics over the years.

And to our students and our readers: Thank you for allowing us the opportunity to enter your professional world through our work. You continue to inspire and motivate us. We hope this book will be a useful and thought-provoking addition to your academic and professional library.

I

# OVERVIEW OF ETHICS AND DECISION MAKING IN COUNSELING AND PSYCHOTHERAPY

# INTRODUCTION TO ETHICAL ISSUES AND DECISION MAKING IN COUNSELING AND PSYCHOTHERAPY

## OBJECTIVES

- To understand ethical terminology and define an ethical dilemma.
- To distinguish philosophical ethics and morality from professional ethics and morality.
- To distinguish professionally mandated ethics from legally mandated ethical standards.
- To explain the importance of professional organizations, especially those that define and enforce ethical standards.
- To define the terms licensure, certification, and accreditation, and identify acceptable certification and accreditation bodies in counseling, psychology, social work, and marital/family therapy.
- To explain the system of ethics governance in counseling.
- To define skills necessary to become a professional decision maker.

Aside from theory in counseling and psychotherapy, there is probably no other area of study that is more related to the everyday practice of counseling than the area of professional ethics. (The term **counseling** is used as a generic term to represent counseling and psychotherapy. Likewise, the term **counselors** is used to also include psychotherapists, regardless of their professional training.) Counselors are frequently confronted with ethical dilemmas. An **ethical dilemma is a circumstance that stymies or confuses the counselor because (a) there are competing or conflicting ethical standards that apply, (b) there is a conflict between what is ethical and moral, (c) the situation is such that complexities make application of ethical standards unclear, or (d) some other circumstance prevents a clear application of standards.** When counselors are faced with an ethical dilemma, they must be alert to ethical and legal standards. They must be educated as to what is considered acceptable and competent counseling practice. They should be educated about the ethical nuances involved in practice with special populations or in types of specialty practice. They must have a sense of their own morals and values and how those morals and values interplay with professional standards. Counselors must know how to recognize ethical dilemmas, so that they may make informed and ethical decisions. In day-to-day practice, this means counselors must, from the very beginning of each case, act in a way that is ethically sensitive.

The primary goal of this textbook is to help you to become ethically sensitive—so that you know when you face a dilemma—and, importantly, to give you direction on how to handle the dilemma in a professional way. This textbook should greatly expand your knowledge of ethics in counseling and psychotherapy. And, as a result of reading the text, you should learn ways to make ethical decisions. Practicing counselors make many decisions throughout any single day of practice. By studying decision-making processes and models, your decisional power should be enhanced. So, the intent is to give you, the reader, the knowledge to understand professional ethics and the means to make wise professional decisions when faced with an ethical challenge.

**Ethical standards are the rules that apply to any professional practice,** including counseling. Ethical standards do not arise in a vacuum. They derive from the judgments of individuals who are members of established and respected professional associations, such as the American Counseling Association (ACA), the American Psychological Association (APA), the National Association of Social Workers (NASW), and the American Association for Marriage and Family Therapy (AAMFT). These professional associations act much like the guilds of old, representing individuals of related professional interests. Not only do professional organizations provide a meeting ground for practitioners, educators, and researchers, they also play a political role in advocating for the profession. These organizations must communicate to many audiences that the represented professionals are competent, needed, and guided by standards (e.g., ethical codes) that act to minimize or to prevent harm to the individuals they serve. A profession without enforceable ethical standards is a questionable profession. Therefore, counselors must be alert to political and professional issues in counseling, psychology, and the other mental health professions.

This text focuses on ethical and professional issues in counseling, psychology, social work, and marriage/family therapy. Part I introduces ethical and professional issues, presents definitions and case-related scenarios, and introduces the reader to value issues and decision-making processes. (Two ethical decision-making models are described in detail.) Ethical principles and ethical standards are introduced and defined. Part II addresses each standard related to specialty practices in the following areas: clinical mental health, health and rehabilitation, couple and family therapy, school counseling, addictions, group counseling, career counseling, clinical supervision, and forensic practice. Part III presents current challenges in the field, including ethical climate, office and administrative practices, and technology. Finally, Part IV reviews the role of the counselor as an ethical practitioner, including the counselor's duties and responsibilities in ethically compromising circumstances. This text provides the professional counselor and psychotherapist with more than a cursory review of ethical issues; its purpose is to instill ethical responsibility through informed practice.

## DEFINING ETHICS

The terminology related to ethics is sometimes confusing because the technical definitions used by philosophers and the definitions used by the lay public and mental health professionals do not match perfectly. **Ethics in philosophy generally refers to theories about what is acceptable behavior.** When the term **philosophical ethics** is used, it implies a discussion of theory. Many theories are related to ethics, and the behaviors that are defined as "good" or "right" that derive from one theory may be quite different than those that derive from another theory. For example, Friedrich Nietzsche, a 19th-century German philosopher, developed an ethics theory of "evolutionary naturalism," wherein right and wrong result from what is naturally selected (following Darwin's theory of evolution). What is "weak" in terms of survival is not valued by a literal interpretation of Nietzsche's (1888/1968a; 1891/1968b) work. In *The Antichrist*, Nietzsche (1888/1968a) stated: "The weak and the failures shall perish. . . . And they shall even be given every possible assistance" (p. 570). Immanuel Kant's (undated/1949) "categorical imperative" stands in contrast. In his view, the decision maker must consider that the decision may become a universal standard—even applying to the decision maker. Kant's "categorical imperative" has been reduced to the golden rule—do unto others as you would have others do unto you. Consider how a person with a serious disability would view these two philosophies. By one philosophy, the disabled person would be viewed as dispensable; by the other philosophy, the person may be viewed as valuable. In some ways, what is good according to Nietzsche's theory is in conflict with Kant's. So what is right or valuable by one theory may not be right or valuable by another theory. Ethical theory ultimately directs interpretation of what is "good" or "bad." These examples demonstrate that *philosophical ethics is theoretical*. The study of philosophical ethics shows that what is defined as a "good act" clearly derives from the theoretical orientation.

In philosophy, the term **morality stands in contrast to ethics. Morality relates more to the application of ethical philosophy** than to actual specified actions. Johnson (1999) stated:

Philosophers have generally, for purposes of clarity, confined the usage of the terms morals and morality to the realm of practice. When they say that someone is morally good, they mean that the actions of that person are praiseworthy. Ethics is a term that refers not directly to practice but rather to theory. Philosophers would not ordinarily say that someone is an ethically good person, but rather a good ethicist, meaning that the person's theories about ethics are worthy of serious consideration. This difference in usage, although generally accepted in philosophical circles, is not followed by people in general. In particular, the terms ethics and ethical are often used in place of morality and moral. For instance, we commonly speak of business ethics rather than business morality and we ask of someone's action "Was that ethical?" rather than "Was that moral?" (p. 2)

So, in philosophy, when an act is in question, it is a moral question. Whether the act is considered moral depends on the ethical theory that is applied.

Outside of philosophical circles, ethics and morality are intermixed and difficult to distinguish (Johnson, 1999). This is especially true when considering the professional ethics of counselors and psychotherapists. In fact, the philosophical definitions just described almost seem at odds with the application of these terms in professional ethics. One often hears the term **professional ethics**, meaning that a practitioner is acting according to standards of practice defined as acceptable by the profession. (Remember, "actions" in philosophy were reserved for "morals.") The term "moral" often implies that a person has a firm philosophical foundation, sometimes based on religious dogma or standards. In common parlance, when one says someone has morals, it means the person is guided by higher principles. So, in common usage, the terms "ethics" and "morals" are almost used to mean the opposite of what is acceptable in the academic discipline of philosophy.

For clarity, when this text uses the term "ethics" as it applies to the discipline of philosophy, the term will be identified as **philosophical ethics**. In those cases, the discussion will center on ethics as theory (as in the case of Nietzsche or Kant). When the term **ethics** is used without the qualifier (philosophical), it is used to mean **professional ethics**. Thus, when the term ethics stands alone, the reference is to professional ethics and the actions of professionals according to standards applied by the profession. When the term morality is used to apply to the discipline of philosophy, it is identified as **philosophical morality**. When the term morality (or morals) is used without the qualifier (philosophical), it is used to mean morality in the everyday sense. So when the term morals or morality stands alone, the reference is to principles or beliefs that guide an individual, sometimes deriving from a religious standard. The definitions, then, are as follows:

- **Philosophical ethics**—the theoretical analysis of what is "good," "right," or "worthy."

- **Professionally mandated ethics or ethics**—acceptable or good practice according to agreed-upon rules or standards of practice established by a profession, as in counseling, psychology, social work, or marriage/family therapy.

- **Philosophical morality**—assessment of actions of a person against a theory in philosophical ethics. Philosophical morality always refers to an act.
- **Morality**—the principles that guide an individual, sometimes deriving from a religious standard; sometimes referred to as moral principles.

In this text, the terms ethics and morality are addressed more often than are their philosophical alternatives. This is a text on professional ethics and practice, and, although reference is made to philosophical ethics and philosophical morality, the focus is clearly on the applied practice of ethics in counseling and psychotherapy.

To further clarify the use of these terms, consider the following examples. What is ethical (even legal) practice in medicine may be immoral by certain religious standards (e.g., abortion). What is ethical in counseling practice also may be immoral by certain religious standards. For example, a fundamentalist Christian may be faced with a dilemma in counseling gay partners specifically about their sexuality. A Roman Catholic counselor may be uncomfortable providing birth control information to a teenage client. In professional practice in the United States, ethics is separated from morality at the level of professional and legal directives. Consider the situation presented in Box 1.1 to assist in exploring your moral positions. Professional and legal standards tend to correspond to what is ethical. However, individual professionals may choose not to separate the moral from the ethical; for example, some physicians may refuse to perform abortions on moral grounds.

---

## BOX 1.1  Clarification of Morals Exercise

What are your morals? As part of the self-exploration process that is critical to anticipating how you will handle ethical dilemmas, take a few minutes to define and assess some of your basic moral principles—those principles that guide you broadly in your daily life. Consider also that these moral principles may translate to specific actions as you are faced with difficult choices as a counselor. For example, what is your stand on abortion? Is it guided by a religious standard? Would you counsel someone considering an abortion? Consider another moral issue: the taking of another person's life. What is your moral stance? Is it ever justifiable to take another person's life? If you believe taking a life can be justified, under what circumstances is it justified? Under what conditions would you counsel a client who has taken someone's life in a way that you do not believe is justifiable? Consider sexual relations outside of marriage. Are they acceptable or unacceptable? Does your religion guide you on this matter? Would you "keep the secret" from a spouse while counseling a person who admits, without remorse, to an extramarital sexual relationship? Attempt to define several guiding and absolute principles that influence you in your day-to-day life. What are the foundations of these beliefs? Finally, consider circumstances that would modify your stance.

## PROFESSIONAL ETHICS VERSUS LEGALLY MANDATED ETHICS

Now that the terms ethics and morals have been clarified, a distinction also must be drawn between what is considered **"professional" ethics** and **"legally mandated" ethics**. In the United States, professionals such as counselors or psychotherapists are directed and bound by the ethical standards of the professional organization or organizations to which they belong. Most counselors are members of the ACA. Psychologists will likely have membership in the APA. The NASW represents social workers and has a code of ethics. Likewise, marriage/family therapists align with, and follow the ethical dictates of, the AAMFT. The ACA, the APA, the NASW, and the AAMFT are professional organizations that provide a forum for counselors and psychotherapists to address their educational, professional, and personal needs. Both the ACA and the APA have divisions devoted to specialty interests. For example, two divisions of the ACA are the American Rehabilitation Counseling Association (ARCA) and the National Career Development Association (NCDA). Rehabilitation counselors and career counselors attend the ACA conference and also attend meetings and professional presentations sponsored by their respective specialty groups. The APA is similar—divisions of the association (e.g., counseling psychology, rehabilitation psychology, family psychology) organize activities and presentations for the national APA conference. The NASW has specialty interest sections that also organize activities and training in specialty practice areas. The AAMFT currently does not have specialty practice divisions. The ACA, APA, NASW, and AAMFT also make malpractice and other types of personal insurance available to members. Additionally, the professional organizations have established professional standards through committees that oversee ethical rules (including disciplinary procedures) and practice. The codes of ethics of the professional organizations can be viewed at the following websites:

| | |
|---|---|
| American Counseling Association: | www.counseling.org/knowledge-center/ethics |
| American Psychological Association: | www.apa.org/ethics/code/index.aspx |
| National Association of Social Workers: | http://socialworkers.org/pubs/code/code.asp |
| American Association for Marriage and Family Therapy: | http://aamft.org/iMIS15/AAMFT/Content/Legal_Ethics/Code_of_Ethics.aspx |

An organization's code of ethics directs members who are faced with an ethical concern or ethical dilemma. Such a circumstance requires the professional to decide if an action is right or wrong (before or at the time of the act) when competing or mutually exclusive ethical, moral, or legal standards are involved. (Remember the definition of an ethical dilemma discussed in the first paragraph of this chapter.) It is possible that competing standards of right and wrong may be at the root of an ethical dilemma. The codes of the major professional organizations, such as the ACA, APA, NASW, and AAMFT, are considered *professional* (as opposed to legal) ethical standards.

Counselors, psychologists, social workers, and marriage/family therapists are licensed to practice in individual states. Licensees are also directed by the ethical code referenced in the relevant state's licensure statute or the specific disciplinary rules that the licensure board adopts. In fact, one of the main reasons for the licensure of professions (especially the mental health professions) is to protect the public from unqualified or unethical practitioners. Counselors or psychotherapists who act unethically, as judged by a licensure authority according to the authority's accepted standards, are subject to penalties as severe as suspension or revocation of a professional license. **Licensure allows a person to practice a profession and prevents the practice of a profession by those who are unlicensed** (Anderson, 1996; Dorken, 1976). **Revocation of a license, therefore, is a loss of the right to practice in the state's jurisdiction. Suspension of a license is a temporary loss of the right to practice the profession within the jurisdiction.** Licenses are not easy to attain. To be licensed as a professional counselor, social worker, or marriage/family therapist in most states requires a master's degree with one or more years of supervised professional (postdegree) practice; licensure candidates must also pass a stringent examination in their respective profession. The standards in psychology are similar, except a doctoral degree is required. Consequently, the prospect of losing a professional license means the loss of a livelihood. Whereas a breach of the code of ethics of a professional organization (such as the ACA, APA, NASW, or AAMFT) can result in professional censure or even loss of membership, the breach of an ethical standard required by regulatory law (legally mandated, for example, by a licensure statute) may result in the loss of a license to practice and/or other legal penalty. The distinction, therefore, between "professional" and "legally mandated" ethical standards is a crucial one.

**Legally mandated ethics** are ethics defined by laws that require one to act in a certain manner as set forth by state or federal legislatures, boards, or departments, or as set forth in the case law opinions of judges (Wheeler & Bertram, 2015); legally mandated ethics requires one to act according to applicable laws, especially as they pertain to those in the helping professions.

In some cases, state licensure statutes or regulations simply reference the professional association's code of ethics. States may develop their own standards, but ethical standards in licensure statutes are usually similar to (or based in large part on) those of the professional association. In counseling, for example, the American Association of State Counseling Boards (AASCB) provides guidance to individual state licensure boards on matters related to ethical standards and enforcement. Members of the AASCB are representatives from state licensure boards. In other words, it is the professional association for the state licensure boards and the members of those boards. This organization works to improve the technical proficiency of these regulatory licensure boards and to enhance the consistency of standards in licensing counselors among all states. It also addresses issues of **reciprocity of licensure**, or what is called **portability** (Altekruse, 2001). **Licensing reciprocity is a process whereby a licensed counselor's credentials in one state are recognized by another state for licensure purposes without additional imposed requirements.** In psychology, the Association of State and Provincial Psychology Boards (ASPPB), a group made up of state psychology licensing board representatives, has its own code of ethics. (See Sinclair [2004] for a comparison of the ASPPB code of conduct and the APA and Canadian Psychological Association codes of ethics.) The ASPPB has also set up a credential bank for individuals who meet quality licensure standards to facilitate reciprocity between states—the Certificate of Professional Qualification (CPQ) in psychology. The CPQ is accepted by many states as a credential that meets licensure standards. In social work, the Association of Social Work Boards serves the same purpose as the AASCB and the ASPPB, and the Association of Marital and Family Therapy Regulatory Boards represents the state marriage/family therapy licensure boards. These important license-related organizations influence the ethical and professional training standards required for individuals to be admitted and retained in the professions.

Mental health professionals need to know both the professional and legal ethical standards that direct their practices. Professionals are obligated to know these standards beyond the knowledge gained by a cursory reading of a code. Counselors should commit to memory the general principles that operate in ethical practice, and they should regularly discuss with other counselors or psychotherapists how such principles apply to professional practice. (See Box 1.2 for a statement made by a counselor who volunteered to share his own experience related to a serious breach of professional ethics.) Chapter 6 will be helpful in describing **ethical standards (the rules of ethical practice)**, because it provides a summary of ethical issues and describes **ethical principles (broad philosophical guidelines,** defined in Chapter 5) that are associated with specific ethical standards. Chapters in Part II provide case scenarios with practice-relevant contexts for understanding the ethical standards.

---

### BOX 1.2  Ethical Errors: Serious and Painful—A Letter From a Counselor Accused of Serious Ethical Misconduct

I remember the day all too well. It was the worst day of my professional life. "My God! What have I done?" Panic surged through my body. My mind raced with worry on the day my boss confronted me with my worst nightmare. He informed me that a former client of mine had accused me of the most serious of ethical violations. Specifically, I was being accused of having a detrimental relationship with this client—a sexual relationship. My boss had tears in his eyes as if he was saying, "Please tell me it isn't true." But, I could not deny the truth. I had been denying the truth for 10 months. It was time to come clean and try to salvage what little integrity I had left. This is my story. It is serious and extraordinarily painful. I hurt many people. My behavior was completely irresponsible. I have lived through it, and I keep what I did in front of me as a teaching tool. I can never forget what I did, or I may become vulnerable again. It doesn't really

(continued)

## BOX 1.2  Ethical Errors: Serious and Painful—A Letter From a Counselor Accused of Serious Ethical Misconduct (*continued*)

matter what is known intellectually about ethical errors. Anyone can read and understand that there are certain things that must not be done, and there are many gray areas as well. But what happens when the human, vulnerable side surfaces? What happens when buttons get pushed and countertransference issues arise? I hope what happens is that the truth is faced, that a boss or trusted colleague is consulted, or that personal counseling is undertaken. I didn't face the truth. As a result, I had to talk to a lawyer, to an ethics committee, and to my insurance company. I lost my job, my license, and lots of money. This was certainly an expensive lesson. What I did was wrong. My punishment was deserved.

What I gained from this ordeal was something very important: I gained myself. I'm sure most students of counseling and most practicing professionals have heard the many reasons why people pursue counseling professionally, including meeting one's own personal needs. This was certainly true for me. My need was to be needed. Therefore, I've been vulnerable to needy clients. When clients were hurting, I wanted to rescue and take care of them. I knew this prior to acting out, but I didn't know how strong this need was and how I could lose myself and my professional boundaries.

One of the many ironies is that I could see what was happening. I remember reviewing the ethical guidelines concerning potentially detrimental relationships. I even informed my spouse that I was attracted to a client prior to acting out. But I was blinded by needs. I needed help, but was ashamed to ask for it. My denial took over and deception began. I held this shameful secret inside. My strong word of caution: Don't keep secrets. Secrets have powerful and destructive energy.

All counselors will be faced with ethical dilemmas throughout their careers. There are no simple answers and no complete guidebook to inform how to respond to the many difficult and ambiguous situations. Experience is a great teacher, but it cannot help with every possible concern. Furthermore, experience often teaches the hard way, by giving the test first, followed by the lesson.

There is little guidance to help those who have been cited for ethical misconduct or legal wrongdoing. A legal specialist for psychologists and counselors informed me that approximately 50% of mental health professionals will face some ethical or legal hardship during the course of their careers. How does one prepare for this behaviorally and emotionally? It is all too easy to say, "Just don't make any ethical mistakes." This statement is unrealistic and naive. Like shadows, mistakes lurk in the darkness and catch a person off guard, when one is most vulnerable.

If for some reason you are accused of some wrongdoing, whether you are guilty or not, it will most likely shock your system. Be prepared for an emotional roller coaster. Get help, but be cautious. Get a lawyer if necessary; inform your insurance company if your lawyer recommends that you do so (make sure you carry insurance); and be careful about what you tell friends, family, and colleagues. By all means, talk to a therapist if you are personally struggling.

(continued)

### BOX 1.2  Ethical Errors: Serious and Painful—A Letter From a Counselor Accused of Serious Ethical Misconduct (continued)

I experienced a plethora of emotions. That dear old question, "How did it make you feel?" certainly became real for me. I was angry at my client, at first, for turning me in; after all, my client was a willing participant who encouraged my involvement. My denial was still strong for the only person I should have been angry at—myself. A client places a counselor in an authority position whether welcomed or not. I abused my position. I should have been angry at myself for allowing this to happen.

Once I was able to accept complete responsibility for what I did, I could begin to grieve. Those were extraordinarily tough days. I had to endure many losses. I experienced many days of depression. For months I was completely ashamed of myself as a human being and could not imagine ever counseling again. Eventually, I realized that although I did a terrible thing, I was not a terrible person. I was a counselor who let personal issues get in the way of my professional responsibilities. Today I am very remorseful for what I did, and I am fortunate that I received a great deal of support when I began to tell the truth.

Not all people forgave me for what I did, and I understand this. I am very sorry for my behavior and I wish I could make amends to all those who suffered. I have developed many resources to help me personally, especially when I'm feeling stressed and overwhelmed, and I use my resources rather than just talk about them. I encourage all counselors to do the same. My resources are personal therapy, a 12-step program, my spouse, and a personal accountability program. It is very easy for counselors to talk and to listen, but more difficult for them to do their own personal work. Frankly, I believe that many counselors are compulsive about their jobs while neglecting themselves personally. Regardless, counselors owe it to their clients, to their profession, to their families, and most of all, to themselves, to take care of themselves.

Well, that is my story. I wouldn't wish it upon anyone. I have to live with myself every day knowing what I did. Sometimes it is very difficult and painful for me. But it is important for me to keep my pain and my story in front of me. I need to remind myself of what I did so I can prevent myself from ever doing it again. Mistakes are best prevented by taking an honest accounting of one's life and one's situation. Be alert to "red flags," and consult supervisors, colleagues, friends, or a therapist if personal needs begin to blind you to your professional responsibilities.

I wish you well on your journey.

## ETHICS GOVERNANCE[1]

Methods to govern ethical practice are necessary to give meaning to professional standards and to enhance the societal stature of the profession. Since counselors are professionals and have professional responsibility, they are subject to

---

[1] This section is adapted from Tarvydas (2012). Copyright 2012 by Springer Publishing Company. Used by permission of Springer Publishing Company.

discipline if they breach ethical standards. The process of ethical governance is intimately linked to the process of professional discipline. If counselors do not practice within the prescribed standards, ethical governance processes may be engaged to discipline them. Ethical standards of practice can be thought of as being either **mandatory** or **aspirational** in the level of direction they provide the practitioner (Corey, Corey, Corey, & Callanan, 2014). The most basic level of ethical functioning is guided by **mandatory ethics, wherein individuals focus on compliance with the law and the dictates of the professional codes of ethics that apply to their practice.** At this level, counselors are concerned with remaining safe from legal action and professional censure. At the more ethically sophisticated level, the aspirational level, individuals additionally reflect on the effects of the situation on the welfare of their clients and the effects of their actions on the profession as a whole. **Aspirational ethics define ideal practice but may not provide specific directives for action.**

These same concepts of mandatory and aspirational ethics can be applied to counseling's standards of practice. It is important to reiterate that specific codes of ethics are binding only on persons who hold that particular credential or membership. If a credential holder or a member of a professional group violates an applicable code of ethics, the organization has the responsibility to provide a disciplinary procedure to enforce its standards. In the case of a professional association, the ultimate sanction would typically be loss of membership, with possible referral of the findings of an ethics committee to other professional or legal jurisdictions. This referral may be accomplished by providing information to the AASCB or the ASPPB for dissemination to member licensing boards or directly to the professional's licensure or certification board. For a credentialing body such as the National Board for Certified Counselors (NBCC), the largest certifying body for professional counselors, or for a counselor licensure board in one of the licensing states, violators could face the more serious option of certificate or license revocation, thus possibly removing their ability to practice. Less serious levels of sanction, such as a reprimand or a period of probation, are also utilized. In the case of a reprimand or probation, there is often an additional requirement for educational or rehabilitative remedies, meaning the sanctioned counselor must take an educational course on ethics, treat an addiction, be further supervised in practice, or follow other remedies to assist in regaining an appropriate level of functioning ethically and/or personally. The assessment of the level of seriousness of the ethical violation will affect the actual choice of sanction once an individual is found to be in violation of the code of ethics. Factors often considered include whether the act was intentional, the degree of risk or actual harm to the client, the motivation or ability of the violator to change, and the recidivism of the violator (Johnston, Tarvydas, & Butler, 2016; Koocher & Keith-Spiegel, 1998).

Responsible practitioners supplement the mandatory level of ethics awareness with advanced knowledge of the scholarly literature on accepted ethical practice. They also consult colleagues who may have experience addressing challenging ethical circumstances and who are respected in the community as ethically wise practitioners. In addition, they may gain guidance from other codes of ethics and specialty guidelines. Sophisticated practitioners will seek these sources to supplement the required mandatory ethical standards with the more aspirational principles. In fact, for certain situations, the course of action suggested by the aspirational guidelines may contradict or exceed those required by mandatory standards. Such situations create stressful ethical dilemmas and place practitioners in need of means to reconcile them responsibly (see Chapter 4 on decision-making processes for further guidance on making ethical decisions when involved in ethical dilemmas).

There are several levels of ethics governance for counselors, and various organizations are involved at different levels. These organizations, taken as a whole, constitute an interconnected network that performs a diversity of functions. Each entity plays a role in the creation of a system of ethics governance.

Colleges and universities provide professional education and research services. Professional programs at universities or colleges in counseling, psychology, social work, or marriage/family therapy usually operate under the review of professional accrediting organizations. **Accreditation** allows for clear recognition of a program (its nature, intent, and quality). The accreditation review process is a means to certify that the school program meets standards set by the accrediting body. **Professional accreditation is the process whereby a college or university professional program (e.g., counseling, psychology, social work, marriage/family therapy) voluntarily undergoes review by an accrediting body.** Mental health professional accrediting bodies include the Commission on Rehabilitation Education (CORE, for rehabilitation counselor education programs and is now affiliated with the next organization, CACREP), the Commission on the Accreditation of Counseling and Related Educational Programs (CACREP, for counselor education programs), the APA Commission on Accreditation (CoA, for psychology education programs), the Council on Social Work Education (CSWE, for social work education programs), and the AAMFT's Commission on Accreditation for Marriage and Family Therapy Education (COAMFTE, for marriage/family therapy education programs). CORE, CACREP, the APA CoA, CSWE, and COAMFTE are **professional accrediting bodies** that evaluate graduate education programs in rehabilitation counseling, counseling, psychology, social work, and marriage/family therapy, respectively. Professional accrediting bodies essentially qualify educational programs as meeting standards beyond those required of colleges or universities to offer degrees; they certify that the educational institution meets these high professional standards. Professional accrediting bodies have the broadest function to provide aspirational educational guidance in ethics. They help to establish the structural foundation for ethical governance. Additionally, they help to build the theoretical and research base for understanding ethical issues, decision-making processes, and ethical educational methods. These aspects of the aspirational knowledge base are needed to support the ethical development of a profession. Colleges and universities also ensure that proper preservice education and professional socialization occur to inculcate future practitioners and educators with the proper ethics base. Educators play an important part in role modeling and supporting ethical analysis and ethical behavior in teaching, supervision, and actual clinical practice. Educational institutions also serve as a resource to other professional organizations and regulatory bodies to provide teaching, research, and service that support aspirational and mandatory ethical practice.

Another level is composed of the professional organizations with aspirational codes of ethics but with no internal mandatory enforcement mechanisms. The International Association of Marriage and Family Counselors (IAMFC) and the Association for Specialists in Group Work (ASGW), as divisions of the ACA, are examples. For such organizations, the primary task is to encourage aspirational ethical practice of their members and the application of ethical standards in specific specialty contexts. Mandatory enforcement is not undertaken by such professional organizations due to factors such as: (a) the lack of access to, and by, consumers for protecting the consumer to discipline the unethical profession; (b) the absence of appropriate remedies for serious infractions; and (c) the lack of substantial financial, staff, and professional resources necessary for responsible enforcement. In some cases, the mandatory enforcement function of the organization is referred to a parent organization (e.g., to ACA in the case of the IAMFC or the ASGW) or the complainant is referred to another appropriate jurisdiction (e.g., a state licensure board) to initiate a disciplinary process.

Nonetheless, professional organizations with aspirational codes perform several significant functions within the ethics governance structure. They typically provide their members with supplemental codes of ethics that extend and illuminate other, more general codes. Such documents provide guidelines for ethical practice for particular, frequently encountered ethical issues or professional activities. For couple and family counselors such issues might be (a) confidentiality issues when more than one person is seen in counseling, (b) different modes of service delivery, (c) value issues, such as handling discussion of divorce or dissolution of a marriage, and (d) the responsibility to "relationships" rather than one individual in counseling. A supplemental code may take the form of guidelines for practice that address specialty setting or function-specific issues, as is done by the IAMFC, a division of the ACA. The IAMFC (Hendricks, Bradley, Southern, Oliver, & Birdsall, 2011) has an aspirational ethics code, which gives guidance to couple and family counselors. In addition to maintaining supplementary, specialty ethical standards or guidelines, some professional organizations at the aspirational level collect information regarding ethical trends and needs for revision of either the specialty or generalist ethics codes. Their leaders also participate in revision and writing of both types of codes. These organizations identify and supply qualified professionals to serve on the various mandatory enforcement bodies. They provide educational programs to extend the knowledge base and to define better quality ethical practice, performing significant educational and socialization functions. A new and innovative role for these organizations, one that is potentially most meaningful, is identifying or providing remediation or rehabilitation programs for impaired professionals who have been found in violation (or are at risk for violation) of ethical standards.

Another level of ethical governance is that of professional organizations that maintain and enforce a mandatory code of ethics (such as the ACA, APA, NASW, and AAMFT). These organizations provide an entry-level mandatory code and enforcement process for their members and, in the case of the ACA,

APA, and NASW, enforce the standards or guidelines of their respective divisions (specialty or special interest groups). Organizations at this level consult with certification and licensing bodies and the specialty professional organizations to ensure active participation of all parties in ethics enforcement. They also provide educational programs to increase practitioner knowledge.

In addition, a level of ethics governance includes professional regulatory bodies that either certify or license professionals, and those that constitute the preeminent enforcers of a mandatory code (see Box 1.3). **Certification** indicates that the professional has met those standards that are expected by the profession (NBCC, 2015). National certification bodies, such as the NBCC, the Commission on Rehabilitation Counselor Certification (CRCC), the American Board of Professional Psychology (ABPP), and the NASW (which provides certificates for members meeting certain standards) as well as state counseling, psychology, social work, and marriage/family therapy licensure boards, operate at this level. They perform a pivotal role in the promulgation and enforcement of ethical standards. They do not develop completely novel internal standards; rather, they draw their specific codes of ethical standards from the organizations that constitute the professional body or their constituent counseling communities, and then regulate based on the profession's own internal standards. They also may provide information and consultation to professional organizations in revising and maintaining current codes of ethics. Beyond their ethical regulatory function, these bodies encourage ethical proficiency of their licensees and certificate holders by requiring graduate degree program education and continuing (postgraduate) education, often in the area of ethics.

The courts are the pinnacle of the ethics governance hierarchy. One of the primary mechanisms for this type of governance is adjudication of **malpractice** in the civil courts. **In malpractice actions, establishing a violation of duty is**

---

## BOX 1.3 Ethics Governance and One State's Standard

To consider ethics governance related to mandatory licensure standards, consider a State of Missouri dictate that addresses sexual intimacies with clients. The ethics code referenced in the rules and regulations of the Missouri State Committee for Professional Counselors has a stipulation that bans "sexual intimacies" with clients. The standard, however, defines "sexual intimacies" very broadly, including sexual intercourse and sodomy, of course, but also including "hugging or caressing by either the licensed professional counselor or the client" or "touching" a person's "legs, stomach, chest, breasts, genitals or buttocks." Has the Missouri dictate gone too far, or is it right on target? If a counselor touches someone's knee, should that be considered unethical? How about a hug abruptly initiated by a client leaving the office—is that unethical? How about a counselor hugging a distressed child in a school context? Remember, this is a mandatory standard, and a person's license is at risk if there is a breach of ethical standards.

**one of the central points.** The standard for determining what constitutes "good professional practice," as applied to the matter at hand, is required. "Good professional practice" is sometimes hard to define and requires many types of considerations. It is not unusual to call various expert witnesses to testify regarding such practices. Additionally, one party to the action might attempt to establish that a blatant violation of the general rules of the profession occurred by reference to the profession's ethical standards (Thompson, 1990; Wheeler & Bertram, 2015).

Another standard of practice applied in court may be consideration of whether the action or service in question was within the **scope of practice** of both the profession and the practitioner; **scope of practice is the extent and limits of activities considered "acceptable" by individuals licensed or certified in a profession or specialty.** "Scope of practice" is the term used to describe specific activities, and the limits of activities, that a professional can perform as part of professional practice. For example, it is in the scope of practice of a licensed physician to do surgery and to prescribe medications. Importantly, even though all physicians are licensed to do surgery (it is within the profession's scope of practice), it would be unethical for a physician who has no personal training in surgery to do specialized surgical procedures—it is not within the *individual* physician's scope of practice. So when scope of practice is addressed, it must be clear whether the profession's or the individual professional's scope of practice is in question. A physician doing brain surgery who has never performed or been trained in brain surgery would be acting outside of his or her personal scope of practice, even though he or she might be licensed to do surgery. State licensed counselors, psychologists, social workers, and marriage/family therapists are governed by the scope of practice described in state statutes, and licensees may be required to declare their personal scopes of practice or their limits of training at the time they are licensed or when renewing a license (e.g., school counseling, clinical psychology). Practitioners are ethically bound to limit their own scopes of practice to areas within those of the profession and in specialties within which they have obtained appropriate training and supervision. For example, a licensed counselor primarily trained in school counseling should not be doing marriage/family therapy, unless additional education and supervision have been obtained. Counselors and psychotherapists must be able to demonstrate that they are competent to practice by virtue of appropriate education, supervision, and professional experience, and they must practice within the scope of their professional license.

This overall description of the professional governance structure shows that it constitutes a network of mandatory and aspirational ethics. An interactive system of research, education, and enforcement shapes and regulates the ethical practice of counselors. This structure provides a system of knowledge, traditions, rules, and laws, but does not provide practitioners with possibly the most crucial tool for ethical practice—knowledge and experience in applying their ethical decisions.

Although professionals may sometimes become caught up in the technicalities of ethics governance, it is important to keep in mind that preventing harm to others and benefiting them through a professional relationship is the primary purpose of professional ethics. It is crucial to keep the client's welfare in mind. Box 1.4 is a statement by a former client of a psychologist who breached the client–psychologist sexual relationship ban of his profession. The statement was volunteered by the victim and is published with her full permission. It is disguised to prevent identification, but is a true account of her feelings through the process of her personal relationship with the psychologist.

---

### BOX 1.4  A Client's Story

For about a year, I sat "in the chair," trying to understand what had brought me to therapy. Across from me sat my therapist, my confidant, my partner in piecing together the puzzle that had become my life. I began by explaining that I was hurting inside because of the young woman I had become. I felt angry, defensive, alone. I had detached myself from all those who were dear to me, except for my family. They, however, were kept at arm's length. My temper had become short and my list of reasons for not going out with my friends had become long. I was confused by these changes in myself because I was unable to identify the source. I was sad about the changes because I did not like living such a negative, un-peopled existence. This existence was nothing like what I had lived the previous 22 years.

The day I realized why I was "in the chair" remains etched vividly in my mind. With bowed head and long curls hiding my face, I choked out the words with humiliation, shame, fear, and pain: I was raped. I told the therapist the story from the beginning—a story which began as one of friendship, laughter, and fun. Then I recounted how suddenly, without warning, the man I had chosen to call friend turned into someone I no longer knew. I told of the day he hovered above my head with eyes full of hate as he spoke with venom, and how because of shock and fear, I could not move. He hurt me with his body and he hurt me with his words. I described how it seemed like hours later, that he dropped me off in front of my apartment. It was at that time that he grabbed the back of my head once again, pressed his mouth angrily onto mine and told me he'd like to do that again sometime—that it was fun.

The pain I went through by finally acknowledging the rape was deep. Making sense of how it had affected my life forced me to open myself up to feel all that the experience was for me. I told the therapist that I felt robbed. I was robbed of my virginity and robbed of my innocence. Perhaps most critical, however, was that I felt I was robbed of my confidence. I felt I could no longer judge who or what was safe. This rapist had been my friend for months. I had gone willingly to his apartment. I completely trusted the boundary I felt existed between us. Then he raped me. Then, he acted like it wasn't rape. Instead, he acted as if I had an equal role in creating what had happened.

My sense of industry and self-power was badly shaken. I trudged through it all with the therapist. He was the only one who knew my secret and as such, I funneled my only bit of trust into the therapeutic relationship. As I worked through the details of the rape, I began focusing on self and my interaction with others. In an attempt to learn to trust again but this time with wisdom, I opened my life completely to the therapist. I chiseled away at the walls that I had built as a means of protection.

(continued)

## BOX 1.4  A Client's Story (*continued*)

After several years of being in and out of therapy with this man, in one session, he said he'd like to have a beer with me. At this point, I trusted him implicitly. He had validated my feelings through the therapeutic relationship and I felt very connected to him. I agreed to have a beer with him. A decision could not be made as to where we would go that next week, so he suggested we just meet in his office. The following week, he brought a six pack of beer and I "sat in the chair." I remember feeling drawn to him on some level. I think the connection was so strong for me because of the work we had done together in therapy. He had become the only man I trusted aside from those in my family. On another level, I knew it was wrong for me to have a beer with my therapist. I also felt it was wrong for me to feel an attraction to him.

I continued seeing him therapeutically after that, but there was no more alcohol involved. After several months, I terminated the therapeutic relationship for good. I felt I was ready to build healthy relationships without being too fearful of making a decision that was unsafe or wrong for me.

Several years later, I wrote my then ex-therapist a note explaining my marriage was ending. After getting the note, my ex-therapist called and asked me to go get a beer. Again, the decision was made to meet at his office. Again, he brought the beer. Again, I sat "in the chair." After catching up for several hours, it was time to go. We stood up and hugged one another, which we had never done before. After a few minutes, he looked down on me and kissed me. The embrace became very sexual very quickly. As his hands moved to places previously associated with pain, I was not sure how to respond. I was certainly shocked and a little scared that he was touching me in this way. I kept my arms around his waist, not touching him in a sexual way. In addition to feeling shocked and a bit scared, because of my past, I also wanted so desperately for someone I trusted to touch me in a loving way that was full of care and tenderness. Based upon the words he whispered in my ear, it seemed he wanted to show me what tender, loving touch was like. I did not stop him from touching me. I was a willing participant, but also felt uneasy for I knew it was wrong for both of us to be doing.

I could not sleep that night. I was so full of self-condemnation—it horrified me to consider what my loved ones would think if they knew I had engaged in this type of relationship with my ex-therapist. For days afterward, when it entered my mind, a chill ran through my body. I was shocked that it had even happened.

After a few weeks, he called again. This time, he would come to my apartment. His visits became weekly. By this time, we were in a mutually sexual relationship. I could hardly fathom the fact that my ex-therapist and I were touching one another in a sexual way. It seemed the more he needed to be with me, the less comfortable I felt with what was happening. It seemed strange inside to think that the person I had needed for so long in therapy could somehow need something from me.

Several times, I expressed my difficulty with the situation and that I felt it wasn't right. His response at those times was related to us both being adults and it said

(continued)

**BOX 1.4  A Client's Story (*continued*)**

implicitly that we were making the choice to be there with one another. As his comfort level began to increase as the relationship wore on, he began to speak his mind and act more freely. My unease became increasingly worse. Eventually, there were times when he touched me in a way that was painful, and he spoke to me in language that was crude. None of this felt loving. When I continued to bring up my uneasiness, he continued to tell me that we were adults. At this point, he was clearly no longer validating my experience. It was like I was not allowed to discuss this with him. The power differential was still present, despite the fact that the therapeutic relationship had ended. I couldn't help but feel that if I had received these types of responses from a man other than my ex-therapist, my response or action would have been much different.

I finally recognized the physical and emotional pain I was in due to this relationship. I ended my involvement with my ex-therapist and was overwhelmed by the fall-out. I felt angry, defensive, alone. I had detached myself from other individuals who were dear to me. I was ashamed, humiliated, full of guilt, and full of pain. Perhaps most importantly, however, was that my sense of being able to judge who or what was safe for myself was shaken. This man had been my therapist. I had trusted him for years. I completely trusted the boundary I thought existed between us. In this case, it was a trust that I was safe from harm with him. I don't think he intended to hurt me, but his involvement with me reinjured me related to my original therapeutic issues.

## DECISION-MAKING SKILLS

Professional counselors have advanced degrees and are highly educated professionals. An important aspect of professionalism is exercising excellent ethical decision making, and so professional counselors must be well trained in decision-making skills.

In practice, counselors face life-relevant situations, and each decision must be made in a way that will maximize the benefit to clients while minimizing potential harm. In effect, counselors must be viewed as "intellectuals"—individuals who apply higher level knowledge to solve complex human problems. At the foundation of decision making is an intellectual attitude. Counselors must believe that they can make educated and informed decisions in a systematic and deliberate way.

To make wise decisions, counselors must have information that is relevant to making such decisions. To gain such information, counselors must have good research skills, be able to define the critical issues, and to search for up-to-date information related to the decision to be made. Professional organizations typically publish journals so that practitioners have current information on contemporary approaches to practice. Professional journals are a source of information about what is currently accepted as ethical practice, and oftentimes professional journals have sections that specifically address ethical issues and how dilemmas should be best approached by practicing professionals.

Counselors and psychotherapists must also have a framework for making ethical decisions. One of the themes of this book is that decision making and daily practice go hand in hand. Competent professionals are competent decision makers. One must always consider that a professional decision can be challenged, and, as a professional, one must always be able to defend a decision. If an accepted decision-making model was used to make the decision, and a counselor can demonstrate adherence to an accepted process of decision making, then it becomes much easier to defend the decision. On the other hand, hodgepodge practice, or practice without a framework or theory to guide decisions, is indefensible. Counselors should embrace a well-respected decision-making model, and they should use the model regularly until it becomes routine. Decision-making models can become habitual and effortless—where decision making is committed to memory. In this way, practicing an acceptable decision-making model becomes second nature.

Counselors also must be invested in their profession. This means they respect the profession and choose to associate with colleagues through professional organizations. They, in other words, must embrace professionalism and work for the benefit of their clients and the profession. This investment means accepting, to a large degree, the ethical dictates of the profession. Not all ethical standards may be viewed as fair—there may be some standards that are ill-conceived or out of date—but counselors must be willing to adhere to the ethical standards of the profession, and when standards need to be changed, they need to become active in facilitating the change. Professional status is an honor, but it is also a responsibility.

## CONCLUSION

Knowledge of professional ethics is crucial to the everyday practice of counseling and psychotherapy. Counselors who are faced with an ethical dilemma must be alert to ethical and legal standards. Professional organizations provide standards and codes that guide mental health professionals.

Philosophical ethics is the theoretical analysis of what is good, right, or worthy. The concept of professional ethics refers to what is acceptable or good practice according to agreed-on rules or standards of practice established by a profession. Philosophical morality is the assessment of actions of a person against a theory in philosophical ethics and always refers to an act. Morality refers to the principles that guide an individual and often derive from a religious standard.

Licensure allows a person to practice a profession and prevents the practice of a profession by those who are unlicensed. Licenses can be revoked or suspended for violation of codes of ethics.

The professional structure governing ethics for counselors and psychotherapists includes: (a) colleges/universities; (b) professional organizations with aspirational codes of ethics but without internal enforcement mechanisms;

(c) professional organizations that maintain and enforce a mandatory code of ethics; (d) professional certification and licensure bodies that enforce mandatory codes; and (e) the courts.

Finally, decision making is a cornerstone of professionalism. Counselors must be viewed, and must view themselves, as intellectuals—highly educated problem solvers. They must have a higher level understanding of the complexities involved in solving human problems. They must seek out current information related to practical dilemmas that arise. They must be guided by ethical decision-making models that become habitual and ingrained in their daily practice. They must also invest in their profession and be actively engaged in professional activities that better the profession and those served by the profession.

# THE MENTAL HEALTH PROFESSIONS AND COUNSELING SPECIALTIES

## OBJECTIVES

- To provide a brief history of the counseling profession.
- To distinguish counseling from psychology and the other mental health professions.
- To summarize education requirements, postdegree training, licensure, certification, and scope of practice for the mental health professions.

Membership in a "profession" offers an individual status and responsibility. Law and medicine, both considered models of professionalism, are founded on a body of knowledge, technique, and practice. They are grounded in academic studies, have a scholarly base, and provide guidance to practitioners in the form of ethical and moral standards (e.g., medicine's Hippocratic oath). They allow practitioners several avenues of practice, even independent or freestanding practice. Over time, social work, marriage/family therapy, psychology, and counseling have become established as independent professions, technically on par with established professions such as medicine and law. To present oneself as a counselor or psychotherapist means that one has accomplished much—graduate education, postgraduate training, admission to a profession by competitive examination, and linkage to a professional community with strict ethical standards. There is pride in such accomplishment.

Today, there are a number of competitive mental health professions, each with its own history and traditions. It is important for any practicing mental health professional to be alert to the mental health professions and the standards of each. Medicine's specialty of psychiatry is the oldest established mental health profession. The youngest, in terms of pervasive legislative support, is marriage and family therapy. Social work and psychiatric nursing are two other mental health professions. Counseling, social work, marriage/family therapy, psychiatry, psychiatric nursing, and psychology professionals make up the core of mental health providers.

In the mental health service arena, the core mental health professions both compete and cooperate. Within all types of practice, it is likely that counselors will work with other mental health professions in the best interests of their clients. For example, many clients served by counselors in private practice may receive medication from a physician (either a primary care provider or a psychiatrist). It is crucial for independently practicing counselors to have working relationships with the prescribing physician. Many **managed care organizations, organizations that act as intermediaries to the mental health service provider and the insurance company paying for services**, require nonphysician providers to have established cooperative service arrangements with board-certified psychiatrists. Counselors working in agencies often work with a team of professionals assigned to the care of individual clients. Team members need to be alert to the limits of practice of other professionals. They also need to know the specialized skills associated with professional affiliation. It is unlikely that counselors will be involved in cases in which they are the only provider of mental health services.

## COUNSELING AND PSYCHOLOGY: TWO CLOSELY RELATED BUT NOW DISTINCT MENTAL HEALTH PROFESSIONS

Counseling and psychology were once considered sister occupations. They developed side-by-side as advances occurred in measurement/assessment, counseling theory, and mental health services. Counseling emerged from (and is still deeply embedded in) educational settings, whereas psychology emerged as an academic discipline with applications in mental health settings. The first psychological clinic was founded in 1896 at the University of Pennsylvania (Fowler, 1996). Psychology's professional development preceded counseling by approximately 20 or 30 years, especially as related to licensure and independent mental health practice. The psychology specialty of counseling psychology is a bridge that spans the two professions; counseling psychology also acts as a boundary marker between them. If there is any doubt that the professions of counseling and psychology overlap in regard to activities and scope of practice, counseling psychology acts as a symbol of their similarity. On the other hand, if there are any doubts that the former sister occupations have emerged as discrete and competitive mental health professions, licensure standards of the two groups stand as distinguishing criteria. For example, Heppner, Casas, Carter, and Stone (2000), reporting on a personal communication with Norm Gysbers (former president of what is now the American Counseling Association [ACA]) about actions that caused some divergence of the ACA and American Psychological Association (APA) on matters that would be relevant to "counseling psychology," stated:

> Norm Gysbers noted that a major shift occurred between the two organizations as third-party payments became more prevalent in the early 1980's, which placed increasing emphasis on accreditation and licensure as entrance into the psychology profession. In essence, the APA began to focus on credentialing *psychologists*, while the ACA then concentrated on credentialing *counselors*. (p. 23) [italics in original quote]

Historically, counseling psychologists may have qualified for licenses in either psychology or counseling, even though requisite coursework or other requirements may be different between the two professions, requiring the licensure applicant to seek training beyond courses required for a degree. In more recent years as all 50 states have achieved counselor licensure, the focus of counselor licensure laws and regulations has become increasingly restrictive to requiring graduation from accredited master's-level counselor education programs, thus increasingly limiting the access for individuals who do not possess this academic preparation. Master's-level counselors do not meet licensure standards for psychology in states that adopt APA standards, which require a doctoral degree in psychology. Even doctoral-level-trained counselors find it difficult to meet psychology licensure standards, as degree requirements for psychology clearly require a degree title in "psychology" (counseling, education, or counselor education doctorates do not qualify). The provinces of the professions have been defined.

In regard to practice, there is little that differentiates the licensed professional counselor from the licensed psychologist. Both provide counseling (or psychotherapy). Both professional licenses typically allow for assessment of individuals with standardized measurement instruments, such as intelligence tests or personality tests. Both licensed professional counselors and licensed psychologists provide individual or group treatments. The two professions compete in the same market of mental or behavioral health services. Of all the mental health professions, counseling and psychology are probably the most similar in philosophy and practice. As Fretz and Simon (1992) stated:

> Ideally, attention will continue to be devoted to recognizing the legitimate overlap of functions of various levels and specialties of counselors and psychologists, as well as the meaningful differences in philosophy and practice that can support the continuing viability of the variety of mental health professions. A high degree of overlap in professional role functioning does not have to lead to hegemony by one profession; a clear specification of both unique and complementary professional roles can lead to a collaboration of professions that can benefit consumers as well as acknowledge unique professional competencies. (p. 23)

Gelso and Fretz (1992) defined several unifying themes of counseling psychology that apply to counseling as well: (a) "the focus on intact, as opposed to severely disturbed, personalities"; (b) "the focus on people's assets and strengths and on positive mental health regardless of the degree of disturbance"; (c) "an emphasis on brief interventions"; (d) "an emphasis on person-environment interactions, rather than an exclusive focus on either the person or the environment"; and (e) "an emphasis on educational and career development of individuals and on educational and vocational environments" (pp. 7–9). These "themes" may act as points in common shared by counselors and counseling psychologists. Counseling is not as closely aligned, either philosophically or historically, to the other mental health professions: psychiatry, social work, marital and family therapy, and psychiatric nursing.

In practical terms, the manner and scope in which these related types of professionals practice in their various settings are defined by the terms of the licensure and credentialing regulations that govern their respective practice areas. The following section describes credentials in counseling and the other mental health professions.

## LICENSING AND CREDENTIALING IN THE MENTAL HEALTH PROFESSIONS

Beyond having a good understanding of the ethical principles that direct the mental health professions, it is especially important to know each profession's credentials and **limits or scope of practice (the boundaries that demarcate the acceptable activities associated with a profession).**

The following section summarizes professional identification and practice-related issues in counseling and the other established mental health professions.

### Counseling

Counseling is a mental health profession that developed from the field of professional education. All 50 states, the District of Columbia, and Puerto Rico regulate the independent practice of counseling, which essentially enables the practice outside of schools or other educational or exempted settings. Because of counseling's historical linkage to schools, most professional counselors are educated in college or university departments or schools of education (where they usually have the option of receiving training to become school or nonschool clinical counselors).

The standard educational credential is the master's degree in counseling. Typically, the specific degree titles are the Master of Education (MEd), the Master of Arts (MA) in education or counseling, the Master of Science (MS) in education or counseling, or the Master of Counseling (MC) degree. Doctoral-level practitioners may hold the Doctor of Philosophy (PhD) in education or counseling. The PhD is considered the highest academic degree in the United States, and traditionally has been viewed as a research degree and a practitioner degree in the mental health field. Some practitioners may hold the Doctor of Education (EdD) in counseling, which is considered a professional degree in education, much like the Doctor of Medicine (MD) credential is a professional degree in medicine. During much of the 20th century, many EdD programs were similar in focus to those of PhD programs. In the past 10 years, however, there has been a renewed focus to distinguish the EdD from the PhD (Shulman, Golde, Bueschel, & Garabedian, 2006). While PhD programs have traditionally focused on preparing doctoral students to engage in research, EdD programs particularly focus on preparing doctoral students to be educators (Zambo, Zambo, Buss, Perry, & Williams, 2014).

In most states, certified school counselors must have a master's degree plus documentation of specific coursework in education. Certification is usually granted to individual school counselors and is regulated by the state's department of education. Certification as a school counselor by such a department usually allows counseling practice only within elementary, middle, and secondary schools within the state. School certification in no way implies that the counselor has been credentialed to practice counseling independently (i.e., in private practice for a fee).

The independent practice of counseling is typically regulated by state licensure statutes. **Licensure is a type of regulation that may restrict both the use of a professional title, such as "counselor," and the practice of counseling in fee-for-service, independent practice. Independent practice is the practice of counseling outside of an exempt institutional or another setting (exempt from oversight by the licensure authority).** For example, counselors working for a state government may be exempt from the licensing requirement. Because the state hires counselors based on some standard, and their practice is supervised and monitored by the authority of the state agency, it may be unnecessary to require that these employees meet additional state licensure requirements. Exemptions from licensure, if any, vary from state to state, and counselors should know the generally accepted exemptions to identify counselors who are practicing legally or illegally. In many states, counselors employed by a state's mental health, vocational rehabilitation, or family services agency may not be required by statute to be licensed by the regulatory board. In some states new counselors who practice under the supervision of a fully licensed counselor do not need to have their own license. However, in other states they may be required to hold a license, sometimes termed an associate or provisional license, that denotes that they are practicing under the supervision of someone with a license. Counselors in any of these exempted statuses may practice counseling consistent with and within the bounds of their employment; however, a counselor who works in an exempt setting as an employee is not able to practice independently for a fee outside of that employment. A private practice as a second job, no matter how small the practice, remains under the jurisdiction of the licensure authority.

Each licensure statute defines the nature and limits of counseling practice controlled by the law and defines exceptions (exempt practice). For example, Christian Science practitioners are often exempted—as long as they practice within the bounds of religious doctrine, they may counsel Christian Scientists about religious and personal issues. Typical exemptions include pastoral counselors, state and/or federal employees, school counselors (as long as they are certified by the state's department of education), hypnotists, and substance abuse treatment personnel. Each state's exemptions may be unique to the politics involved in passing the licensure statute in that state. Exemptions are usually listed in the statute itself.

Counselor licensure for independent practice in most states requires a relevant master's degree from an acceptable educational institution with coursework in identified core areas (such as assessment, group counseling, counseling ethics, and counseling theories). States often require 1 or 2 years of post-master's degree supervised experience. Additionally, the license candidate must pass an examination of knowledge in the core areas of counseling by achieving an acceptable passing, or "cut," score, which is usually at or near the national mean. The newly licensed professional counselor (often designated "LPC" or other letters representing the state's title) is then allowed to charge clients for providing counseling services independent of any institutional oversight. Although practice is considered "independent," licensed professional counselors are obligated to follow ethical and legal rules set forth by the state's licensure board, which has the right to suspend or revoke the license for unethical or illegal practice. Additionally, licensure boards typically require continuing education of licensed professionals and may impose other requirements to maintain a license. Licensure boards often adopt nationally accepted ethical codes, often the ACA's code or some derivative, and adopt administrative or disciplinary rules that constitute mandatory standards of practice to protect consumers.

In addition to licensure of independent practice and state regulation or certification of counselors in the schools, another type of credential is sought by mental health professionals—specialty certification.

**Specialty certification** (such as in the specialties of rehabilitation, mental health, family, or addiction counseling) **is a voluntary means for professionals to identify themselves as trained and qualified specialists. Overseen by freestanding, nongovernmental, and national specialty certification boards, specialty certification identifies professionals who hold specialized training or experience in a circumscribed practice of counseling, usually assisting a unique subpopulation of clients.** As examples, certified rehabilitation counselors (CRCs) specialize in assisting individuals with disabilities; marriage or family counseling specialists serve couples or families; addiction counselors work with individuals with chemical dependencies or other addictions. Specialists often limit their practices to clients who need their particular type of treatment. In effect, specialty certification is a means to identify and to designate counselors who have met specialty standards and who, to some degree, limit their practices to those activities consistent with the specialty.

Many specialty certification boards are given approval or credibility by a large, national professional association. In counseling, the Commission on Rehabilitation Counselor Certification (CRCC) certifies rehabilitation counselors. CRCC was organized with the support of the American Rehabilitation Counseling Association, an affiliate of what is now the ACA, and in conjunction with the National Rehabilitation Counseling Association (NRCA), a division of the National Rehabilitation Association. These organizations originally had seats on the commission, which, since 2013, has been composed of individuals representing various general competency and constituency groups. The CRC credential is the oldest and most widely recognized professional counseling specialty designation. The National Board for Certified Counselors (NBCC) is the largest recognized specialty board in professional counseling. NBCC certifies general counselor and several specialty practitioner groups, such as addiction counselors and mental health counselors. (See Box 2.1 for information on contacting the ACA, NBCC, CRCC, and the American Association of State Counseling Boards [AASCB].)    ↑ oldest, most established

Ordinarily, specialty certification requirements are equivalent to or more stringent than licensure standards. However, some counselors may be certified by a specialty board but may not be licensed to practice independently. Specialty certification is simply a way of identifying a practitioner's level of training and limits of practice; it is not a legal right to practice for a fee. Counselors employed by a state government's vocational rehabilitation agency (usually a license-exempt setting) may attain the CRC credential to demonstrate their commitment and allegiance to their specialty, even though they may be required by law to restrict their practice to their state government job (if they are not licensed).

The surest route to proper credentialing and licensure as endorsed by the counseling profession is by getting a master's degree from a counselor education program accredited by the Commission on the Accreditation of Counseling and Related Educational Programs (CACREP) or its affiliate, Commission on Rehabilitation Education (CORE), state licensure as a licensed professional counselor, and certification in a specialty area of focus through the counselor certification bodies of CRCC or NBCC. The mental health field has seen a proliferation of questionable certifications. Anyone can set up a specialty certification by incorporating a "board," getting a post office box, and developing application forms. A number of boards advertised in professional newspapers and journals have questionable or nonexistent connections to legitimate professional organizations. These boards may charge exorbitant fees to provide impressive-sounding credentials. However, most professionals consider such certification as worthless, except perhaps in deceiving the public. Wise and ethical practitioners

## BOX 2.1  Counseling Professional Organizations and Credentialing Bodies

The largest professional group representing professional counselors is the American Counseling Association (ACA), 6101 Stevenson Avenue, Alexandria, VA 22304-3540; phone 800-347-6647; the ACA website is www.counseling.org. The National Board for Certified Counselors (NBCC) is located at 3 Terrace Way, Greensboro, NC 27403-3660; phone 336-547-0607; the NBCC website is www.nbcc.org. The address of the Commission on Rehabilitation Counselor Certification (CRCC) is 1699 E. Woodfield Road, Suite 300, Schaumburg, IL 60173; phone 847-944-1325; the CRCC website is www.crccertification.com. The address of the American Association of State Counseling Boards (AASCB) is 305 N. Beech Circle, Broken Arrow, OK 74012; phone 918-994-4413; the AASCB website is www.aascb.org.

seek certification only by specialty boards that are well respected in the professional community and have established relationships with recognized organizations that represent a profession (such as the ACA). Practitioners who purchase credentials from freestanding and unrecognized certification bodies to imply a level of expertise or training may be considered unethical, if such an action misrepresents their professional qualifications.

The terms most commonly used to describe **specialty designation—certification through a national specialty certifying board**—in the counseling and mental health professions are **certification, board certification,** or **diplomate** (such as the diplomate of the American Board of Professional Psychology [ABPP]). These terms are generally synonymous and mean a specialty certification has been attained.

## Psychiatry

Psychiatry, the oldest recognized mental health profession, is a medical specialty. All psychiatrists must be physicians and, therefore, must have a medical or equivalent degree. Two academic–professional degrees in the United States allow for licensure as a fully qualified physician—the Doctor of Medicine (MD) and the Doctor of Osteopathy (DO). The Doctor of Chiropractic (DC) degree, which sometimes allows for the title of "Chiropractic Physician," is not consistent with licensure for the full range of treatments typically associated with medical practice (e.g., chiropractors in most states are not allowed to prescribe medication). Graduates of medical schools outside the United States may have the MD degree or some variation, but once they pass a state's licensure standards for the Doctor of Medicine, they may legitimately use the "MD" designation after their names.

The DO degree is awarded by schools of osteopathy. Such schools are typically not associated with universities. **Osteopathy is considered an alternative to the traditional training model of the profession of medicine, which is technically called "allopathy."** It is a relatively young profession, developed as an offshoot of medicine based on philosophical differences. Osteopaths believe that physical structure is often implicated in the disease process, and physical manipulation is a primary osteopathic treatment. Additionally, osteopaths focus on the individual patient more holistically and view medication as an adjunct to other treatments. Regardless, osteopaths are licensed to provide the full range of medical treatment, including surgery and the prescription of medication. In fact, many states license osteopathic physicians and allopathic physicians (MDs) through the same board of healing arts. In a substantial portion of academic curricula and in actual practice, there may be little that distinguishes an osteopathic physician from a physician holding an MD. In fact, some DOs specialize in psychiatry, seeking additional residency training after the education required for licensure as an osteopath.

A licensed physician must have the appropriate degree from an accepted school of medicine or osteopathy. Additionally, a 1-year, general medical "internship" must be completed in a hospital. Candidates are granted a license to practice as a physician upon completion of the internship and after passing the required licensure examinations (sometimes called "state board" examinations). This license allows the physician to perform all medical procedures and to prescribe medicine. Licensed physicians can practice independently—that is, in private practice. However, many hospitals will not grant a physician **hospital privileges (the right to admit patients to and treat patients in the hospital)** without postinternship training. Hospitals usually require a physician to show evidence of 3 or more years of additional training in a specialty—a residency. A **specialty residency is a 3-year or more, hospital-based training program that prepares the physician to practice diagnosis, general treatment, and specialty procedures in a specific area of medical practice,** such as orthopedic surgery, internal medicine (diagnostics), pediatrics, dermatology, family practice, or psychiatry. There are many specialties in medicine and osteopathy. Physicians who have completed a specialty residency can legitimately claim to be specialists and can perform procedures, usually within hospitals where they have been granted hospital privileges. Many physicians who have completed specialty residencies also seek **specialty designation**. Specialty designation through such a board has become the benchmark for advanced specialty practice.

The national certifying body in psychiatry is the American Board of Psychiatry and Neurology (ABPN; see Box 2.2). Physicians who have been licensed and have completed an approved (by the relevant specialty board) specialty residency may then sit for a specialty examination, a rigorous test of knowledge within the specialty. Upon passing the test, physicians are granted "diplomate" status—essentially receiving a diploma of completion of specialty training. Diplomates of a specialty board may describe themselves as "board-certified" specialists.

It is not necessary to be a board-certified specialist to practice a specialty. However, to legitimately and ethically practice a specialty, a physician should have at least completed an approved specialty residency. Many psychiatrists practice without the ABPN designation.

## BOX 2.2  Psychiatry Professional Organizations and Credentialing Bodies

The largest professional association representing psychiatrists is the American Medical Association (AMA). Specifically related to psychiatry, however, the American Psychiatric Association is the largest professional group representing psychiatrists. The American Psychiatric Association is located at 1000 Wilson Boulevard, Suite 1825, Arlington, VA 22209-3901; phone 1-888-357-7924; the website is www.psychiatry.org. The American Board of Psychiatry and Neurology (ABPN) address is 2150 E. Lake Cook Road, Suite 900, Buffalo Grove, IL 60089; phone 847-229-6500; the ABPN website is www.abpn.com.

Board certification is no guarantee of competence, just as not having board certification is no indication of incompetence. However, board certification helps to identify duly trained and knowledgeable specialty practitioners.

Psychiatrists can perform physically intrusive procedures (e.g., surgery, blood tests), electroconvulsive therapy (ECT), psychotherapy, and medicinal treatment or pharmacotherapy. Additionally, by virtue of their general medical training, they may practice any and all procedures within general medicine. This training allows the psychiatrist to be uniquely qualified to understand and address the biochemical and medical aspects of mental disorders. By nature of their training, psychiatrists have a knowledge base to understand and to treat any comorbid physical illness in individuals with mental disorders.

## Psychology

Psychologists, unlike psychiatrists, cannot prescribe medications or perform other treatments or diagnostic procedures that are intrusive or invasive of the physical structure of the body. (It is noteworthy, however, that some psychologists, at the direction of some leaders of the APA, are actively petitioning state legislatures for the right to prescribe medication; three states, at the time of writing, have granted psychologists the right to prescribe medication—New Mexico, Louisiana, and Illinois.) Psychologists, like counselors, can assess individuals with normative tests (such as IQ, aptitude, personality, or interest tests). Psychiatrists are not typically trained in psychometrics or psychological testing procedures and interpretation, and they should not be involved in such activity without appropriate training and supervision. Psychiatrists, psychologists, and counselors, however, are all trained and licensed to perform psychotherapy or counseling.

Psychologists must be educated to the level of the academic doctorate (PhD; EdD; or Doctor of Psychology [PsyD]). The PsyD is usually awarded by freestanding, nonuniversity-affiliated schools of psychology; as such, institutions granting the PsyD degree typically do not seek to prepare psychologists for potential research or academic roles. Freestanding schools of psychology primarily train individuals for clinical practice. The PhD is usually awarded in clinical psychology or counseling psychology at university colleges of arts and science. Schools of education at universities or colleges may award the PhD or the EdD in counseling, educational, or school psychology. Any of these psychology degrees, if obtained from a legitimately accredited college or university, may signify doctoral-level training in psychology. Increasingly, however, the preferred national standard for academic psychology programs is accreditation through the APA's Committee on Accreditation.

To become licensed as a psychologist, candidates must complete the doctorate from an appropriately accredited program and perform 1 or 2 years of postdoctoral practice supervised by a licensed psychologist in a psychology service delivery program that is accepted or approved by the state licensure authority. Additionally, candidates must pass a stringent licensure examination. Once licensed, psychologists can independently provide the full range of psychological delivery services for a fee.

---

**BOX 2.3  Psychology Professional Organizations and Credentialing Bodies**

The address of the American Psychological Association (APA) is 750 First Street, N.E., Washington, DC 20002-4242; phone 800-374-2721; the APA website is www.apa.org. The American Board of Professional Psychology (ABPP) is located at 600 Market Street, Suite 201 Chapel Hill, NC 27516; phone 919-537-8031; the ABPP website is www.abpp.org.

---

Psychologists may become board-certified through the ABPP, which has linkage to the APA (see Box 2.3). Board certification by the ABPP is a highly recognized and respected clinical credential. Specialties designated by the ABPP include clinical, counseling, family, rehabilitation, and neuropsychology. ABPP specialty certification requires up to 5 years of postdoctoral specialized experience under the supervision of a board-certified specialist, plus an acceptable score on an examination of knowledge in the specialty.

The largest professional association representing psychologists in the United States is the APA.

## Marriage and Family Therapy

Marriage and family therapists are licensed in all 50 states and the District of Columbia. Marital therapy focuses on concerns experienced by couples. The focus is on the relationship itself, with an implied obligation to assist the partners to solve problems so that they can maintain their relationship. Family therapy is a treatment approach that treats social concerns or individual problems (including psychopathology) within the context of the family (whether the family is defined by genetics, law, common law, or choice) or recognized household. Other individuals may be involved in a family's problem and may be asked to participate in treatment; for example, a dating partner of a household member may be asked to attend a session.

Marital and family therapists are trained to treat relationships from a dyad (a two-person system) to a family system of three (a triad) or more individuals. Unlike other mental health professions that focus primarily on individual treatment, marital and family therapists are trained in theories of relationships and relationship treatment, which typically are grounded in social systems theory (Cottone, 2012b). This unique theoretical and clinical training constitutes a critical difference in how therapists conceptualize and practice their profession; relationships clearly become the focus.

There is controversy over the existence of marriage and family therapy as a separate or independent mental health profession. Larger, more inclusive professions, such as psychology and counseling, have taken the stance that marital therapy and family therapy are actually treatment approaches that counselors or psychologists may choose with appropriate training and experience. They argue that marriage and family therapy is not a profession unto itself, but rather reflects a body of specialized techniques. Accordingly, freestanding licenses for marriage and family therapists are criticized by some psychologists and counselors who believe that any trained psychiatrist, psychologist, or counselor with specialty training can practice marital and family therapy. Because marital and family therapy is within the scope of practice of the other mental health professions in many states (e.g., counseling, psychology), it is considered a specialty of those professions rather than a separate profession. In fact, a number of individuals affiliated with the ACA helped to establish the National Credentialing Academy for Certified Family Therapists, which certifies counselors as meeting criteria to be "Certified Family Therapists."

Marriage and family therapists represented by the American Association for Marriage and Family Therapy (AAMFT; see Box 2.4) have taken the position that specialty training and specialty designation are not enough. They argue that in-depth, master's-level professional training is needed, primarily with grounding in social systems theory. Further, they have argued convincingly before state legislators that marriage and family therapy should be licensed as a freestanding mental health profession. As a result, all states license marriage and family therapy separately from other mental health professions.

To be licensed as a marriage and family therapist requires a master's degree in marital and family therapy (or a closely related degree), with specialized coursework in systems theory, marital and family treatment approaches, and marital and family therapy ethics, among more general areas. The college or university degrees most often awarded are the Master of Science (MS) or Master of Arts (MA). One or 2 years of post-master's supervision of practice is also required. Upon completion of the supervised experience, applicants must pass an examination covering core knowledge areas.

Currently, there are no formally credentialed subspecialties of marriage and family therapy and, consequently, there are no specialty designations. In time, there will likely be specialty boards in marriage counseling, family work, children's issues, and other areas addressed by marriage and family therapists.

---

### BOX 2.4  Marriage and Family Therapy Professional Organizations and Credentialing Bodies

The address of the American Association for Marriage and Family Therapy (AAMFT) is 112 South Alfred Street, Alexandria, VA 22314-3061; phone 703-838-9808; the AAMFT website is www.aamft.org. The International Association of Marriage and Family Counselors is an affiliate of the American Counseling Association (ACA) and can be contacted through the ACA at 6101 Stevenson Avenue, Alexandria, VA 22304-3540; phone 703-823-9800 or toll free 800-347-6647; the ACA website is www.counseling.org. The National Credentialing Academy (NCA; for Certified Family Therapists [CFTs]) is located at 13566 Camino De Plata Ct, Corpus Christi, TX 78418; the NCA website is www.nationalcredentialingacademy.com.

The AAMFT has a restricted membership composed of already licensed or highly trained and supervised professionals. The AAMFT offers an advanced membership level (clinical member), which acts much like a credential because the criteria for "clinical membership" are stringent. Interestingly, no examination is required to become a clinical member of the AAMFT. Rather, it requires 2 years of close supervision by an AAMFT "approved supervisor" once candidates have completed basic master's-level coursework. The emphasis on the supervisory relationship, rather than on an examination, appears to reflect the overall emphasis of the profession on "relationship."

## Psychiatric Nursing

Psychiatric nursing has established itself as a mental health specialty through general certification in psychiatric and mental health nursing and through advanced "clinical specialist" certification as a mental health nurse. Training for the general practice of nursing requires at least 2 years of college-level preparation leading to state "registration" as a nurse (an RN). This registration is akin to the state licensure of other health professions. To become an RN, an individual must have an acceptable degree in nursing and must pass an examination concerning nursing theory and practice and meet other registration requirements. There are three educational routes to meet educational requirements: the 2-year associate's degree; the 3-year diploma from a hospital-based "school" of nursing; and the bachelor's degree in nursing from a college- or university-affiliated nursing school. There is a trend away from the associate's degree and toward the bachelor of nursing degree as an entry-level training requirement.

RNs are allowed to provide the full range of nursing services, primarily treating patients under the direction of a physician. However, in the psychiatric nursing area, certified "clinical specialists" in mental health nursing are master's-degree–trained nurses who have completed specialized coursework in psychotherapeutic approaches. Certified clinical specialists in mental health nursing make the case that they are trained to the level necessary to provide mental health treatments independent of physician oversight. Nurses are not licensed to administer psychological or educational tests or to independently prescribe medications.

The primary certifying body for professional nurses is the American Nurses Credentialing Center (ANCC; see Box 2.5). The ANCC was established under

---

**BOX 2.5  Nursing Professional Organizations and Credentialing Bodies**

The address of the National League for Nursing (NLN) is 2600 Virginia Avenue NW, Washington, DC 20037; phone 800-669-1656; the NLN website is www .nln.org. The American Nurses Association (ANA) and the American Nurses Credentialing Center (ANCC) are located at 8515 Georgia Ave, Suite 400, Silver Spring, MD 20910-3492; phone 1-800-274-4262; the ANA and ANCC website is www.nursingworld.org.

the auspices of the American Nurses Association (ANA). Over 90,000 nurses are certified by the ANCC. The ANCC certifies only those nurses holding the baccalaureate in nursing, regardless of state registration to practice nursing. Synopses of the two certifications in mental health nursing provided by the ANCC are as follows:

1. "Psychiatric–mental health nursing" certification. Generally, this level of certification requires the RN, documented experience in psychiatric nursing, 30 contact hours of continuing education in coursework relevant to mental health practice, and a passing score on an examination concerning topics including theories/concepts, psychopathology, treatment modalities and nursing interventions, and professional issues and trends.
2. The "Adult Psychiatric–Mental Health Clinical Nurse Specialist" or "Child/ Adolescent Psychiatric–Mental Health Clinical Nurse Specialist" certification. Generally, this level of certification requires the RN, documented experience in psychiatric nursing, documentation of experience in treatment modalities, a master's degree in psychiatric nursing or a closely related field, post-master's experience in psychiatric nursing, and a passing score on an examination that includes theories, psychopathology, treatment modalities, trends and issues, and other areas.

In addition to the ANA, the National League for Nursing (NLN) is respected as a professional nursing organization.

## Social Work

Generally, social workers trained to the level of the master's degree specialize in one of two areas: public policy or clinical social work. In the mental health field, the clinical or psychiatric social worker is trained to practice as an independent mental health professional.

The degree required for independent practice in clinical social work is the Master of Social Work (MSW) degree, which generally requires 60 to 72 semester hours of graduate coursework. Individuals seeking to be mental health professionals usually follow a graduate coursework track that focuses on psychotherapeutic treatment (rather than on social policy). Social workers often are trained to provide group and family treatments as well as individual psychotherapy, depending on the focus of the degree program. Social workers are not trained or licensed to administer psychological or educational tests or to prescribe psychotropic medications.

Licensure of social workers generally requires the MSW and 1 to 2 years of post-master's supervised experience. A passing score on a licensure examination covering social work theory and practice often is required. Psychotherapy, group therapy, and couple or family therapy are all within the scope of practice of most social work licenses.

Master's-level–trained social workers who wish to be certified may seek credentialing through the Academy of Certified Social Workers (ACSW), which then allows its initials to be used after a social worker's name to designate advanced

---

**BOX 2.6  Social Work Professional Organization and Credentialing Body**

The address of the National Association of Social Workers (NASW) is 750 First Street N.E., Suite 800, Washington, DC 20002-8011; phone 202-408-8600; the NASW website is www.socialworkers.org.

---

certification. The ACSW is a widely recognized and respected social work credential and is awarded under the direction of the National Association of Social Workers (NASW; see Box 2.6). The NASW is the largest national organization representing social workers. To be an ACSW, one must have a master's degree in social work, 2 years of post-master's paid experience in social work practice under the supervision of a social worker, and an acceptable score on an examination over social work knowledge in assessment and service planning, intervention, professional development, ethical standards, and administration. The ACSW is a generic credential and does not necessarily reflect qualifications in "clinical" practice.

Social workers who are specialists in clinical practice may seek listing in the NASW "Register of Clinical Social Workers." There are two levels of certification in the "clinical" category: the "Qualified Clinical Social Worker" and the "Diplomate in Clinical Social Work." Both clinical credentials require a master's or doctoral degree in social work from a program accredited by the Council on Social Work Education, the social work accrediting body. Additionally, the ACSW credential or state licensure in social work and 2 years of supervised experience in "clinical" social work are needed. No examination is needed for the "Qualified Clinical Social Worker" credential, but candidates must pass an advanced examination to be a "Diplomate." The diplomate credential also requires 3 additional years of practice.

Another social work certification is the "Certified School Social Work Specialist." This specialist must have a master's degree in social work from an accredited program, 2 years of postgraduate supervised school social work experience, and a passing score on a specialty test for school social workers. The ACSW is not needed.

Social work has established itself as a viable mental health profession. In fact, by the level of education, it is the profession that competes most closely with master's-level professional counseling. Counselors and social workers may compete for similar jobs in mental health centers, hospitals, educational institutions, and other settings not requiring doctoral-trained professionals.

## CONCLUSION

Psychiatrists are licensed physicians who hold either the MD or DO degree. Candidates are granted a license to practice as a physician upon completion of an internship and after passing licensure (state board) exams. A specialty residency is usually a 3-year, hospital-based training program that prepares the physician to practice diagnosis, general treatment, and specialty procedures. A specialty designation is certification through a national specialty certifying board. Professional organizations and credentialing bodies for psychiatrists include the American Medical Association (AMA), the American Psychiatric Association, and the ABPN.

Psychologists treat individuals with psychotherapy and counseling, and assess individuals with IQ, aptitude, personality, and interest tests. They cannot prescribe medications (in most states) or perform treatments or intrusive diagnostic procedures. Psychologists must be educated to the level of the academic doctorate and must perform 1 or 2 years of postdoctoral service supervised by licensed psychologists. They must pass a stringent licensure exam. Counseling psychologists provide counseling and psychotherapy and assess individuals with standardized measurement instruments, such as intelligence tests and personality tests in both individual and group treatment.

Professional organizations and credentialing bodies for psychologists include the APA and the ABPP. Professional counselors hold a master's degree in counseling. Doctoral-level practitioners may hold a PhD in education or counseling; some practitioners may hold an EdD in counseling. Certified school counselors require a master's degree plus specific coursework in education. Licensure is a type of regulation that restricts both the use of a professional title and the practice of counseling in fee-for-service independent practice. Specialty certification is a voluntary means for professionals to identify themselves as trained and qualified specialists that is overseen by national specialty certification boards. Professional organizations and credentialing bodies for counselors include the ACA, the NBCC, and the CRCC.

Marriage and family therapists focus on relationship concerns experienced by couples or families. A master's degree, specialized coursework, and 1 or 2 years of post-master's supervision of practice, and successful completion of an exam are required. Professional organizations and credentialing bodies for marriage and family therapists include the AAMFT, the ACA's International Association of Marriage and Family Counselors (IAMFC), and the National Credentialing Academy for Certified Family Therapists.

Psychiatric nurses are master's-degree–trained nurses with specialized coursework in psychotherapeutic approaches. Two certifications are provided: psychiatric and mental health nurse, and clinical specialist. Professional organizations and credentialing bodies for psychiatric nurses include the NLN and the ANA.

Social workers generally specialize in public policy or clinical social work. A master's degree and 1 to 2 years of post-master's degree supervised experience are required. The NASW is the professional organization and credentialing body for social workers.

# VALUE ISSUES IN COUNSELING AND PSYCHOTHERAPY

## OBJECTIVES

- ■ To explain the value-laden nature of counseling.
- ■ To define and contrast the concepts of ethics, morals, and values.
- ■ To explain the historical and ongoing role of values in the counseling process.
- ■ To identify and discuss the processes used to examine and to work with value systems, values clarification, and values conflict resolution.

Human beings inherently have values, even if those values are not clearly known to the person. Thus, each individual counselor has his or her own set of values, as does every client who comes to counseling. Counselors and their clients focus on issues of values and the meaning of life as they solve problems, develop strategies to address problems, and work toward goals. They use interpretations of what is good, bad, right, wrong, joyous, and painful in their experiences to guide them. Both clients and counselors hold values, whether or not they are able to articulate them. When clients come to counselors for assistance in making choices or changing their lives, both parties enact values, either knowingly or unknowingly. It is of the utmost importance that counselors are fully aware of what they value, especially since such values will, in some measure, be brought to the counseling session and thus will potentially affect the client.

## VALUES

**Values involve that which is intrinsically worthwhile or worthy of esteem; values reflect the value holder's worldview, culture, or understanding of the world** (Box 3.1). For example, one can value a relationship with another person, or one can value love, freedom, democracy, or family. Values arise from individuals' experiences and interactions with their culture, the world, and the people around them, such as their parents, friends, religious leaders, and neighbors. Thus, values vary among individuals, but are likely to vary less among persons growing up within similar systems, such as specific cultures or religions. **A value system is a hierarchical ranking of the degree of preference for the values expressed by a particular person or social entity** (Lewis & Hardin, 2002).

Values focus our activities and choices. In a sermon given in Georgia on February 4, 1968, during the height of the Civil Rights movement, the Reverend Martin Luther King, Jr., spoke eloquently about what it takes to truly be a helper. He encouraged everyone to remember that all people can serve, because sophisticated skills or education is not needed, but rather love of others, grace, and a heart dedicated to service. As Rev. King demonstrated, values, such as service to others, powerfully affect behavior and drive choices about what one wishes to do and what one likes to have.

Values are often mistakenly thought of as involving a simple expression of personal interest or preference, such as a preference for an automatic rather than a standard transmission in a new car. Actually, values are more complex—they involve a set of beliefs that include evaluative, emotional, and existential aspects. Values may have elements of goodness or obligation. Values may have associated positive or negative emotions. Values may provide a sense of the meaningfulness or choice attached to the object of the valuing process. Values are not directly observable, but they guide human choice and action through the preferences expressed in human choices and goals, and they may also be expressed verbally (see the recommended activity to establish a health care directive in Box 3.2).

Reflect on the following scenarios and assess any emotion attached to these situations: the experience parents have when they hug their children after returning from a long journey; the feeling one might have watching the beating of an innocent individual on television news; or the sense one might experience when

---

### BOX 3.1 The Relationship Between Morals, Ethics, and Values—An Example

**Values** are things you hold to be worthwhile. For example, you value your relationship to your spouse or partner. Other relevant values: love, family relations.

**Ethics** are the standards that specifically guide how to act in a specific circumstance. For example, "married people do not cheat on their spouses" is an ethical standard.

**Morals** are based on principles that guide behavior, sometimes deriving from religious standards. For example, fidelity is viewed as a moral prerogative—one must honor one's spouse or lover by remaining faithful. It is an issue of principle.

## BOX 3.2 End-of-Life Choices as Enacted Values

Anyone who has worked with or been close to someone who is near death knows that the final choices about how one dies take on a stark personal meaning. Being near death is sometimes referred to as "instant values clarification." It is important to discuss your final wishes about terminal care with medical caregivers and family while you are healthy and able to express your desires. For example, if you were terminally ill, in a coma, and would likely not come out of your coma, would you want your health care providers to prolong your life if possible, or would you want them to not prolong your life if to do so would be painful and ultimately result in only a few more days of life?

By making these decisions before you become ill with a life-threatening condition, your choices will be based on clear thinking and on your personal values about the end of life. Forethought on these matters is a prerequisite to establishing a legally executed living will, an advanced directive for health care, and/or durable power of attorney for health care. Many state bar associations have example documents on these matters, which may be used to start the process of addressing these issues. Discuss your choices and answers with those closest to you. In class, discuss what you discovered about yourself and your values in doing this important bit of personal business.

seeing a beautiful sunrise or feeling gentle, pine-scented breezes. The beliefs and preferences that underlie values can be articulated—love of family, respect for life and personal freedom, and respect for nature and our responsibility to care for these resources. Values are formed over the years through experiences with **"significant others" (people in one's social network)** on matters of beliefs and choices, and through exposure to cultural institutions, such as school and places of worship. Values are ingrained and held as worthwhile. New developments in ethics, such as virtue ethics, multiculturalism, feminist streams of thought, and the increasing attention in professional codes of ethics regarding expected professional behavior when personal and professional values may conflict, illustrate how values and worldview-based analyses can be reframed to accommodate the diverse lives and perspectives of all people in counseling. The issues that surround ethical judgment involve a complex interplay of morals, values, and priorities that people hold in relationship to themselves, their clients, their colleagues, and other professionals. Ethical principles of practice (i.e., autonomy, beneficence, nonmaleficence, fidelity, justice, and veracity, which are described in Chapter 5) are interrelated with, but distinguishable from, concepts such as morals, values, and codes of ethics. Taken together, they form the heart and soul of counseling.

## MORALS, ETHICS, AND VALUES

Values can be either moral or nonmoral in nature—they may or may not involve preferences concerning what is morally right or wrong. Remember, morals are based on principles that guide behavior, sometimes deriving from religious standards. For example, a person's choice to become a vegetarian might be based on nonmoral or moral value grounds. It might stem from belief in the importance of social status and a wish to follow the lead of a charismatic friend, or to be "politically correct" (nonmoral values of manner or custom); or the choice might be based on a spiritual belief that all forms of life should be respected and protected from discomfort and violence (a moral standard). Thus, any situation, choice, or action may be valued or prized in a number of different and possibly competing ways by different individuals or groups. It also is possible for one individual to hold two or more conflicting values about a particular object or situation, resulting in some level of **dissonance (discomfort with the difference)** if the person becomes aware of the conflicting values. The vegetarian who believes in the sanctity of all life forms may also value respect for family tradition and a mother's wishes (thus eating Thanksgiving turkey once a year at the family gathering). So the relationships of morals to ethics and values are complex, but generally, morals address the biggest issues—the principles that are held at the highest level directing behavior, whereas values relate to things that are worthwhile (valuable) and may be related to morals or may not be related to morals.

The process of socializing new students into a profession can also be thought of as introducing them to the profession's specific core values. For example, new students will learn the high value that counselors place on protecting the privacy of clients by hearing instructors and fellow students discuss the need for privacy in class. Or a situation may arise in supervision that demonstrates the importance of privacy, such as student observing clinical supervisors struggling to keep client information confidential by claiming privilege in the face of a **subpoena (a court request for information).** This socialization process can be seen as a way of assisting individuals in adopting a specific subculture or worldview that will enhance a professional perspective, judgment, and the ability to function responsibly in a new professional role. Rokeach and Regan (1980) noted two dimensions of values that are relevant to counseling: (a) standards of competency versus standards of morals and (b) terminal (desirable end states) versus instrumental (behaviors useful to reach end state) values. Wisdom (more desirable than foolishness), truthfulness (more desirable than deceit), and freedom (more desirable than enslavement) are examples of terminal values. Instrumental values concern those idealized or desirable types of behavior that are useful in attaining the end state, such as being organized or industrious. They are not necessarily good in and of themselves. For example, the instrumental value of industriousness may serve either a thief or a saint, but to very different ends. These dimensions add richness to the consideration of ethics concepts. Thus, unethical practices can be seen as stemming from either ignorance or inadequate training and supervision (violations of the value concerning standards of competency), as well as from personal profit motive, need for self-enhancement, or the need to maintain power and status (terminal values). These latter motivations may be related to personal values that are nonmoral values, and are in conflict with the moral values embedded in a profession's values as reflected in its standards regarding particular situations.

Another important differentiation involves acknowledging that some values can be seen as universal, or, at least, widely respected. Historically, anthropologists see such values as the prohibition against killing, a prohibition on marriage or sexual intercourse between members of the immediate family, respect for ownership of property, and truthfulness as values shared by most human cultures (Brandt, 1959; Kluckhorn, 1951). Nevertheless, culturally permissible exceptions under specific circumstances are allowed, such as killing to defend one's own life or in battle in a war. This acknowledgment is not tantamount to ethical relativism or situational ethics. These exceptions are related to limited circumstances that make the exception permissible. Further, these exceptions are widely understood and largely supported by a cultural group. In more recent work, the quest to identify universal values relevant to counseling while still respecting human diversity continues.

After reviewing the scholarly and religious literature concerning universal values and values central to the major streams of world culture, Kinnier, Kernes, and Dautheribes (2000) compiled a list of universal moral values to assist counselors and clients in examining the implications of value conflicts. Kinnier, Dixon, Barratt, and Moyer (2008) subsequently asserted that universalism is, and should be, the dominant viewpoint in the counseling profession.

Examine these values as presented in Box 3.3 and think about whether they are universal. How should a counselor feel about using them in counseling? Are they "universal" enough to be used with clients of diverse cultural, ethnic, and religious backgrounds? How might examining them assist both the counselor and the client in resolving the issues presented in counseling?

**Questions for Reflection:** Suppose that you are a counselor and are meeting with a new client who would like to discuss with you the decision to undergo gender reassignment (essentially, the client is thinking about becoming a person of the opposite sex, both physically and emotionally). What personal values do you hold about persons being other than the gender they were identified as having at birth? As per the American Counseling Association (ACA) 2014 *Code of Ethics*, counselors "bracket—set aside—personal values that are not in line with the legitimate counseling goals of the client" (Martz & Kaplan, 2014, p. 24). How would you bracket those values that you held that were not in some way consistent with the values of the client? What steps would you take to ensure that any differing values you held would not be imposed on the client or be allowed to adversely affect the counselor–client relationship?

## VALUES IN COUNSELING

### Historical Perspective

Do all members of the human race share common values? To what degree should a counselor's values influence clients? These questions constitute some of the most significant debates in counseling and date back to the beginning of psychotherapy's development with Sigmund Freud's psychodynamic approach. In his system of therapy, the therapist was to work assiduously to maintain an absolute neutrality of response to the patient, thus providing a "blank screen" on which

BOX 3.3  The Short List of Universal Moral Values: Are They Really Universal?

I.   Commitment to something greater than oneself.
     To recognize the existence of and be committed to a Supreme Being, higher principle, transcendent purpose or meaning to one's existence.
     To seek the truth (or truths).
     To seek justice.
II.  Self-respect, but with humility, self-discipline, and acceptance of personal responsibility.
     To respect and care for oneself.
     To not exalt oneself or overindulge—to show humility and avoid gluttony, greed, or other forms of selfishness or self-centeredness.
     To act in accordance with one's conscience and to accept responsibility for one's behavior.
III. Respect and caring for others (i.e., the Golden Rule).
     To recognize the connectedness between all people.
     To serve humankind and to be helpful to individuals.
     To be caring, respectful, compassionate, tolerant, and forgiving of others.
     To not hurt others (e.g., do not murder, abuse, steal from, cheat, or lie to others).
IV.  Caring for other living things and the environment.

*Source:* Kinnier, Kernes, and Dautheribes (2000). Copyright 2000 by the American Counseling Association. Reprinted with permission.

the patient could project and play out intrapsychic conflicts. The desired result of this process was **transference reaction. Patients would project the persona of an important figure from their earlier psychic development and engage this persona in reparatory work by playing out conflicts with this figure in the therapist–patient relationship.** It was essential that characteristics of the therapist, including values and morals, were not conveyed to the patient, thereby encouraging the projection process.

The substance of orthodox Freudian psychodynamic therapy as well as the enthusiastic adoption of the objective, scientific paradigm continued to influence the development of all forms of psychotherapy. This legacy resulted in a long-term supposition that counselors and therapists could and should be value-neutral, a belief that persisted into the 1950s (Ginsberg & Herma, 1953; Walters, 1958). Later, professionals began acknowledging the value-based nature of counseling (Bergin, 1985; London, 1986; Pietrofesa, Hoffman, Splete, & Pinto, 1978). Education and research have continued to value and to develop the scientific and technical aspects of professional practice in subsequent decades. However, it is just as critical for counselors to acknowledge and develop the ability to address the moral and value dimensions of their expertise (Corey, Corey, Corey, & Callanan, 2014; London, 1986). Herr and Niles (1988) noted that *the counselor's*

## BOX 3.4  Value-Charged Issues in Counseling

| | | |
|---|---|---|
| Abortion | Assisted suicide | Pre- or extramarital sex |
| Sexual identity issues | Child custody | Spousal abuse |
| Substance abuse | Illegal means of support | Interracial relationships |
| Cross-racial adoption | Unsafe sexual activity | Child neglect/abuse |
| Controversial religious beliefs | Racist behavior/attitudes | Dishonesty |
| Birth control | Unwed pregnancy | Discipline of children |
| Infertility/childlessness | Cosmetic surgery | Death and dying |
| Unusual sexual practices | Gang membership | Suicide |

*values determine the process of counseling, whereas the client's values determine the content of counseling.* In addition, the content of the problem the client brings to counseling may be value-laden in and of itself for both the counselor and the client, such as whether or not to have premarital sex. Clients also may attempt to camouflage or to avoid certain issues due to struggles with their value systems, such as refusing to discuss their struggles with issues of gender identity. Box 3.4 provides examples of the myriad value-charged issues that clients may bring to counseling. Counselors should examine their own values and biases in these areas and see how they compare with the values of clients they may potentially counsel.

A counselor's personal and professional value systems will influence the course of the counseling interaction through a wide range of mechanisms: (a) if and how the client will be diagnosed, (b) whether certain topics will be addressed or discussed at all through specific direction or more subtle verbal or nonverbal reinforcement, (c) which goals are considered possible or appropriate for the counseling work they will do, and (d) how they will be evaluated (Strupp, 1980).

## VALUES OF COUNSELORS AND THE COUNSELING RELATIONSHIP

Counselors should become intensely involved in assessing their own values and how such values affect the counseling process (Corey et al., 2014; Herr & Niles, 1988). It is highly unethical for a counselor to impose values on a client, "especially when the counselor's values are inconsistent with the client's goals or are discriminatory in nature" (American Counseling Association [ACA], 2014, A.4.b). For example, some counselors have pressured homosexual clients who are content with that status to become involved in conversion or reparative role recovery therapy. It is unethical to even subtly coerce clients to undergo therapy they do not desire. Although not specifically mentioning reparative therapies, the new ACA (2014) *Code of Ethics* clearly prohibits application of treatments where there is substantial evidence of harm to clients (reparative therapies fall in this category), even if requested by the client. The American Psychological Association (APA), National Association of Social Workers (NASW), and American Association for Marriage and Family Therapy (AAMFT) codes do not have a specific standard that addresses application of harmful practices requested by clients. Counselor values should not direct counselors to partake in activities that are harmful or not in the best interest or benefit to clients.

Harmful practices aside, it may be helpful for the counselor to disclose values in conflict with a client's values. The APA (2010) and the NASW (2008) ethical codes' recognition of the ethical principle of "integrity" and the newly adopted ACA ethical principle of "veracity" (ACA, 2014) are guides for counselors to disclose their values and philosophical orientations directly to clients. This discussion might occur either within the context of specific issues that arise within the course of counseling or as part of the processes of **informed consent and professional disclosure (established to provide clients with information before they commit to treatment).** Clients should be fully informed on counseling-relevant matters at the outset of counseling (ACA, 2014; Tjelveit, 1986).

As with any advanced counseling technique, such as **confrontation (challenging a client assertively),** the counselor should disclose values carefully. This disclosure should be intentional, focused on enhancing the client's interests, and presented in an open, nonjudgmental manner that carries with it the sense that the counselor's values may be accepted or rejected without risking the counseling relationship. In keeping with the principle of nonmaleficence, counselors should consider (in consultation with colleagues or supervisors) whether the disclosure of the counselor's values might actually harm the client or the counselor–client relationship, and, if so, then the counselor "should refrain from such a self-disclosure and attempt to resolve the conflict in a different way" (Kocet & Herlihy, 2014, p. 182).

> **Question for Reflection:** Your client makes this statement in session: "I hate Jews. It's too bad Hitler wasn't able to finish what he started." You are Jewish. What, if anything, do you say in response to this statement?

The client might experience the same personal values held by the counselor, as well as a more general body of shared values. Traditionally, these shared values have been described as mental health values (Jensen & Bergin, 1988) or essential therapeutic values (Strupp, 1980). A national survey by Jensen and Bergin (1988) examined the degree of consensus of counselors with key mental health values including autonomy and independence, skill in interpersonal communication, honesty, and self-control. They found a substantial consensus among surveyed counselors that these are central counseling values, although contemporary theory is beginning to challenge such a consensus (Cottone, 2014). (Cottone [2014], for example, challenges the concept of autonomy as a guiding principle in counseling; he argued for the more social concept of "accordance," or social agreement, as a means to acknowledge and accomplish counseling goals.)

The essential therapeutic values described by Strupp (1980) are that people (a) have rights, privileges, and responsibilities; (b) have the right to personal freedom; (c) have responsibilities to others; (d) should be responsible for conducting their own affairs, as much as they are able; (e) should have their individuality respected; (f) should not be dominated, manipulated, coerced, or indoctrinated; and (g) are entitled to make their own mistakes and learn from them. Values may be observed interpersonally within the counseling relationship through studying the perceived operation of (a) *support*, the receiving of encouragement, understanding, and kindness from others; (b) *conformity*, the following of rules and observation of societal regulations; (c) *recognition*, the attraction of favorable notice and being considered important; (d) *independence*, seeing oneself as being free to make one's own decisions and acting autonomously; (e) *benevolence*, the experience of sharing, helping, and acting generously toward others; and (f) *leadership*, the sense of having responsibility, power, and authority over others (Gordon, 1976). Clearly, the values of counselors are expressed through specific behaviors that affect the client in the counseling relationship.

In addition to these more global value orientations, some theoretical orientations embody and promote specific philosophical or value positions as part of the therapeutic system. To the degree that counselors follow these specific systems of therapy, they will directly influence the philosophy and values of their clients, hopefully with the client's direct awareness and consent. Examples of such approaches and associated values include (a) Adlerian psychotherapy's emphasis on social striving and social interest; (b) reality therapy and its focus on personal responsibility and the quality of the individual lifestyle; (c) existential therapy and its emphasis on learning this particular philosophical system, including such concepts as self-determination and freedom with responsibility; and (d) Ellis's rational emotive behavior therapy and its goal of indoctrinating the client with a new set of rational beliefs and values. A counselor's theoretical approach, philosophy, and underlying value system also have an influence on clients. Therefore, the counselor should include these beliefs in the informed consent procedures at the outset of the relationship. These issues should be thoroughly discussed in terms that prospective clients can understand to ensure that they comprehend these aspects of counseling, how the issues might influence their treatment, and whether the values are compatible with their own value system.

When there appears to be serious value incompatibilities or extreme levels of discomfort, counselors must determine how they can continue working with clients. For example, value differences may require that the counselor "bracket—set aside—personal values that are not in line with the legitimate counseling goals of the client" (Martz & Kaplan, 2014, p. 24). The codes of ethics of the professional associations across the board protect individuals by virtue of issues such as "age, culture, disability, ethnicity, race, religion/spirituality, gender, gender identity, sexual orientation, marital/partnership status, language preference, socioeconomic status, immigration status, or any proscribed by law" (wording taken from the ACA [2014, C.5]). Thus, counselors must take steps to ensure that any personal values or discomfort concerning any of these client characteristics do not adversely affect the client.

> **Question for Reflection:** Your 16-year-old client informs you that she is pregnant by her 17-year-old boyfriend. She tells you that she does not love her boyfriend and was thinking about ending the relationship prior to the pregnancy. She wants to have an abortion and needs your help. You are pro-life and do not support abortion; however, you work in a public school that does not have a policy prohibiting counselors from working with students considering abortion. What do you do in terms of working with the client and how do you manage your own reaction?

Essentially, all clients must be treated with respect. Counselors often either overestimate or underestimate their ability to work with clients who arouse biased reactions in them. In such instances, counselors must make every effort to be honest with themselves. Supervision by a skilled senior colleague is invaluable in this determination. As a last resort, if the counselor is actually placing the client at risk or impeding progress, an appropriate referral made in a positive, constructive manner may be necessary. In other instances, proper safeguards such as a skilled supervisor, consultant, or cotherapy can be arranged. Then, with client consent, counseling can proceed effectively. Such situations help counselors increase their ability to understand the viewpoints of others that may be challenging to them.

*Research has demonstrated that the degree to which the values of the counselor and client are congruent influences the outcome of the counseling process.* For example, clients who adopt values like those of their counselors tended to have more positive outcomes (Beutler, Pollack, & Jobe, 1978; Landfield & Nawas, 1964; Welkowitz, Cohen, & Ortmeyer, 1967). Similarly, there is support for the view that religious clients prefer counselors who employ counseling interventions that are of a religious nature, thus indicating the need for counselors to be familiar with and amenable to engaging in such interventions (Schaffner & Dixon, 2003). This important effect of differing counselor and client value systems demonstrates the increasing importance of the counselor being culturally sensitive. Counselors must become aware of the value systems of their clients from different cultures and of their own cultural assumptions and biases. They must also be willing and able to apply the skills necessary to accommodate and to work across these diverse cultural perspectives (Kocet & Herlihy, 2014; Pederson, 1985; Sue, 1996).

> **Question for Reflection:** Your client, a member of the Lakota Sioux, recently lost her husband in an automobile accident and is seeing you for counseling. She reports that she saw her deceased husband and he told her to "watch for the eagle." She has been maintaining evening vigils in wait of her husband's request. You become concerned because she seems to be experiencing hallucinations. What will you do?

## VALUES, CULTURAL WORLDVIEWS, AND MULTICULTURALISM

A deep appreciation and understanding of the values of various cultural, social, and racial groups may provide a window into the relationship with a client who is from a nonmajority group. Counselors must understand how individuals from different cultures see the world and how they value different situations or ways of being—their worldviews. In a diverse society, counselors can no longer presume that all people hold common, universal values that will be expressed in the same way. Even when people from diverse cultures do hold common values, they may apply them to specific circumstances very differently. The actual choices and behaviors they choose are more likely culture specific.

The values of different cultures have been described using a variety of dimensions upon which cultural groups may differ. While these various descriptors may be confusing, they do reflect the rich differences in what human beings value and how they see the world. Themes or dimensions for cultural values include nature, time, social relations, activity, humanity, customs, traditions, and religion (Hopkins, 1997). In contrast, Hofstede (1980) researched cultural differences relevant to public life and work behavior and found four major cultural dimensions: (a) power distances, (b) uncertainty avoidance, (c) individualism/collectivism, and (d) masculinity (or valuing assertiveness and materialism) rather than femininity (concern for people and quality of life).

Becoming culturally sensitive is not an easy pursuit for counselors and constitutes a lifelong area for personal and professional development. Corey et al. (2014), strident proponents of this type of value learning and exploration, noted that often counselors must challenge the stereotypical beliefs that are associated with stereotypical assumptions, including: (a) assuming the client's readiness to engage in and value self-disclosure; (b) assumptions about directness and assertiveness as "good" even when culturally they may show a lack of respect; (c) believe that self-actualization is important and that a trusting relationship can be quickly formed; and (d) assuming the universality of nonverbal behaviors rather than recognizing differences across cultures (Corey et al., 2014). Counselors must continuously strive to learn more about different cultures and varying value systems related to the lives of their clients. Learning about these value themes or dimensions by listening to clients with openness and a desire to enter into their frame of reference is an important obligation.

## VALUES CLARIFICATION

How can counselors best prepare themselves to recognize their values and the implications of these values in their work? This task can be daunting. **Values clarification is a means to assess one's own values in relationship to the work of a professional counselor.**

The work of Raths, Harmin, and Simon (1966, 1978) sparked a tremendously successful movement among educators, counselors, other helping professionals, and even the public that focused attention on the importance and understanding of values. These scholars addressed the vacuum that many people felt in the 1950s in terms of establishing a sense of meaning and the importance of values within their lives and work. This movement appeared to be a reaction to the value-neutral influence of the scientific tradition and the increasing popularity of the humanistic philosophical and therapeutic movements of the late 1950s to the 1970s. The groundbreaking work of Rogers, Perls, Maslow, and others encouraged self-determination, examination of one's own perspectives, and the search for personal meaning and truth through self-examination (Kinnier, 1995). It is within that context that Raths et al. (1966) noted that many individuals were unaware of the values they held and suffered from a lack of focus in their personal and professional relationships and even in the sense of personal identity.

Values clarification helps individuals clarify their beliefs through a method that focuses on the process surrounding assigning value rather than on the content of what is valued (Raths et al., 1966). Distinct steps in the values clarification process involve the three main functions: prizing, choosing, and acting on one's values. Values chosen through this process are considered clarified values.

Kirschenbaum (2000) became convinced that values clarification should be an element in a more comprehensive approach that includes the original seven valuing processes described by Raths et al. (1978) that are contained in the facilitating stage of his (revised) model, but also adds the processes of inculcation of positive values and character, modeling of values and character, and skill building necessary to live a satisfying and constructive life (Kirschenbaum, 2000; see Box 3.5).

Kirschenbaum's revision addressed the criticisms of those authorities who faulted values clarification for being concerned only with the process rather than the outcome of the process. Kirschenbaum's revision concerns itself with both the process and the hoped-for outcomes of values education. Box 3.6 lists activities that are consistent with this tradition.

---

### BOX 3.5 The Comprehensive Values Education Process (Includes the Seven Values Clarification Steps in the Facilitation Process)

I. Inculcating
II. Modeling
III. Facilitating
   A. Prizing beliefs and behaviors
      1. Prizing and cherishing
      2. Publicly affirming, when appropriate
   B. Choosing beliefs and behaviors
      3. Choosing from alternatives
      4. Choosing after consideration of consequences
      5. Choosing freely
   C. Acting on beliefs
      6. Acting
      7. Acting with a pattern, consistency and repetition

Adapted from Kirschenbaum (2000). Copyright 2000 by the American Counseling Association. Adapted with permission.

## BOX 3.6  What Are Some of My Values?

The following activities are consistent with the values clarification tradition. After completing the activities, discuss your answers in a group. Conduct an open, thought-provoking discussion with your peers, examine the consequences of your position, and publicly affirm your beliefs.

*Activity 1.* Imagine that your doctor has told you that you have an aggressive form of cancer and you will be dead soon. You have decided to write your own eulogy. What are the unique traits or meaningful accomplishments that you especially want to include? Why are they particularly important to you? Which one is the most important to you? Why? Which one is most important to your parents? Which one is most important to your spouse, partner, or closest friend? Do these perspectives differ? Why or why not?

*Activity 2.* Imagine you are in a long-standing relationship with your partner that is very happy, except for one thing—you and your partner are not able to have a biological child despite wanting one badly. You have decided to adopt a child, but are not able to receive a healthy infant of your own race. You are offered the opportunity to choose from among the following babies: a biracial baby, a baby who is moderately intellectually disabled, a baby whose biological mother is HIV positive, a 2-year-old who appears to be hyperactive, a child with facial deformities that can only be partially corrected by surgeries, and a toddler who survived the murder–suicide of his biological parents. Would you adopt one of these children or choose not to have a child? If so, which child would you select and why? For each of the children you did not select, what was your reasoning?

Countless individuals have taken part and benefited from this type of activity. This approach offers opportunities to examine countless aspects of our personal and professional relationships and lifestyle choices. It is likely to stimulate lively discussion and serious self-examination. The activities can be tailored to the concerns and needs of quite disparate types of people, including counselors-in-training. For example:

- What do you anticipate will be your ideal type of client to work with? Why? Your most dreaded? Why?

- What will make you happiest about your work as a counselor? Over what do you think you will become the most upset or afraid?

- Who is the living person who has most influenced your desire to work in counseling? Why and how?

- What historical or prominent celebrity figure has most influenced your desire to work in counseling? Why and how?

- What do you anticipate will be the greatest boost to your effectiveness as a counselor and why?

- What do you anticipate will be the biggest threat to your effectiveness as a counselor and why?

- What makes you proudest about your choice to be a counselor?

- What about the counseling profession makes you proud?

## VALUES CONFLICT RESOLUTION

Clearly, the ways in which human experience can be explored through values clarification are vast. Nevertheless, values clarification began to lose favor and to be heavily critiqued. The most common area of concern involves the apparently value-neutral position of the group leader or teacher. The concern was that this experience might create a permissive, self-absorbed atmosphere, and in its extreme, allow abusive or abhorrent values to go unchallenged. Kinnier (1995) suggested that extremist positions (sometimes prejudicial), a therapeutic paradigm shift away from humanistic philosophy, and the inherent flaws within humanistic theory itself are the major forces that have dampened earlier enthusiasm for values clarification. He recommended several changes to resolve specific problems and extend the usefulness of this approach. Kinnier (1995) recommended focusing on one concrete and specific values conflict at a time in a specific area of the person's life, because people do not effectively evaluate values in single, abstract form. The emphasis should not be on rank-ordering values, but rather on determining which values are in conflict and the degree of conflict, as well as arriving at an overall statement of how the key values in conflict can be reconciled. This approach would provide a more specific goal to the process—resolution of a specified values conflict as it usually occurs in real

---

### BOX 3.7  Strategies for Intrapersonal Values Conflict Resolution

**Rational Strategies**

Defining the conflict clearly

Gathering information systematically

Comparing alternatives and considering consequences logically

Eliminating alternatives systematically

Being vigilant for maladaptive affect regarding the conflict, resolution, or both (e.g., excessive worry, postdecisional regret, irrational beliefs) and using cognitive restructuring, emotional inoculation, or stress-reduction techniques to counter maladaptive affect

**Intuition-Enhancing Strategies**

Emotional focusing

Brainstorming/Free association

Life review

Psychodrama or guided imagery to enhance focus

Personal rituals

Incubation (e.g., meditation)

Self-confrontational exercises such as the devil's advocate or the two-chair exercise, and confrontation with one's own mortality that involves both rational discourse and a focus on affective reactions

Adapted from Kinnier (1995). Copyright 1995 by the American Counseling Association. Adapted with permission.

settings. Kinnier (1995) suggested how more effective interventions could be tailored to assist in this conflict resolution (Box 3.7). The interventions are divided between rational and intuitive types to accommodate differing personal styles of those in conflict.

Other issues have arisen as counselors attempt to apply the individualistically oriented concepts of values clarification to group or marriage and family counseling issues. The role of interdependence in healthy human relationships and the social, political, and cultural context of the individual's experience are an important aspect of the counseling therapeutic and theoretical worldviews that are beyond the scope of more limited specialty area perspectives. For example, Sue (1996) noted that counseling practices that impose monocultural value systems or biases on clients from diverse cultural backgrounds are discriminatory and unethical. Thus, counselors must actively guard against imposing such values when counseling their clients (Kocet & Herlihy, 2014).

Marriage and family counselors have long struggled with issues of reconciling the conceptualization of the individual's values with those in the relationships of the group or family as a whole. Doherty and Boss (1991) reviewed the literature on value issues and ethics in the practice of marriage and family therapy. They note that the idea of value neutrality on the part of the therapist is no longer viable, and the emphasis in the field should be on accommodating values within the therapeutic process. Thomas (1994) provided a model of value analysis within marriage and family counseling that attempts to meld personal and systematically oriented value systems in addressing value dilemmas. He noted that counselors must analyze and reconcile values at (a) the individual level of the counselor microsystem, (b) the family level of the client's microsystem, and (c) the level of the overlapping counseling process itself (mesosystem). These operations are embedded in the context of societal values surrounding the dilemma (macrosystem). While this analysis may be couched in marriage and family therapy language, it is important for counselors in all settings to consider contextual or hierarchical levels that affect their ethical and values analysis (Tarvydas & Cottone, 1991). Constantine and Sue (2005) believed a recognition and application of systems interventions will be necessary for ethical practice as counselors recognize that clients often have experiences embedded in the systems in which they are nested.

**Questions for Reflection:** Given this chapter's discussion of counseling clients whose beliefs, preferences, values, and lifestyles may be inconsistent with your own, what do you think your level of comfort (or discomfort) would be when counseling such clients? If you feel that you would have more than a mild level of distress, then consider whether counseling is the right profession for you. If not, you may be able to go into other careers that do not require that you set aside your values when they conflict with those you work with. If you are committed to being in the counseling profession, there are ways to work on being able to bracket your values and still be able to help the client.

(continued)

**Questions for Reflection (*continued*)**
   One final note to consider is that members of other professions, such as attorneys, routinely set aside their personal values when working with clients. A long-honored value in the practice of law is that all clients deserve the best legal representation possible. This commitment is illustrated in the 1993 movie *Philadelphia* (with Tom Hanks and Denzel Washington). Washington's character, an attorney, represented Hank's character, who was terminated from his job because he had AIDS. Although Washington's character stated, "I don't like homosexuals," he still represented Hank's character in a wrongful termination lawsuit, which they ultimately won. What is your reaction to this perspective as applied to the professional who engages in counseling and psychotherapy?

The negotiation of values involves reconciling disparate and often competing values orientations. Counselors must acknowledge the implications of negotiating values with clients. The counselor should establish conditions for a more interactive alliance around particular value perspectives. Huber (1994) described these key assumptions based on the earlier work of Dell (1983). The practitioner must recognize that:

1. No such phenomenon as an absolute value exists that is objectively true or good. Rather, values are a result of the person's processing or reaction of a system's values.
2. All persons must take responsibility for selecting, interpreting, and holding their own values; thus, no one can be held ultimately responsible for changing another's values.
3. Therapists must accept responsibility for the tendency to pathologize their clients, or to see them in terms of their pathologies or problems, thus deemphasizing the role of their own values in the process.
4. Counselors must accept that "what is, is." They must allow clients to be accepted for who they are, rather than being judged as bad or sick because of behaviors that do not conform to the counselor's values or preferences.

The value assumptions just described are only working assumptions and must be examined critically. Nevertheless, these assumptions, if acknowledged and incorporated within the values negotiation process, will allow the negotiation to occur in a constructive and productive manner. The core components of value negotiation are (a) recognition of mutual obligations and entitlements within the relationships among the parties, or the "give and take" of human interactions; (b) the acknowledgment of those things to which others are entitled and the valid claims of others; and (c) the balance of fairness (Huber, 1994). While attending to these principles and the value negotiation process may appear to add greatly to counseling's complexity, in reality these considerations recognize and respect the shared nature of the important relationship between people of diverse backgrounds. Value issues that arise between counselor and client from the dazzlingly numerous sources of interpersonal diversity have the potential to enrich the counselor and the client and their relationship, if they are directly addressed within the valuing process.

**Question for Reflection:** You counseled a couple for approximately 1 year and the marriage ended in divorce. The husband is suing his wife for custody of their two children. You have received a subpoena from the husband's attorney to appear in court to testify about the wife's emotional instability. Although there was evidence of the wife's emotional instability during counseling, you do not think it is serious enough to warrant an "unfit mother" verdict. To complicate matters, you find out that the wife has employed the most incompetent attorney in the city and you are afraid he will not represent her well. What will you do?

## CONCLUSION

The issues surrounding ethical judgment involve a complex interplay of values that people hold in relationship to themselves, their colleagues, and other professionals. Values are enduring beliefs of what is worthwhile and reflect the value holder's worldview, culture, or understanding of the world.

Values clarification and the value negotiation process are general processes that assist counselors in working with value systems of clients. Values clarification involves three steps: prizing, choosing, and acting on one's values. Values chosen through this process are called clarified values. The negotiation of values is a means for counselors and clients to address value conflicts. Counseling is a value-laden process.

# ETHICAL DECISION-MAKING PROCESSES[1]

*Key Chapter*

This chapter presents a scholarly review of ethical decision-making models. It also presents details of two decision-making models developed by the authors. Tarvydas developed the first model; it is an integration model that blends the best of what is known about decision making in counseling to the date of this writing. An example of how this model might be applied to resolve an ethical dilemma is provided. Cottone developed the second model; it is a theoretically based model designed using a radical social constructivism philosophy. It is as pure a model built on philosophy as is known in the literature. Beyond showcasing the authors' models, it is hoped you will get a sense of their commitment to applying ethics best practices in the field, and to their theoretical, philosophical,

---

[1] Parts of this chapter draw heavily and directly from two works published in the American Counseling Association's (ACA's) *Journal of Counseling & Development*—Cottone (2001) and Cottone and Claus (2000) with permission of the ACA; from Tarvydas (2012; copyright by Springer Publishing Company); and from Barnett and Klimik (2012).

and empirical inclinations. Presenting both models is also intended to give students and professors some choice and flexibility in approaching ethical decision making within and outside of the classroom. The models are quite distinct. It is hoped readers will gain by a comparative analysis of the models.

> **Questions for Reflection:** Reflect on your last major decision, such as choosing an undergraduate or graduate program, becoming engaged or married, making a major purchase, or choosing a job. Think about the process you experienced as you made the decision. Did you do some background research? What individuals were involved in discussion about the decision? What values affected your decision? Who communicated these values to you during your personal development? What social or cultural factors may have influenced your decision? Was the process smooth or abrupt? What emotions did you experience? Did you have a chance to reflect or reconsider your decision after you made it but before you implemented it? What actions did you take to implement the decision? Looking back, do you feel it was a wise decision?

## ETHICAL JUDGMENT

The practice of counseling is an art as well as a science, requiring the practitioner to make both value-laden and rational decisions. Rather than being incompatible stances, facts and values must be considered together if counselors are to make good decisions.

An ethics code provides counselors with guidance for the specific situations they experience in their practices. However, authorities have long recognized that ethics codes must be general enough to apply across a wide range of practice settings. They are also reactive in nature; that is, they address situations that have already been part of the profession's experience (Kitchener, 1984; Mabe & Rollin, 1986). As a result, even with the knowledge of the profession's code of ethics, counselors may not find sufficient guidance to resolve a dilemma. They may find that the particular situation they face is not addressed in their code, is addressed by more than one code providing conflicting direction, or that conflicting provisions within one code appear to apply to the situation. Thus, counselors must be prepared to exercise their ethical and professional judgment responsibly. Ethical dilemmas are not so much a failure of ethical codes as a natural and appropriate indicator of the importance of professional judgment. The need to use ethical judgment is affirmation that one is involved in the "practice of a profession," rather than "doing a job," however skilled.

To exercise professional judgment, counselors must be prepared to recognize underlying ethical principles and conflicts among competing interests, as well as to apply appropriate decision-making skills to resolve the dilemma and act ethically (Francouer, 1983; Kitchener, 1984; Kitchener & Anderson, 2011; Tarvydas, 1987). Fortunately, professionals are assisted in this task by examination and refinement of their ordinary moral sense, as well as the availability of thoughtful models for the ethical decision-making process. Many components of ethical decision making involve teachable, learnable skills to supplement the professional's developing judgment.

Several models exist that explain and structure the process of ethical decision making. Some are highly theoretical; others are empirical or philosophical. Some are clinically sound approaches derived from practices that have been known to resolve significant ethical dilemmas. Others are based on anecdotal evidence alone—given credence in stories that have become ethical folklore. The mental health professions increasingly have emphasized the importance of learning ethical decision-making models to ethical best practices. The professions' codes have added standards that require professionals to learn and apply a credible ethical decision-making model (ACA, 2014; Commission on Rehabilitation Counselor Certification, 2010). Because ethical decision making is so critical to the practice of the counseling profession, this chapter provides a thorough scholarly review of the literature on the topic. There are many ethical decision-making models in counseling, but only some are philosophically, empirically, or theoretically founded.

## A REVIEW OF ETHICAL DECISION-MAKING MODELS

In 1984, Kitchener published a seminal work related to ethical decision making in counseling and counseling psychology. Kitchener argued that in the absence of clear ethical guidelines, relying on personal value judgments (as some other authors had proposed) was inadequate because "independent of . . . external considerations, not all value judgments are equally valid" (p. 44). She argued that counseling professionals should "develop a deeper understanding of the basis for ethical decision-making" (p. 44). She then presented a model that integrates Hare's (1981) work on levels of moral thinking (intuitive and critical-evaluative), and Beauchamp and Childress' (1979) suggested ethical "principles" (autonomy, beneficence, nonmaleficence, and justice), and the ethical "rule" of fidelity. Subsequent to Kitchener's 1984 publication, there have been many publications on ethical issues in counseling.

Since Kitchener's (1984) article was published, Beauchamp and Childress' (1979) text, *Principles of Biomedical Ethics*, has been revised several times; it is a highly cited work in its seventh edition (Beauchamp & Childress, 2012) that has laid the groundwork for other authors. Although the Beauchamp and Childress (2012) text is a foundation text that provides guiding principles for ethical decision making, it fails to address decision-making models or processes with any depth. Instead, the authors provide a thorough analysis of ethical theory, including criteria of theory construction and an overview of widely recognized ethical theories (e.g., utilitarianism, Kantianism, liberal individualism). In a work published in 1994, Beauchamp and Walters provided a "set of considerations" or "methods" for resolving moral disagreements as a way "of easing and perhaps settling controversies" (p. 4). The methods included: (a) "obtaining objective information," (b) "providing definitional clarity," (c) "adopting a code," (d) "using examples and counterexamples," and (e) "analyzing arguments" (pp. 4–7). Beauchamp and Walters (1994) did not present a review of decision-making processes, but they took a position and presented a basic model for judging ethical decisions.

Historically there was a lack of in-depth discussion of ethical decision-making processes in the literature. Rather, those authors who included a model in their work simply listed the actual act of making a decision as a step, or they did not list it as a step at all. In either case, many authors in the past did not address an explanatory framework for the decision process itself. Some models are exceptions (i.e., these models explain the actual decision process), especially those involving theoretical and philosophical foundations.

In 2000, Cottone and Claus produced a review of the literature on ethical decision-making models in counseling. That review provided a classification framework for defining ethical decision-making models. Models were classified as one of the following: (a) theoretical or philosophy-based models, (b) practice-based models, or (c) models developed for specialty practice. A major conclusion of the Cottone and Claus work was that there were few empirical studies of ethical decision making in counseling; although there were numerous models, few had been tested against each other or against some other standard.

In 2012, in a chapter in the *APA Handbook of Ethics in Psychology*, Cottone (2012a) developed an updated organization framework for classifying ethical decision-making models applied in mental health contexts. His schema provided a summary of major intellectual movements in the decision-making literature. Three intellectual movements were defined: (a) principle ethics; (b) virtue ethics; and (c) relational ethics. Further, he classified "multicultural sensitivity" as a decision-making "theme" that crossed the three intellectual movements. He further subcategorized models as follows: (a) grounded in the philosophy of individual choice; (b) grounded in quantification (empirical justification) as a means to individual choice; (c) practice-derived models of individual choice; and (d) models of relational influence (where individuals do not make decisions separate from the social context—relationships affect choices).

## THEORETICAL OR PHILOSOPHICAL MODELS OF INDIVIDUAL CHOICE

Several authors made an attempt to ground ethical decision making on some theory or philosophy—notably, Hare's (1991) "The Philosophical Basis of Psychiatric Ethics," which in its original 1981 form was used by Kitchener as a guiding work. Hare argued that absolute thinking (dealing with rights and duties) and utilitarian thinking (doing the greatest good for the greatest number; considering the interests of patients) were both involved in ethical decision making. He then invoked two levels of moral reasoning to address ethical dilemmas—the "intuitive" and "critical" levels:

> That we have a duty to serve the interests of the patient, and that we have a duty to respect his rights, can both perhaps be ascertained by consulting our intuitions at the bottom level. But if we ask which duty or which intuition ought to carry the day, we need some means other than intuition, some higher kind of thinking (let us call it "critical moral thinking") to settle the question between them. . . . (p. 35)

Hare believed that the "intuitive level, with its prima facie duties and principles, is the main locus of everyday moral decisions" (p. 35). However, he argued that it is "not sufficient" (p. 36), and must be superseded by critical (utilitarian) thinking when "no appeal to intuitions" can "settle the dispute" (p. 38). Although Hare's work was applied to psychiatry, it has direct relevance to counseling. Many have followed the lead of Kitchener and incorporated Hare's ideas in their works.

Rest (1984) produced another work that is cited often in the literature. He published extensively on the topic of developmental issues related to moral reasoning (e.g., Rest, Cooper, Coder, Maganz, & Anderson, 1974; Rest, Davison, & Robbins, 1978). His 1984 work, written specifically for the applied ethics of psychology, drew heavily on theories of moral development (e.g., Kohlberg, 1969, 1980) and research findings (e.g., Schwartz, 1977) to present a four-component model of "processes involved in the production of moral behavior" (p. 19). The components are: (a) "to interpret the situation in terms of how one's actions affect the welfare of others"; (b) "to formulate what a moral course of action would be; to identify the moral ideal in a specific situation"; (c) "to select among competing value outcomes of ideals, the one to act upon; deciding whether or not to try to fulfill one's moral ideal"; and (d) "to execute and implement what one intends to do" (p. 20). The four components are not temporally linear and they are not virtues or traits of individuals. Rather, "they are major units of analysis in tracing out how a particular course of action was produced in the context of a particular situation" (p. 20). Rest argued that: "The four component model provides a framework for ordering existing research on moral development, identifying needed research and deriving implications for moral education. There are many directives for the moral education of counselors that come from this research" (p. 27). For instance, he believed an assessment instrument could be developed for each component to assess counseling students entering training or the outcomes of training programs themselves. In a later work, Rest (1994) reviewed the works of Kohlberg and gave an up-to-date summary of research findings related to Kohlberg's theory. He also offered a revision of the four-component model. He defined the four components as "the major determinants of moral behavior" (p. 22) and he summarized the components as: (a) "moral sensitivity," (b) "moral judgment," (c) "moral motivation," and (d) "moral character" (pp. 23–24). He stated:

> In summary, moral failure can occur because of deficiency in any component. All four components are determinants of moral action. In fact, there are complex interactions among the four components, and it is not supposed that the four represent a temporal order such that a person performs one, then two, then three, then four—rather the four components comprise a logical analysis of what it takes to behave morally. (p. 24)

Rest's model is clearly theoretically linked to cognitive theory through the works of Kohlberg, and he has one of the most empirically well-grounded approaches for analyzing moral behavior.

## QUANTIFICATION AS A MEANS TO INDIVIDUAL CHOICE

Gutheil, Bursztajn, Brodsky, and Alexander (1991), in a text on decision making in psychiatry and law, provided a chapter titled "Probability, Decision Analysis, and Conscious Gambling." The chapter reviewed the mechanistic and probabilistic paradigms in science and took a stand that decision making must account for some level of uncertainty (probability). They made an argument in favor of "decision analysis" as a formal decision-making tool:

> Decision analysis is a step-by-step procedure enabling us to break down a decision into its components, to lay them out in an orderly fashion, and to trace the sequence of events that might follow from choosing one course of action or another. This procedure offers several benefits. It can help us to make the best possible decision in a given situation. Moreover, it can help us to clarify our values, that is, the preferences among possible outcomes by which we judge what the best decision might be. Decision analysis can also be used to build logic and rationality into our intuitive decision-making—to educate our intuition about probabilities and about the paths of contingency by which our actions, in combination with chance or "outside" events, lead to outcomes. (p. 41)

Decision analysis involves several approaches, including: (a) acknowledging the decision; (b) listing the pros and cons; (c) structuring the decision (including development of a decision "tree" to graph decisional paths and subsequent decisional branches); (d) estimating probabilities and values; and (e) calculating expected value. Estimating probabilities by means of a decision tree may involve calculating "the relative frequency with which the event in question occurs over a large number of trials in similar circumstances" (p. 46). The authors contrast decision analysis to decision making as gambling. Their model is clearly linked to nonmechanistic, probability theory in science (e.g., the uncertainty principle).

## PRACTICE-DERIVED MODELS OF INDIVIDUAL CHOICE

Some authors have proposed models based on pragmatic procedures derived largely from experience or intended primarily as practical guides for counselors. These models tend to be less theory specific or philosophically pure than those discussed previously. Table 4.1 summarizes practice-based, decision-making models and provides a step-by-step comparative layout. Although the steps may not align perfectly in the table, it does present a basic visual picture that allows for a comparative analysis. (For a more in-depth discussion of these approaches, see the chapter published by Cottone [2012a].)

## MODELS OF RELATIONAL INFLUENCE

Based on a theory of feminism, Hill, Glaser, and Harden (1995) proposed a model for ethical decision making. They value the emotional responses of the counselor and the social context in which the therapeutic relationship takes place. In accord with feminist beliefs regarding power, the client is engaged as fully as possible in the decision-making process. At each step, the feminist model includes a rational–evaluative procedure with corresponding emotional and intuitive queries to assist the counselor. This model includes a review process in

**TABLE 4.1 Summary of Ethical Decision-Making Models**

| Corey, Corey, and Callanan (2007) | Forester-Miller and Davis (1996) | Hass and Malouf (2005) | Keith-Spiegel and Koocher (1985) | Sperry (2007) | Welfel (2006) |
|---|---|---|---|---|---|
| 1. Identify the problem | 1. Identify the problem | 1. Identify the ethical problem | 1. Describe the parameters | 1. Enhance ethical sensitivity and anticipation | 1. Develop ethical sensitivity |
| 2. Identify potential issues involved | 2. Apply the ACA *Code of Ethics* | 2. Identify legitimate stakeholders | 2. Define the potential issues | 2. Identify the problem | 2. Identify relevant facts and stakeholders |
| 3. Review relevant ethical guidelines | 3. Determine the nature of dilemma | 3. Identify relevant standards | 3. Consult legal and ethical guidelines | 3. Identify participants affected by the decision | 3. Define central issues in the dilemma and available options |
| 4. Know applicable laws and regulations | 4. Generate potential courses of action | 4. Review the relevance of the existing standard | 4. Evaluate the rights, responsibilities, and welfare of involved parties | 4. Identify courses of action and benefit/risks for participants | 4. Examine relevant ethical standards, laws, and regulations |
| 5. Obtain consultation, consider possible and probable courses of action | 5. Consider potential consequences, determine course of action | 5. Evaluate the ethical dimensions of the issue and specify a primary ethical dimension if possible | 5. Generate alternate decisions | 5. Evaluate benefits/risks context considerations | 5. Search out ethics scholarship |
| 6. Consider possible and probable courses of action | | 6. Consult and review codes of ethics, review literature, consider ethical principles | 6. Enumerate the consequences of each decision | 6. Consult with peers and experts | 6. Apply ethical principles to the situation |
| 7. Enumerate consequences of various decisions | | 7. Generate a list of possible actions | 7. Estimate probability for outcomes of each decision | | 7. Consult with supervisor and respected colleagues |

*don't have to memorize all ☆ know what its about.*

(continued)

**TABLE 4.1  Summary of Ethical Decision-Making Models** *(continued)*

| Corey, Corey, and Callanan (2007) | Forester-Miller and Davis (1996) | Hass and Malouf (2005) | Keith-Spiegel and Koocher (1985) | Sperry (2007) | Welfel (2006) |
|---|---|---|---|---|---|
| 8. Decide on the best course of action | | 8. Do cost/benefit analysis and choose based on optimum resolution for greatest number | 8. Make the decision | 7. Decide the most feasible option and document the decision process | 8. Deliberate and decide |
| | 6. Evaluate selected course of action | 9. Evaluate the new course of action for effect on people and unforeseen ethical problems | | | |
| | 7. Implement course of action | 10. Judge whether course of action can be implemented | | 8. Implement, evaluate, and document the decision | 9. Inform supervisor and take action |
| | | 11. Implement the chosen course of action | | | 10. Reflect on the experience |

ACA, American Counseling Association.

Reprinted with permission from Barnett and Klimik (2012). Copyright by American Psychological Association.

which the counselor considers the impact of personal values, the universality of the proposed solution, and the intuitive feel of the proposed solution. Because personal characteristics affect ethical decisions, Hill et al. believe integration of this factor into their model improves the decision-making process.

Betan (1997) proposed a hermeneutic perspective of ethical decision making. He stated that "hermeneutics represents a shift in views of the nature of knowledge and the process of how we come to know" . . . since . . . "knowledge is situated in the context of human relationships in which the interpreter (as knowledge is interpretation) participates in narrating meaning" (p. 352). He advocated that hermeneutics adds to, rather than replaces, the principled approaches of Kitchener (1984) and Rest (1984): "The context of the therapeutic relationship and the clinician's psychological needs and dynamics are fundamental considerations in the interpretation and application of ethical principles" (p. 356). Further, he stated:

> A linear, logical-reductionistic approach to ethics, such as that offered by Kitchener (1984) and Rest (1984), can lead to a false dichotomy between the rational and the intuitive, and the universal and the subjective. The key in this hermeneutic approach is to acknowledge the dialectic of the universal and the subjective of human relations, in which each informs the other. That is, our sense of what is universal (in this regard, a standard or principle) is a product of shared subjective experiences, which in turn are embedded in a context of cultural interpretation. (p. 356)

The prima facie obligation of ethical principles asserted by Kitchener must instead, according to Betan, be applied in the context of personal and cultural values. That an ethical truth is constructed in the framework of one's conception of self, others, and the world holds implications for counselor training; counselors must work to gain awareness of ethical dilemmas, their own personal and moral values, and the interaction between ethical principles and context.

Cottone (2001, 2004, 2012a) took an even more radical relational position than that of Betan (1997). Cottone (2001) proposed an ethical decision-making approach based on social constructivism. He argued that decision making is not a psychological process. Rather, decision making always involves interaction with other individuals. Building on the works of Gergen (1985) in social psychology and the works of Maturana (1978, 1988; Maturana & Varela, 1980) in the biology of cognition, Cottone (2001) argued that ethical decisions "are not compelled internally; rather, they are socially compelled" (p. 6). Further, he asserted that ethical decision making occurs in the interactive processes of negotiating, consensualizing, and arbitrating. An individual's psychological process is not involved. The social constructivism perspective of ethical decision making takes the decision out of the "head," so to speak, and places it in the interactive process between people. Cottone's model is presented later in this chapter.

## EMPIRICAL FINDINGS ON MODELS OR PREMISES

Two empirical studies in the published literature had direct theoretical linkage. Cottone, Tarvydas, and House (1994) derived hypotheses about how counseling students in a graduate program make decisions based on social systems theory. According to social systems theory, they posited that "all thinking and decision-making would be highly socially and relationally influenced, and both number and types of relationships would potentially influence how individuals act and think" (p. 57). They concluded:

> The results indicate that interpersonal relations influenced the ethical decision-making of graduate counseling student participants when they were asked to reconsider a decision. In other words, relationships seem to influence ethical decision-making linearly and cumulatively. Additionally, there seems to be an interaction between the number and type of consulted relationships in a way that eludes simple explanation. Although there was only a small interaction effect size, the results support a conclusion that ethical decision-making in a reconsideration circumstance is a relatively complex issue, with at least the number and type of relationships interacting. (p. 63)

The results support a conclusion of social influence over ethical choice. The second study was a test of Janis and Mann's (1977) theory of decision making under stress by Hinkeldey and Spokane (1985). Hinkeldey and Spokane concluded that "consistent with Janis and Mann's theory, results showed that decision-making was affected negatively by pressure but that participants relied little on legal guidelines in making responses to ethical conflict dilemmas" (p. 240).

Dinger (1997) presented dissertation findings on a study that compared Kitchener's (1984) Ethical Justification Model to the A-B-C-D-E Worksheet Model of Sileo and Kopala (1993) and concluded that the Kitchener model better served participants in identifying the ethical issues presented in different scenarios.

## WILLINGNESS OR RESOLUTENESS AS A FACTOR IN DECISION MAKING

There are obvious cases where a well-educated professional, knowledgeable about ethical principles and standards in the field, can still make poor decisions or fail to act ethically when faced with a dilemma. Cottone (2012a) addressed this in a response to the question, "Will the application of a decision-making model ensure an ethical action?" The answer is "No." Mental health professionals must be willing to act ethically—they must be resolute in carrying out ethical directives. Cottone (2012a) stated:

> But research has shown that some intuitive (ethical) judgments may be overridden or even blocked under certain circumstances (Kahneman, 2003). And what about blind spots, those dilemmas prone to bias or that may be confused by personal feelings (Cottone & Tarvydas [2007])? In those cases, it becomes a question of ethical willingness and resoluteness (cf. Bernard & Jara, 1986; Bernard, Murphy, & Little, 1987; Betan & Stanton, 1999). Typically, publications that address ethical willingness document empirically that students of psychology or professional practitioners are unwilling in certain cases to take ethical action. Scenarios presented in such research

typically involve a decision to report a peer who was behaving unethically. In as many as 50% of responses, participants admit that they would "do less than what they realized they should do" (Bernard et al., 1987, p. 490). In effect, the psychologists (or trainees) who responded to these surveys were blinded by personal factors. (p. 114)

So knowledge and training alone are not enough. Factors specific to the decision maker enter into the equation as to whether a report of unethical conduct will be made or addressed. The factors specific to the decision maker may be summarized in the terms "willingness" or "resoluteness."

## THE TARVYDAS INTEGRATIVE DECISION-MAKING MODEL OF ETHICAL BEHAVIOR

The Tarvydas Integrative Decision-Making Model of Ethical Behavior (Tarvydas, 2012) incorporates the most prominent principle and virtue aspects of several decision-making approaches and introduces some contextual considerations into the process. Generally, ethical decision-making models can be thought of as having the characteristics of either principle or virtue ethics (Corey, Corey, Corey, & Callanan, 2014). **Principle ethics focuses on the objective, rational, and cognitive aspects of the process.** Practitioners who adhere to this perspective tend to view the application of universal, impartial ethical principles, rules, codes, and law as the core elements of ethics. **Virtue ethics considers the characteristics of the counselors themselves as the critical element for responsible practice.** Thus, proponents of virtue ethics approaches tend to concern themselves more with counselors reflecting on and clarifying their moral and value positions. Additionally, they examine other personal issues that might influence their ethical practice, such as unresolved emotional needs that might negatively affect their work with clients. Many argue that it is preferable that ethical decision making includes both aspects (Corey, Corey, & Callanan, 2003; Meara, Schmidt, & Day, 1996). Among other positive contributions of such a synergistic approach, Meara, Schmidt, and Day (1996) and Vasquez (1996) speculated that the addition of virtue ethical perspectives would improve ethical conduct in multicultural and diverse interactions and settings. The Tarvydas Integrative Model emphasizes the constant process of interaction between the principle and virtue elements, and places a reflective attitude at the heart of the process. The model also focuses on the actual production of ethical behavior within a specified context, rather than prematurely terminating analysis by merely selecting the best ethical course of action. This approach respects the importance of setting and environmental factors that are crucial in counseling. Indeed, in reviewing the various approaches to ethical decision making, Garcia, Cartwright, Winston, and Borzuchowska (2003) observed that this model uses virtue ethics and behavioral strategies that are consistent with a multicultural approach to counseling and ethical decision making. They proposed an Integrative Transcultural Ethical Decision-Making Model that is based primarily on the Tarvydas Integrative Model.

## Conceptual Origins

The Tarvydas Integrative Model builds on several well-known decision-making models used widely by professionals in the mental health and counseling communities. The seminal works of Rest (1984) and Kitchener (1984) are foundational. Rest (1984) provided the Tarvydas Integrative Model with its core understanding of ethical decision making as a psychological process that involves distinct cognitive–affective elements interacting in each component. Cognitions and emotions are seen as unavoidably intertwined at each component of the decision-making process and in the production of ethical behavior. Rest (1984) conceptualized ethical decision making as more than a direct expression of moral or value traits or a stage in a moral developmental process. He emphasized considering the completion of ethical behavior as the necessary point for consideration, rather than merely arriving at a cognitive decision or intent to do an ethical act. Therefore, Rest's (1984) ethical decision-making components and many of his considerations are the foundation of the Tarvydas Integrative Model.

Kitchener (1984) provided other core elements to the Tarvydas Integrative Model. She made a use of Hare's (1981) distinction between the intuitive and critical-evaluative levels of ethical decision making, thus providing a forum to incorporate the richness and influence of the everyday personal and professional moral wisdom into the individual professional's process of ethical decision making. This personal and professional wisdom informs the first level of the process—the intuitive level, where both nonconscious and conscious levels of awareness lead to decisions that call into play the individual's existing morals, beliefs, and experiences. These morals, beliefs, and experiences that constitute our ordinary moral sense also include professional learning and experiences. Kitchener noted that the intuitive level of process often is the professional's main decision-making tool when a situation is not perceived as novel, unusual, or requiring an unusual level of care. The intuitive level of analysis always constitutes the first platform of decision making, even when the situation requires the more stringent level of analysis involved in the critical-evaluative level of consideration. Thus, a person's ordinary moral sense is relevant to one's ethical decision-making process, reinforcing the concerns raised by proponents of the virtue ethics perspective.

If the ethical issue is not resolved at the intuitive level, the counselor progresses to Kitchener's (1984) critical-evaluative level of ethical analysis. This level involves three hierarchical stages of examination to resolve the dilemma. At the first stage, the counselor determines if any laws or ethical rules exist that would provide a solution for the dilemma. If they do not exist, or if they exist but provide conflicting dictates, the counselor progresses to the second stage by considering how the core ethical principles apply to the situation. The seminal work of Beauchamp and Childress (1994) identified autonomy, beneficence, nonmaleficence, and justice as the core ethical principles that govern ethical behavior. Kitchener (1984) subsequently added fidelity to these core principles for helping professionals, resulting in five core ethical principles to be considered in ethical decision making.

If counselors are still uncertain as to the appropriate ethical course of action, they proceed to the third stage—assessing the positions suggested by ethical theory. Patterson (1992) recommended that counselors should be concerned with normative ethical theory and may benefit from considering whether they prefer their action to be based on a general or a universal law. Kitchener (1984) suggested applying the "good reasons" approach, in which counselors attempt to make a decision based on what they would wish for themselves or someone dear to them. Another standard suggested by Kitchener is to take the action that will result in the least amount of harm.

The final conceptual influence on the Tarvydas Integrative Model is the four-level model of ethical practice introduced by Tarvydas and Cottone (1991). This approach extends consideration of the **contextual forces** acting on ethical practice beyond the singular focus of the individual practitioner in relationship to the individual client. The four levels are hierarchical, moving to increasingly broader levels of social contexts within which ethical practice is influenced. **The four levels are (a) the clinical counseling level, (b) the clinical interdisciplinary level, (c) the institutional/agency level, and (d) the societal resource/public policy level.** The relationships among the levels are seen as interactive. Peak ethical efficiency and lowest levels of ethical stress are reached when each level holds compatible values and standards or endorses a mutually acceptable mechanism for ethical dilemma resolution. The first (or micro) level in the hierarchy is the traditionally central clinical counseling core, in which the counselor–client relationship is the focus. The second level is the clinical interdisciplinary team interaction. At this point, practitioner-to-practitioner dynamics are considered. Team members may be physically dispersed, but functionally remain a team in terms of collaboration or coordinated work with respect to the client's care. Team communications often occur by telephone or electronic means, with only infrequent meetings or staffings. Nonetheless, they constitute an important clinical and ethical force in the client's life. Team relationships and leadership, collaboration skills, and the interplay of the differing ethical codes and traditions become important to the process. At the third level, the institutional or agency context and its constraints enter into the process. Dictates of agency policy, practitioner–supervisor styles and practices, and staffing patterns are factors that might have an influence. Corporate or administrative operations such as institutional goals, marketing strategies, and corporate oversight processes may also play a role. At the fourth (or macro) level, the effects of overall societal resources and public policy are considered. Social concern for scarce health care resources, the changes in behavioral health care models, insurance and policies, and the privatization of mental health care are examples of broad themes and related policies that may affect ethical practices at the practitioner level. Societal values related to such areas as independence and self-sufficiency, work and productivity, physical appearance, what constitutes an unacceptable lifestyle, and other types of behavior do influence the work of counselors extensively (Gatens-Robinson & Rubin, 1995). Societal values are also expressed in more concrete ways that may affect counselor practices through such influences as the climate created by local public opinion and various legislative and regulatory codes.

## Themes and Attitudes

In addition to the specific elements or steps of the Tarvydas Integrative Model, four underlying themes or attitudes are necessary for the professional counselor (Box 4.1). These attitudes involve mindfully attending to the tasks of (a) maintaining a stance of reflection concerning one's own conscious awareness of personal issues, values, and decision-making skills, as well as extending an effort to understand those of all others concerned with the situation, and their relationship to the decision maker; (b) addressing the balance among various issues, people, and perspectives within the process; (c) maintaining an appropriate level of attention to the context of the situation in question, allowing awareness of the counselor–client, treatment team, organizational, and societal implications of the ethical elements; and (d) seeking to use a process of collaboration with all rightful parties to the decision, but most especially the client.

By adopting these background attitudes of reflection, balance, context, and collaboration, counselors engage in a more thorough process that will help preserve the integrity and dignity of all parties involved. This will be the case even when outcomes are not considered equally positive for all participants in the process, as is often true in a serious dilemma when such attitudes can be particularly meaningful. Indeed, Betan and Stanton (1999) studied students' responses to ethical dilemmas, analyzing how emotions and concerns influence willingness to implement ethical knowledge. They concluded that "subjectivity and emotional involvement are essential tools for determining ethical action, but they must be integrated with rational analysis" (Betan & Stanton, 1999, p. 295).

Reflection is the overriding attitude of importance throughout the enactment of the specific elements of stages and components that constitute the steps of the Tarvydas Integrative Model. Many complex decision-making processes easily become overwhelming, either in their innate complexity or in the real-life press of the speed or intensity of events. In the current approach, the counselor is urged to always "stop and think!" at each point in the process. The order of operations is neither critical nor absolute, or more important than being reflective and invested in a calm, dignified, respectful, and thorough analysis of the situation. It is not until we recognize that we are involved in the process and appreciate its critical aspects that we can call forth other resources to assist the process and persons within it. Such an attitude of reflection will serve the counselor well at all stages of this process.

---

### BOX 4.1 Themes or Attitudes in the Tarvydas Integrative Model

Maintain an attitude of reflection.
Address balance between issues and parties to the ethical dilemma.
Pay close attention to the context(s) of the situation.
Utilize a process of collaboration with all rightful parties to the situation.

## CASE SCENARIO 4.1  Themes and Attitudes

Jimmy W. is in fifth grade and has been sent to see you, his school counselor, by Mrs. James, his teacher. This has been a difficult year for you professionally and personally. You have felt overwhelmed by an increasing number of students assigned to you. You have had also difficulty concentrating since your rather acrimonious divorce, which was finalized during the summer. Jimmy has continued to do good work in class since his parents' divorce 8 months ago. However, Mrs. James has noticed that Jimmy tears up his worksheets and art projects as soon as they are graded and is not showing his usual enthusiasm for school work. She has talked to him about the situation, but Jimmy denies that anything is wrong. Jimmy finally confides to you that his mother will no longer allow him to send letters and his completed school work to his father who lives in another state. He misses his father and his correspondence with him; he also thinks his work is meaningless and not important enough to be seen by his dad. He asks you if you will send his letters and school work to his father occasionally. Jimmy finally gives you permission to discuss his concerns with his mother. Jimmy's mother angrily forbids you to communicate with Jimmy's father in any way. She informs you that she is the sole custodial parent and guardian, and that Mr. W. moved away rather than "be bothered with the responsibility of Jimmy." She reluctantly allows you to continue counseling Jimmy about his "behavior problems" in school, but tells you not to raise his hopes about seeing or communicating with his father. While you will continue to provide supportive counseling to Jimmy, you consider the matter of contact with Mr. W. closed. By the end of the school year, you have not heard from Mr. or Mrs. W. and Jimmy's problems have not worsened. Were you correct?

PROBABLY NOT. When you stop and reflect on this situation outside of the furor of the meeting with Jimmy and his mom, you realize that two factors probably clouded your thinking. The first factor was your own painful divorce and custody problems. The second factor involved recent situations in which your school principal criticized you before the school staff for refusing to reveal to him confidential information in a controversial case about a student's family financial matters. Your anger at your former spouse and your fear of the principal have blinded you to other questions you must explore. You may discover that either the mother has incorrectly reported the custody arrangements, or the father does have some legal right to the communication his son desires. Even if Mr. W. does not have a legal right to correspondence from his son, Jimmy's rights and desires must be considered primary, and his father may have some moral claim to continue contact with his son apart from the custody decree specifics. Although counseling must occur with parental consent, it might be possible to counsel Jimmy and his mom to preserve some acceptable type and level of contact with Jimmy's father. A greater ability to communicate might facilitate Jimmy's adjustment and future co-operative communication regarding other aspects of Jimmy's welfare. These deeper considerations would include themes of balancing the moral claims of all parties to the situation regardless of the legal aspects of the situation. It also introduces the attitude of collaboration to the decisions involving Jimmy's well-being. None of these issues would have been available for your consideration unless you had first systematically practiced the attitude of reflection about a decision you initially thought was obvious.

## Stages and Components

The specific elements that constitute the operations within the Tarvydas Integrative Model have four main stages with several components and steps within each stage (Box 4.2). As previously stated, the concepts summarized in the following sections are primarily from Rest (1984), Kitchener (1984), and Tarvydas and Cottone (1991).

### Stage I: Interpreting the Situation Through Awareness and Fact Finding

At this stage, the primary task of counselors is to be sensitive and aware of the needs and welfare of the people around them, and the ethical implications of these situations. This level of awareness allows counselors to imagine and to investigate the effects of the situation on the parties involved and the possible effects of various actions and conditions. This research and awareness must also include emotional as well as cognitive and fact-based considerations. Three components constitute the counselors' operations in this stage.

Component 1 involves enhancing one's sensitivity and awareness. In Component 2, the counselor takes an inventory of the people who are major stakeholders in the outcome of the situation. It is important to reflect on any parties who will be affected and play a major role in the client's life, as well as considering what their exact relationship is ethically and legally to the person at the center of the issue—the client. In Case Scenario 4.1, Jimmy may be best served by some contact with his father, assuming that the father is interested and not abusive. Imagine dropping a rock into a pond: The point of impact is where the central figure, the client, is situated. However, the client is surrounded by people at varying levels of closeness, such as parents, foster parents, intimate partners, spouse, children, employer, friends, and neighbors. They radiate out from the client in decreasing levels of intimacy and responsibility to the client.

There are multiple spheres of influence of stakeholders in any client's life, as well as the stakeholders at each of the four levels in the professional world of the counselor. Remember, the four levels of influence on the counselor are: (a) the clinical counseling level, (b) the clinical interdisciplinary level, (c) the institutional/agency level, and (d) the societal resource/public policy level. The influence of client and counselor stakeholders may intersect. This way of thinking about the relationships between the different stakeholders in the situation allows for a fuller appreciation of the specific people and contexts of the counselor's practice and the client's situation. A number of people and levels of the service hierarchy will (or should) play a part in the ethics decision. These social forces will create both positive and negative influences in the ethical situation and should be taken into account in the ethical analysis. The ethical claims of these parties on the counselor's level of duty are not uniform. Almost all codes of ethics in counseling make it clear that the client is the person to whom the first duty is owed, but there are others to whom the counselor has lesser, but important, levels of duty. It is always important to determine whether any surrogate decision makers for the client exist, such as a guardian or person with power of

*Know stages, not all components, tho.*

## BOX 4.2 The Stages and Components of the Tarvydas Model

### Stage I: Interpreting the Situation Through Awareness and Fact Finding
Component 1    Enhance sensitivity and awareness
Component 2    Determine the major stakeholders and their ethical claims in the situation
Component 3    Engage in the fact-finding process

### Stage II: Formulating an Ethical Decision
Component 1    Review the problem or dilemma
Component 2    Determine what ethical codes, laws, ethical principles, and institutional policies and procedures exist that apply to the dilemma
Component 3    Generate possible and probable courses of action
Component 4    Consider potential positive and negative consequences for each course of action
Component 5    Consult with supervisors and other knowledgeable professionals
Component 6    Select the best ethical course of action

### Stage III: Selecting an Action by Weighing Competing, Nonmoral Values, Personal Blind Spots, or Prejudices
Component 1    Engage in reflective recognition and analysis of personal competing nonmoral values, personal blind spots, or prejudices
Component 2    Consider contextual influences on values selection at the counselor–client, team, institutional, and societal levels
Component 3    Select the preferred course of action

### Stage IV: Planning and Executing the Selected Course of Action
Component 1    Figure out a reasonable sequence of concrete actions to be taken
Component 2    Anticipate and work out personal and contextual barriers to effective execution of the plan of action, and effective countermeasures for them
Component 3    Carry out, document, and evaluate the course of action as planned

attorney, so that they may be brought into the central "circle of duty" early in the process. In Case Scenario 4.1, the mother must be counseled. The noncustodial parent has many rights to contact his son and even decision-making authority in some jurisdictions. It is useful to be sensitive and proactive in working through situations in which the legal relationships involved do not coincide with the social and emotional bonds between the client and other people involved in the dilemma.

In the final element in Stage I, Component 3, the counselor undertakes an extensive fact-finding investigation of a scope appropriate to the situation. The nature of the fact-finding process should be carefully considered, and does not focus on the professional resources available such as the code of ethics or in-depth legal information (that comes later); but rather the nature of the clinical situation, the facts related to it, and the people directly involved in it, as well as their actions and reactions to it. It is not intended to be a formal investigative or quasi-legal process. The counselor should carefully review, understand the information at hand, and seek out new information. Only information that is appropriately available to a counselor should be involved. The scope and depth of information that would be rightfully available to the counselor is surprising, but it is often underutilized. For example, information might be gained from such sources as further discussion or clarification with the client, contacts with family (with appropriate permission of the client), case records, expert consultation and reports, legal resources, or agency policy and procedures. In Case Scenario 4.1, the exact legal nature of the father–son relationship and the mother–father relationship should be explored.

### Stage II: Formulating an Ethical Decision

Although this aspect of the process is most widely known by professionals, many may erroneously think it is the end of the process. The central task in this stage is to identify which of the possible ethical courses of action appears to come closest to the moral ideal in the situation under consideration (Rest, 1984). Many decision-making models in other areas of counseling can be applied as a template at this stage, but the following components are drawn from the work of Van Hoose and Kottler (1985).

Component 1 suggests that the counselor review the problem or dilemma to be sure that it is clearly understood in light of any new information obtained in Stage I. In Component 2, the counselor researches the standards of law and practice applicable to the situation. This component includes Kitchener's (1984) attention to ethical codes, laws, and ethical principles; and Tarvydas and Cottone's (1991) concern for the team and organizational context in the examination of institutional policies and procedures to make mention of other useful areas for consideration. If you were the counselor in Case Scenario 4.1, at this point you would need to ensure that you were familiar with the requirements of the Family Educational Rights and Privacy Act of 1974. You need to be sure about the protection afforded to your counseling notes and which records about Jimmy would be released to Jimmy's parents upon their request. The counselor would also analyze which of the six core ethical principles (autonomy, beneficence, nonmaleficence, justice, fidelity, and veracity) are either supported or compromised by the types of actions that are being contemplated. This operation is formally known as principle analysis and is one of the most challenging, yet critical, aspects of the ethical analysis of a dilemma. The core, or main principle, analysis concerns the ethical obligations owed to the client rather than those owed to other parties in the situation. Component 3 initiates the process of formally envisioning and generating possible and probable courses of action. As with all decision-making processes, it is important not to truncate this exploratory process by prematurely censoring the possibilities, or succumbing to a sense of being too overwhelmed or too limited in options. Component 4 is the logical outgrowth of considering courses of action—positive and negative consequences are identified and assessed in light of the risks, as well as the material and personal resources available. In Component 5, the counselor is reminded to consult with supervisors and trusted, knowledgeable colleagues for guidance, if this has not been done before this point. Professional standards of practice emphasize the importance of appropriate collegial consultation to resolve difficult clinical and ethical dilemmas. Research has also demonstrated that such consultations can have a significant influence on those seeking such consultation (Cottone, Tarvydas, & House, 1994). At this time, it is valuable to review the reasoning employed so far in working through the ethical dilemma, and the solutions and consequences envisioned, to be sure that all potentially useful and appropriate considerations have been taken into account. Finally, the best ethical course of action is determined and articulated in Component 6. The ethical decision at this stage of the model should be contrasted with the actual decision made by the counselor—which is the product of Stage III.

Stage II of the Tarvydas model might be the end of most decision processes applied in other stage models. One comes to a decision—and it is implemented. *But the Tarvydas model has two more stages, which are unique to the decision-making literature.* Tarvydas asks the decision maker to weigh other factors before a finalized decision is made. The decision arrived upon in Stage II is only preliminary—it acts as a stimulus for further reflection and weighing of factors that are not typically considered by other models of decision making. Her model requires weighing of competing "nonmoral" values, personal blind spots, or biases.

### Stage III: Selecting an Action by Weighing Competing, Nonmoral Values, Personal Blind Spots, and Prejudices

Many people would think the ethical decision-making process is concluded at the end of Stage II. This impression is limited by the realization that many additional forces may affect the counselor. As a result, the counselor may not actually execute the selected ethical course of action. Component 1 of Stage III interjects a period of reflection and active processing of what the counselor intends to do in view of competing, nonmoral values (Rest, 1984). At this point, the counselor considers any personal factors that might intervene to pull him or her away from choosing the ethical action or cause that action to be substantially modified. Nonmoral values involve anything that the counselor may prize or desire that is not, in and of itself, a moral value, such as justice, valuing social harmony, spending time with friends or working on one's hobby, or having personal wealth. In this component, counselors are also called upon to examine themselves to determine if they have some personal blind spots or prejudices that might affect their judgment or resolve to do the ethical thing, such as a fear of HIV infection or the conviction that men who are homosexual are also likely to molest children. This portion of the model provides an excellent opportunity for counselors to carefully evaluate whether they have adequately incorporated multicultural considerations and competencies in their work on this ethical dilemma. They need to be sure that they are not operating from a culturally encapsulated frame of reference. In Case Scenario 4.1, the counselor might have realized upon reflection that her need to avoid controversy with the principal, or her identification with Jimmy's mother's anger with her ex-husband (a noncustodial parent), and her wish to be seen as supportive of the rights of a single mother may be competing with her knowledge of what is legally or ethically right.

*It is important that counselors allow themselves to become aware of the strength and attractiveness of other values they hold that may influence whether they will discharge their ethical obligations.* This stage is particularly critical in introducing the type of analysis of blind spots or prejudices that keep counselors from practicing ethics in a manner that is truly multiculturally competent and in keeping with social justice aims of the profession. Additionally, counselors may have a variety of other personal experiences or predispositions that make them vulnerable to potentially biased judgments. If they are self-aware, they may compensate for their conflicted impulses at this point more effectively and honestly. They may have a visceral distaste for a certain type of client, an overriding need to protect minor children, or a sexual or emotional attraction to a particular client. Counselors may have strong needs for acceptance by peers or supervisors, prestige, influence, to avoid controversy, or to be financially successful. These values may come into conflict with the course of action necessary to proceed ethically and must be reconciled with the ethical requirements if the client is to be served ethically. On the other hand, counselors may place a high value on being moral, ethical, and accepted as respected professionals with high ethical standards. They may value the esteem of colleagues who place a high value on ethical professional behavior. Those forces should enhance the tendency to select ethical behavioral options. (The influence of the ethical climate on the ethical behavior of the counselor is more fully explored in Chapter 12.) The importance of selecting and maintaining ethically sensitized and positive professional and personal cultures is critical to full professional functioning, as the next component suggests.

In Component 2 of Stage III, counselors systematically inventory the contextual influences on their choices at the clinical counselor–client, team, institutional, and societal levels. While this is not a simple process of weighing influences, it should serve as an inventory of influences that may be either dysfunctional or constructive for selecting the ethical course over other types of values present in these other interactions. Counselors may also use this type of information to think strategically about the influences they will need to overcome to provide ethical service in the situation. Beyond the immediate situation, it is important to recognize that counselors should control their exposure to contexts that consistently reinforce values that run counter to the dictates of good ethical practices. In Case Scenario 4.1, Jimmy's counselor might be influenced in one direction if she spends most of her personal and professional time with staff who are primarily concerned with getting ahead in the school hierarchy and being seen favorably by the administration, in contrast with having a few strong relationships with colleagues who take great pride in their professional identities and reputations. This problem might result in terminating or curtailing certain relationships, changing employment, or selecting another aspect of counseling service to provide.

Component 3 is the final aspect of Stage III. At this time, the counselor selects the preferred course of action or the behavior that he or she plans to undertake. This decision may be a reaffirmation of the intention to take the ethical course of action as determined at the conclusion of Stage II. However, it may be some other course of action that may even be unethical or a modified version of the ethical course of action selected in Stage II. Whatever the choice, the counselor selects it after this more extensive reflection on his or her own competing values and personal blind spots, as well as the contextual influences on him or her in the situation in question.

### Stage IV: Planning and Executing the Selected Course of Action

Rest (1984) described the essential tasks of this stage as planning to implement and execute what one decides to do. This operation includes Component 1, in which the counselor determines a reasonable sequence of concrete actions to be taken. In Component 2, the task is to anticipate and work out all personal and contextual barriers to effectively executing the plan. It is useful to prepare countermeasures for barriers that may arise. In Case Scenario 4.1, if Jimmy's father indeed has a legal and ethical right, as well as a personal interest in Jimmy, what barriers might arise if Jimmy is given the opportunity to contact him? It is here that the earlier attention to other stakeholders and their concerns may suggest problems or allies to the process. Additionally, earlier consideration of the contextual influences in Stage III assists the counselor in this type of strategic planning. Component 3 is the final step of this model. It provides for the execution, documentation, and evaluation of the course of action as planned. Rest (1984) noted that the actual behavioral execution of ethics is often not a simple task, frequently drawing heavily on the personal, emotional qualities and professional and interpersonal skills of the counselor. He mentions such qualities as firmness of resolve, ego strength, and social assertiveness. Countless skills such as persistence, tact, time management, assertiveness skills, team collaboration, and conflict-resolution skills could be added to this list. Considerations are limited only by the characteristics and requirements of the counselor and the specific situation involved. To protect the interests of both counselor and client, document the entire plan and the rationale behind it thoroughly, and take ethical decision-making steps in response to the ethical dilemma as the process unfolds. The information gained in this documentation process will prove critical in evaluating the effectiveness of the entire ethical decision-making process.

## Practicing the Tarvydas Integrative Model

Like the basic counseling microskills, the skills of ethical decision making do not come automatically, or even easily, after merely reading concepts in a book. A gradual progression in gaining practical skills and sensitive, accurate ethical knowledge is achieved by solving mock ethical dilemmas; working to address actual ethical dilemmas under the supervision of an ethically knowledgeable instructor, clinical supervisor, master counselor or mentor; and incorporating ethical analysis into the clinical training process.

## The Theoretical Contribution of the Tarvydas Model

Although the Tarvydas model is complex, it is representative of the best theory applied to decision making (Box 4.3). It applies principle, virtue, and relational ethics. It involves a degree of intuition, but it maintains a clear focus on data gathering. It requires an analysis of contextual factors. It does not stop with a simple application of standards to a situation; rather it requires reflection on personal and cultural factors that may be less than obvious—sometimes called "blind spots" or biases. It requires a step beyond the models based on practice and requires that the decision maker quickly analyzes the consequences of actions for stakeholders. As a model, it is an integrative marker of the best of contemporary decision-making theory and practice. Due to its integrative nature, it allows for linkages with influential areas of emerging ethical thought. Recently, Tarvydas and her associates have expanded their analysis of the influence and role of the client's active involvement in the ethical decision-making process. This model of applied participatory ethics emphasizes the participation of the client in the process as a means of client empowerment, and as a vehicle for responding to the relationship and social justice foci in counseling in counseling ethics (Tarvydas, Vazquez-Ramos, & Estrada-Hernandez, 2015).

## COTTONE'S SOCIAL CONSTRUCTIVISM MODEL OF ETHICAL DECISION MAKING

The "social constructivism" model of ethical decision making was first introduced in the literature in 2001. This model is based purely on philosophy, incorporating the ideas of the social constructivism movement into mental health services without integration of other ideas historically valued in the ethical decision-making literature. Whereas the Tarvydas model builds on the best that is known about ethical decision making as a psychological and social process to date, the Cottone model diverges by presenting a model that is incompatible with the emphasis of established models on psychological theory. It is a purely social/relational model.

The term **social constructivism** is used here to represent an intellectual movement in the mental health field that has emerged from both the psychological and systemic-relational paradigms of mental health services (see the related

---

**BOX 4.3  The Tarvydas Model—Unique Contributions to Ethical Decision-Making Theory**

It is integrative of psychological and social processes.
It is integrative of intuitive and rational processes.
It involves a degree of reflection after an initial formulation is made, requiring reassessment considering additional personal factors.
It considers the professional context in which decision making is carried out.

*[handwritten margin note: pure social model – not psychology]*

discussions in Lyddon [1995] and Cottone [1992]). Generally, social constructivism **implies that what is real is not an objective fact; rather, what is real evolves through interpersonal interaction and agreement as to what is "fact"** (Ginter et al., 1996). The "radical constructivist" position, which represents an extreme view and a complete break from psychological theory, is derived from the works of von Foerster (1984), von Glasersfeld (1984), and specifically Maturana (Maturana, 1978, 1988; Maturana & Varela, 1980). The radical constructivism position has been embraced by theorists in the field as an offshoot of social systems theory (a comprehensive theory of relationships). It is a unique, biologically grounded theory (the biology of cognition) that ultimately allows for a *biosocial* interpretation of what is "real." In essence, biologically based social constructivism argues that all that is known is known through biological and social relationships (biosocial). Psychological processes are not involved. Knowledge derives from complex physiological relations wherein observing organisms interact socially to construct an understanding of reality. Literally, that means that when we are interacting with other people, we are physically and perceptually affected by the presence of the other person, while at the same time we are communicating socially. Our biology is engaged perceptually while, simultaneously, we are socially engaged. So, as an example, when two people look at a growth on a tree (a perceptual process) and define it as "fruit" (a social process), then it becomes understood as fruit within the confines of that relationship.

The social constructionist movement in psychology (e.g., Gergen, 1985) is more rooted in the social psychology literature and avoids in-depth theorizing about biological bases. However, the social constructionism movement (make note of the slightly different spelling of "constructionism" and "constructivism") has uncanny similarities to the ideas presented by radical constructivists. Gergen (1985, 1991, 1994), a social psychologist, has thrown down a broad theoretical gauntlet arguing for a social-relational interpretation of human understanding. Gergen (1991) stated: "The reality of the individual is giving way to relational reality" (p. 160). The term "social constructivism," therefore, is used here to represent the biologically rooted but radical social constructivism deriving primarily from the works of Maturana, while acknowledging the seminal works of Gergen, which are grounded in social psychology (see Cottone, 2012b).

The need for a radical social constructivism model of ethical decision making is threefold. First, it provides a distinct view of the decision-making process—it is based purely on a relational view of reality. Other models tend to portray the decision maker as a psychological entity that makes the decision alone or within some social context. For example, Kitchener, in her highly cited 1984 work, described ethical decisions as those involving the decision maker's intuitive and critical-evaluative reasoning. In contrast, the social constructivism perspective places the decision in the social context itself, not in the head of the decision maker; decision making becomes an interpersonal process of "negotiating," "consensualizing," and "arbitrating" (three terms defined later in this chapter). A second rationale for developing a social constructivism model is that it may lead to empirical testing of social versus psychologically based ethical decision-making models. Because a constructivism approach is so unique theoretically, it provides a competitive perspective to more psychologically based models. Critical paradigm experiments (Cottone, 1989a, 1989b, 2012b) may be designed to test the social perspective against the more traditional psychological perspective. Such experiments help researchers and practitioners weigh the relative merits of one approach against another, providing an empirical foundation that is sorely needed in this area of study. The third rationale for a social constructivism model is its appeal to practitioners as an alternative perspective for framing ethical decisions. Although there are a plethora of ethical decision-making models, this model provides an alternative to psychological or hybrid models for practitioners who are more aligned with a systemic or relational worldview. The model is parsimonious and does not involve complex steps or stages, so it may be easier for counselors to implement in the stressful times that accompany an ethical challenge.

In a follow-up article on the model, invited by the editors of the *Canadian Journal of Counselling*, Cottone (2004) stated:

> To truly appreciate a social constructivism model of ethical decision-making, one must first transform one's thinking to accept a radical position: the psychology of the individual can be displaced by relational (biosocial) theory. Social constructivism is founded on ideas that allow for all conclusions about human functioning to be understood based on the biological and social forces that affect behaviour. Psychology that focuses primarily on an individual can be viewed as excess baggage, a social creation itself that provides little or no descriptive power beyond biological and social factors. In other words, all behaviour can be viewed as biologically affected and manifested through social relationships. This is a difficult position for some people to accept. After all, many current mental health professionals have been inculcated with psychological theory. The thought that the psychology of the individual is superfluous is not easily accommodated. (p. 6)

To understand the model, one must be willing to set aside thinking in psychological terms—that is, thinking about people as individuals with free will and individual choice. One must be willing to suspend judgment long enough to accept that all that is known about ethical dilemmas derives from relationships, at many levels.

## APPLYING THE SOCIAL CONSTRUCTIVISM MODEL OF ETHICAL DECISION MAKING

### "Objectivity in Parentheses"

What social constructivism means to ethical decision making is that decisions can no longer be viewed as occurring internally. Many other decision-making models portray the decision as the responsibility of the individual decision maker. For example, an individual is asked to decide on the best course of action (Corey et al., 2014), select an action by weighing competing values in a given context (Tarvydas model), make the decision (Keith-Spiegel & Koocher, 1985), or deliberate and decide (Welfel, 2002). From a constructivism perspective, decisions are moved out of the intrapsychic process and into the interpersonal realm. As Gergen (1985) wrote:

> From this perspective, knowledge is not something people possess somewhere in their heads, but rather, something people do together. Languages are essentially shared activities. Indeed, until the sounds or markings come to be shared within a community, it is inappropriate to speak of language at all. In effect, we may cease inquiry into the psychological basis of language (which account would inevitably form but a subtext or miniature language) and focus on the performative use of language in human affairs. (p. 270)

Further, Gergen said: "The mind becomes a form of social myth; the self-concept is removed from the head and placed within the sphere of social discourse" (p. 271). From this vantage point, all that is done, all activity, and all to which language is applied, is a reflection of what has been shared previously in the community. Language is not generated spontaneously; it is transmitted socially (as per Wittgenstein [1953/1958], language is a "convention"). All that is done (in language or otherwise) is bound to heritage. Decisions, therefore, cannot be located "in" the individual. Rather, they are in the social matrix. There is no free will or choice, because all decisions are biologically and socially compelled within a person's network of relationships. And free will or free choice as concepts would have to be culture free—and no concept in language is culture free. As Gergen (2001) concluded (applying Wittgenstein's [1953/1958] ideas): "There can be no private language" (p. 805). So if language is culturally situated and transmitted, any claim to "subjectivity" in language collapses, because any language represents symbolic transmission of culture. There is no subjectivity in language or symbolism, because language and symbolism are derived from socially shared activities.

The social constructivism position is contrary to the positions taken by ethicists in counseling who appear to be bound predominantly to psychological theorizing about how decisions are made. Decision-making models tend to lay out steps for ethical choice (see Cottone & Claus, 2000), but almost across the board they fail to describe adequately how that choice occurs; it somehow disappears into the head (or mind) of the individual making the decision, either intuitively or based on utilitarian values (cf. Hare, 1991). For example, how are values weighed by the individual? Few models actually answer that question. For example, Gutheil et al. (1991) grounded their decision model in probability theory and weighing probabilities. With most models, how a decision is made is a psychological mystery.

The social constructivism approach to ethical decision making places the ethical decision out in the open—in the interaction between individuals as they operate in what Maturana (1978) identified as the "consensual domain" (p. 47). A decision is never made in a social vacuum. A decision is always made in interaction with at least one other individual. The interactive aspects of a decision are undeniable. In professional ethics, a decision to enter into an intimate relationship with a client is a decision made in interaction with the client. Likewise, a decision to breach a client's confidentiality is a decision made in relation to a third party. Decisions are not compelled internally; rather, they are compelled socially. This is the social constructivism position.

Some decisions may be viewed as "good" within a social context, while others may be viewed as "bad" within a social context. But that is not to say that decisions are "relative." What differentiates the social constructivism approach from purely relative models of right or wrong (where right and wrong are relative truths held by individuals) is that the social constructivism approach defines the view within a social-consensual domain as absolutely true within that social context (Cottone, 2011). As Maturana (1988) described it, "objectivity" is "in parentheses," where the parentheses are the boundaries of human interaction. In other words, what is known is known through a social construction process, and within the social context, it is an absolutist's view. To demonstrate this point, consider that there can be competitive social consensualities—competitive absolute truths, so to speak. Understanding that there can be competitive absolute truths (a logical contradiction) helps to clarify the distinction between social constructivism and objectivism (where there is one absolute truth) and relativism (where truth is relative to each individual). Cottone (2011) called these consensualities **bracketed absolute truths, where truths reside within the brackets of a group's social interaction.** Social constructivism stands apart from objectivism and relativism in the primacy of relationships. In effect, there are pockets of objectivities, and each pocket is demarcated by the group that acts according to what is believed to be true. For example, according to social constructivism, there can be several competitive truths, even competitive "gods." Each of a number of competitive gods represents absolute truth within a social-consensual domain represented by the religion's adherents. Each such god effectively competes for what is absolutely true against other gods (other socially consensually constructed truths). Ironically, some people literally war over some religions; but there is no irony from a social constructivism perspective. In those cases, the warring individuals believe absolutely in the "truths" represented by their god and will fight to the death to preserve such principles. This demonstrates the power of shared beliefs—beliefs acknowledged within a social (in this case a religious) group. From within a group, the group's truth looks absolute; it only looks relative when it is viewed by outsiders from outside the group, who then impose a claim of relativity on what they observe. (See Cottone's [2011] book *Toward a Positive Psychology of Religion*, for a more thorough analysis of religion from a postmodern perspective.)

Just as people fight wars over religion, so too can mental health professionals war over what is believed to be ethical practice. Past court cases have frequently represented the battlefield. The classic and well-known Tarasoff legal decision is a good example. In that case, a University of California therapist took what he believed were acceptable actions to warn authorities of a dangerous client. The therapist took actions that were, up to that moment, directed by the professional consensus as to obligations of psychologists in that circumstance. The surprise was that the courts ruled in favor of a different view—siding with the family of the murdered individual targeted by the client—and the courts assessed liability. VandeCreek and Knapp (1993) explained:

The decision was based, to a large extent, on the affirmative duty to act which arises out of the "special relationship" between a psychotherapist and a patient. According to the common law, an individual usually has no duty to control the behavior of another in order to protect a third party. Nevertheless, once a "special relationship" has been established, the law may require affirmative obligations. These socially recognized relationships, such as parent to child or possessor of land to renter, imply a legal duty to attempt to protect others from harm, or to warn them of potential harm. (p. 5)

The professionals involved were essentially trying to protect the confidentiality of the client consistent with ethical standards to that date. But, in interaction with the legal system, the actions and the defense did not hold weight. Accordingly, serious implications for professional ethics in counseling derive from a social constructivism perspective because no single, socially constructed ethical stance can be considered inherently better than another—predominance only derives from negotiation, consensus building, and/or arbitration. As with the Tarasoff decision, the involved parties were acting according to what was directed socially by the consensus of their communities. The fact that there was an unresolved clash of consensualities led to arbitration.

## Conflicting Consensualities

Professionals must identify the levels of consensus that operate around an action or a dilemma. The fact that there is a dilemma means there may be a disagreement—a conflict of consensualities—between groups of people with which the professional has interacted.

The codes of the ACA, the National Association of Social Workers (NASW), the American Association for Marriage and Family Therapy (AAMFT), and the APA reflect consensualities as to what is acceptable practice; membership in the APA, NASW, AAMFT, or the ACA indicates that the member is interacting with the consensualizing process the association represents. Counselors also interact with clients and client families, lawyers, judges, physicians, and other mental health professionals. Each interaction may represent the coming together of systems of thought. Each may represent a distinct consensus on an issue. When there is a disagreement over an ethically sensitive issue that is resistant to easy negotiation, there is a conflict of consensualities. Take, for example, one of the most salient cases of a breach of ethical standards—sexual intimacies with a client. The counselor who enters into a sexual relationship with a client acts in a way that represents rejection of the professional standard banning sexual intimacies while acting in a way that represents acceptance of the risks of the social/sexual relationship. The sexual relationship may also represent linkage to a system, which may not fit well within the constraints of a secret, professionally banned relationship. For example, the client may have family, friends, or an attorney who advise that such a relationship is "wrong." When a disagreement arises between the professional and the client's system, a clash of consensualities may result (a disagreement over the nature or course of the relationship), with potential legal and professional threat to the counselor. The decision to enter into such a relationship is an act of vulnerability for the professional—the counselor's livelihood is at stake. Nothing professionally damaging may occur, but there is a possibility that the couple's initial consensus that the relationship exists (or may be acceptable at some level) may deteriorate under the strain of other relationships and competing consensualities that come to bear on their interaction. Of course, there is a consensus established in the professional literature that sexual intimacies with clients are unethical (see the ACA and APA codes) and harmful (e.g., Bouhoutsos, Holroyd, Lerman, Forer, & Greenberg, 1983; Pope, 1988; Sonne, 2012). Therefore, a counselor would be well served to avoid such a detrimental relationship. There is little support for an offending professional, given current ethical and professional standards.

A decision to breach an ethical standard (as with an offending counselor) or the decision to challenge a professional's ethics (as with the educated client) is a decision that derives from past and present interactions. There are no psychological determinants, but only biological and social forces that affect interactions one way or another. In other words, the actions of the client and the counselor can be completely conceptualized as resulting from physical and social forces, not psychological needs. The action to mount an ethical challenge to the counselor also derives from physical and social factors impinging the client. What appears to be an ethical (or unethical) decision is simply an action taken in concert with the emerging social consensus of the moment.

Social constructivism ethical decision making means that the professional must avoid linkages of vulnerability and cultivate linkages of professional responsibility. Relationships should be cultivated in accord with the larger sociolegal consensus that pervades professional practice. Ethical decision making occurs well before a crisis of consensualities arises. It is implicit in the professional culture. It means a rich, professional network is established and actions are taken to prevent and to avoid contact with social networks where challenges of "right" and "wrong" must be answered.

So, social constructivism ethical decision making is not classic psychological decision making at all. It is linkage to professional culture. One either does or does not fully enter into a professional culture. Those interactions that help to engage a professional fully in the ethical professional climate are actions of ethical choice. Such activity happens most basically in educational institutions where counselors are introduced by seasoned clinicians to a professional culture and to the rules that guide acceptable practice. At that level, the profession is responsible for conveying the importance of linkage to a professional culture so that communicating on ethical issues becomes an ongoing activity of the student professional.

## The Interpersonal Process of Negotiating, Consensualizing, and Arbitrating

Counseling practice is complex and ethical dilemmas arise as new challenges confront practitioners. Even a counselor who is closely aligned with an ethically sensitive professional community may face an ethical challenge. Should there be accusations of unethical practice, counselors must act to protect their own interests and the interests of their clients. In such cases, the social constructivism ethical decision-making alternative to psychologically based ethical decision making must occur. It does not occur internally or "in the head." Instead, social constructivism ethical decision making is a process of negotiating (when necessary), consensualizing, and arbitrating (when necessary) that occurs in the interpersonal process of relations that come to bear at critical moments of professional practice.

**Negotiating is the process of discussing and debating an issue wherein at least two individuals indicate some degree of disagreement.** For example, if a client's attorney contacts a counselor about testifying at a worker's compensation or disability hearing, the counselor should first request permission from the client to release confidential information (in order to talk to the attorney). Next, the counselor should consult with the attorney and negotiate as to whether the testimony is crucial to the client's case. If there is a formal request to testify, a waiver of privileged communication might be necessary, depending on laws in the jurisdiction. If there is a disagreement over the nature of the testimony or its potential effects, the counselor might refuse to testify, recognizing that a court-ordered subpoena might result. Negotiation, therefore, is a process of discussing and debating a position taken by the counselor; negotiation requires operation in language and some level of expressed disagreement.

**Consensualizing is a process wherein at least two individuals act in agreement and in coordination on an issue.** Consensus is viewed as an ongoing interactive process, not a final outcome or "thing." Cottone (1992) stated: "The idea of consensus must not be viewed solely as a formal language-based activity. In fact, consensus is probably best understood by the actions of individuals as they relate mutually, verbally and non-verbally, within certain interpersonal contexts" (p. 269). Where there is language, social interaction, and co-operation, there is an evolving consensuality. (Notice that the word "co-operation" is hyphenated; the hyphen is purposeful and indicates that individuals operate—act—in a coordinated fashion.) Maturana (1970) described this as the "consensual domain" (p. 50). Individuals who consensualize may have been involved in negotiation, but it is not necessary to negotiate to consensualize. Negotiation requires that there was some degree of disagreement, whereas consensualizing may or may not involve disagreement. For example, if an attorney requests that a counselor testify, the counselor may agree (with minimal discussion or no debate) and may just show up at the scheduled hearing ready to testify. In this case, the attorney and the counselor have consensualized by coordinated action as to the request to testify. Consensualizing is the process of socially constructing a reality. If there is disagreement or discordant action (consensualizing is not evident), arbitration may be necessary.

**Arbitrating is a process whereby a negotiator or negotiators seek the judgment of consensually accepted individuals (alone or in groups) who are socially approved as representatives of sociolegal consensus—arbitrators.** Arbitrators make judgments in interaction with each other, complainants, defendants, the authority of agreed-upon rules or law, and past judgments (e.g., case law). In most cases, the arbitrator has the final say, unless, of course, there is an appeal to a higher consensually accepted arbitrator (e.g., a court of appeals). Arbitrating is the social process that imposes a socially constructed reality.

## Response to a Challenge

When a professional is accused or questioned about ethical misconduct, he or she may respond in a way that acknowledges, disputes, or further questions the alleged or questionable behavior. The counselor's response probably derives as much from the nature of the relationship to the accuser or inquirer as to the nature of the alleged misconduct. To deny an accusation of a "nemesis" may prevent meaningful negotiation, even in the case of acceptable conduct, setting up an adversarial circumstance and a clash of consensualities to be settled by consensually agreed-upon higher authorities (e.g., the courts). Denial to a friendly colleague, on the other hand, may bring about negotiation as to whether a breach has occurred (against some agreed-upon standard, such as an ethical standard in a code of ethics). The moment of accusation or inquiry is a critical moment, and social forces influence what may appear to outsiders as a "decision."

## The Social Constructivism Process of Ethical Decision Making

At critical moments, such as when a concern arises or when there has been an accusation or inquiry, the ethically sensitive professional operating from a social constructivism mode would take several steps: (a) obtain information from those involved; (b) assess the nature of the relationships operating at that moment in time; (c) consult valued colleagues and professional expert opinion (including ethics codes and literature); (d) negotiate when there is a disagreement; and (e) respond in a way that allows for a reasonable consensus as to what should happen or what really occurred. Every involved relationship must be examined for potential linkage to another (possibly adversarial) system of thought. Additionally, every involved relationship must be assessed for a potential conflict of opinion over what should or did happen. If consensus is not possible, further negotiation, interactive reflection, or arbitration may be necessary (see Figure 4.1).

After information is obtained, the nature of relationships is assessed and valued colleagues and experts are consulted (Figure 4.1). The interactive process of socially constructing an outcome to an ethical dilemma involves negotiating (if necessary), consensualizing, and arbitrating (if necessary). The ultimate goal is to establish consensus among involved parties about what should or did happen in questionable circumstances. When consensualizing fails, parties may partake in "interactive reflection," a process of conversation with trusted individuals to come to agreement as to whether arbitration should be sought or whether a position needs to be modified to re-enter negotiation. If consensualizing fails after interactive reflection, arbitration is necessary.

## "A Truth" Versus "The Truth"

Conflicts between people can, hopefully, be addressed by open discussion or reasonable negotiation of what should happen (or what actually occurred). Unfortunately, "the truth" may be a matter of dispute. If, in fact, counselors plan to break the rules (or have broken the rules), they should accept the consequences of their actions imposed by the sociolegal consensus in the profession and the

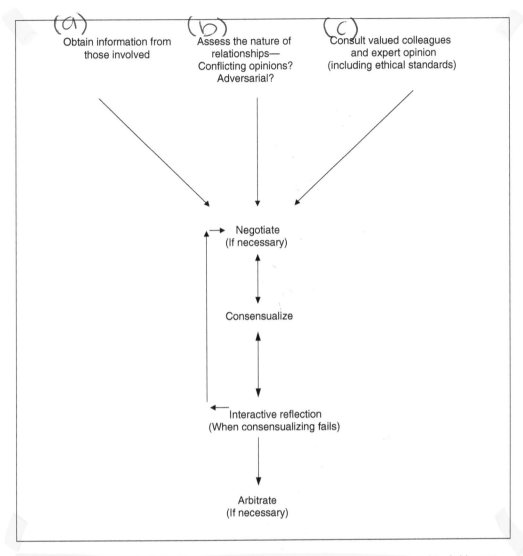

**FIGURE 4.1** The interactive process of socially constructing an outcome to an ethical dilemma.

courts. Otherwise, they might act to protect their own professional interests by denying a wrongdoing, possibly at the expense of clients.

It may be that only a client and a professional know the actions that have occurred. When there is a difference of opinion about an act—a conflict of consensualities—arbitration may be the only answer. In such cases, the "truth" may never be known to others, even though a judgment may occur. Aside from arbitration, when there is a dispute (i.e., there are competing truths), only in cases of repeated offenses can a "truth" be established. Where there are repeated offenses, such a "truth" is established around the victims, whose stories combine to constitute a systemic imperative for legal or professional action. Some professionals may "come clean" in such a circumstance. Other professionals may resist acceptance of professional or legal mores (or possibly be the victims of a conspiracy, however unlikely). Whatever the professional's action, it reflects the physical and social forces affecting the counselor at that moment in time.

Once an ethical course of action has been chosen, it is wise for counselors to take additional steps in line with the recommendation of Tarvydas (see her model in this chapter) to engage in a period of reflection and active processing of what the counselor intends to do. From a social constructivism position, however, reflection is not a process of mind—rather, it is a continued reappraisal of actions in context and in consultation with others who can provide a perspective that represents their linkage to the professional community. It is a continued process of seeking alternative opinions or perspectives. If different perspectives emerge that allow for different views and a negotiated settlement (prior to an arbitrated decision), it is not too late to reappraise the circumstance. In the constructivism model, such reflection takes the form of "interactive reflection."

### CASE SCENARIO 4.2  Negotiating, Consensualizing, and Arbitrating

Counseling is provided to a 12-year-old girl through a family counseling agency funded by both private and government funds. The girl lives with her grandmother, who signs the consent for treatment as the child's legal guardian. After several counseling sessions, the grandmother demands to know what the child reported. The child, in counseling, reports to the counselor that the grandmother is not her legal guardian, which is substantiated (assessment of the nature of relationships). Her mother is identified as the legal guardian (assessment of the nature of relationships). The mother lives 60 miles from the counseling center and has not been involved with the child for some time. The counselor is faced with a dilemma—technically there has been no informed consent because the grandmother fraudulently signed the consent form as the legal guardian. Yet the counselor has an ethical "responsibility" to the child according to ethical standards. The counselor consults the executive director of the agency (a noncounselor) who informs her that counseling cannot continue without informed consent or procedures would be breached, threatening the service contract (consultation of colleagues). The clinical service supervisor is consulted and informs the counselor that, aside from informed consent, she still has an obligation to the child (consultation of colleagues). The counselor attempts to seek the mother's permission, but fails on several phone attempts (obtaining information from involved parties). She even arranged through certified mail to meet the mother, drove 60 miles, and was disappointed when the mother did not show for the scheduled meeting at the arranged site (attempt to negotiate). The counselor then sought the joint counsel of her clinical supervisor and the executive director (consultation with colleagues). The executive director took a firm legal stance and directed her not to work with the child without legally executed informed consent by the responsible adult. An agreement was reached among the professionals to request the grandmother's assistance in procuring the informed consent of the mother (consensualizing). The grandmother agreed (consensualizing), but faced with the non–co-operation of the mother (nonconsensus), the grandmother obtained legal custody of the child only after threatening the mother with charges of child neglect (threat of arbitration leading to renegotiation and coordinated action between the mother and grandmother). Counseling was reinitiated with the consent of the grandmother as the legal guardian. The child was informed that the grandmother had legal access to information provided in counseling.

Case Scenario 4.2 is based on an actual case discussed in a graduate course on ethical issues in counseling. The case demonstrates the interactive processes involved in decision making. Terms associated with the social process of ethical decision making are bracketed as related to the flowchart shown in Figure 4.1.

As Case Scenario 4.2 demonstrates, the outcome of an ethical dilemma is highly social and can be clearly conceptualized as an interactive, not intrapsychic, process.

## How the Social Constructivism Model Interfaces With Multiculturalism

Because the social constructivism model of ethical decision making is based on relational theory and fully acknowledges the "communities of understanding" that each person represents, it is fully sensitive to cultural issues. In fact, the social constructivism model not only acknowledges cultural diversity (by accepting culturally derived truths), but it also helps to define the limits of multiculturalism (Cottone, 2004). The limits of multiculturalism are defined by the ethical constraints of a situation—those ethical consensualities established by the profession that define acceptable limits about permissible behavior in and out of the counseling context. In 2004, Cottone presented a case scenario that is helpful in describing both the model's facility at incorporating diversity issues, while delimiting ethical constraints on behaviors, no matter how culturally grounded those behaviors may be. Consider a hypothetical case of a young teenage African girl who lives in America with her parents, who are citizens of an African nation. The girl and the parents have temporary permission to live in the United States. The girl is enrolled in a school, where she reports to the counselor that she fears a planned visit to her homeland, because her parents plan to have her undergo a ritual female circumcision, a procedure that is common in her homeland. She fears the circumcision and does not want to go back to the homeland or to participate in the ritual. The counselor is faced with a dilemma—there are laws in the state of residence that would define such an act as child abuse, whereas the counselor found (through researching the ritual) that, indeed, it is a culturally accepted practice in the child's homeland. The counselor followed a process that exemplified the social constructivism model, consulting the parents, the legal authorities, and ethics professor, and a professor of multicultural counseling. Although the parents disagreed, a consensus was established among the other consulted individuals—regardless of cultural tradition, in this case, state statutes protecting children prevailed. The counselor decided that, if the parents insisted that the child would have to undergo the procedure, the child abuse authorities in the state of current residence would be called.

In effect, multiculturalism has limitations. Counselors cannot condone certain actions that are dangerous to others, for example, no matter what cultural tradition directs a behavior. If a client is a part of a group that defines a behavior as acceptable, that alone does not allow for acceptance of that behavior, especially if the behavior is antithetical to ethical principles at the foundation of counseling practice. There are limits as to what can be defined as "accepted" behavior by nature of counseling ethical principles; for example, acceptance of a "hate group" philosophy, where such a hate group is known to act on the philosophy, would be antithetical to counseling practice. The social constructivism ethical decision-making model, therefore, brings all community mores and traditions to bear on a situation—those of the cultural traditions of the client *and* those of the professional culture of counseling. In the end, there is reconciliation of these "consensualities" around the defined acceptable limits of counseling practice as a counselor consults with others to define a course of action. If there is a clash of consensualities, as with the case example of the parents from an African nation, then the counselor must take a position that appears to be beneficent, nonmaleficent, just, faithful to the client, truthful, and respecting of the client's freedom of choice.

## Concluding Words About the Social Constructivism Model

Gergen (1991) stated: "When individuals declare right and wrong in a given situation they are only acting as local representatives for larger relationships in which they are enmeshed. Their relationships speak through them" (pp. 168–169). The social constructivism approach to ethical decision making is a purely social interpretation of the decision-making process. The social constructivism decision-making approach is a process of negotiating and consensualizing. All behavior occurs in a social context. From the constructivism perspective, decisions occur always in interaction. Professionals are less vulnerable to ethical challenges if they are linked to a rich professional culture, which is not supportive of a breach of ethical standards. When concerns arise at crucial moments of professional practice, the social constructivist obtains information from those involved, assesses the nature of relationships operating at that moment, consults valued colleagues and professional expert opinion (including ethical codes), negotiates when necessary, and responds in a way that allows for a reasonable consensus. Where negotiation must occur—when there is a conflict of consensualities—the counselor may accept or challenge an opposing position, knowing that an adversarial relationship may be established and judgment may occur in consensually agreed-upon "courts" of arbitration. The social constructivism model also acknowledges multiculturalism, and by nature of accepted ethical standards, it helps to define the limits of multiculturalism.

## CONCLUSION

Counselors must exercise their ethical and professional judgment responsibly. They must recognize an ethical dilemma and apply appropriate decision-making skills to resolve the dilemma. Several models exist that explain and structure the process of ethical decision making: (a) theoretically or philosophically based models; and (b) practice-based models.

Theoretically or philosophically based models ground ethical decision making on a theory or philosophy. These models include absolute thinking (Hare); moral reasoning (Rest); decision analysis (Gutheil, Bursztajn, Brodsky, & Alexander); transactional analysis (Berne); feminist (Hill, Glaser, & Harden); hermeneutic (Betan); and social constructivism (Cottone).

Practice-based models are based on pragmatic procedures derived from experience or intended as practical guides for counselors. They are less theory-specific or philosophically pure than theoretical models and have characteristics of either principle or virtue ethics. Principle ethics focuses on the objective, rational, and cognitive aspects of a process. Virtue ethics considers the characteristics of the counselors themselves as the critical element for responsible practice. The Tarvydas Integrative Model is a four-stage model that builds on the Rest and Kitchener models and has a four-level approach: (a) clinical counseling level, (b) clinical interdisciplinary level, (c) institutional/agency level, and (d) societal resource/public policy level. The Tarvydas model has four underlying themes: stance of reflection, balance, attention to the context, and collaboration. It requires decision makers to go beyond a simple weighing of factors—requiring reflective analysis of nonmoral values, blind spots, or biases before a final decision is made and implemented.

Cottone's social constructivism model provides an alternative to practitioners who are more aligned with a systemic or relational worldview. In this view, decisions are not viewed as occurring internally; decisions are moved out of the intrapsychic process and into the interpersonal realm. Social constructivism ethical decision making is a process of negotiating, consensualizing, and arbitrating. Negotiating is the process of discussing and debating an issue wherein at least two individuals indicate some degree of disagreement. Consensualizing is a process wherein at least two individuals act in agreement and in coordination on an issue. Arbitrating is a process whereby a negotiator seeks the judgment of consensually accepted individuals who are socially approved as representatives of sociolegal consensus. Overall, social constructivism ethical decision making directs counselors to avoid linkages of vulnerability while cultivating linkages of professional responsibility.

# INTRODUCTION TO ETHICAL PRINCIPLES IN COUNSELING AND PSYCHOTHERAPY

## OBJECTIVES

■ To explain the six "ethical principles" that guide the helping professions: autonomy, nonmaleficence, beneficence, justice, fidelity, and veracity.

■ To define the basic relationship between ethical principles and the ethical principle intellectual movement in counseling and psychotherapy.

Counselors must deal with a variety of ethical issues and dilemmas. Specific standards guide their practices, including those that are defined fully in Chapter 6: confidentiality and privacy, privileged communication, roles and relationship boundaries, informed consent, professional responsibility, and competence. Those ethical "standards" will be addressed at length in Chapter 6. Counseling and psychotherapy are also guided by encompassing ethical guidelines, defined as **ethical principles (high standards for ethical behavior),** which have been applied to the helping professions, primarily deriving from the field of biomedical ethics. Six ethical principles underlie ethical counseling practice; they are autonomy, nonmaleficence, beneficence, justice, fidelity, and veracity (Box 5.1).

BOX 5.1  A Simplified Summary of the Six Ethical Principles

Autonomy—To allow opportunity for self-determination and unfettered decision
  making; to honor the right to individual decision making.
Nonmaleficence—"Primum non nocere" ("First let us do no harm"); to act so that
  harm is not done to clients.
Beneficence—To do good; to help clients and benefit them.
Justice—To be fair and egalitarian.
Fidelity—To be loyal, honest, and to keep promises.
Veracity—To be truthful in relationships with clients and other involved parties/
  stakeholders. Veracity means dealing truthfully with individuals with whom
  counselors come into professional contact.

## BACKGROUND

In the most recent edition of *Principles of Biomedical Ethics* (Seventh Edition),
Beauchamp and Childress (2012) described four general principles of ethical
medical practice:

> (1) *respect for autonomy* (a norm of respecting and supporting autonomous
> decisions), (2) *nonmaleficence* (a norm of avoiding the causation of harm),
> (3) *beneficence* (a group of norms pertaining to relieving, lessening, or
> preventing harm and providing benefits and balancing benefits against
> risks and costs), and (4) *justice* (a group of norms for fairly distributing
> benefits, risks, and costs). (pp. 12–13) [italics in original quote]

These four ethical principles have been applied to other human service professions since the first edition of the Beauchamp and Childress (1979) book. In
counseling, the principles are recognized as foundational guidelines for the specific ethical standards that address everyday practice. In fact, Kitchener (1984)
published a seminal work applying the four ethical principles plus the "ethical
rule" of fidelity to counseling psychology. Beauchamp and Childress defined an
ethical rule as more content-specific and more restricted in scope than a principle—more like an ethical standard. According to Beauchamp and Childress,
fidelity involves being true to one's word, and it also implies "trust" in the professional providing services and "loyalty" to the person being served. For example, Beauchamp and Childress (2012) stated, "Abandonment of a patient is an
example of a breach of fidelity that amounts to disloyalty" (p. 324). A counselor
should not abandon (discontinue services without adequate cause) a client in the
middle of a contracted service. Kitchener believed that the four ethical principles
(respect for autonomy, nonmaleficence, beneficence, and justice) and the ethical
rule of fidelity were foundational to ethical standards in counseling. In the literature of counseling, there has been widespread acceptance of these foundational

principles, and, following Kitchener's lead, the rule of "fidelity" has been uncritically incorporated as an equal "principle" to the other four principles originally defined by Beauchamp and Childress.

In 2014, the American Counseling Association (ACA) added another of the Beauchamp and Childress (2012) ethical rules—*veracity*—to the list of ethical principles to guide the profession of counseling (ACA, 2014). In the medical setting, **veracity** is honesty "in all professional interactions" (Beauchamp & Childress, 2012, p. 302). Beauchamp and Childress further stated that "veracity in health care refers to accurate, timely, objective, and comprehensive transmission of information, as well as to the way the professional fosters the patient's or subject's understanding" (p. 303). The addition of veracity to the list of ethical principles communicates a message that counselors must not be deceptive in any way in their dealings with clients or others who are legitimately involved with a case. The ACA *Code of Ethics* defines veracity as "dealing truthfully with individuals with whom counselors come into professional contact" (ACA, 2014, p. 3).

## THE HISTORICAL IMPORTANCE OF ETHICAL PRINCIPLES TO MENTAL HEALTH PROFESSIONS

**Ethical principles constitute high standards for ethical behavior.** The mental health professions have largely espoused "principle ethics," the model of ethical reasoning traditionally dominant in medicine and bioethics. **Principle ethics involves objectively applying a system of ethical principles to take the right decision when a counselor is faced with an ethical dilemma.** Principle ethics are in contrast to what is called *virtue ethics*, or *relational ethics*, as described in Chapter 4. One major difference between principle ethics and virtue ethics is that **virtue ethics** emphasize "the person taking action rather than the actions taken by that person" (Cottone, Glosoff, & Kocet, 2005). And certainly, with relational ethics, the influence of stakeholders is prominent in the decision process.

Principle ethics involve reasoning about the ethical dilemma or choice by *specifying* and *balancing* the ethical principles in an analysis to arrive at an ethical solution to the dilemma. **Specifying involves determining and naming the principles that are involved in the situation being considered. Balancing involves weighing which principles are more applicable or important in the analysis** (Meara, Schmidt, & Day, 1996). Several principles are usually involved in a dilemma. These principles are said to have **prima facie merit in the analysis; that is, these principles must be considered in every case and, if set aside, valid and compelling reasons must be given.** Such reasons are usually based on the specific facts in the situation and the greater importance of other core principles to the issue. This process allows for maintaining the general structure of obligations within a society without thoughtlessly forcing its members into slavish, absolutist compliance with standards that do not fit specific situations. The six ethical principles (autonomy, beneficence, nonmaleficence, justice, fidelity, and veracity) form the substrate on which enduring professional ethical obligations are based.

## THE PRINCIPLES

### Respect for Autonomy

**Autonomy is a right to self-determination of choice and freedom from the control of others** (Case Scenario 5.1). Kitchener (1984) noted that there is a difference between freedom of action and freedom of choice: While people should have freedom to make choices, their ability to act on these choices is limited by the autonomy of others. If a person's (person X's) choice abridges the freedom or autonomy of another person (person Y), as in murder, it would be ethical to deny the autonomy of person X in that instance. Counselors create conditions of autonomy for their clients when they do not interfere unnecessarily in the decisions of clients; when they provide all necessary information to their clients in a manner clients can understand; and when it is determined that the clients have the ability to use this information to assess their choices, plan them, and carry them out (Howie, Gatens-Robinson, & Rubin, 1992). *The necessary conditions for autonomy are voluntariness, competence, and full disclosure of information.* The specific professional ethical standards, which will be addressed fully in the next chapter, that relate directly to the principle of autonomy are: professional disclosure, informed consent, right to privacy/confidentiality, and determination of client competency for the types of decisions involved in the situation.

Kitchener (see Kitchener & Anderson, 2011) is very careful to differentiate the ethical principle of *respect for autonomy* from misinterpretation as some sort of implied personality type or characteristic. Respect for autonomy is not about people being mavericks. It is not about valuing people as sole arbiters of right and wrong. Rather, it is a position that respects a client's (and others') rights to be free from controlling interference in decision making and choice. Her position respects the individual as an agent of choice, but not as a freestanding personality predisposition. Counselors and psychotherapists are expected to honor and respect the client's prerogative—to give weight to decisions and actions

### CASE SCENARIO 5.1  Autonomy

A counselor at a community mental health center has been seeing a client for approximately 6 months. The counselor's client initially presented substance use concerns, but has not been complying with treatment goals for reducing substance use. The psychiatrist who manages the client's medications has suggested to the counselor that this client needs to be in a structured treatment program. At the client's next appointment, the counselor tells the client that arrangements for the client to participate in the agency's treatment program have been made "for her own good." The client is visibly upset at this news and replies that she has no desire to be in the program. The counselor tells the client, "It's too bad, you're already in it." Is this a violation of the client's autonomy?

Yes. The counselor has ignored the client's right to self-determination or autonomy by making a treatment decision for the client without presenting information to the client in order for the client to make her own decisions.

that directly flow from the client. It is a nuanced position, but one that clearly articulates the idea of "respect" as part of the decision process.

## Beneficence and Nonmaleficence

The principles of beneficence and nonmaleficence are closely related, and in some ways represent different aspects of the same concept. **Beneficence involves a more active concept of contributing to the well-being of others** (Case Scenario 5.2), whereas **nonmaleficence involves being passive or refraining** from taking **some action that might harm another** (Case Scenario 5.3). At its most basic level, it involves the general social obligation to provide mutual aid to members of our society who are in need of assistance. This obligation for mutual aid applies as long as (a) doing so involves a significant need on the part of the other; (b) the person who might assist the other has some particular qualification, such as knowledge or skill to assist the other; (c) the action would have a high probability of succeeding; and (d) the risk or burden to the person rendering aid is not greater than that to the person needing aid (Beauchamp & Childress, 1983).

In addition to the societal obligation for beneficence, all members of a profession such as counseling have additional obligations to assist their clients. The entire existence of a profession is based on the society's recognition of special skills and knowledge, as well as a purpose to help members of the society with certain types of problems and situations. Important professional duties stemming from beneficence include the obligation to ensure that professionals establish, reach, and maintain an appropriate level of competency in terms of their knowledge, skills, and ethical practices. They must balance their decisions to influence the client or actively undertake a course of action that, in their professional judgment, will result in the client's increased growth or well-being against the possibilities that they might, at the same time, sacrifice some of the client's autonomy or do harm to the client. Counselors must not assume a **paternalistic stance (assuming an authoritative attitude)** toward their clients. Another related term is "parentalism" (Kitchener & Anderson, 2011, p. 32). "**Parentalism**

---

**CASE SCENARIO 5.2 Beneficence**

A client comes to a university counseling center with an eating disorder. No one on staff has expertise in this area, but the client is in need of services and is assigned to a female counselor. The counselor is aware that she lacks the knowledge and skills to work effectively with this client's issues, and seeks consultation and supervision from a private practitioner who specializes in eating disorders. Is the counselor acting in the best interest of her client?

Yes. This scenario illustrates the principle of beneficence. Counselors are obligated to possess appropriate levels of competence in terms of knowledge and skills to work with particular client issues. When no other qualified counselor is available within a particular agency, it is appropriate and the counselor's ethical obligation to seek consultation and supervision.

**CASE SCENARIO 5.3** Nonmaleficence

A counselor in private practice utilizes a particular therapy technique only with his female clients. He firmly believes that clients with past sexual abuse issues can only make progress in treatment if they have sex with a caring, male counselor. He regularly encourages his female clients to consider, as part of the treatment plan, engaging in sexual relations with him to "work through past trauma." Is this ethical?

No. This scenario illustrates a violation of the principle of nonmaleficence. There is absolutely no research evidence to suggest that client–counselor sexual relations are therapeutic. Quite to the contrary, sexual relations between client and counselor are considered to be harmful to the client and are a clear ethical violation.

**means literally acting like a parent toward a person"** (Kitchener & Anderson, 2011, p. 32). When working with clients of different backgrounds, classes, races, religions, or abilities, counselors must be ever cautious about assuming that they know better than the clients or their families concerning what is in the best interests of clients. Howie et al. (1992) offered specific guidelines for determining when paternalistic beneficent action might be justified; but being an expert does not automatically entitle the professional to the moral authority to take paternalistic action on behalf of a client. For example, counselors may be taking a morally wrong action if they discuss only traditional female career choices with female clients. If they assume that female clients would benefit more from traditional career choices than from the challenges of a nontraditional career, they are acting paternalistically.

Nonmaleficence is one of the oldest moral principles in the professions, probably best known as the cornerstone of the Hippocratic Oath taken by ancient Greek physicians to "above all, do no harm." Nonmaleficence is refraining from any action that might cause harm, in addition to not intentionally harming others. This principle is often considered the most pressing obligation for professionals because their activities have the potential to do either good or harm. As a result of the client's trust and the counselor's advanced knowledge, the counselor often has access to special information or opportunities to injure clients either intentionally or unintentionally.

Kitchener (1984) discussed the responsibilities involved in diagnosis of clients as an especially powerful occasion to help or to harm the client. In conjunction with the client, the counselor must determine whether the benefits of diagnosis outweigh the possible harm of going through the assessment and diagnostic processes. Because diagnosis is related closely to treatment planning, funding, and the effects of labeling, these are important concerns. Kitchener noted that the experience of distress or discomfort is often unavoidable—even necessary—during diagnosis and treatment. This realization may make it difficult to discern what constitutes a sufficient level of harm to justify nonpursuit of a particular course in counseling. Even counselors who do not diagnose clients directly are not absolved from concerns about diagnosis and misdiagnosis. In reality, psychiatrists, psychologists, counselors, and other mental health professionals who assign diagnoses often must rely on a variety of records, comments, evaluations, and judgments that are (or should be) conveyed to them to assist in making an appropriate diagnosis. Counselors must ensure that their observations are included in this process, or that an inappropriate diagnosis is reevaluated. The increased use of managed health care and the medical model to access psychotherapy has resulted in heavy pressures on mental health professionals to provide diagnoses for funding of care. These pressures are likely to increase the incidence of misdiagnosis or overdiagnosis, while increasing the possibility of harm to clients.

## Justice

The concept of **justice involves fairness and equality in access to resources and treatment** (Case Scenario 5.4). Counselors are obligated to ensure that their processes, agencies, and services do not discriminate. They must not operate in a manner that advances discrimination at the hands of others. **Distributive justice** involves **access to resources and services that may be considered scarce** (Howie et al., 1992). All of the policies and rules of agencies, institutions, eligibility criteria, laws, and social policies that affect the mental health practice should meet acceptable criteria for just distribution. If counselors determine that serious inequalities exist, they must determine what types of advocacy (both within and outside of the given system) are needed to address the injustice and undertake advocacy efforts to remedy the situation.

Some criteria for distributive justice that might be considered include (a) equal shares, (b) distribution by need, (c) distribution by motivation or effort, (d) distribution by contribution of person, (e) free market exchange or purchase, and (f) fair opportunity, or equalizing unequal opportunity (Howie et al., 1992). The process of determining a model of justice for a particular purpose and

---

### CASE SCENARIO 5.4 Justice

Agency X is located in a small community and provides a variety of psychological, social, and vocational services for its clients. One staff member in particular has expertise in the area of vocational and career counseling. She sees two new clients, both with work-related problems. One client, a well-respected member of the community, is a department head at the county courthouse. The other client works as a night custodian at a local factory and has had some legal difficulties. The counselor recommends a full career assessment for the first client in response to the client's request for career exploration. She tells the second client that career counseling services are not offered at this agency, only job placement. She also tells him that he is experiencing job stress that will soon pass if he "just works hard enough." Is this discriminatory?

Yes. This scenario illustrates a violation of the principle of justice. By not making the same recommendation for both clients in response to similar requests for career counseling, the counselor is discriminating against the second client based on his personal characteristics. The counselor is ethically obligated to provide equal access to resources and services to all clients.

**CASE SCENARIO 5.5** Fidelity

A client in need of a more structured living environment does not fully meet the criteria for admission to the local care facility or hospital. The client has been suicidal in the past and has been recently faced with some extraordinary situational stressors. The client has been very compliant with treatment, has been working hard to improve, and has expressed real discomfort to the counselor about the prospect of being hospitalized. Two staff members in a community agency consult with one another and decide to say that the client is in need of hospitalization for suicidal ideation. The underlying purpose is to have him meet the qualifications for admission into the care facility. Is this in the client's best interest?

No. This scenario illustrates a violation of the principle of fidelity. Although it may be in the client's best interests to be in the care facility, the staff members are misrepresenting the truth to justify the client's admission and they are doing so knowing that the client has communicated a desire to stay out of the hospital.

justifying that particular approach is a complex and important aspect of enacting the ideal of justice. Counseling practices such as due process considerations, access to grievance processes, and techniques of systems intervention and advocacy are examples of activities related to this principle.

Regardless, the principle of justice requires that counselors act in a way that is fair to clients, especially in avoiding prejudicial decisions or favoritism.

## Fidelity

**Promise keeping, keeping commitments, and loyalty are characteristics of the principle of fidelity** (Case Scenario 5.5). Because the bond of trust in the counseling relationship is considered to be of utmost importance to its effectiveness, this principle holds particular meaning for individuals in counseling and the related professions. Indeed, many counseling theorists, such as Rogers (1951), place particular importance on the healing characteristics engendered by the very qualities nurtured by fidelity. Some interpretations of fidelity emphasize the nature of the promises made to clients and the social contract between professional and client, and not just the legal contracts written at the onset of a counseling relationship. Reducing this concept to a legalistic concern that recognizes only specific, direct promises, and not those implied within the nature of the relationship, is inappropriate to the richness of the counselor–client relationship. Counseling practices, such as professional disclosure, informed consent, maintenance of confidentiality, and avoiding harmful relationships, are obligations that flow from the important principle of fidelity; these practices are addressed in Chapter 6.

## Veracity

The ACA *Code of Ethics* defines **veracity** as **"dealing truthfully with individuals with whom counselors come into professional contact"** (ACA, 2014; Box 5.2). Honesty is the principal characteristic of the principle of veracity

(Case Scenario 5.6). Counselors should not misrepresent information, withhold the truth, or lie to clients or others legitimately involved in the case. As a new addition to the list of principles valued by the profession, veracity as a concept implies that the profession values counselors who are forthcoming with information, not deceitful, and open to communication about issues of relevance to counseling process and content.

---

## BOX 5.2  Ethical Principles of Professional Organizations

### Ethical Principles of the American Counseling Association (ACA, 2014)

The fundamental principles of professional ethical behavior are:

*autonomy*, or fostering the right to control the direction of one's life;

*nonmaleficence*, or avoiding actions that cause harm;

*beneficence*, or working for the good of the individual and society by promoting mental health and well-being;

*justice*, or treating individuals equitably and fostering fairness and equality;

*fidelity*, or honoring commitments and keeping promises, including fulfilling one's responsibilities of trust in professional relationships; and

*veracity*, or dealing truthfully with individuals with whom counselors come into professional contact.

### Ethical Principles of the National Association of Social Workers (NASW, 2008)

Social workers' primary goal is to help people in need and to address social problems.

Social workers challenge social injustice.

Social workers respect the inherent dignity and worth of the person.

Social workers recognize the central importance of human relationships.

Social workers behave in a trustworthy manner.

Social workers practice within their areas of competence and develop and enhance their professional expertise.

### Ethical Principles of Psychologists and Code of Conduct (American Psychological Association [APA], 2010)

Principle A: Beneficence and Nonmaleficence

Principle B: Fidelity and Responsibility

Principle C: Integrity

Principle D: Justice

Principle E: Respect for People's Rights and Dignity

*(continued)*

## BOX 5.2   Ethical Principles of Professional Organizations (*continued*)

### *Code of Ethics* of the American Association for Marriage and Family Therapy (AAMFT, 2015)

The AAMFT *Code of Ethics* does not list ethical principles explicitly, but they are embedded in, or referenced by, specific standards, primarily as "aspirational" guides. For example, Standard I, "Responsibility to Clients," states that marriage and family therapists advance the welfare of families and individual clients (another way of saying "beneficence"). Standard 1.1 is about nondiscrimination (addressing fairness). Section 1.8 addresses "client autonomy in decision making." Standard II states: "Therapists respect and guard the confidences of each individual client," which addresses fidelity. In other standards, therapists are directed to not exploit (3.8; 4.1), harass (3.7), or have sexual intimacies with clients or their family members (1.5); these standards all relate to the concept of nonmaleficence. And the association lists "integrity" as a core value, relating this to honest behavior by members (essentially veracity).

## CASE SCENARIO 5.6   Veracity

An 18-year-old client has been diagnosed by a psychiatrist at a psychiatric hospital with schizophrenia. The client's symptoms are both classic of schizophrenia and ominous. A counselor is assigned to the case and family counseling is requested, with full client permission. The counselor meets with the family, and the parents of the client ask the counselor what the prognosis is for their son. They have high hopes for their son, as he is intelligent and motivated to get a higher education for a professional career. The counselor decides to minimize the negative ramifications of the disease, and the counselor implies that "everything will be alright." Has the counselor been deceitful?

LIKELY. Although counselors should not provide only a pessimistic prognostication, being overly optimistic and ignoring the wealth of literature about the full implications of a diagnosis of schizophrenia is a breach of the principle of veracity. The counselor can discuss the opportunity that vocational rehabilitation provides and certainly can direct the client and the family to services provided by rehabilitation professionals. However, realistic expectations should be communicated in a way that does not squelch hope.

## PRINCIPLES, CHALLENGES TO THE PRINCIPLES, AND CODES OF ETHICS

The six ethical principles are drawn from broader, sociocultural understandings of what is right and good. Therefore, they have great explanatory power regarding how certain professional practices and rules, such as professional codes of ethics, agree with the general sense of morals communicated in Western society. They are at the heart of any well-written ethical standard or common clinical practice.

Although the mental health professions now have competing theories of ethical decision making (virtue ethics and relationship ethics), principle ethics still dominates the scene, as mental health codes of ethics are constructed typically with acknowledgment (sometimes explicitly, sometimes implicitly) of ethical principles as their foundation. So even though the virtue ethics and relational ethics movements are potent in offering different views of the decision-making process (see Chapter 4), the principle ethics movement has been adopted as the guiding framework for construction of codes of ethics. However, there has, for the first time, emerged a pubic challenge to one of the principles. Cottone (2012a, 2014) provided a challenge to the ethical principle of autonomy, claiming that it is out of sync with the other ethical principles, which are all relationship focused. Cottone also claimed that the ethical principle of autonomy is an offshoot of Western culture's emphasis on the individual decision maker—independent, freestanding individuals who are somehow insulated from the effects of social influence. Cottone (2014) argued that the ethical principle of autonomy should be replaced with an alternative principle—accordance—which fully accepts the client's position as being embedded in social and cultural domains of influence. **Accordance is a concept that means agreement, collaboration, and cooperation in the decision-making process.** Decisions are made in consultation and not by an individual acting alone or outside the influence of those that have current or historical linkage to the individual. In other words, the decision process is embedded in the social process. Accordance, he argued, is more fully a relational concept and is more aligned with the relational nature of the other ethical principles. Cottone's critique of the ethical principle of autonomy constitutes the first challenge to a principle on philosophical grounds since the adaption of principle ethics in the mental health professions in the 1980s. Cottone (2014) argued that ethical principles are not "set in stone," and they should be viewed as debatable and even open to replacement. Regardless, the ethical codes of major mental health professions (the American Psychological Association [APA], ACA, American Association for Marriage and Family Therapy [AAMFT], and National Association of Social Workers [NASW] codes) all appear heavily weighted by the influence of the widely accepted ethical principles of autonomy, nonmaleficence, beneficence, justice, fidelity, and veracity.

## BEYOND ETHICAL PRINCIPLES: DEFINING ETHICAL STANDARDS

Even though the various professions and professional specialties in counseling have many codes of ethics, all can be analyzed in terms of the ethical principles underlying the specific *ethical standards* of the codes. **Ethical standards are specific profession-relevant directives or guidelines that reflect the best ethical practice of professionals. In other words, an ethical standard is an established guideline defined by a professional group to direct professionals when they are addressing ethical dilemmas.** Chapter 6 outlines the most widely applied ethical standards in mental health professional practice. Codes of ethics usually are a compendium of ethical standards. Interestingly, the codes of the mental health professions are surprisingly similar in their basic conceptualizations of ethical practices. Of course, differences exist in specific areas and in how the details of the core obligations are discharged. Nevertheless, it can be said that all mental health professions endorse (through the standards in their codes of ethics) the core ethical obligations embodied in the six ethical principles.

## CONCLUSION

Six principles guide ethical standards in the helping professions: autonomy, nonmaleficence, beneficence, justice, fidelity, and veracity. These principles provide the "big picture" in what is called the "principle ethics" movement in the mental health professions. The principle ethics "intellectual movement" (Cottone, 2012a) is the first and most widely applied framework for defining ethical standards and decision making in the mental health professions. It is at the foundation of the ethics codes that direct mental health practitioners across disciplines, and therefore, it is a movement that is established and well recognized as a guide for counselors and psychotherapists. The ethical principles are well established, and until recently, they have been unchallenged in the professional ethical literature on philosophical grounds.

# 6

# INTRODUCTION TO ETHICAL STANDARDS IN COUNSELING AND PSYCHOTHERAPY

## OBJECTIVES

■ To apply the six "ethical principles" that guide counseling practice and to establish best practice guidelines in the form of "ethical standards."

■ To understand the specific standards commonly found in ethical codes that guide practices in counseling and psychotherapy, including confidentiality, privacy, privileged communication, roles and relationship boundary issues, informed consent, responsibility, and competence.

Counselors must deal with a variety of ethical issues and dilemmas. Specific standards guide their practice, including confidentiality and privacy, privileged communication, roles and relationship boundary standards, informed consent, professional responsibility, and competence. As defined in Chapter 1, **ethical standards** are the rules that apply to any professional practice, including counseling. In Chapter 5, the six ethical principles that underlie the ethical standards in the practice of counseling (autonomy, nonmaleficence, beneficence, justice, fidelity, and veracity) were introduced.

It is useful to select a particular standard from a code of ethics to delimit the ethical principles that support it. This activity has been used by the Ethical Case Management Practice Training Program developed by Rubin and associates

(Wilson, Rubin, & Millard, 1991). This analysis is helpful in strengthening the counselor's level of familiarity and comfort with the application of the specific ethical principles. It also strengthens the ability to discern the underlying principles behind any number of ethically charged rules, policies, or client situations. Of course, the application of the ethical principles is also a critical stage of the ethical decision-making process as described by many authorities (see Chapter 4).

Consider the six foundational principles listed in Box 6.1 as you read the following section, which describes the ethical standards of counseling. Each ethical standard is, to some degree, an application of one or more of the guiding ethical principles. The ethical standards of counseling are defined in the following section.

## ETHICAL STANDARDS IN MENTAL HEALTH PRACTICE

This section introduces and defines the ethical standards applied to mental health practice in general. The chapters that follow define and expand upon the ethical standards as they are applied in specialty practice. Those chapters define the nuances of applications of the standards to the very specific circumstances that arise in practices in specialties such as school counseling, clinical mental health, career, rehabilitation, addictions, group, forensic practice, couples/family treatment, and clinical supervision. The intent of the presentation of standards that follows in this chapter is to provide a general definition and a brief overview of the concept in practice.

### Confidentiality and Privacy

The American Psychological Association (APA; Section 4), American Association for Marriage and Family Therapy (AAMFT; Standard II), National Association of Social Workers (NASW; Section 1.07), and American Counseling Association (ACA; Section B) codes of ethics address the issues of privacy and confidentiality as related terms. The concepts are related, but there are differences. Privacy is a broader issue—mental health professionals, by nature of their work, are privy to the most personal and intimate information about their clients. The very fact of attending counseling is a very private matter for some individuals. U.S. culture generally respects the fact that individuals have a right to maintain certain personal information as "private"—meaning it is not to be shared in an open forum. **Privacy is a person's right to keep information about himself or herself from being divulged to others** (ACA, 2014). **Thus, in counseling, privacy is the client's right to keep the counseling relationship a secret.** Privacy relates not only to communications made to and by counselors, but also to issues such as the disposal of client records, the provision of a private waiting room area, the security of electronic recordings of counseling sessions or digitized communications (e.g., faxes), the use of credit cards for billing, the use of computer services for scoring of tests, billing, e-mail, electronic transmission of information, and other documentary or business activities of the counselor. For example, if a client

---

## BOX 6.1  Counseling Practices and the Ethical Principles That Underlie Them

Everyday counseling practice involves actions that are based on ethical principles. Inspect the following list of principles and practices associated with each principle. Can you think of other practices that represent some of the principles? Are there other principles (not included in the six listed principles) that may be operating in a counseling practice?

**Respect for Autonomy**
Obtaining consent from a client to counsel the client after ensuring the client is fully informed and provided thorough information.
Obtaining an evaluation of a client's competency (to make decisions).
Obtaining client consent/assent to treatment plans.
Respecting a client's freedom of choice related to participation in counseling, in general, or in certain procedures.

**Nonmaleficence**
Avoiding counseling in areas where one is not competent.
Avoiding harmful roles or relationships with clients.
Informing clients of risks associated with procedures and freedom of choice to undertake procedures.

**Beneficence**
Doing the best one can for one's clients within counseling parameters.
Working within one's limits of competence and training.
Heeding the duty to warn or protect endangered parties.
Terminating counseling or referring clients who are not benefiting from services.

**Justice**
Advocating against discrimination or against practices or rules that discriminate.
Respecting cultural differences.
Doing some work for the needy for no charge (pro bono publico).
Ensuring that services are accessible to those with limitations.

**Fidelity**
Being loyal to clients and employees and keeping promises.
Advocating for clients.
Respecting a client's privacy and confidentiality.
Being loyal to one's colleagues and the profession of counseling.

**Veracity**
Being truthful and honest with clients and other individuals legitimately involved with the case.
Maintaining accurate documentation.

---

pays for services with a credit card, and the counselor lists a counseling agency name or profession on the receipt, the credit card company effectively has information that the individual paid for services to a counselor, which is a breach of privacy. If sessions are scheduled in a way that others may observe clients in a waiting room, privacy may be compromised. The ethics codes of the AAMFT, NASW, ACA, and APA state that an individual's privacy should be respected. Counselors must be mindful of this overriding standard.

"Confidentiality" is related to, but different than, privacy. **Confidentiality more specifically addresses the need to keep information communicated in the counseling session contained within the counseling relationship** and was developed as something akin to an antigossip guarantee. **Confidentiality** is the ethical obligation of counseling professionals to safeguard the "client's identity, identifying characteristics, and private communications" (ACA, 2014, p. 20). When information is communicated in the privacy of the formal counselor–client relationship, it is to be maintained as a secret within that relationship. Confidentiality is an ethical concept almost universally referenced in both professional association codes of ethics and legal ethical standards.

**When confidentiality is referenced by law or statute, it is referred to as "legal confidentiality." Legal confidentiality is a mandate that prevents the discussion of private communications (with a counselor in a professional context) from being revealed to other individuals.** For example, the Illinois Mental Health and Developmental Disabilities Confidentiality Act (1978) defines "confidential communication" and specifies when such communications can and cannot be disclosed. Counselors cannot reveal to other individuals what is communicated in counseling without potential penalty of law. For example, Section 16 of the Illinois act states that one who intentionally violates the act is guilty of a misdemeanor.

Confidentiality guaranteed by a professional association alone (nonlegal confidentiality) does not carry the weight of law; however, it does carry the weight of the professional association, which can censure members or remove them from association membership. For example, ACA has its own *Policies and Procedures for Processing Complaints of Ethical Violations* (ACA, 2005a), which specifies the steps involved in lodging and processing a complaint against a counselor. Possible sanctions against ACA members who have been found to have committed an ethical violation include remediation, probation, suspension from ACA membership, or permanent expulsion.

Confidentiality is a guarantee to clients that what they communicate privately in professional counseling will be held "in confidence"—for the ears and eyes of the counselor alone—unless clients specifically release the counselor from the promise.

There are limits and exceptions to both professionally mandated and legal confidentiality. In a classic court case, *Tarasoff v. the California Board of Regents* (VandeCreek & Knapp, 1993), a judgment was made that a psychologist had the "duty to warn" an endangered party when a counseling client made a direct threat on a life. In this case, the psychologist, a counselor at a University of California counseling center, warned the police of the threat. Unfortunately, he failed to warn the threatened individual, whom the client later murdered. The legal judgment that followed the incident stated that in such cases, **confidentiality is overridden by the duty to warn—to inform endangered individuals of an identifiable threat.** In fact, in 2004, the California State Supreme Court extended the "duty to warn" in a decision against a therapist (David Goldstein) who chose

not to inform an endangered party (Keith Ewing) when the parents of Goldstein's client informed Goldstein that their son (Geno Colello) threatened to hurt
Ewing. Goldstein, the therapist, felt he was immune from responsibility, since
the client did not tell him of the threat. But the courts ruled against Goldstein,
even in this situation where a third party warns of a direct threat to an identified
victim. The Court held Goldstein responsible for not breaking confidentiality
and warning the endangered party. Some believe that the California Supreme
Court went too far in this case, since the credibility of third parties cannot be
assessed. The question becomes, "Have the courts gone too far in extending the
duty to warn?" Certainly, counselors have an obligation to protect a person's
confidentiality, but what constitutes the boundary between a choice of keeping a
promise or protecting the public? The message of the California Supreme Court
is clear: Threats to individuals should not be taken lightly; the authorities and the
potential victim must be warned. Most ethical codes in the mental health professions incorporate the practices suggested by the original *Tarasoff* decision (when
a client makes a direct threat to an identifiable party), and counselors should be
alert to this limit of confidentiality. Certainly, if information is communicated by
a third party (known to be credible by the counselor) about a threat by a client
to harm someone or to act against society (e.g., terrorism), the counselor would
be wise to use a formal decision-making model to assist in making a decision to
break confidentiality (see Box 6.2).

*[handwritten margin note: 3rd party ↓ duty to protect]*

---

## BOX 6.2  Assessing Clients for Potential to Harm Self or Others

(*Note:* See also the section in Chapter 7 on suicide statistics, signs of potential
suicide, and recommended actions following the guidelines of the American
Association of Suicidology, 2013a.)

When a client poses a risk to self or others, it is imperative for the counselor to
consider actions to protect (a) the client (if threatening suicide or self-harm, for
example), (b) an endangered party (if threatening an identifiable third party), or
(c) potential innocent bystanders. This "risk" assessment is crucial to the concepts
of "Duty to Warn" or "Duty to Protect."

Generally, a counselor must assess the client first for either suicidal ideation
(thoughts) or assault/homicidal ideation (thoughts). It is not unusual for a
person to have fleeting suicidal thoughts when under pressure or in difficult
circumstances. Even the healthiest people sometimes have fleeting thoughts of
self-harm, or they may even have thoughts of harm to others who have "done
them wrong." By themselves, suicidal ideation or assault/homicidal ideation is
not necessarily a warning sign of impending action by a client. However, when
suicidal or assault/homicidal ideation is accompanied by **plans (they know how
they are going to accomplish harm to self or others), intentions (they know when they
are going to accomplish harm to self or others), or means (they have the instruments
available that are necessary to carry out the action, such as available overdose drugs
or a weapon),** then the concern reaches a level requiring the counselor to take

(continued)

## BOX 6.2  Assessing Clients for Potential to Harm Self or Others (*continued*)

direct and ethical action. A general rule of clinical practice is that if a client has intentions, plans, or means to do self or other harm, the counselor must act to protect the client or the identified endangered party. But, assessing suicide risk, for example, is not as simple as evaluating for intentions, plans, or means. Carrier (2004) provided a detailed chapter on assessing suicide risk. In addition to assessing for plans, he recommends assessing for a number of other predictive factors, including: means and opportunity to carry out the plan; previous suicide attempts; a diagnosed mood disorder (e.g., depression, bipolar disorder); drug or alcohol use; hopelessness; social isolation; gender (more women than men attempt suicide, but more men than women complete a suicide attempt); anger; psychosocial stressors (such as unemployment, financial or relationship problems); and a family history of suicide. With assault/homicidal threat, a number of those factors apply, plus the client must be assessed for a history of doing harm to others or to animals. Carrier (2004) provided a nice review of assessment instruments used to assess suicide potential, and his review is worth reading. Regardless, if a counselor believes that a client is a risk for suicide or harm to others, the counselor must act to protect the endangered party. For suicide, the client should be taken to the nearest hospital emergency department, or precautions should be taken to ensure the client is never left alone. A "no suicide" or "no harm" contract, although recommended, is not enough in such circumstances, since people contemplating self or other harm may not be in a clear state of mind. If there is an identified endangered third party—a potential victim or victims—action should be taken to alert the endangered individuals and the authorities. The counselor would also be wise to use a well-known decision-making model to determine if others are in danger and should be warned (e.g., family members or bystanders). State laws may require additional actions in such circumstances, and counselors should be alert to legal precedent on matters of duty to warn and duty to protect in jurisdictions where they practice.

Other common limits to confidentiality typically referenced in professional codes or statutes involve the following:

1. Required revelation to authorities of any case of substantiated or suspected child abuse or neglect
2. Required revelation to authorities of a client's communicated intent to do harm to an identified individual or to society (e.g., through an illegal act)
3. Required revelation of counseling information to a parent or legal guardian of a client who is a minor child, on the request of the parent or legal guardian

4. In-case consultation with other professionals or when educating students of counseling (often, however, identifying information must be disguised)

Counselors should inform clients prior to counseling of any professional and/or legal limits to the confidential relationship. Otherwise, they may share confidential information with others only with the direct written consent of clients.

In 1996, the Public Law 104-191, the federal Health Insurance Portability and Accountability Act (HIPAA), was signed into law. The HIPAA law was designed to improve the continuity of health insurance coverage and to ensure that individuals could obtain insurance in a way that health insurance companies would not abuse information in health records. This law has a provision that is very specifically targeted to mental health professionals. Beyond standard and strict provisions for the exchange of information for billing, insurance, and other purposes, there is a restriction on the sharing of "psychotherapy" notes (Health Insurance Reform Security Standards, 2003). On April 14, 2001, the U.S. Department of Health and Human Services (DHHS) instituted rules related to the HIPAA law, providing new federal standards for the privacy of health records. Information about medication prescription, medication monitoring, start and stop times of counseling sessions, type and frequency of treatment, and test results and summaries may be released with a standard request. *Psychotherapy notes*, which contain very intimate information about clients, *cannot be shared as standard procedure when a client gives permission generally to release information* (New Patient Records Privacy Rule Takes Effect, 2001). **Psychotherapy notes (essentially case progress notes that describe the content and process of counseling sessions)** can be shared only with a client's permission on a detailed release form that addresses the release of psychotherapy notes specifically. In other words, *general "release of information" forms are not acceptable for the sharing of psychotherapy notes.* This law helps to protect clients from undue invasion of privacy by individuals who really do not need to know the private information relayed during counseling sessions. The central aspect of the privacy rule is *minimum necessary* disclosure; in this way, individuals are assured that only what is necessary is shared in order to address their health and disability concerns.

Confidentiality is not only a legal issue at the state level; federal laws and regulations also address it. For example, federal rules (such as HIPAA) and federal law affect the release of specialized information; a federal law prohibits the disclosure of information of individuals treated for chemical dependency (see Chapter 7).

**Questions for Reflection:** What value is the counseling profession if counseled individuals cannot be assured of confidentiality? If confidentiality cannot be guaranteed for an individual (or a group of individuals), what is the risk of nontreatment? Will individuals choose not to seek counseling if their confidentiality is not guaranteed? What is the risk to society if such individuals do not seek counseling?

Although confidentiality appears to be a straightforward concept, challenging situations may arise that make judgments difficult. One area of contemporary concern is related to individuals with HIV who may transmit the virus to others through intimate relations. Should the counselor breach confidentiality and warn a partner of an HIV-positive individual? Does *Tarasoff* apply? What are a counselor's responsibilities? These questions have received attention in the literature (e.g., Cohen, 1990; Harding, Gray, & Neal, 1993; Schlossberger & Hecker, 1996; Stanard & Hazler, 1995), but there are no clear answers; especially in more recent years when advances in treatment of the disease have rendered it to be more a chronic serious disorder rather than a life-threatening one. The mental health professional codes do not give unquestionable guidance. However, an evolving norm to break confidentiality appears to be emerging in recent legal case law if the following criteria are met: (a) there is an identifiable party at risk; (b) there is a significant risk of infection; (c) a warning is likely to be effective in preventing infection; and (d) efforts to get the infected individual to reveal the infection to the endangered party have failed (see Reaves, 1999). Revelation appears justified if the criteria are met. Like all complicated legal matters, there have been exceptions to the prevailing case law. In a Texas Supreme Court ruling (*Santa Rosa Health Care Corporation v. Garcia*, 1998), a provider was not held responsible to inform the wife of a hemophiliac of her possible exposure to HIV. The issue becomes a balancing act. Which is most critical—the risk of a life, the risk to society, or the risk of a most basic ethical standard at the foundation of a profession?

Acceptable ethical standards are often established after a serious concern has been raised in the literature or in the courts. Counselors must remain current with the professional literature (see Box 6.3) to ensure that they are alert to potential ethical dilemmas; by doing so they can act to prevent a breach of ethics before it happens (Case Scenarios 6.1–6.4).

## CASE SCENARIO 6.1 Confidentiality

The mother of a 21-year-old female client calls, concerned about her daughter, and wishes to share information with the counselor in private practice about the daughter's status. In the course of the conversation between the mother and the counselor, the mother asks about the daughter's progress in counseling. Should the counselor answer?

NO. The counselor should not answer without specific written consent from the client that allows communications with the mother. In fact, counselors should not even acknowledge that they are seeing any clients to anyone over the phone, especially without the client's written consent. This is true of anyone seeking information about an individual's participation in counseling, even an identified lawyer or judge. Counselors should be leery about communicating about clients over the phone on incoming calls, but may more safely communicate to individuals on calls they place with the permission of their clients.

## CASE SCENARIO 6.2 Confidentiality

A counselor at a party meets a social worker who referred a client to the counselor. The social worker begins to discuss the client with the counselor while other individuals are milling around. Should the counselor discuss the case?

NO. The counselor should communicate to the social worker that they should not talk about cases at the party. With appropriate permission from the client, they should talk about the case only in a private, professional (not social) context. At that time, they should discuss only information directly pertinent to the social worker's role in the case and allowed by client consent. It is also prudent in this day of advanced technology (e.g., e-mail and cellular phones) to evaluate the privacy of any professional conversation, however proper, to ensure that confidentiality or privacy is not unintentionally breached.

## CASE SCENARIO 6.3 Confidentiality

The spouse of a counselor meets the counselor at the counselor's office and sees a client walk out of the counseling office. The spouse asks, "What's his problem?" Should the counselor discuss the case with the spouse?

NO. A counselor's confidentiality does not extend to a spouse. In some cases, it does extend to coworkers in agencies or to other professional colleagues, but even in these cases, the coworkers or colleagues must be informed of the confidential nature of the information and must guarantee that they will maintain confidentiality. Regardless, the service-providing counselor is ultimately responsible ethically if confidentiality is breached.

## CASE SCENARIO 6.4 Confidentiality

A counselor has had a rough day and goes to a local cosmetology salon after work. The counselor begins discussing tough cases with the cosmetologist but is careful to disguise names and identifying information about specific clients. Has anything unethical occurred?

YES. If it is possible that someone can identify a client by context, confidentiality has been breached. If, for example, a relative or friend of a client overhears such a conversation and can piece together the information, thereby identifying the client, an unethical act has occurred. Only in certain professional situations can a general discussion of disguised cases be ethical, such as a professor's discussion of a case in a relevant college class. Even if the risk of identifying a client is not significant, any practice of public discussion of cases is generally harmful of the trust of confidentiality. It risks decreasing the confidence of the lay public in the profession of counseling and subjects both clients and other counselors to misunderstanding or even ridicule.

## BOX 6.3  Confidentiality as Defined in the Codes of Ethics of the Professions

**American Counseling Association *Code of Ethics* (ACA, 2014)**
The introduction to Section B (Confidentiality and Privacy) reads: "Counselors
recognize that trust is a cornerstone of the counseling relationship. Counselors
aspire to earn the trust of clients by creating an ongoing partnership, establishing
and upholding appropriate boundaries, and maintain confidentiality. Counselors
communicate the parameters of confidentiality in a culturally competent manner."

**Ethical Principles of the National Association of Social Workers
(NASW, 2008)**
**1.07 Privacy and Confidentiality**
(a) Social workers should respect clients' right to privacy. Social workers should
not solicit private information from clients unless it is essential to providing
services or conducting social work evaluation or research. Once private
information is shared, standards of confidentiality apply.
(b) Social workers may disclose confidential information when appropriate with
valid consent from a client or a person legally authorized to consent on behalf
of a client.
(c) Social workers should protect the confidentiality of all information obtained in
the course of professional service, except for compelling professional reasons.
The general expectation that social workers will keep information confidential
does not apply when disclosure is necessary to prevent serious, foreseeable,
and imminent harm to a client or other identifiable person. In all instances,
social workers should disclose the least amount of confidential information
necessary to achieve the desired purpose; only information that is directly
relevant to the purpose for which the disclosure is made should be revealed.

**Ethical Principles of Psychologists and Code of Conduct (APA, 2010)**
**4.01 Maintaining confidentiality**
Psychologists have a primary obligation and take reasonable precautions to
protect confidential information obtained through or stored in any medium,
recognizing that the extent and limits of confidentiality may be regulated by law
or established by institutional rules or professional or scientific relationship. (See
also Standard 2.05, Delegation of Work to Others.)

**Code of Ethics of the American Association for Marriage and Family
Therapy (AAMFT, 2015)**
The AAMFT code reads as follows:
Marriage and family therapists have unique confidentiality concerns because the
client in a therapeutic relationship may be more than one person. Therapists
respect and guard the confidences of each individual client.

**2.1 Disclosing Limits of Confidentiality.**
Marriage and family therapists disclose to clients and other interested parties at
the outset of services the nature of confidentiality and possible limitations of the
clients' right to confidentiality. Therapists review with clients the circumstances
where confidential information may be requested and where disclosure of
confidential information may be legally required. Circumstances may necessitate
repeated disclosures.

## Privileged Communication

**Privileged communication** is a legal right of clients found in state or federal statutes. **Privileged communication is a client's right to prevent the revelation of confidential information in a legal proceeding** (e.g., in a legal hearing or courtroom). A counselor cannot be forced to testify on a client's case if the privilege stands. Privileged communication is owned by the client, and only the client can waive the privilege allowing testimony (Hummel, Talbutt, & Alexander, 1985; Reaves, 1999; Wheeler & Bertram, 2015). *Privileged communication, being a legal right, is not found in professional codes of ethics; it is* **statutory (in state or federal laws).**

Like confidentiality, there are limits to privileged communication. In many states, stipulations override any psychotherapist or counselor privileged communication in cases of substantiated or suspected child abuse or neglect. In such cases, a judge can order a counselor to testify on otherwise confidential information. Such disclosure is not illegal, and the counselor is given immunity from prosecution (i.e., cannot be found guilty of breaching privileged communication). Privilege also may not stand when a client sues a counselor (Wheeler & Bertram, 2015).

> **Question for Reflection:** Confidentiality and privileged communication are related concepts, although privileged communication applies strictly to legal settings (e.g., preventing revelation of confidential information before the courts). Which of the six ethical principles underpin the concepts of confidentiality and privileged communication (autonomy, nonmaleficence, beneficence, justice, fidelity, or veracity)?

In some states, communications are "privileged" in civil but not criminal cases by licensure statute. **Criminal law cases involve the illegal actions of a person—such as murder or theft—and they are resolved in the criminal court** (Wheeler & Bertram, 2015). **Civil law cases involve disagreements between people in some legal relationship (marriage, a contracted work relationship, employment) that need to be resolved by legal authority.** If a client is charged with a felony and goes to criminal court, attorneys can request the counseling case files and the judge can order the counselor to testify. **A court request to provide information is called a subpoena.** While subpoenas may be easily initiated by a lawyer with the clerk of the court, such a subpoena does not necessarily require the counselor to comply. Whenever a counselor receives a subpoena requesting confidential information, the counselor should always and immediately seek legal counsel to see whether the counselor should comply with the subpoena or whether compliance should be contested, for example, by filing a motion to quash the subpoena (Wheeler & Bertram, 2015). **If the judge orders that the information must be provided, it is usually called a "court order."** If this occurs in a state where there is no privileged communication on criminal court cases, then the counselor would have to comply. On the other hand, where civil law allows for privileged communication, when a civil court (not a criminal court) such as a divorce court, subpoenas a counselor, the counselor must refuse to provide information about a client's case on the grounds of the client's lawful right to privileged communication. Other examples of civil cases in which a counselor may be asked to provide information or even to testify include workers' compensation disability/injury hearings, social security disability hearings, child custody hearings, termination of parental rights hearings (unless there is an allegation of child abuse or neglect and an exemption to privileged communication), and other legal proceedings in which a crime allegedly has not been committed. As with confidentiality, counselors must know the limits of privileged communication written into licensure laws or other state statutes. (See the general review of privileged communications laws across several mental health professions by Glosoff, Herlihy, and Spence [2000].) The ethics committee of a state counseling association or a licensure board of a state can help a counselor identify those laws that affect professional practice. Most ethical codes require that counselors respect the laws in the jurisdiction within which they practice.

On June 13, 1996, the U.S. Supreme Court ruled that communications between psychotherapists and their clients are confidential and privileged. The decision specifically extended federal privilege, which, according to the ACA (1996), "already applies to psychiatrists and psychologists." The actual Supreme Court case, *Jaffee v. Redmond et al.* (1996), extended privilege to a licensed social worker who was described with the broader term "psychotherapist" in the suit, which, according to the ACA (1996), "leave[s] the door open for inclusion of other providers of psychotherapy" (p. 10). In *Jaffee*, a police officer, Redmond, killed a suspect during an arrest. The officer later sought counseling from a licensed clinical social worker. Jaffee, administering the estate of the deceased on behalf of the family, requested the social work case notes, and the social worker refused to turn over those notes to the court. The original decision went against the social worker, and damages were awarded to the family. On appeal, the decision was overturned on the basis of the confidential relationship between the police officer and her social worker therapist. The Supreme Court upheld the appellate court's decision to overturn the original decision. This ruling was groundbreaking because it has federal implications (not limited to one state) and because it was liberal in its definition of psychotherapist and psychotherapy. Glosoff et al. (2000) stated:

> Although no state legislature licenses "psychotherapists," and the *Jaffee*
> court did not define its use of the term, it seems likely that the precedent
> established in *Jaffee* may be acknowledged for relationships between
> licensed counselors and their clients in future federal cases in which only
> federal laws are at issue (Remley et al., 1997). In cases in federal court
> in which state law is at issue, Federal Rule of Evidence 501 requires that
> questions of privilege be determined in accordance with the law of that
> state. Counselors in states where no privileged communication statute exists
> or where the number or types of exceptions weaken the privilege might
> nonetheless use the court's reasoning in *Jaffee* when they want to persuade
> a judge to extend privilege in a case or when they are working with state
> legislatures to establish or strengthen counselor–client privilege. (p. 456)

Only time will tell the implications of the *Jaffee* decision for the counseling, psychology, and marriage and family therapy professions, although the ruling appears to apply clearly to social workers who have "psychotherapy" clearly referenced in their scope of practice by licensure statute (Case Scenarios 6.5–6.7).

---

**CASE SCENARIO 6.5** Privileged Communication

A vocational rehabilitation counselor is hired by a workers' compensation insurance company to assess an alleged injured worker. The insurance claims adjuster refers the case and is suspicious that the claimant is malingering (faking an injury or illness) to collect workers' compensation injury benefits. The claims adjuster requests that the counselor evaluate the client to plan and to recommend rehabilitation services, if necessary. The counselor does not explain any limits of confidentiality and does not have the claimant sign a waiver of privileged communication. Counseling clients in the counselor's state are afforded privileged communication in civil legal proceedings. Later, the counselor is asked to testify on the case by a workers' compensation administrative law judge. The counselor was hired by the workers' compensation insurance company, so the counseling information is owned by the insurance carrier. Therefore, the counselor must testify. True or false?

FALSE. The client/claimant owns the privilege, and only the client can waive the privilege in a civil case. If it appears that court testimony is going to be part of a case assessment, the counselor should obtain a written waiver of privileged communication before assessing the client. This issue also involves another ethical standard, informed consent, which we address later in this chapter.

---

**CASE SCENARIO 6.6** Privileged Communication

A marriage counselor sees a husband and wife in counseling conjointly. The counselor is subpoenaed by a judge regarding divorce proceedings at the request of the husband's attorney. The husband claims that the counselor had evidence of the wife's mental instability from previous medical and hospital records as well as from observation of the wife in marriage counseling. The husband believes the marriage counselor can testify as to the effects of the wife's mental disorder on the marriage. The husband waives privileged communication. The counselor refuses to testify on the basis of the privileged communication of the wife. Is the counselor acting legally?

IT DEPENDS. In some states, privileged communication stands only in cases in which there has been one-on-one communication between a client and a therapist. If other persons are present (as in group counseling or marriage, couple, or family counseling) the privilege may not stand. Whether privilege stands depends on how the statute is written and on past case law. In some states, relationship theory and family counseling are referenced into the definition of practice in the psychology or counselor licensure statute. Therefore, it can be assumed by the law itself that privilege extends to circumstances involving relational treatment or family counseling. If there is no state case law on this issue, a final conclusion on this issue is not possible. A counselor who is unsure whether privileged communication applies should consult or hire an attorney before attending any legal proceeding, thereby seeking representation on that issue before the court.

### CASE SCENARIO 6.7 Privileged Communication

An allegation of child abuse is made against a counselor's client, who is the parent of the child in question. The counselor is subpoenaed by a hearing officer to attend a parental rights termination hearing. The counselor must go to testify. True or false?

TRUE. In states where privileged communication is overridden by licensure or other statutes in cases of child abuse or neglect, the counselor should appear and be prepared to testify in those cases. However, the counselor should alert the judge or hearing officer of the client's right to privileged communication and should formally request that the privilege be overridden as a part of the record, based on the relevant statute. Even in such cases, the counselor is advised to consult with his or her own attorney prior to testifying or otherwise providing information. The counselor should also consider contacting his or her professional liability insurance carrier, which may provide representation in some instances.

## Counselor Roles and Relationship Boundaries With Clients and Other Involved Parties

### Historical Use of the Terms "Dual" and "Multiple" Relationships

The literature of the mental health professions historically associated the term **dual relationship (a relationship in addition to the contracted counseling relationship)** with a misuse of therapist power or authority. Such relationships were viewed as a second role with the client, and that second role was always viewed as harmful. This is reflected in the older codes of ethics; for example, the outdated AAMFT *Code of Ethics* stated that therapists "make every effort to avoid dual relationships with clients that could impair professional judgment or increase the risk of exploitation" (AAMFT, 1991). The ACA (1995) code stated that "dual relationships" should be avoided "when possible." The term "dual relationship" has lost favor in the recent literature because it is unclear and, to some degree, misleading. For example, every counselor in private practice is in a dual (or for that matter, "multiple") relationship with clients by nature of counseling. The counselor is a professional helper and is also involved in a contracted financial arrangement and a record-keeping arrangement. The therapist in private practice is at least involved in three professional relationships with clients: helper, business service provider, and record keeper. The term "dual relationship," therefore, is not necessarily a negative term, and most codes acknowledge this by qualifying any discussion of dual relationships with a statement addressing "harm" or "exploitation" of clients. A dual relationship that is harmful or an exploitive relationship is wrong. Across the board, codes of ethics place a ban on "harm" to clients. Unfortunately, the term "dual relationship," in and of itself, holds an undeserved negative connotation, and the newer codes of ethics have begun to modify terminology in discussing these matters.

Historically, ethical breaches in this area of counseling were the most prevalent and potentially damaging to clients and the profession of counseling as a whole. Part of the problem may have been related to inexact terminology and unclear ethical guidance on the "dual relationship" issue. Accordingly, Cottone and Tarvydas (2003) made some sweeping recommendations related to terminology as applied to this area of ethics. The first code of ethics to revise the terminology on this matter was the *Code of Professional Ethics for Rehabilitation Counselors* (Commission on Rehabilitation Counselor Certification [CRCC], 2001), revised under the direction of R. Rocco Cottone as chair of the ethics code rewrite task force. Cottone made a compelling case that the "dual" (or even the "multiple") relationship terminology was misleading and unclear. He recommended a revision of the term around crucial roles and relationships that counselors enter with clients and other involved parties. In a letter to the CRCC explaining the need to revise the code's terminology, he redefined the term "dual relationship" as three separate and distinct kinds of interactions: (a) sexual and romantic interactions with clients and/or family members of clients; (b) nonprofessional interactions with clients (excepting sexual or romantic interactions), such as attending a client's wedding or a client's graduation or a party after such an event, some of which he defined as "potentially beneficial"; and (c) contiguous professional relationships (professional roles in addition to an existing contracted role; such roles are undertaken sequentially or simultaneously to the preexisting role). The commission revised the rehabilitation counseling standards; this action represents the first direct action by a professional body to revise the "dual" relationship terminology.

Part of the negative connotation associated with the outdated term "dual" relationship has to do with the associated concern of exploitive sexual relationships. Ethical codes in the mental health professions ban sexual relationships with current clients, and, in the case of former clients, ban involvement for a period of 2 to 5 years subsequent to professional involvement. There is unanimous agreement among ethical codes: Sexual intimacies with clients are unethical. In states where psychotherapeutic practice is regulated, such relationships are also illegal. They are considered a breach of the most basic trust between a mental health professional and a client. This ban is not just a moral issue; research evidence indicates that such relationships are damaging to clients; see the discussion in Pope (1988), and the study by Bouhoutsos, Holroyd, Lerman, Forer, and Greenberg (1983), and Sonne (2012). There are no compelling reasons in defense of sexual relations with current or recent clients. Counselors would have difficulty defending themselves in cases of substantiated or acknowledged sexual activity of this sort. In any discussion of roles and relationships with clients or former clients, sexual intimacies stand alone and deserve to be addressed directly and unequivocally. Related to legal repercussions of sexual relations with clients, Reaves (1999) stated, "the largest civil judgments have been reserved for those professionals that engage in such heinous conduct" (p. 23). The mental health professional codes of ethics make it clear in freestanding sections that sexual intimacies with clients are unethical. The codes ban sexual intimacy with former clients for a period of time, but allow for professional scrutiny even after that time has passed.

Licensure boards often report that mental health professionals have had licenses suspended or revoked on the basis of improper sexual intimacies with patients or trainees under their supervision. The sexual contact issue between patients and counselors is very commonly the charge that leads to suspension or revocation of a professional license on ethical grounds. The Association of State and Provincial Psychology Boards (ASPPB, the professional association of licensure boards), which keeps statistics on disciplinary actions of its boards, reported that the highest number of reported disciplinary actions against psychologists fits into the category of "sexual/dual relationship with patient"; 715 of 2,206 disciplinary actions were in the sexual/dual relationship category (ASPPB, 2001).

Aside from the issue of sexual intimacies with current or former clients, the term "multiple" relationships gained favor in some professional circles, implying two or more therapist–client relationships. The term is used in some ethical codes; for example, the APA (2010) *Code of Ethics*. Typically, the term "multiple relationship" is linked to the issue of exploitation or harm to clients. Exploitive or harmful multiple roles are considered unethical.

### Harmful Versus Nonharmful Interactions

Although it is wise to avoid potentially harmful relationships with clients or trainees, not all relationships with clients outside of counseling are technically illegal or unethical; see the analysis by Anderson and Kitchener (1998). Certainly, an unplanned, accidental social contact is not unethical; for example, a counselor could hardly be blamed for running into a client at a party or athletic event. Other cases also may not be unethical:

1. A professor of counseling is impressed by a student. After the student graduates, she hires the student to work in a counseling service that she owns.
2. A supervisor of counselor licensure candidates gets to know his supervisees over several years of supervision. Friendships develop that last beyond the formal supervision agreement.
3. A counselor encounters a former client whose counseling was terminated several years earlier. The counselor remembers that the client provided a professional service, which he currently needs. He then negotiates to purchase the services from the former client.

These relationships are not illegal or technically unethical, but still warrant scrutiny. Counselors generally know if a relationship holds the potential of harming the client or compromising the client's best interests or well-being (Kitchener, 1988). In fact, the term **"exploitation" can be defined as an action by a counselor that benefits the counselor while it compromises the best interest or well-being of a client.** Counselors should also consider the appearance of impropriety as well as the unintended level of coercion or influence they may have on impressionable clients. The general rule is: Avoid potentially harmful or exploitive relationships, or, if such a relationship is imminent, clearly examine the ethical or legal ramifications and act to minimize or rectify any harm.

Some have argued that a total ban on relationships outside the contracted therapeutic relationship is unjustified. Lazarus (2001) and Lazarus and Zur (2002) have been vocal critics of such bans in psychotherapy in general. Tomm (1993), in the area of marriage and family therapy, has also been adamant in arguing against a total ban on extra-therapy interactions. Their positions are founded on personal experiences wherein clients or trainees actually benefited by interactions outside of the counseling or supervising process. These authors have argued that an outright ban on all nontreatment (or nonsupervision) interaction misses the point—the issue is really harm or exploitation by unethical practitioners. They maintain that the focus should be on banning exploitation or harmful interactions, not on banning all nonprofessional interactions. For example, should a counselor feel guilty about buying Girl Scout cookies from a client? By some, this could be viewed as unethical, but it certainly is not likely to be harmful, and in some sense, it might be beneficial to the client. Although buying cookies from a client can be viewed as a trite example, there are many examples wherein therapists are put in positions of interacting with clients in ways that are innocent to the therapeutic relationship and may actually be beneficial to the client—attending a ceremony or family funeral, accompanying a client on an anxiety-producing activity, purchasing a product or service in a way that does not compromise counseling, or attending a wedding or graduation ceremony. An outright ban appears to be unjustified.

However, there may be a *slippery slope* (one step on a slippery slope may lead to a fall). **The "slippery slope" analogy applied to professional ethics implies a slow and gradual erosion of ethical safeguards.** Haug (1993) has made a case that involvement in interactions outside of counseling with a client may lead to potentially detrimental relationships (the fall on the slippery slope). By banning all extra-therapeutic interactions, ethical authorities may act to prevent truly harmful ethical breaches.

Counselors and therapists are human. No licensure board or ethical authority can control feelings. Pope, Keith-Spiegel, and Tabachnick (1986) found that "attraction to clients is a prevalent experience among both male and female psychologists" (p. 155). Feelings may develop and may be uncontrollable, but there are controls on actions of professionals. In fact, there is evidence that psychologists frequently contemplate entering into sexual relationships with clients (Lamb, Catanzaro, & Moorman, 2004). In a survey of male counselors, Thoreson and his associates found that "although relatively few respondents (1.7%) reported having engaged in sexual misconduct with clients during a professional relationship, the prevalence rate increased to 17% when the definition of sexual misconduct was expanded to include (a) students and students under supervision, and (b) occurrences of sexual misconduct after the professional relationship" (Thoreson, Shaughnessy, Heppner, & Cook, 1993, p. 429). In a later survey of female counselors: "Counselors viewed sexual contact in current professional relationships as less ethical than contact in subsequent relationships, although relationships with former clients were seen as less ethical than relationships with former trainees. Compared with male counselors from a previous study, female counselors were less likely to report sexual contact in their professional roles" (Thoreson, Shaughnessy, & Frazier, 1995, p. 84). Because sexual feelings and contemplation of sexual relationships with clients and trainees are fairly common, counselor trainees need to be alert to the issues. Educators should train mental health professionals about ethical ways to handle attraction and sexual feelings toward clients (Harris, 2001; Lamb et al., 2004; Vasquez, 1988). Certainly all nonprofessional roles with clients should be managed carefully (Younggren & Gottlieb, 2004).

As to whether there is danger of physical or emotional harm, a healthy friendship that develops during a formal counseling or supervisory relationship and lasts beyond the formal contracted services may not be considered harmful. Sexual intimacies are another matter. To reiterate, research shows that clients most usually are in danger of emotional harm when involved sexually with a counselor or therapist (Bouhoutsos et al., 1983; Pope, 1988; Sonne, 2012). To cross the line of sexual intimacy is a misuse of power for the therapist. Clients must be viewed, to some degree, as emotionally vulnerable by nature of their status. Seduction by clients is considered a symptom of some emotional disorders. Counselors must take extra precautions against any semblance of these types of nonprofessional relationships.

If there is any question that the therapist may be "set up" by a client, or if there is discomfort regarding a counseling relationship, the counselor should take reasonable precautions. Strategies to consider include leaving the door slightly opened so that a secretary or colleague can see in the office, but in a way that the voice is somehow screened to maintain confidentiality; taping all sessions with client consent; and inviting a second therapist to do cotherapy with the client's permission. Just as care must be taken to protect clients from potential harm from interactions with counselors, care must also be taken to protect counselors from the malicious intentions of some clients.

Controversy exists over the issue of potential harm related to the use of touch in therapy. Some psychotherapeutic techniques actually encourage touch between therapists and clients. Other techniques may involve deep muscle massage or physical contact. Therapists who use these techniques believe that touch is therapeutic. Regardless, the ethical codes clearly ban sexual intimacy—any sexual contact is unacceptable. Therapists who use touch as part of their therapeutic repertoire should use it cautiously and appropriately. Hand-holding may be acceptable; touching a person's knee or thigh can be considered crossing the ethical line. Having a witness available during treatments may also prevent the misinterpretation of touch in therapy or may minimize the therapist's legal vulnerability. Counselors should review state statutes and standards related to physical contact between counselors and clients if they plan to use such modalities. Some state guidelines are stricter than others.

### A Need for Clear Standards

The high number of past complaints, questions, and infractions in the category of "dual" or "multiple" roles in counseling may have been related to confusion over the terms. The terms "dual" and "multiple" relationships are inexact. Although there is historical linkage to these terms, it is recommended that they should be abandoned. Inexact terminology and ambiguous or equivocal standards are problematic for the ethics committees of credentialing bodies. The new ACA *Code of Ethics* standards (ACA, 2014) in Box 6.4 are more exacting, using behavioral-specific terminology. The standards avoid the terms dual and multiple relationships. Banned nonprofessional roles and relationships (Section A.5) are clearly stated. Boundary extensions are also addressed in Section A.6. The focus becomes harm to clients. The recommended standards also allow for potentially beneficial relationships with clients other than the contracted therapeutic relationship, with the client's permission (informed consent), clear forethought, and adequate consideration before the relationship is initiated (excepting, of course, sexual or romantic interactions or relationships).

In other words, the terms "dual" and "multiple" relationships have been deconstructed—analyzed and redefined for what they truly represent. By abandoning global terms, clearer guidance can be given to counselors in compromising situations.

The first two professional codes of ethics rewritten without use of the terms "dual" or "multiple" relationships were: the *Code of Professional Ethics for Rehabilitation Counselors* (CRCC, 2001) and the ACA *Code of Ethics* (ACA, 2005b). The 2014 ACA *Code of Ethics* maintains the intent of the 2005 revision, with some refinement of terminology. Additionally, an analysis of the issue in the field of marriage and family therapy has been published, addressing deficiencies in the profession's ethics code (Cottone, 2005). The newest AAMFT (2015) code does not address the issue. As Tammy Bringaze, a member of the ACA Task Force that rewrote the ACA *Code of Ethics*, stated during the February 5, 2005 Task Force meeting: "Clients don't know what 'dual' or 'multiple' relationships are when they file ethics complaints." A similar argument can be made for the past use of the term "impaired professional judgment," a term found in some codes of ethics. How does a client prove "impaired professional judgment" or even comprehend the concept when making an ethics complaint? These terms appear to have been used for the benefit of therapists rather than the benefit of clients who may have a complaint.

The term "boundaries" is a contemporary term now being applied to professional ethics roles and relationships with clients. Sommers-Flanagan (2012) stated:

> The term boundary is an interesting concept to define in the context of human relationships. People speak of boundaries, boundary breaks, crossings, extensions, and violations almost as if they take up physical space in the world. But in relationships, a boundary is primarily part of the psychological landscape. A boundary is a limit, rule, guideline, or protective space that helps define the relationship or is defined by the relationship. (p. 246)

Newer codes now address role and relationship boundaries with clients, and the term "boundary extension" is now used to refer to cases where beneficial interactions with clients outside of the therapeutic relationship may be allowed.

No ethical standards can give absolute guidance in every case of an ethical dilemma. However, the newer standards may represent an improved way to communicate right and wrong when it comes to interaction with clients in and outside of the therapeutic relationship. And since the standards allow for certain interactions that are potentially beneficial to clients, they reflect a value on "positive ethics"—going beyond prohibitions and sanctions and considering promotion of positive behavior (Handelsman, Knapp, & Gottlieb, 2002).

### Confronting Counselors in Harmful Relationships With Clients or Trainees

As with breaches of all ethical standards, counselors who are aware of colleagues who are involved in harmful relationships with clients or trainees are obligated to confront the counselor in question. Most ethical codes allow a counselor first to confront the suspected unethical practitioner to attempt to rectify the problem before being obligated to report the concern formally to a legal or ethical authority. Colleagues have great potential influence over perpetrators of unethical behavior by addressing ethical concerns openly and by re-educating (or educating, in some cases) the unethical parties of their ethical obligations. However, colleagues should report to authorities serious infractions or persistent concerns subsequent to re-educating or warning the perpetrator. In most cases, the reporting party is **legally immune, or professionally protected from retribution (e.g., immunity from any sort of counter legal suit).** It is a professional counselor's responsibility to confront an unethical colleague. Potential ethical concerns or dilemmas warrant discussion of the concerns with the offending counselor, as well as consultation with an authority on ethical matters (e.g., a member of a professional association's ethical practice committee). Persistent infractions by a counselor, or concerns of a serious or sexual nature, warrant a formal report to authorities.

> **Question for Reflection:** What ethical principle(s) is(are) at the root of the standards in Box 6.4 that relate to avoiding potentially harmful relationships with clients—autonomy, nonmaleficence, beneficence, justice, fidelity, or veracity?

---

**BOX 6.4  ACA *Code of Ethics*—Standards on Counselor "Roles and Relationships," Boundaries, and "Boundary Extensions"**

**A.5. Prohibited Noncounseling Roles and Relationships**
**A.5.a. Sexual and/or Romantic Relationships Prohibited**
Sexual and/or romantic counselor–client interactions or relationships with current clients, their romantic partners, or their family members are prohibited. This prohibition applies to both in-person and electronic interactions or relationships.

**A.5.b. Previous Sexual and/or Romantic Relationships**
Counselors are prohibited from engaging in counseling relationships with persons with whom they have had a previous sexual and/or romantic relationship.

(continued)

### BOX 6.4 ACA *Code of Ethics*—Standards on Counselor "Roles and Relationships," Boundaries, and "Boundary Extensions" (*continued*)

**A.5.c. Sexual and/or Romantic Relationships With Former Clients**

Sexual and/or romantic counselor–client interactions or relationships with former clients, their romantic partners, or their family members are prohibited for a period of 5 years following the last professional contact. This prohibition applies to both in-person and electronic interactions or relationships. Counselors, before engaging in sexual and/or romantic interactions or relationships with former clients, their romantic partners, or their family members, demonstrate forethought and document (in written form) whether the interaction or relationship can be viewed as exploitive in any way and/or whether there is still potential to harm the former client; in cases of potential exploitation and/or harm, the counselor avoids entering into such an interaction or relationship.

**A.5.d. Friends or Family Members**

Counselors are prohibited from engaging in counseling relationships with friends or family members with whom they have an inability to remain objective.

**A.5.e. Personal Virtual Relationships With Current Clients**

Counselors are prohibited from engaging in a personal virtual relationship with individuals with whom they have a current counseling relationship (e.g., through social and other media).

**A.6. Managing and Maintaining Boundaries and Professional Relationships**

**A.6.a. Previous Relationships**

Counselors consider the risks and benefits of accepting as clients those with whom they have had a previous relationship. These potential clients may include individuals with whom the counselor has had a casual, distant, or past relationship. Examples include mutual or past membership in a professional association, organization, or community. When counselors accept these clients, they take appropriate professional precautions such as informed consent, consultation, supervision, and documentation to ensure that judgment is not impaired and no exploitation occurs.

**A.6.b. Extending Counseling Boundaries**

Counselors consider the risks and benefits of extending current counseling relationships beyond conventional parameters. Examples include attending a client's formal ceremony (e.g., a wedding/commitment ceremony or graduation), purchasing a service or product provided by a client (excepting unrestricted bartering), and visiting a client's ill family member in the hospital. In extending these boundaries, counselors take appropriate professional precautions such as informed consent, consultation, supervision, and documentation to ensure that judgment is not impaired and no harm occurs.

**A.6.c. Documenting Boundary Extensions**

If counselors extend boundaries as described in A.6.a. and A.6.b., they must officially document, prior to the interaction (when feasible), the rationale for such

(*continued*)

**BOX 6.4 ACA *Code of Ethics*—Standards on Counselor "Roles and Relationships," Boundaries, and "Boundary Extensions" (*continued*)**

an interaction, the potential benefit, and anticipated consequences for the client or former client and other individuals significantly involved with the client or former client. When unintentional harm occurs to the client or former client, or to an individual significantly involved with the client or former client, the counselor must show evidence of an attempt to remedy such harm.

**A.6.d. Role Changes in the Professional Relationship**
When counselors change a role from the original or most recent contracted relationship, they obtain informed consent from the client and explain the client's right to refuse services related to the change. Examples of role changes include, but are not limited to (a) changing from individual to relationship or family counseling, or vice versa; (b) changing from an evaluative role to a therapeutic role, or vice versa; and (c) changing from a counselor to a mediator role, or vice versa. Clients must be fully informed of any anticipated consequences (e.g., financial, legal, personal, therapeutic) of counselor role changes.

**A.6.e. Nonprofessional Interactions or Relationships (Other Than Sexual or Romantic Interactions or Relationships)**
Counselors avoid entering into nonprofessional relationships with former clients, their romantic partners, or their family members when the interaction is potentially harmful to the client. This applies to both in-person and electronic interactions or relationships.

ACA, American Counseling Association.

**Questions for Reflection:** How are the 2014 ACA standards in Box 6.4 different from the standards in the current APA, AAMFT, or NASW ethics codes (Box 6.5) on the topic of roles/relationships with clients? Which standards do you prefer—those of the ACA, NASW, AAMFT, or APA?

## Informed Consent

Informed consent is the client's right to agree to participate in counseling, assessment, or other professional procedures or services after such services are fully explained and understood. Vesper and Brock (1991) stated: "The doctrine of informed consent was originally designed to require physicians and surgeons to explain medical procedures to patients and to warn them of any risks or dangers that could result from treatment. The intent of the doctrine was to permit the patient to make an intelligent, informed choice as to whether to undergo the proposed treatment or procedure" (p. 50). There have been times in human history

## BOX 6.5   The Issue of Roles and Relationships With Clients Addressed in Other Codes of Ethics

### Ethical Principles of the National Association of Social Workers (NASW, 2008)
### 1.09 Sexual Relationships

(a) Social workers should under no circumstances engage in sexual activities or sexual contact with current clients, whether such contact is consensual or forced.

(b) Social workers should not engage in sexual activities or sexual contact with clients' relatives or other individuals with whom clients maintain a close personal relationship when there is a risk of exploitation or potential harm to the client. Sexual activity or sexual contact with clients' relatives or other individuals with whom clients maintain a personal relationship has the potential to be harmful to the client and may make it difficult for the social worker and client to maintain appropriate professional boundaries. Social workers—not their clients, their clients' relatives, or other individuals with whom the client maintains a personal relationship—assume the full burden for setting clear, appropriate, and culturally sensitive boundaries.

(c) Social workers should not engage in sexual activities or sexual contact with former clients because of the potential for harm to the client. If social workers engage in conduct contrary to this prohibition or claim that an exception to this prohibition is warranted because of extraordinary circumstances, it is social workers—not their clients—who assume the full burden of demonstrating that the former client has not been exploited, coerced, or manipulated, intentionally or unintentionally.

(d) Social workers should not provide clinical services to individuals with whom they have had a prior sexual relationship. Providing clinical services to a former sexual partner has the potential to be harmful to the individual and is likely to make it difficult for the social worker and individual to maintain appropriate professional boundaries.

### Ethical Principles of Psychologists and Code of Conduct (APA, 2010)
### 3.05 Multiple Relationships

(a) A multiple relationship occurs when a psychologist is in a professional role with a person and (1) at the same time is in another role with the same person, (2) at the same time is in a relationship with a person closely associated with or related to the person with whom the psychologist has the professional relationship, or (3) promises to enter into another relationship in the future with the person or a person closely associated with or related to the person. A psychologist refrains from entering into a multiple relationship if the multiple relationship could reasonably be expected to impair the psychologist's objectivity, competence, or effectiveness in performing his or her functions as a psychologist, or otherwise risks exploitation or harm to the person with whom the professional relationship exists. Multiple relationships that would not reasonably be expected to cause impairment or risk exploitation or harm are not unethical.

*(continued)*

### BOX 6.5  The Issue of Roles and Relationships With Clients Addressed in Other Codes of Ethics (*continued*)

(b) If a psychologist finds that, due to unforeseen factors, a potentially harmful multiple relationship has arisen, the psychologist takes reasonable steps to resolve it with due regard for the best interests of the affected person and maximal compliance with the Ethics Code.

(c) When psychologists are required by law, institutional policy, or extraordinary circumstances to serve in more than one role in judicial or administrative proceedings, at the outset they clarify role expectations and the extent of confidentiality and thereafter as changes occur. (See also Standards 3.04, Avoiding Harm, and 3.07, Third-Party Requests for Services.)

**Code of Ethics of the American Association for Marriage and Family Therapy (AAMFT, 2015)**

**1.3 Multiple Relationships**

Marriage and family therapists are aware of their influential positions with respect to clients, and they avoid exploiting the trust and dependency of such persons. Therapists, therefore, make every effort to avoid conditions and multiple relationships with clients that could impair professional judgment or increase the risk of exploitation. Such relationships include, but are not limited to, business or close personal relationships with a client or the client's immediate family. When the risk of impairment or exploitation exists due to conditions or multiple roles, therapists document the appropriate precautions taken.

**1.4 Sexual Intimacy With Current Clients and Others**

Sexual intimacy with current clients or with known members of the client's family system is prohibited.

**1.5 Sexual Intimacy With Former Clients and Others**

Sexual intimacy with former clients or with known members of the client's family system is prohibited.

---

when such a simple concept did not hold weight—a clear example being the "Nazi doctors" doing experiments "on ethnic groups in concentration camps" which led to a "Declaration of Helsinki" at the 1964 World Health Conference. The Declaration of Helsinki affirmed informed consent as a central element of research (Cain, Harkness, Smith, & Markowski, 2003). As with medical patients, clients of counselors have the right to consent to treatment or research participation, or to refuse to submit to treatment or research (see Caudill, 1998).

Clients have the right to know the potential benefits or detriments of therapy or counseling. They should be fully informed of significant facts about procedures, what typically occurs, and the probable outcomes before treatment. Clients should be informed of the credentials or training of treating professionals, especially as related to specialized procedures. There should be no counselor coercion involved in a decision to undergo treatment. In fact, Pomerantz (2012) argues that informed consent should involve "promoting autonomous decision making (empowered collaboration)" (p. 328), arguing that it is both acknowledging of client individuality yet also acknowledging the collaborative therapeutic relationship. Alternative treatments, or alternatives to treatment, should also be addressed; see Caudill (1998), Handelsman and Galvin (1988), and Wheeler and Bertram (2015) for specific issues related to content and format of informed consent procedures.

Counselors generally present this information to clients in writing. The information should be clear and presented at a level that the client can understand (Handelsman, Kemper, Kesson-Craig, McLain, & Johnsrud, 1986). Counselors should ensure that clients are intellectually and emotionally able to understand the information provided so that they can make a true voluntary judgment (Handelsman & Galvin, 1988). Essentially, clients have freedom of choice to participate in counseling services.

Handelsman and Galvin (1988) provided a format for informed consent that lists questions the client can pose to the therapist. This format fosters open discussion of therapeutic issues and helps to establish a professional relationship and rapport. More recently, Handelsman (2001) made a compelling argument that informed consent should be considered a process, not an event. The consent process should be incorporated into the treatment process.

Informed consent alone does not legitimize treatment approaches. Caudill (1998) stated:

> Of course, the fact that informed consent is given does not legitimize treatment approaches which are illegal or unethical. For example, in California there was a case in which therapists allegedly used a technique that involved beating the patient. In fact, they had informed consent forms which purported to authorize such treatment. In Rains versus Superior Court (1984), a California appellate court essentially held that it didn't matter what the consent form said, no such treatment was permissible. In addition, the cases are quite clear that an informed consent form will not legitimize treatment by an individual who does not have the requisite professional license. (p. 7)

Informed consent provisions do not override the responsibility of counselors to be nonmaleficent and to provide competent services.

Obtaining informed consent is not as serious a concern when clients are of legal (adult) age to consent and when they voluntarily seek treatment. However, it becomes a more serious concern when a client is a minor, when clients may not be fully competent to consent to treatment, or when there is a third-party referral. Discussions of informed consent are often juxtaposed with discussions of the issue of **client competency**, which usually refers to **the ability of clients to understand and to make judgments or decisions in their best interests**. Clients judged to be competent to make decisions in their best interests have a right to be fully informed about the nature of treatments or procedures, the professional's qualifications and experience performing procedures or treatments, the risks and benefits of treatments or procedures, and alternative treatments (Caudill, 1998). Generally speaking, children are considered not competent to make such decisions; parents or guardians must be consulted when a child is involved. Also, when counselors treat people who have disabilities, older adults, or those legally defined as not competent to make such decisions, they must consult a guardian for approval before initiating treatment.

A **third-party referral source is another individual, an agency, or an organization that directs the client to the provider of services.** Clients referred by a third party sometimes go willingly and voluntarily submit to treatment. Other times, **therapy is compulsory, meaning it is required for some legal reason.** Compulsory therapy is initiated by a third-party referral source, usually as a form of rehabilitation or ongoing assessment when (a) the client has been involved with, is accused of, or is guilty of an illegal or potentially harmful act, or when (b) treatment is viewed as a means to return a person to gainful activity when the person is receiving benefits or services for disability or other conditions. Examples of compulsory counseling are (a) a judge-ordered referral of an ex-offender who, as part of rehabilitation, must undergo counseling; (b) a workers' compensation company-referred injured client who is at risk of losing benefits and is required to undergo vocational assessment; (c) a chemically dependent parent who is at risk of losing his or her children through parental rights termination unless there is sobriety; and (d) a misbehaving child who is required to undergo assessment or therapy as a condition for return to school or other settings. In all of these cases, a third party requests evaluation or correction of the client's problem or condition. It is a client's right to consent to counseling. Even in cases of compulsory counseling, clients have the right to refuse services. If legal issues are involved, clients have the right to know if their counselor will testify on the case. If a counselor may be called to testify, the client must waive privileged communication, if applicable, and must be informed of the possible outcomes before accepting counseling services.

> **Question for Reflection:** Which ethical principle(s) is(are) at the root of the ethical standard of informed consent—autonomy, nonmaleficence, beneficence, justice, fidelity, or veracity?

Minor children involved in counseling technically do not have the right to consent to treatment; their parents or legal guardians have the right to consent for them. This is true in most states, but there are exceptions. Some states (by statute) allow minor children to seek counseling related to birth control, venereal disease, pregnancy/abortion, or substance abuse/dependence treatment without the consent of a parent or legal guardian; see the discussion in Hartsell and Bernstein (2013) on "mature minor" clauses in laws allowing older adolescents to consent without parental permission on some issues. Barring such exceptions, parents or legal guardians not only have the right to consent to their children's counseling, they also, in most cases, may have the right to know what occurs in counseling and they may request termination of counseling at any time.

It is therapeutically and ethically wise for the counselor to consult a minor about treatment issues and to enlist the minor's participation when parental or guardian consent is given, even if there are limits to the confidential relationship. This is the concept of "assent." **Assent is agreement to participate in counseling by a person who is otherwise unable to give formal informed consent.** Counselors who seek assent of clients (usually minors or those incapable of giving informed consent) are communicating to clients that they value their commitment to counseling and seek their cooperation and collaboration. The limits of confidentiality must be addressed with the minor in a way that the minor understands: The minor must know that what is discussed in counseling can be shared with the parent or legal guardian, even before the minor is asked to assent to treatment.

Some counselors attempt to get a verbal or written agreement from parents or legal guardians that they will respect the minor's or another individual's right to confidentiality. This is no guarantee, however. Unless there is clear statutory provision and case law for a parent or legal guardian's ability to waive informed consent and access to case information, such agreements must be viewed as tenuous, or even potentially misleading. Separate agreements that waive parental rights to informed consent or access to files may not be upheld legally. Certainly, a parent or legal guardian would have the right to cancel such an arrangement at any time.

Obtaining informed consent is even more complicated when elderly or persons with disabilities are involved (Pepper-Smith, Harvey, Silberfeld, Stein, & Rutman, 1992). Can an elderly person with serious mental deterioration (e.g., dementia) consent to psychological or counseling assessment or treatment? Can a relative be consulted or informed? Many elderly clients may have diminished capacity to make informed judgments, yet they may be considered legally "competent." These clients may be in vulnerable circumstances if an unscrupulous practitioner is involved. It is wise to obtain consent to inform and to consult with involved family members or to do family intervention in most cases in which a person's ability to make judgments is diminished. Such a person's "informed consent" to treatment may be in order technically. However, ethically, the involvement of family members may be necessary to ensure appropriate treatment when there is no legal guardian. And, where feasible, assent should be sought (Case Scenarios 6.8 and 6.9).

## CASE SCENARIO 6.8 Informed Consent

A physician writes an order for a counselor to assess the IQ of a geriatric patient at a hospital. The patient consents. The IQ test and a thorough mental status assessment produce results of diminished capacity, but overall the IQ is in the low borderline range of measured intelligence. The counselor sends the bill for the assessment to Medicare and sends a copayment bill to the spouse of the patient, who protests both the rationale for the test and the bill itself. The spouse claims that she should have been informed. Was anything done unethically in this case?

IT DEPENDS. The question on this case is, "Were the IQ testing and mental status assessment necessary for diagnostic or treatment reasons?" If so, nothing was done illegally, although a professional consult with a second opinion would be recommended, and appropriate consultation with family members (with permission) seems justified.

---

**CASE SCENARIO 6.9** Informed Consent

A husband and wife attend their first marriage counseling session. They are never informed about the potential length of treatment, the probable results, or alternative treatments. The counselor simply begins counseling. Is this ethical?

NO. Most codes of ethics (Box 6.6) either explicitly or indirectly require: (a) the counselor to formally present procedure-relevant information, and (b) the client to formally consent before treatment is initiated.

---

## Professional Responsibility

**Professional responsibility is the counselor's obligation to clients and to the counseling profession. It relates to the appropriateness of professional actions.** *In all cases, a professional counselor's responsibility is to advance the welfare of clients* (Margolin, 1982). Counselors must not discriminate against those who seek their services. They cannot subjugate their obligations to their clients for the sake of monetary or other rewards. Counselors and psychotherapists are also obligated to end their services if it becomes clear they are not helping or benefiting their clients (see Box 6.7).

Counselors and psychotherapists are obligated to their employers as well as to their clients. They have a responsibility to serve their employers in a way that demonstrates competence and ethical sensitivity. Sometimes, however, conflicts arise between employing institutions and the best interests of clients. If such conflicts jeopardize the integrity of professional services rendered to clients, the counselor has an obligation to attempt to remedy the compromising conditions. When a reconciliation of institutional and professional conflicts is not forthcoming, the counselor has an obligation to terminate the affiliation with the employing institution, rather than to persist or compound the injustice. Just as physicians should not compromise the health and safety of their patients in a hospital that provides less than minimal standard care, counselors should refuse to treat clients in settings where the best interests of clients are in conflict with institutional interests. Professional counselors should always seek to develop treatment (work) environments where the employing institution's goals and objectives are consistent with a primary responsibility for competent and timely service to clients. (See the related discussion in Chapters 12 and 13 on ethical climate and office/administrative practices.)

**Question for Reflection:** Which ethical principle(s) is(are) at the root of the ethical standard of responsibility—autonomy, nonmaleficence, beneficence, justice, fidelity, or veracity?

As you will learn in Chapter 10 (Professional Responsibility—see the section on Couple and Family Therapy), defining one's professional responsibility

## BOX 6.6  Informed Consent as Defined in the Codes of Ethics of the Professions

### American Counseling Association *Code of Ethics* (ACA, 2014)

The ACA code reads as follows in Section A.2.a. "Informed Consent": Clients have the freedom to choose whether to enter into or remain in a counseling relationship and need adequate information about the counseling process and the counselor. Counselors have an obligation to review in writing and verbally with clients the rights and responsibilities of both counselors and clients. Informed consent is an ongoing part of the counseling process, and counselors appropriately document discussions of informed consent throughout the counseling relationship.

### Ethical Principles of the National Association of Social Workers (NASW, 2008)

The NASW standards define informed consent in Section 1.03 as follows:

(a) Social workers should provide services to clients only in the context of a professional relationship based, when appropriate, on valid informed consent. Social workers should use clear and understandable language to inform clients of the purpose of the services, risks related to the services, limits to services because of the requirements of a third-party payer, relevant costs, reasonable alternatives, clients' right to refuse or withdraw consent, and the time frame covered by the consent. Social workers should provide clients with an opportunity to ask questions.

(b) In instances when clients are not literate or have difficulty understanding the primary language used in the practice setting, social workers should take steps to ensure clients' comprehension. This may include providing clients with a detailed verbal explanation or arranging for a qualified interpreter or translator whenever possible.

(c) In instances when clients lack the capacity to provide informed consent, social workers should protect clients' interests by seeking permission from an appropriate third party, informing clients consistent with the clients' level of understanding. In such instances social workers should seek to ensure that the third party acts in a manner consistent with clients' wishes and interests. Social workers should take reasonable steps to enhance such clients' ability to give informed consent.

(d) In instances when clients are receiving services involuntarily, social workers should provide information about the nature and extent of services and about the extent of clients' right to refuse service.

(e) Social workers who provide services via electronic media (such as computer, telephone, radio, and television) should inform recipients of the limitations and risks associated with such services.

(f) Social workers should obtain clients' informed consent before audiotaping or videotaping clients or permitting observation of services to clients by a third party.

### Ethical Principles of Psychologists and Code of Conduct (APA, 2010)

3.10 Informed consent

(a) When psychologists conduct research or provide assessment, therapy, counseling, or consulting services in person or via electronic transmission

*(continued)*

**BOX 6.6  Informed Consent as Defined in the Codes of Ethics of the Professions (*continued*)**

or other forms of communication, they obtain the informed consent of the individual or individuals using language that is reasonably understandable to that person or persons except when conducting such activities without consent is mandated by law or governmental regulation or as otherwise provided in this Ethics Code. (See also Standards 8.02, Informed Consent to Research; 9.03, Informed Consent in Assessments; and 10.01, Informed Consent to Therapy.)

(b) For persons who are legally incapable of giving informed consent, psychologists nevertheless (1) provide an appropriate explanation, (2) seek the individual's assent, (3) consider such persons' preferences and best interests, and (4) obtain appropriate permission from a legally authorized person, if such substitute consent is permitted or required by law. When consent by a legally authorized person is not permitted or required by law, psychologists take reasonable steps to protect the individual's rights and welfare.

(c) When psychological services are court ordered or otherwise mandated, psychologists inform the individual of the nature of the anticipated services, including whether the services are court ordered or mandated and any limits of confidentiality, before proceeding.

(d) Psychologists appropriately document written or oral consent, permission, and assent. (See also Standards 8.02, Informed Consent to Research; 9.03, Informed Consent in Assessments; and 10.01, Informed Consent to Therapy.)

### *Code of Ethics* of the American Association for Marriage and Family Therapy (AAMFT, 2015)
#### 1.2 Informed Consent

Marriage and family therapists obtain appropriate informed consent to therapy or related procedures and use language that is reasonably understandable to clients. When persons, due to age or mental status, are legally incapable of giving informed consent, marriage and family therapists obtain informed permission from a legally authorized person, if such substitute consent is legally permissible. The content of informed consent may vary depending upon the client and treatment plan; however, informed consent generally necessitates that the client: (a) has the capacity to consent; (b) has been adequately informed of significant information concerning treatment processes and procedures; (c) has been adequately informed of potential risks and benefits of treatments for which generally recognized standards do not yet exist; (d) has freely and without undue influence expressed consent; and (e) has provided consent that is appropriately documented.

for clients becomes complicated when there is more than one person receiving services in the counseling session. For example, who is the counselor responsible for in a marital counseling situation where partners are at odds over a major marital problem (assuming one partner is not endangered)? Can the

## BOX 6.7  Responsibility as Defined in the Codes of Ethics of the Professions

### American Counseling Association *Code of Ethics* (2014)
Section A.1.a. of the ACA code addresses "Primary Responsibility" and reads as
follows: "The primary responsibility of counselors is to respect the dignity and
promote the welfare of clients."

### Ethical Principles of the National Association of Social Workers (NASW, 2008)
Section 1.01 of the code reads as follows: "Social workers' primary responsibility
is to promote the well-being of clients. In general, clients' interests are primary.
However, social workers' responsibility to the larger society or specific legal
obligations may on limited occasions supersede the loyalty owed clients, and clients
should be so advised. (Examples include when a social worker is required by law
to report that a client has abused a child or has threatened to harm self or others.)"

### Ethical Principles of Psychologists and Code of Conduct (APA, 2010)
The APA code addresses responsibility under an ethical principle—Principle B:
Fidelity and Responsibility. It reads in part as follows: "Psychologists establish
relationships of trust with those with whom they work. They are aware of
their professional and scientific responsibilities to society and to the specific
communities in which they work. Psychologists uphold professional standards
of conduct, clarify their professional roles and obligations, accept appropriate
responsibility for their behavior, and seek to manage conflicts of interest that
could lead to exploitation or harm."

### cs of the American Association for Marriage and Family
### ...AMFT, 2015)
de defines responsibility in Standard I. "Responsibility to Clients:
d family therapists advance the welfare of families and individuals
asonable efforts to find the appropriate balance between conflicting
the family system."

counselor take sides, for example, if there has been an infidelity? Can the counselor take the side of one partner at the expense of the other partner? As you
will read in Chapter 8 on informed consent, counselors doing couple or family
therapy often inform clients, before the initiation of treatment, that they avoid
taking sides in disagreements, taking a role of "relationship advocate" (Margolin, 1982). **Relationship advocacy means the counselor's "responsibility"
is to help couples to help themselves save the relationship.** So, in effect, the
responsibility issue becomes complicated depending on the setting and nature
of counseling, and these complications are addressed in later chapters that discuss specialty practice. Regardless, the primary responsibility of counselors is
to their clients, whether counseling occurs with an individual, a couple, a family, or a group.

It is also important to recognize that the client is the person who is served,
not the person or institution paying the bill (Cottone, 1982). Inexperienced

or uninformed counselors or counselors who are unduly influenced by their business interests often mistakenly feel that their obligation is to the paying party. The counselor's principal obligation is always to the person receiving services—the client, patient, or counselee—unless there is potential danger to another individual or to society. In such a case, the counselor has a duty to warn the endangered party and the authorities. The presence of a third party (a person or institution) paying for services does not diminish, redirect, or in any way compromise the counselor's primary obligation to the client, patient, or counselee.

There may be limits to confidentiality or privileged communication if there is a third-party payer. In such cases, clients must be fully informed prior to the onset of treatment of any limits to confidentiality or privileged communication to ensure informed consent. Clients have the right to refuse treatment, even with the presence of a third-party payer, and counselors must respect the rights of clients to refuse treatment. Counselors have a clear and primary responsibility to persons who receive their counseling services.

Persons who refuse treatment when there is third-party oversight may suffer consequences directly related to the relationship between the client and the overseeing person or agency (e.g., a third-party referral source or payer). Those consequences should be clearly circumscribed to the client's relationship with the third party and should not impinge on the client's relationship with the counselor. Counselors have a primary responsibility to assess or treat fully informed clients competently and to communicate their findings only with the clients' consent. Counselors should not be put in a position, or volunteer to be in a position, of strong-arming a potential client by threatening repercussions that come from a third party. Counselors certainly can educate the client about possible repercussions of nonconsent, but any discussion related to a client's hesitance to consent to services should be directed to the third party requiring or paying for such service (Case Scenarios 6.10–6.12).

## Competence

*Professional "competence" focuses on two aspects of professional practice: (a) the quality of provided services and (b) the boundaries or scope of professional activity*

Boundaries of professional activities involve whether the professional is trained, experienced, and licensed appropriately to perform certain procedures or treatments. Counselor competence, in the ethical sense, means that the counselor or therapist is capable of performing a minimum quality of service and that **the service provided is clearly within the limits of his or her training, experience, and practice as defined in professional standards or regulatory statutes (scope of practice).** A counselor who tells a client not to take prescribed medication is unethical and is practicing illegally (literally practicing medicine without a license). A counselor who uses hypnotic technique may be well within the ethical and legal bounds of the counseling profession, depending on the counselor's past training and experience with hypnotic technique and regulation of hypnosis by statute. Both the "quality issue" and the "scope of practice" issue are implied in any discussion of professional competence (see Box 6.8).

Similarly, professional counselors or therapists who may be licensed to practice certain procedures or techniques should not perform those activities without appropriate specialized training in the area of practice in question. Professional licenses often define a scope of practice that is very broad, giving

## CASE SCENARIO 6.10  Responsibility

A counselor receives a referral from a friendly caseworker at the state family services agency. The caseworker communicates with the counselor that he is counseling a woman who is "disturbed." He wants her evaluated presumably for treatment potential, but notes that the information is really needed for possible parental rights termination. The counselor receives many cases from the referring caseworker at the family services agency, and the counselor agrees to assess the referred individual, saying "I'll see what I can do." The client comes with the full intention of later receiving counseling under the auspices of the family service agency. Instead, the client is evaluated and never scheduled for later treatment, and the counselor's report appears as evidence in a parental rights termination hearing. Is this unethical?

PROBABLY. Assuming that the counselor informed the client of limits to confidentiality and/or privileged communication, this is still a probable breach of responsibility. This is especially true if the findings were in any way influenced by the prior stated intent of the caseworker to seek parental rights termination. The client should have been fully informed of the intent of the evaluation and its potential uses. Additionally, the evaluation should be as objective as possible in its recommendations, using standard and accepted means of assessment.

## CASE SCENARIO 6.11  Responsibility

A school counselor/evaluator is given a case referred by a teacher who is a close friend. The teacher communicates to the counselor that the student is a behavior-disordered (BD) student and the teacher wants this child "out of my classroom" and "placed in special education." The counselor finds that much of the problem may be "embedded in" and "specific to" the teacher–student relationship, meaning there is less support for a diagnosis of BD in other settings. Yet the teacher has documented well the misbehavior of this student. The counselor recommends to the special education panel that a diagnosis/classification of BD is warranted. Is this ethical?

POSSIBLY. The counselor has an obligation to assess, historically and otherwise, the student's behavior in other settings with other authority figures. If the counselor's recommendation is primarily based on the friend's documentation and without otherwise independent competent assessment of competing outcome/recommendations, there is a breach of responsibility and probably a case of professional incompetence.

## CASE SCENARIO 6.12 Responsibility

A researcher does a follow-up study on a previously tested hypothesis. The outcome conflicts with the prior conclusion and statistical findings. The researcher writes an article on the initial findings, but fails to acknowledge the follow-up study. The researcher also fails to acknowledge the work of one of her students who collected the data during the original study. The report is later published. Is this unethical?

YES. There is a breach of "responsibility" on two counts. First, the researcher has an obligation to report the findings of the follow-up study, even if it means the article might not be published. This omission is a breach of responsibility to the profession. Second, there is a breach of responsibility to the student who assisted in the study. The student should receive acknowledgment formally on the manuscript.

## BOX 6.8 The Standard of "Competence" in the Codes of Ethics of the Professions

### American Counseling Association (ACA) *Code of Ethics* (2014)

The ACA code addresses competence under the general heading of "professional responsibility" Section C. Standard C.2.a reads: "Counselors practice only within the boundaries of their competence, based on their education, training, supervised experience, state and national professional credentials, and appropriate professional experience."

### Ethical Principles of the National Association of Social Workers (NASW, 2008)

The NASW standard of competence is 1.04. It reads as follows:

"(a) Social workers should provide services and represent themselves as competent only within the boundaries of their education, training, license, certification, consultation received, supervised experience, or other relevant professional experience.

(b) Social workers should provide services in substantive areas or use intervention techniques or approaches that are new to them only after engaging in appropriate study, training, consultation, and supervision from people who are competent in those interventions or techniques.

(c) When generally recognized standards do not exist with respect to an emerging area of practice, social workers should exercise careful judgment and take responsible steps (including appropriate education, research, training, consultation, and supervision) to ensure the competence of their work and to protect clients from harm."

### Ethical Principles of Psychologists and Code of Conduct (APA, 2010)

Standard 2, specifically 2.1 (Boundaries of Competence), reads as follows: "(a) Psychologist provide services, teach, and conduct research with populations and in areas only within the boundaries of their competence, based on their education, training, supervised experience, consultation, study, or professional experiences."

(continued)

**BOX 6.8 The Standard of "Competence" in the Codes of Ethics of the Professions (continued)**

*Code of Ethics* **of the American Association for Marriage and Family Therapy (AAMFT, 2015)**
Standard III "Professional Competence and Integrity" addresses the need for therapists to maintain a "high standard" of professional competence and integrity. Standard 3.1 reads: "Marriage and family therapists pursue knowledge of new developments and maintain their competence in marriage and family therapy through education, training, and/or supervised experience."

the licensed professional much latitude in his or her practice. Just because a counselor is licensed to do testing procedures does not mean the counselor can start administering intelligence tests without some training and supervision of that practice. The scope of practice of a license does not supersede the competency of the individual counselor to perform certain procedures. Counselors, who are faced with doing procedures that are new to them, or desire to expand their personal scopes of practice, should request a professional consultation with a specialist who is trained and competent in the area. **A professional consultation is a paid, formal arrangement wherein a consulting counselor obtains a second opinion, professional advice, or even supervision (to the extent of possible cotherapy) on an issue of concern from a knowledgeable, competent colleague.** A licensed counselor with a rehabilitation counseling degree who does marriage counseling without ever having had a course or supervision in marriage counseling is practicing unethically (literally crossing the boundaries of professional competence). In such cases, the rehabilitation counselor has an obligation to refer the client to, or to consult with, an appropriately trained and credentialed marriage counselor. Likewise, a marriage counselor should not suddenly begin chemical dependency treatment with a substance-dependent client without specialized training in chemical dependency; referral to or consultation with an appropriately trained rehabilitation or addiction counselor is in order. Just because a professional is licensed to perform a procedure does not mean he or she can ethically perform the procedure. All physicians are licensed to do brain surgery, yet only those who have specialized training or experience in the procedure should be actively and independently doing it.

Competency, however, is not as simple as what a licensure statute says one can do, or the extent of one's training for providing quality services. There are other issues that are crucial to the profession of counseling. Mental health professional codes of ethics have defined the need for competency related to working with individuals with culturally diverse backgrounds. In the 1990s there were major publications on the need for "multicultural counselor competencies." Notably, Sue, Arrendondo, and McDavis (1992) published "Multicultural counseling competencies: A call to the profession" in the *Journal of Counseling and Development.* That article summarized work that began in April of 1991, when the Association for Multicultural Counseling and Development (AMCD) outlined the need for a multicultural perspective in counseling. Subsequently, multicultural competencies were defined. The work of Sue et al. (1992) was an attempt to bring the actions of the AMCD membership to the attention of the broader ACA membership. It provided a rationale and a need statement related to a multicultural perspective. Since that time, multicultural counselor competencies have been embraced by the counseling profession. Subsequent publications have outlined how multicultural competencies can be integrated into counseling practice (e.g., Arrendondo, 1998; Hansen, Pepitone-Arreola-Rockwell, & Green, 2000).

**Question for Reflection:** Which ethical principle(s) appear(s) foundational to the concept of professional competence—autonomy, nonmaleficence, beneficence, justice, fidelity, or veracity?

As a sign of the "technology" times, there are also concerns that counselors must be competent in alternative means of service delivery, most notably through technology. Today, with technological advances, it is possible to do counseling by phone, Internet, or by e-mail, as examples. Assessment may now be computer-assisted. Records are often digital and stored by means of computers. Facsimile (fax) machines or e-mail may transmit records instantaneously. The practice of counseling has been enhanced and complicated by technology. In 1999, the Association for Counselor Education and Supervision (ACES) published its "Technical Competencies for Counselor Education Students: Recommended Guidelines for Program Development" (ACES, 1999). The ACES document not only addressed the need for counseling program graduates to have knowledge of technological applications, but also to "Be knowledgeable of the legal and ethical codes which relate to counseling services via the internet" (ACES, 1999). More recently, the ACA *Code of Ethics* (2014) has substantially increased its attention to the complexities inherent in the growth of communication technology and social media and their use in counseling practice, and provided clearer guidance in the ethical considerations to be contemplated. Counseling can no longer be conceptualized as sitting in a private room with a client. Technology has had a pervasive influence on the way counseling is provided and the resources that can be accessed and used. Smartphones, as a simple example, have made counselors available to clients even when counselors are not near a land-based phone or computer; counselors may be providing counseling to clients while they are in transit. The ethical implications of advances of technology are staggering, and this text devotes a whole chapter to these issues.

Suffice it to say, related to competencies, that the practice of counseling is changing due to a number of developments (e.g., multiculturalism, technology), and counselors are obliged to keep abreast of these concerns and to ensure competent and ethical practice in line with these developments (Case Scenarios 6.13 and 6.14).

## CASE SCENARIO 6.13 Professional Competence

A school counselor has a client who is showing excessive anxiety; the counselor later learns that the client has been diagnosed by a psychiatrist as having "generalized anxiety disorder." The school counselor begins to arrange individual sessions of counseling and performs a technique called systematic desensitization, a behavioral technique used to ameliorate symptoms such as phobic anxiety when the anxiety results from the presentation of a specific object or situation. Is the counselor practicing unethically?

POSSIBLY NOT. If the anxiety is specifically school-related and the counselor has been trained and supervised successfully in systematic desensitization, this activity is within the realm of competent practice. School anxieties, such as a phobia to testing or speaking in public, are treatable ethically by appropriately trained school counselors. On the other hand, if the phobia is not school-related, or if the counselor is attempting to treat the generalized anxiety disorder, this is questionable practice. It is generally understood that generalized anxiety disorder is not best treated by systematic desensitization. Also, the psychiatrist, if he or she were treating the client actively, should have been consulted, even regarding treatment of a circumscribed school phobia.

## CASE SCENARIO 6.14 Professional Competence

A marriage counselor is counseling a couple that is having sexual difficulties. The problem is a complicated one, and the counselor's interventions have not produced a desirable outcome. The counselor has explained to the couple that although he has training to address certain sexual problems, he does not view himself as a sex therapist. Regardless, the husband and wife implore the counselor to continue treatment. They do not want to start over with another professional. The counselor continues to counsel the couple. Is this unethical?

PROBABLY. If other trained sex therapists are available, the counselor should either refer the couple to a sex therapist or professionally consult with one. On the other hand, if no other professional is available, the counselor has an obligation to immediately seek appropriate training or guidance and to serve the couple as best as possible.

## DECISION MAKING IN CONTEXT

This chapter has laid out the ethical standards referenced in ethics codes for the professions of counseling, social work, marriage and family therapy, and psychology. These standards require critical analysis and evaluation. They are not defined by some omnipotent authority. Rather, they result from the consensual process of professionals, enlisted as "experts" by a professional association, who make a sincere effort to ensure that clients are being well served and not harmed by the profession. Regardless, it is obvious that the principle ethics intellectual movement is foundational to the existing mental health professional codes of ethics. The ethical standards, deriving primarily from ethical principles, act as specific guidelines. Together, ethical principles and standards provide guidance to counselors and psychotherapists as they face ethical dilemmas and crucial decisions in clinical practice.

## CONCLUSION

Counselors must abide by the ethical standards of confidentiality/privacy, privileged communication, roles and relationship boundaries, informed consent, professional responsibility, and competence.

Confidentiality is the obligation of professionals to respect the privacy of clients and the information they provide. Counselors cannot reveal to others what is communicated in counseling without potential penalty of law, where there is legal confidentiality.

Privileged communication is a client's right to prevent the revelation of confidential information in a legal proceeding. A counselor cannot be forced to testify on a client's case if the privilege stands.

Harmful counselor–client relationships may involve: (a) sexual or romantic counselor–client interaction or (b) other avoidable detrimental nonprofessional relationships. Mental health professionals engaged in such relationships may face license suspension/revocation and legal consequences. Counselors must also avoid nonprofessional relationships with clients, unless they have a compelling reason to extend boundaries in the client's best interest.

Informed consent is the client's right to agree to participate in counseling, assessment, or other professional procedures and services after such services are fully explained and understood. Clients must be fully informed of significant facts about procedures and possible outcomes before treatment.

Professional responsibility is the counselor's obligation to clients and to the counseling profession. Counselors have a primary responsibility to advance the welfare of their clients. They also bear responsibility to serve their employers in a way that demonstrates competence and ethical sensitivity.

Counselor competence means that the counselor or therapist is capable of performing a minimum quality of service and that the service is clearly within the limits of the counselor's training, experience, and practice (scope of practice) as defined in professional standards or regulatory statutes. Counselors without specialized training in a particular area should refer clients to appropriately trained professionals.

These ethical standards are guidelines that mental health professionals should know well. In Chapters 7 through 11, the ethical standards are addressed as related to specialty practice in counseling. Each chapter will detail how the ethical standards apply in distinct areas of counseling practice, such as school counseling, addictions, couple and family therapy, mental health treatment, career, rehabilitation and health counseling, group counseling, supervision, and forensic practice. The nuances of practicing within counseling specialties are addressed.

# ETHICAL AND LEGAL CHALLENGES ACROSS COUNSELING SPECIALTIES

# PRIVACY, CONFIDENTIALITY, AND PRIVILEGED COMMUNICATION

## OBJECTIVES

- To define two ethical standards—privacy and confidentiality.
- To define a legal standard often associated with confidentiality and privacy—privileged communication.
- To explain differences and similarities of privacy, confidentiality, and privileged communication.
- To outline ethical standards across mental health professions addressing privacy and confidentiality in their codes of ethics.

This chapter is the first of a number of chapters that will address ethical issues and standards according to the designated specialty areas of the mental health professions. This chapter addresses the ethical standards of privacy and confidentiality and the related legal issue of privileged communication. As was described in Chapter 6, **privacy is a broad encompassing standard that protects the client by preventing revelation of the counseling relationship without the client's knowledge or approval. Confidentiality,** a related concept, **protects the actual content of the counseling** (not just the presence of the therapeutic relationship) and is akin to an antigossip guarantee; what is communicated to a counselor or psychotherapist in the counseling relationship is considered protected information, to be shared only when there is a compelling reason to breach confidentiality (e.g., the legal reasons addressed in Chapter 6). **Privileged communication** is a legal right owned by the client. It is statutory—meaning it is written into law. It will not be found in ethics codes, as it is a legal standard. Privileged communication is **the client's right to prevent the revelation of confidential information in a legal proceeding.** Counselors and psychotherapists must be educated on the presence and any limits of privileged communication written into statutes (both state and federal) that apply to their practices.

Not only are oral communications confidential and privileged, but the client has the right to have all written documentation kept private, including the counselor's notes on the client. While case notes are considered part of the client's record and are thus subject to being seen by a third party, counselors should nevertheless "take the clinical notes they need in order to function effectively as professionals" (Remley & Herlihy, 2014, p. 139). This is consistent with the American Counseling Association (ACA) Code (2014), which states "counselors create and maintain records and documentation necessary for rendering professional services" (B.6.a.).

As to how long such documentation should be kept depends on a number of factors. Remley and Herlihy (2014) state that "some state counselor licensure laws dictate that counselors' records be kept for a certain number of years" (p. 148); thus counselors should contact their attorney to ascertain whether such laws exist in their jurisdiction. Further, counselors need to determine whether their agencies have a record-keeping policy, as well as take into account pertinent ethical standards of their profession. For example, the ACA Code (2014) states:

> Counselors store records following termination of services to ensure reasonable future access, maintain records in accordance with federal and state laws and statutes such as licensure laws and policies governing records, and dispose of client records and other sensitive materials in a manner that protects client confidentiality. Counselors apply careful discretion and deliberation before destroying records that may be needed by a court of law, such as notes on child abuse, suicide, sexual harassment, or violence. (Sec. B.6.h.)

Thus, counselors should carefully create and maintain notes, store them for as long as necessary, and properly dispose of such notes when no longer needed and when authorized.

The following sections address these matters as related to specialty practice.

## CLINICAL MENTAL HEALTH

Privacy issues in clinical mental health practice are complicated by the presence of a third paying party, usually an insurance company, sometimes through a managed care overseer or through government or other agencies that fund services. Occasionally, clients pay for counseling out of their own pockets, but not as often as in some specialties of practice in which clients are sometimes willing to pay for services separate from medical insurance (e.g., marriage counseling). As stated in Chapter 6, **privacy is a person's right to keep information about the person**

**from being divulged to others** (ACA, 2014). Privacy is an ethical standard that makes private: (a) the fact that a person has sought counseling and (b) what is communicated in counseling. The client has control over how the information will be used. Privacy and confidentiality, although different concepts, are related; they both involve the right of the client regarding information or behaviors that are shared with a counselor. Whereas privacy issues relate to a constitutional right (Remley & Herlihy, 2014), confidentiality issues address the specific counseling context. Privacy issues extend to such areas as (a) discreet scheduling of sessions to prevent clients from encountering other clients in waiting rooms, (b) billing and administration of case records, (c) use of client information over computers or phones (wireless or otherwise) or through testing services, and (d) other activities that do not necessarily relate to information provided in counseling sessions. Confidentiality is generally understood to deal with the content of counseling sessions. Wilcoxon, Remley, and Gladding (2012) stated: "These [privacy] questions are particularly important when managed care agencies and other third-party payers attempt to gain access to therapy information about clients or when therapists are bound by law and/or professional codes of ethics to break confidentiality" (p. 63). Ethically sensitive counselors do their best to ensure that information about clients is considered private.

The American Mental Health Counselors Association (AMHCA) *Code of Ethics* (2010) gives detailed guidance on the matter of confidentiality. The code specifically addresses 17 separate but relevant issues under the heading of confidentiality. The confidentiality "principle" (as it is defined in the AMHCA *Code of Ethics*) is broad and makes specific reference to such issues as taping (recording) sessions, dealing with minors, working with families, group work, and record keeping (both standard and electronic).

As described in Chapter 6, privileged communication relates to the revelation of confidential information in legal proceedings. As with many specialties of practice, mental health counselors may be called upon to testify at legal proceedings. It is important that mental health counselors know the laws that relate to privileged communication in their states.

In a noteworthy development, the U.S. Department of Health and Human Services (DHHS) issued a major rule related to privacy of individual patient records. Frank-Stromborg (2004) noted:

> Making the Privacy Rules a reality, the Department of Health and Human Services (DHHS) issued its final version of the Privacy Rules on August 14, 2002, under the Health Insurance Portability and Accountability Act (HIPAA) of 1996. As of April 14, 2003, all covered health care entities must comply with the newly implemented national standards. However, compliance for smaller health care entities with annual receipts of $5 million or less is extended until April 14, 2004 (45 CFR chapters 164.534, 164.160.103, 2002). . . . Further the final version means that the government is serious about the newly promulgated rules. In fact, the government is so serious concerning compliance with the Privacy Rules that not only can an employer be penalized with punitive damages, but personal punitive damages can also be a consequence of noncompliance. (p. 13)

The rule "generally gives patients the right to see their records (although not psychotherapy notes), to receive notice of how their records may be disclosed, and to have an accounting of their records that have been released to parties beyond the treating provider" (New Patient Records Privacy Rule Takes Effect, 2001, p. 1). An article in the Practitioner Update of the American Psychological Association (APA) stated:

> Separate patient authorization is required for the release of psychotherapy notes—in addition to consent the patient gives to disclose his or her other records—to parties beyond the treating provider. Psychotherapy notes are the only type of record given heightened privacy protection under this rule. Importantly, a health plan or provider may not make treatment, payment, enrollment or eligibility for benefits conditional on a patient's authorization to release psychotherapy notes. (New Patient Records Privacy Rule Takes Effect, 2001, p. 1)

All agencies or organizations that receive federal funding may not, by law, release confidential psychotherapy notes, unless there is separate signed client permission to do so. Further, the rule covers material from a private counseling session or a group, joint, or family counseling session. "'Psychotherapy notes' excludes medication prescription and monitoring, counseling session start and stop times, the modalities and frequencies of treatment furnished, results of clinical tests, and any summary of the following items: diagnosis, functional status, the treatment plan, symptoms, prognosis, and progress to date" (New Patient Records Privacy Rule Takes Effect, 2001, p. 1). The privacy rules have direct relevance to the related concept of confidentiality, because they limit revelation of the content of counseling sessions.

Mental health practitioners, more so than any other type of counselor (except rehabilitation counselors), counsel adult clients who are not competent to make judgments about such issues as money management, treatment compliance, or privacy issues. It may be too easy for the unethical practitioner to get the permission of an individual with a mental disability to share information with other individuals, or even to share the information in legal proceedings. A common trait of individuals with mental disorders listed in the *Diagnostic and Statistical Manual of Mental Disorders, fifth edition* (DSM-5; American Psychiatric Association, 2013) is the presence of poor judgment. Clients who have limitations of judgment or ability must be given special treatment as related to the confidentiality issue because they may release information inadvertently to serve a counselor's agenda rather than their own needs. Ethical mental health professionals ensure that every effort is made to explain fully the relevant issues so that clients can understand and make fully informed decisions.

As addressed in Chapter 6, confidentiality is akin to an antigossip guarantee. Counselors must be alert to the need to keep information learned in counseling as private as legally possible. Because individuals with mental disorders often manifest behaviors that are odd or unusual, their behaviors make for interesting general conversation. At more than one social gathering, counselors have been overheard entertaining others by talking about the strange behaviors of their clients. Such behavior shows poor respect for individuals in serious personal situations and poor regard for the profession, which allows counselors the privilege of serving people in need. No matter how seriously disturbed a client's behavior may be, it is incumbent on the counselor to respect the individual and to maintain the privacy of client information.

Beyond being an ethical standard, confidentiality may be legally mandated (as well as mandated by a professional code of ethics). Fisher (2012) stated: "Many laws provide legal support for the profession's ethical rule" (p. 333). She went on to describe how confidentiality may be referenced in licensure statutes (giving the standard the force of law) and in other statutes that require confidentiality (or a breach of confidentiality) under certain circumstances. A good example is when there is communication of potential to do harm to an individual or society.

## Duty to Warn

Pietrofesa, Pietrofesa, and Pietrofesa (1990) described the mental health counselor's responsibility related to the "duty to warn" endangered parties. They stated, "It is clear that ethically and legally the mental health counselor is required to protect an identifiable victim of a client from harm" (p. 135). They provided "steps" to be taken when there is potential danger to a client. Costa and Altekruse (1994) also provided guidelines for mental health counselors when duty to warn is an issue. Their duty-to-warn guidelines included (a) get informed consent, (b) plan ahead through consultation, (c) develop contingency plans, (d) obtain professional liability insurance, (e) be selective about clients, (f) involve the client, (g) obtain a detailed history, (h) document in writing, and (i) implement a procedure to warn. Further, they provided vignettes of potential dilemmas in working with families and analyses of the circumstances according to three conditions related to duty to warn: a special relationship, a prediction of harmful conduct, and a foreseeable victim. Duty-to-warn situations may arise in mental health counseling because many of the served clients experience acute symptoms of a serious nature that may affect their judgment. In cases of imminent danger, a breach of confidentiality is acceptable.

## Suicide Statistics, Signs of Potential Suicide, and Recommended Actions

Of course, if there are suicidal concerns, counselors should take action to protect a client from self-harm. The statistics on suicide are compelling. The American Association of Suicidology (AAS) published final data for 2013. In 2013 in the United States, there were 41,149 suicides, with 17.1% of deaths in the age range of 15 to 24 due to suicide. In addition, there were nonfatal outcomes, as there were 1,028,725 attempts. The AAS estimates that suicide "intimately" affects at least six other people. The highest number of deaths was by means of firearms (51.5%), followed by suffocation/hanging (24.5%). The highest suicide death rates per capita were in the following states: Montana, Alaska, and Wyoming. The lowest suicide rates per capita were in New York, Massachusetts, and New Jersey. The AAS published these warning signs: (a) talking about or wanting to die; (b) looking for a way to kill oneself; (c) talking about feeling hopeless or having no purpose; (d) talking about feeling trapped or in unbearable pain; (e) talking about being a burden to others; (f) increasing the use of alcohol or drugs; (g) acting anxious, agitated, or reckless; (h) sleeping too little or too much; (i) withdrawing or feeling isolated; (j) showing rage or talking about seeking revenge; and (k) displaying extreme mood swings. The greater the number of signs, the greater the risk of suicide. Counselors, if they assess potential for suicide using the contributing factors listed, should never leave the person alone or dismiss the person without supervision. Mental health professionals must ensure that the person has no firearms, alcohol, drugs, sharp objects, or other items that can be used to self-harm. Serious consideration should be made to take the person to an emergency department at a local hospital, preferably a hospital with a psychiatry staff. The national suicide prevention hotline can be called at 800-272-TALK (8355) for guidance or for client support. Counselors should take suicide threats seriously and immediately go into a protective mode of action.

## HEALTH AND REHABILITATION

Rehabilitation counselors may have particularly pressing issues regarding confidentiality in their work. Issues regarding confidentiality that emerged in a survey of certified rehabilitation counselors (CRCs; Patterson & Settles, 1992) were (a) maintaining confidentiality in institutional settings, (b) knowing that a client is driving a car with poorly controlled seizures, (c) recommending to an employer a client who is suspected of abusing substances, (d) sharing information with family members about a client with chronic mental illness, (e) conflicts between workers' compensation and state laws related to confidentiality, (f) the requirement to report client information to an agency that results in disciplinary action against the client, (g) learning that a client who has AIDS is not practicing safe sex, and (h) discussing clients with others without signed, written consent.

Many rehabilitation counselors are involved in legal and third-party consultant roles as vocational experts in civil court matters, administrative hearings, and Social Security or workers' compensation work (Blackwell, Martin, & Scalia, 1994). Practices involving vocational or forensic expert services often involve indirect services provision. (See the section Forensic Practice.) The rules of confidentiality are different under these circumstances than is typical of professional counseling service delivery. The Commission on Rehabilitation Counselor Certification (CRCC, 2010) defined **indirect services** in its revised *Code of Ethics Professional Ethics for Rehabilitation Counselors* (the "CRCC Code") as services provided when rehabilitation counselors are employed by a third party, whether or not they engage in direct communication with the client, and where **there is no intent to provide rehabilitation counseling services directly to the person with the disability or medical condition.** This type of service typically involves evaluation for expert witness testimony or consultation on cases. In those cases where there is a face-to-face relationship, rehabilitation counselors "fully disclose to the individual (and/or his or her designee) the rehabilitation counselor's role and limits of the rehabilitation counselor–client relationship" (Section A2a, p. 3). Case Scenario 7.1 describes the complexities of this type of disclosure. In such instances, they must clearly address confidentiality limitations with all the individuals involved. Havranek (1997) examined the application of ethical principles in forensic rehabilitation and noted the different demands of this practice in various settings and with specific populations. He further alerted rehabilitation counselors to the necessity of remaining objective despite expectations of the party who may have retained their services. The CRCC *Code of Professional Ethics for Rehabilitation Counselors* (CRCC, 2010) provides a rule that embodies well-accepted advice in such situations in the areas of informed consent and privileged communications, to "provide unbiased, objective opinions" (Section A3b, p. 4). Clients must know from the start any limits of confidentiality and privileged communication.

The clarity and timeliness of disclosure of professional role limitations is crucial to good ethical practice for the rehabilitation counselor. Unless so informed, it is not unreasonable that the client would assume that all information obtained would be held in confidence. If an uninformed client's benefits were canceled as a result of the rehabilitation counselor's report provided to a third party that employs the rehabilitation counselor, the client justifiably feels that trust and confidence was violated. Such situations are a common source of ethics complaints.

Rehabilitation counselors should not assume that privileged communication extends to their practices. Some may erroneously think that their national specialty certification through the CRCC provides privilege to their counselor–client relationships. Remember, privileged communication is a legal directive. It is statutory. A professional certification (e.g., the CRC designation of the CRCC) does not carry the right to privileged communication. Rehabilitation counselors must carefully research the legal protections afforded to their clients in the jurisdiction of practice. In cases where privileged communication is legally extended to clients of rehabilitation counselors by nature of licensure statutes, it only applies to those who hold a license in that jurisdiction. Unfortunately, rehabilitation counselors' involvement in the state-by-state counselor licensure movement has been inconsistent and unintegrated compared with that of some counseling specialties, such as mental health counseling.

Multidisciplinary or interdisciplinary teams are a frequent aspect of the rehabilitation counseling practice and tradition. Team treatment is an important asset to the client's counseling process, but it offers an additional challenge to ethical practice. These teams may not necessarily work in physical proximity or have similar levels of training or understanding regarding ethical obligations to the client. Also, the rehabilitation counselor must communicate client information to team members involved in the client's treatment or employment plan. While this transfer of information is usually standard practice and done to benefit the client, clients must be fully informed of what type of information will be shared, and when, how, and with whom information will be shared. Client consent to this disclosure should not be taken for granted nor obtained under pressure to give blanket permission. Counselors "carefully consider implications"

**CASE SCENARIO 7.1** Indirect Services and
Client Confusion

James is a new client being seen by Dawn, a vocational rehabilitation counselor
working for the RehabCo Insurance Company in its long-term disability policy
rehabilitation service program. James, a nurse, has been off work and on disability
with a severe back injury that has resolved into a chronic back pain condition.
Several different physicians and clinics made a variety of attempts to provide James
with medical services, all resulting in no substantial improvement. James has been
out of work for 12 months and his current physician says that he cannot carry out
the physical requirements of his job. Dawn is assigned to assess whether James can
benefit from rehabilitation services through a medical and vocational file review.
During this process, she interviews James by phone and he states that he is not
willing to consider alternative types of employment because he does not want to lose
his benefits. James is still hopeful he can return to his old job as a nurse even though
his employer is unwilling to consider job modification or light-duty employment. Dawn
recommends an independent medical evaluation, after which James is declared
medically able to return to work. As a result, James's benefits are terminated. James
is angry with Dawn and lodges a complaint that she did not advocate for him. He
expected that Dawn would work with him to assist him in returning to work with his
previous employer. Was Dawn unethical?

MAYBE. This scenario presents an all-too-frequent situation when rehabilitation
counselors provide indirect services on behalf of a third party—the insurance
company, in this case. The client who has a disability may not understand what
to expect from this professional. The key issues here are whether or not proper
professional disclosure and fully informed consent occurred at the onset of the
involvement with James. He should have been fully informed that Dawn was only
calling to verify information regarding his medical and vocational status and that she
would not be providing direct services to him (professional disclosure). In addition,
she should have told him that all information he gave her would be provided to the
insurance company to determine the status of his disability claim. Dawn should have
clearly explained to James his choices and the consequences of each choice for his
benefits (informed consent). If she had done so and truthfully reported her opinion
to the insurer based on objective facts, she would have been providing ethically
appropriate services to James that unfortunately resulted in an outcome he did not
desire.

when revealing information to collaborative team members (CRCC, 2010, Code,
Section B3b, p. 8).

Minimal disclosure is another important ethical practice intended to further safeguard client confidentiality. Minimal disclosure (CRCC, 2010, Code,
Section B2d, p. 8) requires that even where client consent is given, the rehabilitation counselor only reveals the minimum amount of information necessary.
Just being a member of the treatment team does not entitle one automatically to
know whether a young man with a spinal cord injury is capable of erection and
penile penetration while having sex, or that a student involved in a work-study
placement through a high school is a victim of incest. Some information is not to
be shared as it may have nothing to do with the treatment goals. The standard

of minimum disclosure also applies to disclosure of case records and other client information provided to other team members or professionals. Whenever disclosure does occur, the rehabilitation counselor must take care that team members have specific rules they follow on confidentiality, that they reinforce the need to preserve client confidentiality, and that the client is informed of this disclosure to the team (Strein & Hershenson, 1991).

Confidentiality issues for rehabilitation counselors may be more prevalent or complex in certain settings or within particular groups of clients such as those with addiction, psychiatric, correctional, or HIV/AIDS disabilities. Certain types of services such as group counseling or treatment present extraordinary confidentiality challenges. Rehabilitation counselors may offer group services ranging from skills training groups for job seeking or social skills training, to psychosocial treatment oriented groups that assist in the therapeutic or personal adjustment of their clients. While the rehabilitation counselor may take appropriate measures to set the expectation of confidentiality among group members, all clients must be informed that confidentiality cannot be guaranteed in a group setting (CRCC, 2010, Code, Section B4a, p. 8). They must also be told that privileged communication is generally not extended to group counseling by the legal system. Some other confidentiality issues are specific to particular settings. Examples include: (a) legal restrictions placed on access to educational records of minor students provided by the federal Family Educational Rights and Privacy Act (FERPA; see the section on School Counseling), (b) conflicting legal dictates in state and federal law regarding the privacy rights of people who are HIV-positive and the public's need to know about individuals with fatal, contagious diseases (see Anderson & Barret, 2001, for an excellent discussion), and (c) the laws extending stricter confidentiality to those in treatment in any addiction treatment facility receiving federal funding (see the section on addiction counseling).

## COUPLE AND FAMILY THERAPY

Confidentiality, as an antigossip guarantee, is designed to prevent revelation of privately communicated information to other individuals. In the classic one-client and one-counselor relationship, confidentiality is a simple issue of counselor responsibility. Counselors are bound by their ethical codes or legal ethical standards (e.g., ethical standards in licensure statutes) to maintain the information communicated in counseling sessions in confidence—that is, in a way that does not share information with others unless there are extenuating circumstances in which confidentiality would not stand (recognized exemptions). Couple or family counseling, however, presents complications. First, such counseling almost always involves more than one person as a client. Couple and family counselors, by philosophy, often treat relationship "systems" as the unit or target of intervention. Often, therefore, one or more people overhear what other individuals communicate to a counselor in a session. In this sense, there is no one-to-one confidential relationship.

Most ethical codes and licensure statutes were designed primarily for one-to-one counseling relationships. However, the American Association for Marriage and Family Therapy (AAMFT) *Code of Ethics* does address the issue of more than one person being the unit of treatment. The AAMFT (2015) *Code of Ethics* states:

> Marriage and family therapists have unique confidentiality concerns because the client in a therapeutic relationship may be more than one person. Therapists respect and guard the confidences of each individual client. (Standard II, p. 4)

Further, the code states:

> When providing couple, family, or group treatment, the therapist does not disclose information outside the treatment context without a written authorization from each individual competent to execute a waiver. In the context of couple, family or group treatment, the therapist may not reveal any individual's confidences to others in the client unit without the prior written permission of that individual. (Section 2.2, p. 4)

*Policy on secrets*

Essentially all legally responsible parties in couple or family therapy are required formally to release the information before it can be communicated to other individuals; but not all ethics codes or licensure standards are as clear as the AAMFT *Code of Ethics* on this issue. It is especially important for licensed professionals to examine their licensure statutes and any ethical references in those statutes. First, the statutes must be examined to ensure that provision of standard services to couples or families is clearly within the purview of the practice of the profession, meaning that the scope of practice of the profession must clearly reference couples, marriages, relationships, systems, or family work. Second, if couple or family counseling is referenced in the legal definition of professional practice, ethical standards should then be examined in light of the definition of professional practice. Is a confidential relationship described in the statute's ethical guidelines? Does confidentiality extend to relationships beyond the one-on-one counseling relationship? These questions must be addressed in an examination of relevant ethical standards.

Regardless, unique circumstances in couple and family counseling still exist that are worth noting in any discussion of confidentiality and privileged communication. For example, even in a situation wherein legal confidentiality exists by statute for communications made within the context of relationship treatment, certain information may be communicated to a therapist privately by one member of a family or couple in treatment. In fact, Margolin (1982) stated: "Some therapists, in fact, arrange for sessions with individual family members to actively encourage the sharing of 'secrets' to better understand what is occurring in the family" (p. 791). When one member of a couple or family privately reveals a secret to the counselor (in treatment), the counselor is faced with deciding whether that privately communicated information is confidential in a one-to-one sense. Can that information be communicated subsequently in the context of relationship treatment? What if one member of a couple communicates that he is involved in a secret, extramarital sexual relationship? Obviously this information is crucial to marital counseling, but if it is communicated in a formal counseling setting with no other parties present, it is considered confidential. It is ethically compromising for a counselor to continue relationship counseling with such information (essentially counseling in a way that does not acknowledge the infidelity). Margolin (1982) believed that therapists have several options in such a situation: The therapist can choose (a) to keep the secret, (b) to reveal the secret, or (c) to reveal the secret in certain circumstances. Regardless, *it is crucial that counselors communicate their policy on such matters before counseling is initiated*. Margolin (1982) stated, "The most difficult predicament for the therapist would be if she or he failed to convey a policy on confidentiality" (p. 792). The same is true for any communication made by one individual in private to a counselor when that party is involved in relationship treatment with the counselor. Secrets, such as physical or sexual abuse, child molestation, sexual orientation, infection with a sexually transmitted disease, drug involvement, gambling, or use of Internet pornography, often are revealed to counselors, and counselors must be prepared to reiterate their policy on confidentiality (with legal exceptions noted) and to follow whatever policy has been communicated and agreed to by the involved parties.

There is the additional problem that some secrets may involve illegal activity. For example, adultery is considered a punishable act in some states. If the counselor keeps a secret of illegal adultery from a spouse, it is possible (although highly unlikely) that the counselor could be charged by the spouse with criminal conspiracy or "alienation of affection" (Cottone, Mannis, & Lewis, 1996; Margolin, 1982). Some argue (Cottone et al., 1996) that counselors must not condone illegal activity by keeping secrets. Counselors are most ethically and legally safe when they maintain a policy that such secrets will be openly discussed in counseling sessions with all involved parties present. Otherwise the counselor can choose to reveal in circumstances wherein there is potential significant personal, physical, or emotional harm to unknowing partners or family members, or if the counselor is compromised legally or ethically.

Privileged communication, like confidentiality, is more complicated in the context of couple and family counseling. Privileged communication is referenced in statutes most typically as related to one-to-one communication. In other words, communications made by one person in private to a counselor are considered safe from revelation in a legal proceeding, unless there are legal exceptions or the client waives the privilege. But what about cases in which several people are involved in counseling? As with confidentiality standards, the way the statute is written is critical to interpreting this legal standard. If the statute provides for privileged communication, it must be examined as to whether the privilege extends to all people in a session, or whether it is limited to one-on-one communications made to a counselor. Also, state case law (judgments in past relevant legal cases) is crucial in determining the extent of coverage of privileged communication. Unfortunately, legal standards are often unclear and many states lack definitive case law. Consequently, counselors must act conservatively. Margolin (1982) stated: "Lacking definitive legislation on these issues . . . family therapists cannot comfortably assume that existing privilege statutes protect the communications that occur during family therapy" (p. 794). Clients should know the risks of communicating secrets in circumstances in which there is no clear confidentiality or privileged communication.

## SCHOOL COUNSELING

Confidentiality, the assurance to the client that what is said in a counseling relationship will not be revealed, is an ethical responsibility of counselors in all settings. School counselors have unique challenges in trying to honor that obligation because they work with minors. Remley and Herlihy (2010) noted that legal and ethical requirements seldom conflict, but an exception occurs in counseling minor clients.

Children have an ethical right to privacy and confidentiality. Remley (1985) noted that in the legal structure of the United States, children have some of the protections granted to adults; however, in many ways the protection of children's rights depends on interpretations made by their parents, guardians, or the courts. The legal status pertinent to the discussion of confidentiality is privileged communication, which means that a client is protected from confidential communications being disclosed in a legal proceeding.

Isaacs (1997), Isaacs and Stone (1999), and Glosoff, Herlihy, and Spence (2000) offered a review of privileged communication. Herlihy and Sheeley (1987) and Sheeley and Herlihy (1987) summarized their survey of the provision of privileged communication to the clients of school counselors. In approximately 20 states, students in schools are granted the legal right of privileged communication when talking with a school counselor (Taylor & Adelman, 1989). The restrictions that are placed on the privileged communication vary among the states. School counselors must know whether privilege is granted and examine the limits that exist in relevant statutes.

The level of privilege to which a minor is entitled is a complicated legal determination (Waldo & Malley, 1992) that school counselors must investigate in the state in which they are employed. Additionally, a decision by the U.S. Supreme Court in *Jaffee v. Redmond* (1996) has possible implications about privileged communication for all counselors (Glosoff et al., 2000; Remley, Herlihy, & Herlihy, 1997). In that decision, the Supreme Court ruled that the communications between a master's-level social worker and her client were privileged communication under the Federal Rules of Evidence. The social worker was referred to as "therapist" or "psychotherapist" in the decision and the activities were referred to as "counseling sessions," "counseling," or "psychotherapy." The decision is important for establishing a precedent in an official federal court that provides protection to communications between therapists and their patients (Glosoff et al., 2000; Remley et al., 1997). School counselors need to remain informed about how the implications from that decision may extend to minors and to the school setting.

Regardless of whether privilege has been mandated to protect student communications with counselors, confidentiality within that relationship is imperative. The position statement on the school counselor and confidentiality (American School Counselor Association [ASCA], 1999d) details the obligations of a school counselor for establishing and maintaining confidentiality in schools and places no age limitation on who is entitled to a confidential relationship. The position paper contains definitions and limitations pertinent to school counselors' practice and should be reviewed carefully. One significant point in the statement is that counselors have a responsibility to protect the privacy of information received from students, parents, and teachers. A critical phrase that is repeated throughout the position statement is "confidentiality must not be abridged by the counselor except where there is clear and present danger to the student and/or other persons" (p. 1)

The ASCA Ethical Standards for School Counselors (ASCA, 2010) give detailed guidance on matters of confidentiality, balancing respect for the student and the rights of parents. It encourages school counselors to know the laws that apply to their practices, and it generally reflects the need to prioritize the student's well-being and safety.

Tompkins and Mehring (1993) discussed considerations of privilege and confidentiality, and stated that the third consideration of student–counselor privacy is the policy and expectation of the employer. Counselors are specialized members of the school community who receive requests from teachers, school administration or staff, and others concerned with the educational enterprise. They must respect, and presumably follow, dictates from the school principal and superintendent (Moyer & Sullivan, 2008; O'Connell, 2012). Because teachers and administrators are able to reveal all that a child says to them, it is often difficult for these individuals to understand why school counselors should not do so as well.

The competing demands of maintaining confidentiality for the student and some employer policies further complicate the counselor's responsibilities. Case Scenario 7.2 provides additional attention to the difficulties involved in decisions about how to respond to requests from members of the school community. Before accepting employment, counselors should clarify the policy and expectations of the school.

---

### CASE SCENARIO 7.2 Responding to the Policies of the School and Maintaining Confidentiality

An elementary school counselor is attending an integrated team meeting with administrators, teachers, and a school psychologist about a student, Joey, a third grader who is increasingly withdrawn in the classroom. Joey is not completing his work and is not participating in any classroom activities. The counselor has been working with the child, whose single-parent mother has been diagnosed with an inoperable brain tumor. During the school team meeting, the principal asked the counselor to explain what has been happening to Joey.

Should the counselor provide this information to the principal and the team?

NO. The counselor should maintain the confidentiality of Joey's communication and simply respond that Joey has been encountering some stressful situations and the effects are obviously being expressed in the classroom. The counselor should continue by saying that perhaps, together, she and the school team could determine strategies to help Joey become more engaged in class.

Several options have been proposed to help school counselors in matters related to confidentiality. Remley and Herlihy (2014) identified some pertinent facts about children and confidentiality:

1. Younger children often do not have an understanding of confidentiality or the need for privacy, which is a socially learned concept. Young children may not be nearly as concerned about confidentiality as the counselor is (Huey, 1996) and may not need reassurance of confidentiality (Corr & Balk, 2010).
2. Preadolescents and adolescents may have a heightened desire for privacy that is appropriate to their developmental stage of growth.
3. Some children may not be concerned at all about privacy. It is inappropriate to assume that children do not want their parents or guardians to know information they have told counselors.
4. Children sometimes tell an adult about their concerns hoping that the adult will act as an intermediary in telling their parents.
5. The reasoning capacity of children is limited, and they may not be able to make decisions that are in their best interest because of their age. (p. 225)

Tompkins and Mehring (1993) and Davis and Ritchie (1993) suggested that counselors:

1. Stay informed about the law and written policy in the area of the practice.
2. Operate within the ethical code of the professional organization.
3. Review expectations and policy before employment is accepted.
4. Operate within their personal limits of expertise.
5. Keep the best interest of the children their predominant concern.

By providing informed consent for the parent (and requesting assent by the student) when dealing with sensitive issues or before engaging in long-term counseling, the counselor helps to establish a climate of confidentiality. Remley and Herlihy (2014) suggested that school counselors educate in advance all interested persons (i.e., students, parents, and school personnel) about confidentiality and its exceptions; for example, by providing information on school counseling to parents when the child is first enrolled, by publishing information in student handbooks, and visiting classrooms at the start of classes.

The guidelines provided by Zingaro (1983) included some specifics helpful to the practice of school counseling. He suggested that when it is in the best interest of the child for a significant adult to have information, the counselor may respond by telling the adult how he or she can help the child rather than revealing specific information disclosed by the child. Case Scenario 7.3 provides an example of "need to know" practices. Taylor and Adelman (1989) suggested that counselors should focus on establishing a relationship in which youngsters take the lead in sharing information when appropriate. Those authors provided guidelines for enhancing clients' motivation and choice to resolve their problems by confiding in other adults. Strein and Hershenson (1991) offered suggestions for using a "need-to-know" basis as an alternative guideline to confidentiality when counselors work in situations that are not one-to-one relationships, a common occurrence in schools.

When a parent or guardian demands to know the content of counseling sessions and the student strongly resists this disclosure, school counselors may find the following steps suggested by Remley and Herlihy (2014) useful:

1. Discuss the inquiry with the minor and see if the minor is willing to disclose the content of the counseling session to the adult. Sometimes counselors are more concerned about privacy than a child is. If that doesn't work, go to step 2.
2. Try to persuade the adult that the child's best interests are not served by revealing the information. Attempt to educate the inquiring adult about the nature of the counseling relationship, and assure the adult that information will be given if the child is in danger. If that doesn't work, go to step 3.
3. Schedule a joint session with the adult and the minor. Assume the role of mediator at this session. Hope that the adult's mind will be changed about wanting the information or that the minor will be willing to disclose enough information to satisfy the adult. If that doesn't work, choose step 4 or step 5.
4. Inform the child ahead of time and then disclose the content of the session to the inquiring adult. If the adult is not a parent or guardian, inform the parent or guardian before disclosing the information. Remember that the adult may have a legal right to the information.
5. Refuse to disclose the information to the inquiring adult. Secure approval from your direct administrator before doing this. Remember that the adult may have a legal right to the information. (p. 229)

---

**CASE SCENARIO 7.3** Sharing Information on a "Need-to-Know" Basis: How Would You Respond to This Request?

Teacher: What is going on with Jamie? She has asked to go to your office twice in the last 2 days and she is so testy lately. Every time I speak to her directly, she rolls her eyes and huffs. I hate to stop her from coming to see you, but of course I cannot let her take advantage of my good nature and continue to see you unless I know she has a legitimate reason.

Should you provide the teacher with the specific circumstances that are creating Jamie's difficulty?

NO. You should phrase your response in such a way that protects Jamie's confidentiality yet tells the teacher some specific actions she can take to assist Jamie. An example of such a response follows.

Counselor: I know how well you get along with your students and how interested you are in helping them. Jamie does need time with me right now and I appreciate you letting her come to talk with me when you feel you can. What seems like her frustration with you is probably a result of other concerns. She should be better in time. In the meantime, you might talk with her and arrange a signal to let her know when her reactions are inappropriate so you can have less tense interactions. I remember when you tried that last year with Juan—things went much better for both of you.

Varhely and Cowles (1991) suggested that an overlooked dilemma in conflicts over confidentiality involves the counselor's personal beliefs, experiences, and values. Counselors must strive to determine their personal beliefs about the rights and responsibilities of children, their needs for belonging and a sense of adequacy, and their personal value system. Without a continual process to develop self-awareness in these areas, counselors may further complicate the difficulties inherent in maintaining confidentiality in school settings. Case Scenario 7.4 illustrates a situation in which a counselor's values might shape how a situation is treated.

Some exceptions to confidentiality relate to protecting children from harm—the duty to warn and reporting child abuse. School counselors should be aware that, as with privileged communication, the statutes that determine a counselor's liability in situations of duty to warn and of reporting child abuse are mandated by the state in which the counselor is practicing. Counselors must do a careful review of legislative updates and judicial opinions in their states to make informed decisions (Hopkins & Anderson, 1990).

Counselors must determine actions to take in the delicate balance between confidentiality and the duty to warn others on a case-by-case basis (Sheeley & Herlihy, 1989). They may be vulnerable to a lawsuit if they breach confidentiality. However, if counselors could have prevented an incident, they may be sued if a student client is injured, injures someone else, or commits suicide. Counselors should make the decision with diligence and careful judgment to breach

---

## CASE SCENARIO 7.4 The Influence of Personal Values and Beliefs on Professional Decisions

You are a school counselor on your way home after a long day. A teacher walks you to your car in the school parking lot and starts a discussion about a student you both know. How would you respond?

Eighth-grade teacher to school counselor: Thank goodness I got a chance to see you. You need to do something about that Duvoe child. Danny is in my class and I can't do anything with him! He's so unkempt; his hair is falling over his shoulders! I told him the second day of class that he needed a haircut, but it's as if he is defying me. Now he doesn't even tie it back. It falls all over his face. I can't even see his eyes when I look at him! He should be made to cut his hair and to look me in the eye when I'm talking to him.

Danny's teacher is asking the school counselor to "do something" because his hair is long. Is that a problem in which a counselor should be involved?

NO. While Danny does not appear to be behaving in a manner that indicates he has a personal problem, it is the counselor's responsibility to provide support and assistance to teachers who may be struggling to meet the needs of diverse students. You should attempt to better understand the situation and demonstrate your support to this teacher in a manner that will not encourage undue imposition of either the teacher's or the counselor's values upon Danny. One response might be the following:

"You are concerned about Danny's appearance but I'm not sure I understand how Danny's long hair is a problem." Counselors need to be responsive to teachers to be considered a part of the learning team; however, acting on the teacher's request may not be in line with the values of a counselor who believes in allowing students to be individuals.

confidentiality and warn others. The first step is to be fully informed about state laws and court decisions. Legal mandates and statutes are continually interpreted and revised; keeping abreast of the laws and decisions is an ongoing process. If the school district does not have a policy on confidentiality and its limitations, school counselors should work actively to develop one. That local policy should be adequately disclosed to all students and to all parents.

Sheeley and Herlihy (1989) and Remley and Sparkman (1993) have additional suggestions for school counselors who work with students who may be suicidal. Their suggestions are useful in establishing policy and procedures for this difficult situation:

1. Be able to recognize the warning signs of students with suicidal potential.
2. Have an established plan for dealing with the crisis.
3. Have referral sources for crisis situations.
4. Develop the skills to help students and families if a student threatens suicide.
5. Take action if it is determined that a student is at risk of harming himself or herself.
6. Consider actions that are the least intrusive steps, but that will nevertheless ensure the safety of the person who is suicidal.
7. Consult with colleagues in determining risk as well as the appropriate action to take.
8. Inform school administrators and parents when counselors have determined that a student client is at risk of attempting suicide.
9. If these adults are reluctant to become involved, school counselors have an ethical responsibility to do all they can do to prevent the suicide.

Eating disorders, substance abuse, reckless sexual behavior, cult membership, criminal activity, and other dangerous activities may also be viewed as instances of harm to self. School counselors should question the degree to which such behaviors constitute a student's potential for harm to self that might necessitate breaching confidentiality.

Coll (1995) and Sealander, Schwiebert, Oren, and Weekley (1999) discussed the legal and ethical concerns about confidentiality in substance abuse prevention programs. Their review and guidelines may provide additional insights. Federal guidelines (42 U.S.C. 290 dd-3 and ee-3; 42 CFR Part 2) govern the circumstances of disclosure of the records of people who are receiving treatment for substance abuse or who are participating in prevention or referral activities. Generally, the confidentiality of the records is protected. Exceptions are made for medical emergencies, child abuse or neglect, or the endangering of a third party. These are considered situations in which the benefits produced or the harms prevented justify overriding confidentiality. Even in these cases, only information pertinent to the current problem should be revealed. The federal regulations about minors in substance abuse treatment, prevention, or referral programs permit notification of parents unless state laws restrict requiring or prohibiting notice.

Another situation that may call for breaching confidentiality is when a student client indicates intent to harm others. The *Tarasoff* decision was a call for reasonable action by a therapist to protect third parties. In a discussion of this legal duty, Gehring (1982) reviewed and analyzed the court's interpretations of the decision. More recently, Waldo and Malley (1992) concluded that this duty to protect requires several actions on the part of a therapist—not only the duty to warn an intended victim. They explain the four criteria used to assess what might be expected of school counselors in a decision involving the duty to protect:

1. Special relationship to the dangerous person or to the potential victim
2. The presence of a clear threat and the imminence of danger
3. The ability to identify potential victim(s)
4. Reasonable care when making decisions

According to these authors, courts have defined the following obligations of school counselors in such cases: (a) to assemble necessary background information, (b) to confer with a psychiatrist when consultation is needed, and (c) to keep careful records. Seeking professional legal advice is a suggestion but not an obligation. The actions that school counselors may take to protect a person at risk are (a) making referrals by notifying the parents of the student client, (b) notifying a probation officer, (c) notifying the police, (d) designating someone to inform the intended victim, (e) warning the potential victim, (f) detaining the client, and (g) seeking voluntary or involuntary commitment. Counselors may choose one or more of these possibilities (Waldo & Malley, 1992).

Assessing the dangerousness of the situation is difficult. You may want to review Case Scenario 7.5 to get a sense of these complexities. Gross and Robinson (1987) and Thompson and Rudolph (2000) discussed case studies with guidelines and procedures for each situation. Counselors may find these practice scenarios useful.

## CASE SCENARIO 7.5  Assessing Dangerousness

As a school counselor, you have been conducting a small group for children whose parents are recently divorced. A 13-year-old from that group, Eleanor, has told a friend that she cannot stand her life with her mother and the live-in boyfriend at home any more. Her mother's boyfriend is "impossible," no one is paying any attention to her, and her father refuses to intervene. Eleanor has said that she isn't sure how she is going to do it but she's going to end the lives of the people who are making her feel so miserable so that she can go live with her father. Eleanor's friend has told you about these threats.

Should you intervene?

YES. You should assess the dangerousness of the situation before determining how to work with Eleanor to resolve the situation. Determine if Eleanor has a specific plan and the plausibility of the plan, whether she has the means to carry out the plan and how accessible those means are, and how pervasive these thoughts are to her. If you determine the threat is credible, you should tell Eleanor that you must report the situation to her parents and possibly to the police. Make the reports and document the actions. Consultation with another professional is advisable. Proceed simultaneously with other actions that are directed at supporting Eleanor in resolving her difficult situation; for example, arrange an agreement with Eleanor for individual counseling to consider alternative actions, arrange a meeting (with Eleanor's permission) with all the parties to work on acceptable solutions to the home situation, or refer Eleanor to another professional for more intensive counseling.

Counselors also deal with two sensitive dilemmas that involve youth sexuality—counseling minors about birth control or abortion and counseling students with AIDS. McWhirter, McWhirter, McWhirter, and McWhirter (1998) and Gustafson and McNamara (1987) discussed the difficulties in determining whether to tell parents about the sexual activity of a minor, especially in relation to seeking birth control or abortion information. State laws that mandate reporting, or protect counselors from such reports, are as varied as other laws. In some states, minors can discuss sexually transmitted diseases or pregnancy prevention or cessation with counselors without the legal requirement of parents' notification (Stadler, 1989). Other states mandate notification. Counselors should remain informed about the legal issues, consult with colleagues, and be deliberate about their decisions.

Talbutt (1983a) reviewed court cases related to abortions. She noted legal and ethical issues in school employees providing abortion information and concluded that counselors should be familiar with their school district's policy and know the laws and current court rulings that have implications for abortion counseling. Urging minors to discuss plans with parents may be both a legal mandate and a counseling goal. Talbutt noted the need for counselors to establish procedures before taking a crisis approach. The procedure should include family members and local referral agencies.

Stone (2002) also reviewed a recent case concerning abortion and made several recommendations for school counselors, including: (a) taking into account the age and level of development of the student when ascertaining the level of autonomy to give to the student, and (b) taking into account the ethnicity, culture, and religious values of the student (and her parents) when ascertaining the student's views on abortion. Stone also suggested that the school counselor consult with supervisors and colleagues in coming to a carefully considered decision on how to proceed with the student.

As to whether parents should be notified when a child is pregnant, Remley and Herlihy (2014) have considered the issue of whether such disclosure would have a chilling effect and dissuade students from seeking care for their pregnancy, and that it may even be unconstitutional for a school to require that parents must be notified.

Lynch (1993) provided a thoughtful discussion of the process of counseling someone with AIDS in which counselors balance confidentiality concerns with the duty to protect. Her overview is for those who work in college counseling centers, but the dilemmas she recognizes are applicable to other school settings. Both her article and the position statement entitled The School Counselor and AIDS (ASCA, 1999a) promote positive health education, familiarity with current resources, and prudent adherence to the primary role of counselors. McWhirter et al. (1998) suggested that counselors notify state public health agencies of possible communicable or reportable diseases after determining measures to protect confidentiality. Those authors proposed that such disclosure protects the third person and the client's confidentiality and demonstrates the counselor's measures to prevent harm. Current ASCA ethical standards advise counselors to inform a third party who is at risk for contracting a communicable disease if that person has not already been notified of the danger.

The dilemmas associated with school counselors, their clients, and issues of confidentiality provoke much discussion. Isaacs (1999) summarized the factors that affect the choices made by counselors to breach confidentiality and suggested the following:

- Determine in advance the kinds of behaviors and issues that might warrant breach.
- Establish a network of peers.
- Determine alternative actions to breaching confidentiality.

All states require some type of reporting of suspected cases of child abuse. As with other state mandates, the specifics of the laws vary from state to state. Counselors should understand the requirements of the laws in their states and the procedures in their districts. Laws are being revised constantly and must be monitored by school counselors. Sandberg, Crabbs, and Crabbs (1988) provided responses to frequently asked questions about legal issues in child abuse.

The Professional School Counselor and Child Abuse and Neglect Prevention is an ASCA (1999c) position statement that outlines various counselor responsibilities beyond the reporting of child abuse. This statement includes a useful set of definitions and examples of the signs of abuse and neglect.

According to the ASCA position statement (ASCA, 2015), school counselors must report suspected child abuse and neglect and thus need to be familiar with current policies, procedures, reporting requirements, and state laws concerning abuse (See Case Scenario 7.6 on reporting suspected cases of child abuse.) The types of child abuse cited in this statement include:

- Physical abuse
- Neglect or deprivation of necessities
- Medical neglect
- Sexual abuse
- Psychological or emotional maltreatment
- And other forms included in state law

School counselors must also provide to abused children appropriate counseling and services designed to treat the abuse (ASCA, 2015).

Counselors are encouraged to implement activities to educate and to support other school personnel involved in protecting children from abuse and neglect. They are also charged with providing ongoing services to the children and/or the family in the crisis or to refer them to an appropriate agency. Providing child abuse/neglect prevention programs is also among counselors' duties (Minard, 1993). Remley and Fry (1993) identified the multiple roles of the counselor in reporting child abuse: informant, counselor to the victim or perpetrator, employee, liaison, court witness, and counselor to the family. Clearly, the potential for role conflict, as well as the burden of being a resource for so many people, makes this area a difficult one for school counselors. Counselors must have the qualities of awareness, knowledge, commitment, and effective communication skills to face the process of reporting and preventing child abuse and neglect (Howell-Nigrelli, 1988).

## CASE SCENARIO 7.6  Reporting Suspected Cases of Child Abuse

You are a school counselor who has just met with a student referred to you by her classroom teacher. Based on that session, you arranged an appointment that same morning with your school principal. The meeting leaves you conflicted:

School Counselor: Mr. B., I need to report this case of suspected abuse to the state reporting agency. Angela Adams has a series of welts on her back that look like the mark of a belt. In addition, she has a large bruise, just darkening, on her shoulder. Her teacher brought her to see me due to these marks, and Angela said she and her dad got into a fight last weekend. She said that her brother looks worse than she does because, "Dad really beat him up."

Principal: Angela Adams? This is surprising. I met her mom at open house this year, and she and her husband have helped out on several school and community projects. I really doubt that this could be the right story. Angela can be very obstinate, you know. I had her in my office twice last year for not following teacher directives. I think we should wait on this and see if anything further happens. I know the Adams's neighbors. I'll ask if they ever hear anything.

Have you discharged your responsibility to report this suspected child abuse by leaving matters in the principal's hands?

NO. You have both a legal mandate to report suspected abuse and a personal belief that the incident should be reported. If others in the school system do not agree, you should carefully consider the dilemma and be prepared to convince others of your position.

The addition of corporal punishment to the ASCA position statement acknowledges that the abuse of children may also occur at school. This ASCA position statement states that school counselors should not support the use of corporal punishment as a disciplinary tool.

Another issue of abuse that is not addressed clearly in the ethical standards is psychological maltreatment in the schools, either by educators or students' peers. Although ASCA provides no position statement and no ethical standards are available, counselors need to monitor the emerging literature about bullying and psychologically abusive teachers (Neese, 1989). Clearly, students have the right to attend school in a violence-free atmosphere. Counselors also have an ethical responsibility to competently assess and address potential for violent behavior among the students with whom they work, and take steps to prevent any serious harm.

Wheeler and Bertram (2015) discussed antibullying laws and have stated that because of such laws, schools must be prepared to intervene when bullying occurs. Wheeler and Bertram in particular discuss the case of a middle-school student who had been punched in the stomach by a bully. The next day the boy suffered a blood clot, due to the punch, which paralyzed him. The boy sued the school, alleging that it was aware of the bullying but did little about it, in violation of the antibullying law. The boy settled out of court with the school district for $4.2 million. As the suit was settled out of court, legal precedent was not set;

however, this should put school counselors on notice that they need to be aware of antibullying laws that are applicable to their school and, in consultation with the school administration, to intervene when bullying occurs.

Sealander et al. (1999) reviewed the laws that uphold the privacy of student information. The FERPA establishes parameters on accessing and disclosing student records. The Drug Abuse Office and Treatment Act (1976) protects the drug and alcohol treatment records of students in any institution that receives federal assistance. The Individuals with Disabilities Education Act (IDEA) further stipulates the care of the records of students in special education. The ACA (1998b) has compiled a helpful resource that also clarifies federal law on student records.

In November 1974, the FERPA, or the Buckley Amendment, became law. The intent of this federal mandate was to provide parents and eligible students (older than age 18) the right to inspect school records and to protect the dissemination of educational records. Federal funds may be withheld from school districts that do not adhere to the policies of allowing parents access to records and denying access without parental permission. All U.S. school districts develop a records policy statement and procedures for access and protection to explain how the regulations are implemented. Walker and Larrabee (1985) and Fischer and Sorenson (1996) presented the following useful information on the application of FERPA guidelines:

- Parents or eligible students should be informed of their rights under this act. This right is extended to custodial and noncustodial parents, unless a court order restrains the access of the noncustodial parent.

- Information about types of educational records that exist and the procedures for accessing those records is disseminated. The content of educational records may include academic progress, test scores, identification data, home background, health information, educational history, anecdotal remarks, case summaries, and recommendations.

- Parents or eligible students may review educational records, request changes, pursue a hearing if the change is disallowed, and add personal statements as explanations, if necessary.

- Personally identifiable information is not released without prior written consent of a parent or an eligible student.

- Parents and eligible students are allowed to see the school's record of disclosure.

- Records made by educators that remain in the sole possession of the maker and therefore are not accessible or revealed to any other individual are not subject to disclosure under this act (Fischer & Sorenson, 1996). This indicates that private notes do not have to be revealed under this federal act.

School counselors who have administrative responsibility for the educational records of children should comply with local policy, state law, and the Buckley Amendment. Remley (1990) discussed whether counselors have a legal or ethical obligation to keep counseling records and the content of the records. He described circumstances in which personnel may be obligated to disclose counseling records and outlined procedures for maintaining, transferring, and discarding counseling records.

The Education for all Handicapped Children Act is Public Law 94-142. In 1990, that Act was amended by PL 101-476 and renamed the IDEA. The act was revised in 1997. This law guarantees free and appropriate education in the least restrictive environment possible to all students regardless of the nature and degree of their handicapping conditions. While the law does not refer to school counselors specifically, they are involved in offering many services to students with handicapping conditions and may be included in the Individual Education Plan (IEP) for students with exceptionalities. School counselors need to be aware of federal guidelines that apply. Henderson (2001) has compiled a helpful overview of the IDEA and Section 504 of the Rehabilitation Act of 1973. These federal laws provide educators with specifics about the eligibility for services, responsibilities, funding, due process, and evaluation/placement procedures.

## ADDICTIONS

Ethically sensitive treatment requires the counselor to protect clients' sensitive personal information. Due to the social stigma attached to addiction by many, the principle of confidentiality is integral to the ethical provision of care. Confidential communications in the area of addiction counseling is addressed by federal and state laws and regulations. The federal alcohol and other drug confidentiality law requires covered programs to strictly maintain the confidentiality of patient records and limits the release of patient information related to alcohol and drug treatment. These statutes (42 U.S.C. 290dd-2) and the accompanying regulations (42 CFR Part 2) came about through Congress's recognition that safeguards on privacy serve the important purpose of encouraging people with substance abuse problems to seek and succeed at treatment. The lack of privacy could stigmatize clients in their communities and affect the success of substance abuse treatment programs. The law regulates service providers who receive federal funds directly, by way of state distribution, or by way of tax-exempt status. Any provider receiving such funding is bound by federal confidentiality laws. In addition, state laws generally require confidential relations between individuals treated by licensed professionals. The laws are complex. Addiction counselors are encouraged to become familiar with the rules and their application and advised to take advantage of detailed information sources in order to understand the nuances of the law (for instance, see DHHS, 1994, 1996).

In general, a counselor may disclose any information about a client when the client authorizes the disclosure by signing a valid consent form. Valid consent forms, by federal regulation, must include (a) the client's name, (b) the name of the disclosing program, (c) the name and titles of the party receiving the information, (d) the purpose of the information disclosure, narrowly described and corresponding to the information to be released, (e) a statement that the client may revoke the consent at any time, except to the extent that action has been taken in reliance on the consent, (f) a date at which the consent will expire if not revoked, (g) the signature of the client, and (h) the date the consent was signed. A consent is not considered valid unless it contains all of these elements.

Federal law provides the substance abuse client protection beyond that offered by many licensure statutes on confidentiality or privileged communication. The federal confidentiality codes protect information about any client applying for or receiving services, including assessment, diagnosis, counseling, group counseling, or referral for other treatment and apply to all program personnel. Disclosure does not simply refer to explicit statements about an individual's status in treatment, but also includes implicit disclosures. For instance, staff may not confirm that a particular person is a client, even if the inquirer says he or she is a family member and knows the client is attending treatment. Further, the counselor should not leave messages for a client where another person could hear the message; disclose any information by which a client's identity could be inferred; or permit the police to have access to client records without a valid court order. Information about a client protected by federal confidentiality laws may be disclosed or disseminated only with client consent. Individuals who violate the regulations are subject to a criminal penalty in the form of a fine, may be sued for unauthorized disclosure by the concerned client, and place their professional license and certification at risk.

The general prohibition against revealing information that could identify a client does not mean that counselors may never disclose the names of their clients. A counselor may disclose identifying information without indicating that a person has ever sought or received alcohol or other drug services, for instance, when a program is part of a larger organization such as a general hospital. Even without consent, client-identifying information may be disclosed to medical personnel in an emergency that presents a serious threat and requires immediate medical intervention. Counselors should note that a program may not use the medical emergency rule to contact family members or the police without direct client consent.

If a client commits or threatens to commit a crime either on program grounds or against program staff anywhere, the regulations permit the program to disclose client-identifying information to the police. The law does not permit the release of other client names who may have witnessed the crime without their proper written consent. Requests from police to turn over records when a crime was allegedly committed by a client are portrayed in Case Scenario 7.7. Of importance, the rule does not allow a counselor to disclose a client's confession of past crimes, unless the crime was committed on the program grounds or against program staff.

In cases of suspected child abuse or neglect, the federal rule allows a counselor to make reports to the appropriate state or local child abuse hotlines, as required by many state laws. However, without client consent or a court order, client files must be withheld from child protection agencies.

An additional concern related to confidentiality and privileged communication in treatment of individuals with addictions centers on the commonly used method of group therapy. According to some state regulations, communications made in a group setting, even if a licensed professional is involved, may not be considered confidential or privileged in the classic sense of these terms. If group treatment is referenced in a licensure statute, the licensed professional is usually bound to keep group discussions confidential. However, since other group members are peers and not professionals, they are not bound by law to keep private any group discussions. Group members may talk about other group members without legal repercussion. They may also report to others, even authorities, information communicated at group meetings. Therefore, if a client confesses a crime in a group meeting, other group members could take this information to authorities, and even testify as to what was said, without legal repercussion. If a counselor is present, the counselor may be bound to confidentiality, given that group counseling is addressed by state law and that the crime does not come under an exception to the statute's confidentiality provision. Counselors may have group members sign an agreement about keeping group-disclosed information confidential, but such agreements may not be legally binding and may serve only as a promise to not discuss group information in other settings. Accordingly, group members should be informed of the limits of their privacy before they enter a group. Likewise, substance abuse clients should know that federal laws provide them extra protections if they seek treatment in a program that is obligated to honor federal confidentiality law.

Finally, even when a confidential relationship is formed in an individual or group context, privileged communication may not always stand. Many state laws offer the protection of privileged communication for civil court cases but not for criminal court cases. Counselors should study their state statutes closely in this regard. Counselors may be compelled to testify on criminal allegations, even if a revelation of such was made in a confidential counseling context.

## CASE SCENARIO 7.7 Turning Over Records

A licensed professional counselor in private practice was informed by the local police that one of his patients had allegedly committed a felony. This particular client, treated in a group setting, had sought treatment to address issues associated with substance abuse problems, and, in fact, the client used his attendance in group therapy as an alibi. Police officers requested the names, addresses, and case files of all clients who attended the group with the suspect. The counselor refused to provide this information.

Did the counselor act appropriately?

YES. In an actual case (*State of Missouri v. Anthony Genovese*), a counselor refused to turn over the files of other group clients to authorities, which resulted in the police standing outside of the counselor's office requesting identification from anyone attempting to enter her office. The counselor immediately contacted an attorney, who filed a protest with the police department. The police did leave the entrance of the counselor's office. The counselor was then served with a subpoena to provide all group members' information to the police. Clients of counselors in the state are afforded privileged communication in civil cases, but not criminal cases. The counselor requested that her case files of clients not under investigation be considered confidential and privileged, and the court ruled in her favor. Later, when the original felony charge was tried, the counselor's records of all group members were again subpoenaed. Again, the counselor requested the court view her files as confidential and privileged communications, but this time the court ordered all group members' names, addresses, and phone numbers to be released: They were considered public information and crucial to the defendant's alibi. The counselor appealed this decision, and the court's ruling was overturned in favor of the counselor's actions.

In 2000, the DHHS released a set of privacy standards for compliance with the HIPAA of 1996. Substance abuse treatment programs must comply with HIPAA rules. Generally, this means that addiction counselors will follow federal confidentiality rules and should not disclose client information unless they obtain consent or identify an exception to the rule that allows a disclosure. Counselors should then make sure that the disclosure is also permissible under the Privacy Rule (Office of Applied Studies, Substance Abuse and Mental Health Services Administration, 2004).

## GROUP COUNSELING

Complex ethical circumstances arise in groups that do not arise in other counseling situations. In a recently publicized case in a Midwestern state, a member of an Alcoholics Anonymous group confessed to his group that he had committed murder. The revelation was reported in the newspapers, apparently leaked by other group members. The authorities subsequently investigated the individual who made the revelation. Questions of group counseling confidentiality were raised, and the consensus of the mental health community was that there was no confidentiality except as was voluntarily agreed to by the members of the group.

In the absence of a licensed professional, no protection can be given legally to the information provided in a group. But even in the presence of a licensed professional whose clients are afforded legal confidentiality and privileged communication, the presence of other individuals in a group (nonprofessionals) compromises confidentiality—other group members are not required by law to keep information private or secret. In an article addressing confidentiality in a support group for individuals with AIDS, Posey (1988) described some circumstances unique to group treatment:

> In our group, discussions of confidentiality have been triggered by people dropping in, one member identifying another at a bar, issues of how or whether to leave telephone messages, and how to respond to a member's family and friends at the hospital. Initially, a member distributed names and telephone numbers of the group members but recalled them when members expressed discomfort. Once, a news reporter appeared at a meeting and wanted to sit in, and he guaranteed that identities would be protected. The group agreed to discuss his interest but would not allow him to attend the meeting. (p. 226)

Unusual, and sometimes unpredictable, issues of confidentiality arise in group settings. This is partly because nonprofessional group members may reveal information communicated in a group at their discretion, judgment, or in some cases, misjudgment. The 2007 Association for Specialists in Group Work (ASGW) "Best Practice Guidelines" (see Thomas & Pender, 2008, p. 114) document specifically states: "Group workers have the responsibility to inform all group participants of the need for confidentiality, potential consequences of breaching confidentiality and that legal privilege does not apply to group discussions (unless provided by state statute)" (Section A.7.d).

Group counselors must stress the importance of confidentiality and set a norm of confidentiality regarding all group disclosures. The importance of maintaining confidentiality should be emphasized before the group begins and at various times throughout the group sessions. Participants should also know that confidentiality cannot be guaranteed.

It is important for clients to know that although counselors will act to protect the right to confidentiality of clients, counselors cannot enforce a ban on gossip among other members of the group or between members of the group and outsiders.

Confidentiality is also complicated in groups when other individuals have access to records. For example, if a group of minors is being counseled, the parents of the minors technically have the right to information about the nature and content of counseling (unless there is a legal exemption to parental consent or oversight). Parents even have legal access to case file information. Revelation of group counseling case file information to parents of one or more members of a group (such as a group counseling case note) that references other individuals in the group essentially breaches the confidentiality of the other group members, unless those other group members' parents allow for such revelation.

Group counselors have a special responsibility to ensure that case notes for group counseling are written for each individual in the group. Further, information about other group members should be deleted or omitted from the case files of the group member for whom the case notes are written. This situation is complicated further by federal law. The federal FERPA of 1974, which covers all educational institutions that receive federal funding from preschool through university graduate training, clearly states:

> The parents of students [have] the right to inspect and review any and all official records, files, and data directly related to their children, including all material that is incorporated into each student's cumulative record folder. . . . Where such records or data include information on more than one student, the parents of any student shall be entitled to receive or be informed of, that part of such record or data as pertains to their child. (Section 438.[a] [1])

Counselors must ensure that records for each client are kept separate and that group case notes do not reference other individuals specifically. In effect, counselors in educational settings must document group counseling case files carefully in light of a legal standard that allows parents full access to such information, even if a parent's child is referenced in another client's case notes.

Regardless of the specific situation in which an issue of confidentiality arises, the counselor must inform each group participant of the limits of confidentiality before that individual consents to treatment (Gregory & McConnell, 1986). The APA, National Association of Social Workers (NASW), and ACA codes and the ASGW 2007 "Best Practice Guidelines" (see Thomas & Pender, 2008) all agree that the limits of confidentiality must be discussed with clients. Initiation of groups should not occur until all members of the group are privy to and informed of the limits of confidentiality, and clients should be made to acknowledge such awareness (e.g., by signing a statement of understanding). (The AAMFT [2015] code does not address group practice.)

Standard exemptions to confidentiality apply in group counseling just as in individual counseling. Depending on the state law that applies, counselors must typically breach confidentiality in situations in which there is (a) suspected or substantiated child abuse or neglect, (b) evidence or suspicion that a client intends to do harm to an individual or society (e.g., through an illegal act), (c) a request by a parent or legal guardian, (d) client permission to reveal, (e) the need to confer with other involved professionals, and (f) in other cases covered by law or specific ethical standard.

In an interesting study of confidentiality dilemmas in group psychotherapy, Roback and Purdon (1992) examined how group psychotherapists reported handling serious confidentiality issues. They stated:

> The overall findings of this exploratory study suggest that when confronted with a patient disclosure involving psycholegal issues (criminal behavior, threatened harm to others, potential danger to a child, or past physical abuse of an adolescent), experienced group psychotherapists are highly unlikely to deal with the situation totally within the group context. Rather, they attempt to deal with such incidents by adding private, individual therapy sessions for the patient. However, rarely do they take the incident entirely out of the group context. Realistically, there are groups that are too volatile to manage inflammable patient disclosures such as intended homicide, and patients who are too disturbed (e.g., the agitated paranoid) to be defused within the group context. Competent patient care requires the therapist to be sufficiently flexible to discriminate when the group process will be inadequate for a given situation. (p. 6)

Further, they found that male and female therapists acted differently:

> Male group therapists report being more likely to attempt to neutralize patient threats in the group context alone, whereas their female counterparts are more likely to deal with such incidents by augmenting the patient's group sessions with private individual sessions. (p. 6)

Beyond ethical considerations, group counseling process issues arise in such conflicts.

The issue of privileged communication, too, is complicated in group treatment circumstances. Privileged communication prevents the revelation of confidential information in a legal proceeding. A counselor cannot be forced to testify on a client's case if the privilege stands—the client owns the privilege. Privileged communication, historically, has been accorded most usually in one-to-one communication circumstances. As addressed earlier in this chapter, it may not apply to circumstances in which other individuals are present in counseling. Unless group counseling is specifically addressed in laws that provide for privileged communication, it is probably wise to assume that group communications will not be considered privileged, and counselors may be required to testify. On the other hand, if group counseling is referenced in the law that provides for privileged communication, counselors may proceed with the intent to hold information that is communicated in group contexts as privileged. However, even in those cases in which group counseling is referenced in laws providing the privilege, there may be no definitive standard as to whether clients will be protected from revelation of private information in a legal proceeding unless there is clear case law in the legal jurisdiction within which the counselor practices. In such cases, clients should know that there is a possibility that information may be vulnerable to revelation in a legal context, although the counselor will make every effort to prevent such revelation. Counselors should study state statutes and case law carefully.

Some statutes provide for privilege under certain circumstances. Many state licensure statutes allow for privileged communication in civil, not criminal, cases only. Most states allow for revelation of suspected or substantiated child abuse or neglect, and state statutes that cover such matters may override any privileged communication provided to clients of counselors. In group settings where such matters are commonly discussed, clients should have prior knowledge of the limits on their privilege.

Individuals who seek group therapy often are involved in individual therapy as well. This occurs in both private practice and in institutional settings. The complexities of a client being seen in both individual and group therapy are described in Case Scenario 7.8. There should be clear guidelines for the sharing of group information among agency employees in institutional settings. Codes of ethics typically require that when there is a relationship between professionals, there should be a formal agreement regarding issues of confidentiality. When a group counselor consults with a client's individual counselor (with the client's permission), the group counselor should be assured that the information communicated will be held in confidence and protected from revelation to outsiders.

Certainly, there are ethical concerns related to the contiguous professional relationship if a counselor is performing both individual and group treatment (for a nongroup matter) with one client (see Glass, 1998). Counselors must be cautious in this circumstance to prevent contamination of group treatment with information from the individual treatment. Counselors should avoid seeing clients in both the group facilitator and individual counselor roles. Concerns also arise if a client participates in individual treatment with another mental health professional. Glass (1998) said:

> Confidentiality questions about what information is to be shared by the two therapists need to be worked out. There is also a danger that the patient will use the individual sessions to drain off affect elicited in the group instead of dealing with it in the group. Using different individual and group therapists will be most productive if the patient consents to allow both therapists to communicate freely with one another throughout the course of treatment. Otherwise the danger is great that the two therapists may find themselves working at cross purposes. (p. 110)

Glass recommended "only one form of treatment at a time" (p. 110) to prevent the ethical dilemmas that arise.

**CASE SCENARIO 7.8** Introduction of a New Member in Groups

A counselor in a small rural mental health center is seeing a client in individual counseling and has also encouraged the client to join a group the counselor runs for individuals with similar issues. The client joins the group, and in the first session, the counselor proceeds to introduce the client, summarizing her concerns to the other group members.

Has the counselor done something wrong?

PROBABLY. Unless the counselor got permission from the client before the group meeting to reveal information communicated during individual sessions of counseling, there was a breach of confidentiality. As inferred earlier in this chapter, doing both individual and group counseling with a client is an ethical dilemma minefield. Where such an arrangement cannot be avoided, clear ethical boundaries must be defined around the material addressed in the individual sessions and the material addressed by the counselor in group sessions. It would be wise to have a formal written agreement with the client defining any limits of confidentiality across modes of treatment.

## CAREER

Any number of complications can arise for career counselors with regard to confidentiality and privileged communication. As with all professional counselors, the trust engendered by the assurance of confidentiality is the most critical element of the counseling relationship.

Several areas of practice—such as vocational or forensic expert practices—require that career counselors take particular care in observing requirements to guard client confidentiality. These counselors may be asked to provide expertise or testimony on matters of career trajectory, likely earning (current or lifetime), typical job performance or scope of career activity, fair wage, and other legal matters. They must clearly address confidentiality limitations with all of the individuals involved. The 2015 National Career Development Association (NCDA) *Code of Ethics* provides a rule that embodies well-accepted advice in such situations. The Section B Introduction reads as follows: "Career professionals recognize that trust is a cornerstone of the professional relationship. Career professionals work to earn the trust of clients by creating an ongoing partnership, establishing and upholding appropriate boundaries, and maintaining confidentiality. Career professionals communicate the parameters of confidentiality in a culturally competent manner" (p. 6). For example, career counselors may be asked to provide information about a person's employability or earnings potential in divorce cases. In this role as forensic expert in these legal cases, there is no intention that the counselor will actually provide counseling to the client as this is a forensic assessment role only. In such cases, the career counselor must address limits of confidentiality deriving from the forensic assessment role; that is, the career counselor is retained by a third party and may testify in such a situation regardless of client permission.

There are many instances of clients having misunderstood the nature of the services provided by a career counselor. Clients may think that information they provided to the professional will be held in confidence, only to be shocked and angered later to discover that it is included in a report or deposition that resulted in a negative outcome for them, such as a loss of benefits. Such anecdotal reports are unfortunate illustrations of a need for greater care in observing the informed consent procedures regarding confidentiality limitations. The client must be informed clearly when the counselor is employed by a third party. Clients must be helped to understand fully how that relationship will influence any information given to the client, or how services provided to the client will be limited or changed.

Another potentially devastating and costly misunderstanding on the part of career counselors is the uncritical assumption that privileged communication extends to their practices. Because privileged communication is granted only through statute and legal precedent, the types of professionals covered by this privilege vary with jurisdiction (Glosoff et al., 2000). Thus, possessing a national certification in career counseling does not entitle one to legal privilege for therapeutic communications in and of itself. Career counselors must research the nature of the laws governing the granting of privilege in their own areas of practice and in their geographic location. Generally, privileged communication is extended only to licensed professionals. The *Jaffee* ruling by the U.S. Supreme Court underscored this position; so a national specialty certificate does not afford similar protections.

Many career counselors in educational institutions perform their work within a multi- or interdisciplinary team context. Such an arrangement is often considered the intervention of choice, but it does present the counselor with additional factors for consideration of confidentiality. Different team members have varying levels of training and understanding of this ethical obligation, and may have a legitimate desire and need to know information the counselor may have about the client. While, generally, it is acknowledged that professionals may have an appropriate need to communicate information to other people involved in the client's care, the client must be informed clearly and fully of this common limitation to confidentiality at the outset of counseling. Indeed, it is a common and sensible practice to obtain suitable written release of information regarding this and other limitations to confidentiality in a written consent to treatment document. It is also wise to discuss with the client the sharing of information with other professionals. The client should be informed of when, how, to whom, to what extent, and what type of information will be shared with others. This process must be done in such a way as to avoid coercion of clients or the implication that they will not be served if they do not grant blanket permission.

Even when consent is obtained, the career counselor must be circumspect about revealing information to others. The counselor must determine the appropriateness of the disclosure before providing information by asking, "Is it likely that the information that I am about to share with my team member(s) will substantially enhance that person's work with the client?" (Strein & Hershenson, 1991, p. 313). The same analysis should be applied to decisions about including material in case records that will be viewed by these individuals. Strein and

Hershenson provided additional benchmark concepts to be considered when fostering confidentiality within a team context. Their recommendations include taking steps to (a) articulate the specific rules the treatment team will follow regarding confidentiality, (b) reinforce the obligation of confidentiality with the team in any circumstance in which it appears that a team member may not realize the confidentiality of the information, and (c) inform the client before material will be shared with members of the team.

Career counselors also should be aware of other important limitations to confidentiality because it would not be unusual to have a number of clients with issues that could limit confidentiality. Examples might include people with psychiatric or addiction disabilities, HIV/AIDS, and clients with correctional histories who might become dangerous to themselves or others. Clients of career counselors may be involved in group treatment or counseling for purposes ranging from job-seeking skills and support groups to more traditional psychotherapeutic adjustment counseling groups. Counselors must inform their clients of confidentiality limitations (e.g., group counseling). Also, they must also inform clients that the courts generally do not uphold privilege for therapeutic communication in a group setting. It is imperative that the counselor should become skilled and comfortable in providing informed consent opportunities to clients, for it is never possible to anticipate when these issues might arise with any client. Career counselors working in certain specialized settings also must become knowledgeable about specific additional state or federal laws that apply to confidentiality and privilege in those settings. Examples include the access to records of minors by their parents as required by the federal FERPA, and the laws extending stricter confidentiality to those in treatment in any addiction treatment facility that receives federal funding.

## CLINICAL SUPERVISION

Confidentiality in supervision must be considered from the perspective of both the client and the supervisee. From either perspective, the definition is comparable to confidentiality as traditionally referenced in counseling—that is, **confidentiality** is "the ethical duty of counselors to protect a client's identity, identifying characteristics, and private communications" (ACA, 2014, p. 20). The following discussion first considers confidentiality as it relates to the client of the supervisee and then the counselor as supervisee.

Supervisors should make supervisees aware of clients' rights, including protecting clients' right to privacy and confidentiality in the counseling relationship and the information resulting from it. Clients also should be informed that their right to privacy and confidentiality will not be violated by the supervisory relationship. Thus, the supervisor must ensure that the counselor has informed his or her clients of their rights to confidentiality and privileged communication. Clients also should be informed of the limits of confidentiality and privileged communication. The general limits of confidentiality are harm to self or when others are threatened; when the abuse of children, elders, or dependent adults; and in cases when a court compels the counselor to testify and break confidentiality (including those circumstances where a counselor is sued by the client or the client has filed an ethical grievance against the counselor). These are generally accepted limits to confidentiality and privileged communication, but they may be modified by state or federal statute.

Supervisors must also "be sure that their supervisees keep confidential all client information, except for purposes of supervision. Because supervision allows for a third-party discussion of the therapy situation, the supervisee must be reminded that this type of discourse cannot be repeated elsewhere. In group supervision, the supervisor must reiterate this point and take the extra precaution of having cases presented using first names only, with as few demographic details as possible" (Bernard & Goodyear, 2009, p. 68).

With video, electronic, or live supervision, the supervisor needs to re-emphasize the importance of confidentiality. When supervisees tape, they must be reminded they possess confidential documents. Notes should use code numbers rather than names and be guarded with care. Records of the counseling relationship, including interview notes, test data, correspondence, the electronic storage of these documents, and audiotape and videotape recordings, are considered confidential professional information. Supervisors should verify these materials are used in counseling, research, and training and supervision of counselors with the full knowledge of the clients and with permission granted by the applied counseling setting that is offering service to the client. This professional information is to be used for full protection of the client. Written consent from the client (or legal guardian, if a minor) should be secured prior to using such information for instructional, supervisory, and/or research purposes. Agency or organization policies regarding client records also should be followed (See the Association for Counselor Education and Supervision [ACES], 2011, "Best Practices in Clinical Supervision" document for detailed guidance on matters of supervision.)

It is the supervisor's responsibility to keep information obtained during supervision regarding the counselor supervisee confidential and to protect the supervisee's right to privacy. The supervisor must keep and secure supervision records and consider all information gained in supervision as confidential. If records are stored electronically, then the supervisor must ensure that pertinent laws are adhered to and also ensure that supervisees "inform clients on how records are maintained electronically" (ACA, 2014, H.5.a.), including the way such information is secured and how long it will be maintained and stored.

The supervisee should understand the circumstances under which information obtained in supervision can be revealed. Supervisees can make more informed decisions about what to reveal in supervision if they understand that evaluative information from supervision may be passed along or any particular issues troubling the supervisor may be discussed with colleagues (Sherry, 1991).

## FORENSIC PRACTICE

In forensic practice, sometimes attorneys ask a mental health professional to consult on a case privately to address issues of the mental status and mental health of legal clients. Gottlieb and Coleman (2012) stated that professionals in private consultation with attorneys on a case come under the **work product rule, which prevents revelation of the discussion in a legal hearing**. Gottlieb and Coleman stated that "if asked, [the mental health professional] must refuse to disclose their involvement in the case" (p. 105). Further, Gottlieb and Coleman stated, "This issue becomes more complex when attorneys ask forensic psychologists to evaluate their clients" (p. 105), for example, to mitigate imposed punishment by the courts, which would require testimony of the evaluating professional. Confidentiality has limits if there is a formal forensic examination of the client with the intent of presenting the evaluation results in the court or legal proceeding. In those cases, the information provided by clients would not be confidential, and, of course, the client should know this prior to any evaluation (preferably addressed through informed consent). Also, since mental health professionals are skilled at getting clients to reveal information (typically with the intent to treat the client, but not in the case of forensic practice) it is important for the forensic professional to remind the forensic client of the limits of the professional relationship and that revealed information may be shared in a legal proceeding. In other words, forensic professionals and forensic clients must be alert to privacy issues not relevant to the legal questions as well as issues of confidentiality. When a forensic evaluation is court ordered, all the information obtained during assessment is open to the court.

## CONCLUSION

This chapter presented information applied to the nuanced ethical practice of mental health specialties related to privacy, confidentiality, and privileged communication. Counselors and psychotherapists must not only know the general standards of ethical practice that apply to their work, but they must know the issues specific to their specialty practices, and especially the legal rules that may apply to specialty settings. As this chapter made clear, there are different issues across different counseling and mental health specialties. Knowledge of specific issues in specific practices is a prerequisite to ethical specialty practice.

# INFORMED CONSENT

## OBJECTIVES

- To describe the application of the ethical standard of informed consent across counseling specialties.
- To describe distinctive ethical actions in the nuanced practice of a counseling specialty.
- To describe legal issues that are associated with specific counseling specialties that affect informed consent.

This chapter addresses the standard of informed consent across the counseling specialties. Each section will also address any crucial legal issues specific to specialty practice. **Informed consent is the client's right to approve treatment—to agree to services.** It is typically accomplished in a formal way (typically with a written informed consent form) in the initial phase of service provision. However, informed consent should not be viewed as a single event; there may be several points in the counseling process where a client or clients need to address such issues as a change in modality (e.g., from individual to group counseling) or a change in a service provider (a newly assigned counselor). Informed consent is complicated with children, whose parents typically have the right to consent for them, and for those who are deemed not competent to sign a consent form (persons who are profoundly intellectually disabled or have dementia). This chapter, therefore, places the concept in the perspective of the mental health professional practicing in specialty settings or practices.

Koocher and Daniel (2012) outlined the differences among the terms "consent," "permission," and "assent." The term consent, as defined previously, implies that the individual making the decision to participate in services is fully informed, and thereby, the term consent implies "informed consent." **Proxy consent, according to Koocher and Daniel, occurs when someone is not capable of consenting either mentally or legally, as described earlier; a third party (e.g., a parent in the case of a child client) is given permission legally to consent for the client.** In cases of proxy consent, "assent becomes critical" (Koocher & Daniel, 2012, p. 5). **Assent** implies that **the therapist has sought the co-operation of the client, but does not replace the legal role of consent.** Establishing a collaborative and co-operative relationship through assent is ideal, and it is possible that a client unable to give consent, may refuse to assent to services. A refusal to assent to services does not trump legally established informed consent, and services would still need to be initiated by the counselor to at least try to establish a working relationship. It is always best, however, when clients assent to treatment that it is permitted by someone legally able to consent for the client.

The intent of informed consent procedures is that clients should be provided with the information they need to make informed choices about their own counseling process and rehabilitation plan. Even in forensic practice (where there is a legal issue) when no counseling service is offered or is to be offered beyond evaluation, clients or evaluees have the right to know how their participation will affect outcomes. The three elements of informed consent necessary to exercise autonomy through informed choice are: (a) **capacity (the mental ability to use information to make rational judgments)**, (b) **comprehension (the ability to understand the provided information in all forms—written and oral)**, and (c) **voluntariness (the willingness of the individual to act without the undue influence of others)**.

## CLINICAL MENTAL HEALTH

In an actual case, the children of a young woman (diagnosed with a reading disorder, depression, and borderline intelligence) were taken away when she unwittingly signed a form presented to her by a family services agency caseworker. The caseworker had full knowledge of the person's limitations and inability to read and did not inform the woman of the contents of the form fully, even when the woman asked for an explanation. The children later were returned after much legal maneuvering, when it was learned that the client signed a paper she could not read and that was not thoroughly explained to her.

Mental health counselors must be sure that their clients have the capability to consent to treatment. Handelsman, Kemper, Kesson-Craig, McLain, and Johnsrud (1986) found that the readability of consent forms for therapy was difficult—equivalent to an academically oriented periodical. At this level, few clients of even average intelligence can understand a consent document fully. Clients who are emotionally disabled may not be in a state of mind to fully comprehend their rights related to accepting or refusing treatment. Handelsman (2001) outlined general "themes" for "accurate and effective informed consent," and his work provides an excellent context for understanding the process approach to informed consent. He stated, "Think of informed consent as a process rather than an event" (p. 457). In other words, informed consent occurs not only at the onset of counseling, but regularly throughout counseling, especially as new information and new situations arise, which may require disclosure to and acceptance by the client. A process view of informed consent is welcomed, especially with clients whose capability is in question.

The mental health professional codes of ethics give guidance on this issue of informed consent. Further, the consent of a legally authorized person is sought for those who are legally incapable of giving informed consent; yet it is a standard that the incapable person is still consulted and informed of the actions to be taken by the therapist, and that person's "assent" is still sought (see the American Psychological Association [APA] ethics code, 3.10)—assent as described in the preceding implies agreement. The American Mental Health Counselors Association (AMHCA) *Code of Ethics* (AMHCA, 2010) states that "When a client is a minor or is unable to give informed consent mental health counselors act in the client's best interest" (Principle I.B.2.c). These guidelines generally relate to individuals diagnosed as intellectually disabled, organically impaired, or seriously emotionally disturbed. It also applies to individuals under adult age (children/minors) as defined in the legal jurisdiction of practice.

Although there are few legal cases that address mental health practice (Pomerantz, 2012), the case of *Osheroff v. Chestnut Lodge* (1985) provides an example of the importance of informed consent where patients are hospitalized for mental health treatments. Pomerantz (2012) described the importance of this case. A physician was treated at a clinic that did not provide needed medication management of his mental symptoms. The patient was not given adequate information or a choice to participate in the clinic's nonpharmaceutical treatments. When he changed to another institution and was medicated appropriately, he recovered "within a few weeks" (p. 315) and was able to resume his medical practice. As the parties in *Osheroff* settled out of court, the matter did not set legal precedent; however, "it certainly drew attention to the importance of informed consent to psychotherapy" (Pomerantz, 2012, p. 315).

## HEALTH AND REHABILITATION

Rehabilitation counseling has a long-standing philosophical and political tradition that endorses the ideal of the client participating as an equal partner with the counselor in the counseling process. A keystone right in this movement is the normalization principle—the right of persons with disabilities to have access to informed choices. **Normalization** is a rehabilitation principle that **dictates that people with disabilities "should be treated in a manner that allows them to participate both symbolically and actually in roles and lifestyles that are 'normal' for a person of their age and culture"** (Greenspan & Love, 1995, p. 75). This tradition of client participation has become institutionalized in rehabilitation treatment settings in diverse ways, including the powerful accreditation standards for rehabilitation programs such as the Commission on Accreditation of Rehabilitation Facilities (CARF) and the Joint Commission on Accreditation of Healthcare Organizations (JCAHO).

Historically, this point of view is one of the values that distinguishes rehabilitation service from the medical treatment model. It received resounding affirmation through the passage of the Rehabilitation Act of 1973, which emphasized consumer involvement of the client in the state–federal vocational rehabilitation process in a number of its provisions. The most striking example of this focus was the mandated involvement in the rehabilitation services planning process through the completion of an Individual Written Rehabilitation Program (IWRP; Rubin & Roessler, 2015). The Rehabilitation Act Amendments of 1998 elaborated on the concept of informed choice by stating: "Individuals . . . must be active participants in their own rehabilitation programs, including making meaningful and informed choices about the selection of their vocational goals, objectives, and services" (Section 100[a][3][c]). In this plan and its contemporary version—the Individualized Plan for Employment (IPE)—the plan is codeveloped by counselor and client, written, and reviewed periodically by both as part of the ongoing evaluation of the services plan. The required elements of the plan are (a) a statement of the long-term goals for the client and intermediate steps related to it, (b) a statement of the particular rehabilitation services to be provided, (c) the methods to be used in determining whether the intermediate objectives or the long-term goals are being attained, and (d) information from the client regarding how the client was involved in choosing from among alternative goals (Rubin & Roessler, 2015).

It is important that the rehabilitation counselor consider informed consent as an aspect of the rehabilitation counseling process—a collaborative rehabilitation process—rather than just an opportunity for the client to independently decide. This process may involve some preparatory counseling, skill teaching, or motivation-enhancing techniques. Due to their disabilities, some clients may not have had a chance to develop decision-making skills; or they may have a limited base of life experiences or other cognitive or psychological limitations. In a study of counselors' perceptions of barriers to informed choice, participants identified the four most prominent barriers to choice as: (a) unrealistic consumer vocational goals; (b) consumers requesting more services than are necessary to achieve suitable employment; (c) the consumers' desire for the most expensive services rather than reasonable cost/professionally recommended services; and (d) finding ways to balance the expectations of consumers with reality (Patterson, Patrick, & Parker, 2000).

While rehabilitation philosophy clearly is in support of full informed consent and inclusion, it is a significant ethical challenge to rehabilitation counselors to fulfill the actual intent, rather than just the letter, of these guidelines. The determination of when a client is legally or ethically competent to provide informed consent is a critical consideration for rehabilitation counselors. If a client is a minor, but is psychosocially and cognitively mature, has a traumatic brain injury, or appears to be under the influence of a drug, the counselor must think carefully about whether assent is possible, or whether other measures are needed. The counselor still needs to involve a parent or guardian, and should wait until the client is in a better position to provide assent, unless the treatment constitutes a medical or psychological emergency. A **legal guardian is a person who is appointed by the court to make decisions regarding an individual's personal matters or**

**property.** This concept presumes the client is incompetent to make these decisions (Remley & Herlihy, 2014). Haffey (1989) and Stebnicki (1997) provided guidance on the assessment of clinical competency for rehabilitation interventions. Haffey differentiated the legal from the clinicoethical issues involved; Stebnicki utilized a functional assessment approach for determining mental capacity.

Rehabilitation clients may have a legal guardian who has been court appointed to make decisions for them if they have been found to be legally incompetent to do this for themselves. There are a number of ways in which the legal requirements of achieving this consent can be reconciled with the ethical responsibility of respectfully allowing clients to participate in the decision as fully as their abilities allow (Stebnicki, 1997). Therefore, while clients with legal guardians may not be able to provide legal consent to a decision, ethically they should have the opportunity to assent to it. Often clients can be educated about this process over time. If clients undergo involuntary commitment or have guardianship instituted on their behalf, the code of ethics for rehabilitation counselors directs the counselor to take such action only after careful deliberation and to advocate for resumption of client autonomy as quickly as possible (Commission on Rehabilitation Counselor Certification [CRCC], 2010).

## COUPLE AND FAMILY THERAPY

Related to informed consent, there are unique circumstances in couple and family counseling that require special consideration (Knauss & Knauss, 2012). In couple and family counseling it is accepted procedure to have all adult participants (or otherwise competent individuals) sign a statement of "consent to treatment" once treatment issues have been addressed. However, compromising situations exist. One or more competent parties in the family may refuse to sign the consent form; in such a case, family treatment with all family members present cannot proceed. For example, with a family of four with one adult child and one minor child, the parents and the adult child would be required to sign the consent form. If the adult child refused to sign, then that child would have the option of opting out of counseling, potentially at the expense of the family as a whole. In effect, the legal and ethical autonomy of the individual overrides that of the majority of the family members. One person's hesitance can lead to a decision to abandon certain types of relationship counseling. Counselors, therefore, should encourage and should seek the informed consent of all competent adult participants in couple and family counseling. They must honor, accordingly, the rights of any one individual to refuse to consent to treatment.

Family counselors should not be put in the position of strong-arming a client to consent when there is hesitance by one or more family members. It is recommended that family counselors, rather than trying to convince the hesitant party to sign the consent form, should allow the family members to convene in private to discuss the issues. The counselor essentially provides the family members with the information and forms, and then exits the room to allow the family members to discuss the issues. Any pressure to sign would then be confined to the dynamics of the family. The outcome (signature or no signature of the hesitant party) then becomes "grist" for the therapy "mill," meaning that the family consent issues become a potential focus of initial treatment. But the counselor should in no way be aggressive in seeking an individual's consent to treatment.

Both parties in couple counseling must consent to treatment. Generally, any one party may withdraw from counseling, and it is crucial for the counselor to address concerns in a way that will engage both parties. Typically, counselors maintain a **neutrality position,** meaning **they do not take sides on matters of couple disagreement.** Rather, they take a stance of **relationship advocacy** (Butler, Brimhall, & Harper, 2011; Margolin, 1982), which means **they see the partnership or marriage as the client, and they act to help the partners help themselves to improve interaction.** Regardless, if one partner decides he or she does not want to continue in treatment, relationship counseling must end, and the counselor then must decide if either or both require referral to individual counseling. It would be questionable ethics for a counselor to do individual counseling with both of the parties involved in failed couple counseling, as it would appear that the counselor could benefit by doubling a fee by failed conjoint counseling. The ethically wise counselor refers partners needing or requesting individual counseling to other providers to avoid the appearance of impropriety or questionable professional motives. It takes two to initiate couple counseling, but it only takes one to withdraw consent to end couple counseling.

## SCHOOL COUNSELING

Ethical standards stipulate that school counselors inform students about the purposes, goals, techniques, and rules of procedure for counseling in a written disclosure statement. The student should also be informed about the meaning and limits of confidentiality, privileged communication, authoritative restraints, and the possibility that the counselor may want to consult with other professionals. This explanation should occur at or before a counseling relationship begins. The Ethics Committee of American School Counselor Association (ASCA, 1999–2001) has also identified the critical necessity of informing clients of potential limitations of the counseling relationship.

Where students are not able to legally give consent to counseling, their assent should be sought. Obtaining assent from students helps to engage the client in the counseling process and to establish a rapport and a trusting, truthful relationship.

Muro and Kottman (1995) suggested that a written disclosure statement to clients makes the process of informed consent more concrete for students. The language should be simple and appropriate for schoolchildren.

Where required by law, parents must sign consent forms prior to initiation of counseling. In most states, the age of majority is 18, meaning that anyone under 18 must have parental or guardian consent. The issue of parental consent is a tricky issue, and it is one that school counselors should address with the school administration. One option, which has worked well in some school districts, is to have a district-wide counseling consent form provided at the time of school enrollment. The counseling consent form would be part of the enrollment packet that is presented to parents or guardians when the child is formally enrolled in the school district. Such consent forms could address the role of counseling in the educational enterprise—specifically requesting full consent for any ongoing counseling service that addresses educational needs or activities (such as advisement, classroom activities, test or classroom anxiety treatment, classroom behavior). Some school districts additionally (at the time of formal enrollment in the district) request permission to provide a certain number of personal counseling sessions (e.g., three sessions) to address any private or personal matters of the child. If additional counseling is needed beyond the agreed-upon number of sessions, further formal consent from the parent or guardian would be sought. This allows counselors to be sensitive to personal or private student matters, without proceeding on sensitive matters without the full informed consent of the parent or guardian. Regardless, students should know from the beginning of the counseling relationship that their parents or guardians have the right to information about what is communicated in counseling.

It is important to note that some states have what is called a **"mature minor" statute.** Such a statute **"gives minors, at ages 16 or 17, the right to receive therapeutic treatment without the consent of the parents in the areas of drug or alcohol abuse, birth control, sexually transmitted diseases, and some other specific areas"** (Bernstein & Hartsell, 2004, p. 158). Some states even grant such rights to children younger than 16. School counselors should acquaint themselves with current state laws on such matters, as they may be able to address such matters without parental consent.

# ADDICTIONS

## General Requirements

Informed consent with substance abuse clients is complicated by the fact that treatment services may be sought when a person is not in a condition or state to make an informed decision. Treatment services may be needed when an individual is under the direct or recent influence of drugs or alcohol or is suffering the consequences of addictive behavior. In those cases, the counselor must ensure that the potential client is competent to make a decision about beginning treatment. An objective method of assessing competence, such as a structured clinical interview, routine mental status exam, or breathalyzer test, provides the best protection for vulnerable clients (McCrady & Bux, 1999). Further, procedures to maximize the comprehension of consent documents should be considered. Once a client has been treated initially (especially if detoxified), it is incumbent upon the counselor to respect the client's right to further consent to treatment or to withdraw from treatment on his or her own accord.

## Mandated Treatment and Coercion

There are numerous referrals for addiction treatment that can be considered compulsory to a greater or lesser degree. Many states mandate treatment for traffic offenders identified as substance abusers. Judges may also order treatment for other offenders before making rulings about child custody or a criminal sentence. Addiction treatment may be mandated as part of a judicial sentence or condition of parole. In these situations, it must be understood that the client—no matter how the client is referred—still has the right to refuse treatment. It is not the counselor's responsibility to persuade clients sent for compulsory treatment that they must remain in treatment. It is appropriate to explore the alternatives and possible consequences if a client chooses not to participate or prematurely terminates counseling (ACA, 2014). In the case of uninitiated treatment, the counselor should simply report to the referral source that a potential client has not initiated treatment. If a potential client does not initiate treatment, the counselor has no ethical obligation and may report to referral sources the individual's failure to consent to treatment. Also, client consent should be required in order for the counselor to contact referral sources if a client decides later to withdraw from treatment; for example, the original consent to treatment form should have a statement that indicates the counselor has the right (permission) to contact referral sources should treatment be terminated by the client or when the client is noncompliant with counseling directives. In cases where a client ceases treatment or is not compliant with treatment, it is important for the counselor to have obtained consent when treatment began in order to release information about the client's attendance or compliance with mandated treatment.

## Addiction Treatment for Adolescents

Some states make provisions for minors to receive substance abuse treatment without the consent of parents or guardians (the mature minor statutes discussed in the section on School Counseling of this chapter). Most often, however, states require the consent of a parent or guardian before treatment can be initiated. In these cases, parents or guardians have the right to review assessment and treatment files. In cases in which minors do not have the right to consent to their own treatment or are not provided confidentiality protection by law, they should be informed from the outset of treatment that the information they provide is subject to review by parents or legal guardians. Informed consent in addiction treatment, then, has some special circumstances that require ethical sensitivity on the part of the counselor. As with all minors, client "assent" should be sought, subsequent to full disclosure and information on the limits of confidentiality.

## GROUP COUNSELING

In establishing groups, counselors must play a special role that extends beyond the informed consent of clients agreeing to group treatment. Of course, as with any type of counseling, clients have the right to consent to treatment or to refuse treatment. However, it is also true that an individual can be misplaced in a group that is not consistent with the client's interests or concerns. Obviously, the counselor is obligated ethically to screen clients (to make a judgment as to good client–group fit) for entry or exit from groups. Screening in or out of group ensures appropriate placement. Both the American Counseling Association (ACA) and

Association for Specialists in Group Work (ASGW) guidelines emphasize the importance of screening prospective group members. Corey, Williams, and Moline (1995) stated:

> The purpose of screening is twofold: (a) to determine if an individual is compatible for a particular group and (b) for the person to determine if the group is compatible with his or her personal goals. If both the leader and the prospective member are in agreement with respect to the appropriateness of the group for the member, there is a basis for forming what is likely to become a working group. Proper screening and orientation can occur only if the group counselor is clear about the purpose of the group and is able to provide persons with adequate information prior to joining a group. (p. 164)

Methods of screening include individual interviewing, a group interview with prospective group members, an interview done by a team of leaders, or screening through written questionnaires. Care must be given to prevent a serious misplacement, such as putting a victim of sexual abuse in a group of sexual perpetrators, or placing an abstinent drug abuser in a group that abuses substances. Even more subtle misplacement may occur, and the counselor must be alert to the possible consequences of misplacement and must act to prevent problems by careful group assignment. When it is obvious that a misplacement has occurred, procedures should be in place to provide a formal means for an individual to terminate services in a way that is not harmful to any group participant. Termination procedures should be discussed with members of a group before a group begins. Members should know they may leave the group at any time, but there may be repercussions for premature withdrawal from the group (especially in cases of mandatory treatment). A "trial period" after which members can formally exit the group of their own volition is highly recommended. Certainly, clients should be informed of their obligation to alert the group leader and other group members of their concerns or intentions regarding group attendance.

Coercion is not acceptable; a client's rights have been breached if undue group pressure comes to bear on that client's decision to remain in or participate in group activities. Corey et al. (1995) stated: "Some degree of group pressure is inevitable, and it is even therapeutic in many instances. It is essential for group leaders to differentiate between 'destructive pressure' and 'therapeutic pressure.' People may need a certain degree of pressure to aid them in breaking through their usual forms of resistance" (p. 166). Aside from what can be considered "therapeutic pressure," counselors must protect clients from coercion, physical threats, undue pressure, and intimidation.

A counselor has an obligation to provide prospective members with enough information about the group so that they can make fully informed decisions about group attendance. This includes information about the counselor's credentials and background, procedures or rules of the group, the purpose of the group, counselor expectations regarding client behavior, and the rights, responsibilities, and risks of group membership (ASGW, 1998a). Knauss and Knauss (2012) also recommend that clients should be informed of standard termination procedures at the time of screening (before the client commits to treatment), so that there is no confusion about the reasons and procedures that occur at the termination process, whether initiated by the client or the counselor. For example, it is recommended that a client wishing to terminate group counseling should address the reasons with the group, so that there is clarity for the group. The loss of a group member may seriously impact the group (Knauss & Knauss, 2012), and ensuring a clearly understood and smooth process in such cases is a way to minimize negative consequences.

## CAREER

Career counselors may find themselves in situations wherein they are employed by a company to provide outplacement services for an employee who has been fired. If the fired employee has not been fully informed of the limits of confidentiality (e.g., if the employee tells the career counselor she stole money from the company), the counselor is not allowed to inform the employer of this illegal activity.

Career counselors who work in school settings may participate in the development of the Individual Education Plan (IEP) as part of the requirement of providing educational services to students with disabilities. Some clients may not have developed decision-making skills, or they may have a limited base of life experiences or other cognitive or psychological limitations. The determination of when a client is legally or ethically competent to provide informed consent is a critical consideration for career counselors and depends on the laws of the state.

If a client appears to be under the influence of a drug, the counselor must think carefully about whether informed consent is possible, or whether other measures are needed. The counselor might need to wait until the person is in a better position to provide consent.

Some clients may have a parent or legal guardian who must be involved in the informed consent process. Where required, the parent or legal guardian must always consent to services for the client. Assent, as in any case with a minor client or a client not competent to consent, is a demonstration of the counselor's loyalty to the client and communicates the need for agreement by the client to participate in the counseling process.

## CLINICAL SUPERVISION

It is essential that both clients and supervisees understand and agree to the procedures of counseling and supervision prior to these activities. Actively involving all parties throughout the decision-making processes or providing for informed consent throughout these processes enhances the likelihood of attaining successful and ethical outcomes for both the client and the counselor being supervised. Informed consent is not a one-time event; rather, it is a continuing concern that needs to be revisited throughout the counseling and supervision process. Bernard and Goodyear (2009) noted that the supervisor has three levels of responsibility:

> (1) The supervisor must determine that clients have been informed by the supervisee regarding the parameters of therapy; (2) the supervisor must also be sure that clients are aware of the parameters of supervision that will affect them; and (3) the supervisor must provide the supervisee with the opportunity for informed consent. (p. 53)

## Informed Consent With Clients

Counseling and supervision codes of ethics specify that counselors in training or in practice make every effort to ensure clients are aware of the services rendered and the qualifications of the person rendering those services. The supervisor must ensure that supervisees inform clients of their professional status. Supervisors need to ensure that supervisees inform their clients of any status other than being fully qualified for independent practice or licensed. For example, supervisees need to inform their clients if they are students, interns, trainees or, if the counselor is licensed with restrictions, then the nature of the licensure restrictions should be communicated (Association for Counselor Education and Supervision [ACES], 1993).

The types of services and the risks and benefits of counseling also need to be discussed. This discussion by the supervisee should include such specifics as the number and length of sessions, the cost for service, and the opportunity for telephone consultations. The type of services the client will be offered, preferred alternatives, and the risk of receiving no treatment should also be explained to ensure informed consent by the client; in other words, all pertinent information in ethical standard consent must be communicated even in cases where there is a third-party supervisor overseeing the counselor.

## Informed Consent Regarding Supervision

Supervisors should have supervisees inform their clients that they are being supervised and explain all the conditions of their supervision (ACA, 2014, Standard F.1c.). The client must be informed of the supervision procedures, whether sessions will be taped or observed, who will be involved, and how close the supervision will be. Clients should be informed of the limits of confidentiality. Client permission must be obtained before students and supervisees can use any information concerning the counseling relationship in the training process (ACA, 2014, Standard F.1.c.; F.5.c.).

Confidentiality should be fully explained as it applies to both the process of counseling and to supervision. This discussion must also include when confidentiality will be breached. Disney and Stephens (1994) noted, "Supervisees place themselves in a position to be sued for invasion of privacy and breach of it if they do not inform their clients that they will be discussing sessions with their supervisor" (p. 50). A written form to alert clients of the conditions of supervision is a strategy to avoid possible misunderstandings later.

## Informed Consent With Supervisee

Just as the supervisee has a responsibility to secure the client's informed consent, the supervisor is obligated to ensure that the supervisee understands and consents to the conditions of his or her supervision (ACA, 2014, Standard F.4.a.). Supervisees should enter the supervisory experience knowing the conditions that dictate their success or advancement. The responsibilities of both the supervisor and the supervisee should be clear. Supervisors should incorporate the principles of informed consent and participation with clarity of requirements, expectations, roles, and rules in the establishment of policies and procedures for their institutions, program, courses, and individual supervisory relationships. Mechanisms for due process appeal of individual supervisory actions should be established and made available to all supervisees. Supervisors should also inform supervisees of the goals, policies, theoretical orientations toward counseling, training, and supervision model or approach on which the supervision is based (ACES, 1993).

Whiston and Emerson (1989) stated all trainees entering a program should be cognizant that personal counseling may be recommended. Trainees should also be informed regarding the choice of supervisor, the form of supervision, the time allotted for supervision, the expectations of the supervisor, the theoretical orientation of the supervisor, and the type of documentation required for supervision. A written agreement can articulate a supervisory relationship in detail to avoid later misunderstandings. It serves to formalize the relationship, educate the supervisee regarding the nature of supervision, provide a model of how to approach informed consent with clients, and provide security for both parties by structuring the relationship (McCarthy et al., 1995).

## Issues of Due Process in Clinical Supervision

Supervisees have due process rights consistent with the laws in relevant states. These rights should be communicated to supervisees at the time they consent to supervision. Borders (2001) noted that supervisees must be afforded due process, ranging from timely feedback to opportunities for remediation to avenues to report dissatisfaction with supervision. To be ethically and legally sound, supervisors must employ a process that is neither arbitrary nor capricious (Disney & Stephens, 1994). The ACES guidelines are very clear on this issue. Supervisors should incorporate the principles of due process and appeal into the policies and procedures of their institutions, program, courses, and individual supervisory relationships. Mechanisms for due process appeal of individual supervisory actions should be established and made available to all supervisees (ACES, 1993).

The ACES guidelines further specify that supervisors of counselors should meet regularly in face-to-face sessions with their supervisees and provide supervisees with ongoing feedback on their performance. This feedback should take a variety of forms, both formal and informal, and should include verbal and written evaluations. It should be formative during the supervisory experience and summative at the conclusion of the experience. Supervisors should also establish and communicate to supervisees and field supervisors specific procedures regarding consultation, performance review, and evaluation of supervisees (ACES, 1993).

The ACA *Code of Ethics* (2014, Standard F.8.a.) addresses the issue of due process with regard to counselor education and training programs. It states that prior to admission, counselors should orient prospective students to the counselor education or training program's expectations, including but not limited to the following: (a) the values and ethical principles of the profession; (b) the type and level of skill and knowledge acquisition required for successful completion of the training; (c) technology requirements; (d) program training goals, objectives, and mission, and subject matter to be covered; (e) basis for evaluation; (f) training components that encourage self-growth or self-disclosure as part of the training process; (g) the type of supervision settings and requirements of the sites for required clinical field experiences; (h) student and supervisee evaluation and dismissal policies and procedures; and (i) up-to-date employment prospects for graduates (ACA, 2014, Standard F.8.a.). Counselor education and training programs should integrate academic study and supervised practice. Such programs also are required to clearly state to students and supervisees, in advance of training, the levels of competency expected, appraisal methods, and timing of evaluations for both didactic and experiential components. Supervisors are also required to provide students and supervisees with periodic performance evaluations.

Bridge and Bascue (1990) noted the importance of proper documentation of supervision. It is critical that supervisors document the periodic formative as well as the summative evaluations that provide direct feedback to supervisees. Specific competencies and behaviors that are not adequate with behavioral indicators of the target performance to be attained should be noted. The supervision records should be dated and signed. This information should be available to the supervisee so that sufficient time is provided to correct any deficiency. Established notification and grievance procedures should provide recourse for supervisees who are unsuccessful in this process. Evaluations of supervisee performance in universities and in applied counseling settings should be available to supervisees in ways consistent with the Family Rights and Privacy Act and the Buckley Amendment (ACES, 1993).

## FORENSIC PRACTICE

The matter of informed consent is a crucial matter in the forensic practice of counseling. **Forensics** relates to **the use of science or objective scientific methods to address legal issues or crimes.** Counselors may be involved in forensic issues in addressing such matters as a legal disability claim, child custody matters, competency of clients to stand trial or to understand their crimes, and other matters. A classic example would be the employment of a rehabilitation counselor to assess the work capacity of a client who is claiming a work-related injury and worker's compensation benefits. Lawyers representing either or both the client (plaintiff) or the worker's compensation insurance company (the defendant) might request a rehabilitation counselor to assess the client's capacity to work postinjury. The counselor might perform objective tests (e.g., intelligence, achievement, aptitude, or other skill-based tests) to assess the residual functional capacity of the injured party (typically known as the claimant or plaintiff). That objectified evidence would then be presented in a legal hearing. The counselor's opinion as to the work capability of the claimant might be requested, and possible jobs in the prevailing work environment might be identified. The findings of the rehabilitation counselor's evaluation and his or her opinion would be entered into the record. In such a case, the client (claimant) would have to be fully informed of the counselor's role, the nature and process of the evaluation, and what could be communicated in a legal hearing. The claimant has the right to consent to such an evaluation, unless of course it is court ordered, whereby the judge or hearing officer on the case is requiring such evaluation before a decision will be rendered. Typically, such evaluations are court ordered. Where consent is required or sought, the counselor must fully communicate the intent of the evaluation and that the counselor is acting only as an evaluator and is not, and will not, serve as a treating professional. It is possible that a client may consent to evaluation and the results of the evaluation may be used as a foundation for a decision that goes against the wishes of the client. It is not the counselor's role to take sides (or to be a "hired gun," meaning the counselor *always* testifies against either defendants or plaintiffs); rather the counselor's role is to be objective in assessment of the client on matters of law and then to communicate findings, and even opinions, based on objectified evidence.

This process would hold true of a charge against a person for a criminal act, where a counselor is asked to assess the mental status or mental capacity of a criminal. Sometimes, consent is not needed or sought, as in the case where "a person can be evaluated for competency to stand trial, pursuant to a court order, without informed consent" (Gottlieb & Coleman, 2012, p. 103). The counselor in this case could be asked to testify as to the client's mental state. Even in a case where consent is not needed, the mental health professional is wise to try to inform the client of the nature and intent of the evaluation from the outset (Gottlieb & Coleman, 2012). Where consent is needed, it should be fully informed consent, as the client (the defendant in this case) should know how the results of the evaluation could be used.

## CONCLUSION

This chapter has provided a summary of the ethical standard of informed consent across counseling specialties. Although informed consent is a general ethical obligation of counselors, specialty practice concerns do arise. Some of those concerns require the counselor to take specific actions to address consent beyond what is understood as simple client approval and agreement to partake in counseling services. The specialty practice of counseling is nuanced ethical practice, requiring counselors to be alert to, and educated about, issues that align with types of counseling practice.

# ROLES AND RELATIONSHIPS WITH CLIENTS

This chapter further delineates issues that arise in counseling specialty practice regarding roles and relationships with clients. Each counseling specialist faces challenging ethical circumstances. Boundary issues are described, and the ethical practice of boundary extension is explored.

## CLINICAL MENTAL HEALTH

The American Mental Health Counselors Association (AMHCA) *Code of Ethics* (2010) specifically states under Standard I.A.3 "Dual/Multiple Relationships" that "Mental health counselors make every effort to avoid dual/multiple relationships with clients that could impair professional judgment or increase the risk of harm. Examples of such relationships may include, but are not limited to: familial, social, financial, business, or close personal relationships with the clients" (Principle I.A.3). In Section I.A.4 under the same principle, the code states, "Romantic or sexual relationships with clients are strictly prohibited. Mental health counselors do not counsel persons with whom they have had a previous sexual relationship." Sexual intimacies with former clients are banned for 5 years subsequent to termination of services (Section I.A.4.b), and then only with professional scrutiny (for exploitation) of such relations as a qualifying factor.

As described in Chapter 6, the term "dual relationship" is unclear, and the term is not implicitly a negative term, as the standard implies. The AMHCA 2010 standard does not differentiate between professional and nonprofessional "dual" relationships, and they should be separated for clarity. The ban on sexual relationships with former clients for 5 years appears to be consistent with the American Counseling Association (ACA) *Code of Ethics* (2014) Standard A.5.c, and the provision for scrutiny of relationships initiated 5 years subsequent to treatment appears also to be aligned with the ACA standard. See Case Scenario 9.1 to evaluate a situation involving allegations of a sexual relationship with a client. The AMHCA standard gives no guidance for potentially beneficial interactions with clients outside of treatment, as does the new ACA (2014) *Code of Ethics* with its "Extending Counseling Boundaries" Standard A.6.b. Overall, there are some inconsistencies between the AMHCA ethics code and the new ACA ethics code. Those AMHCA members who are also members of ACA are bound by both codes, and application of a recognized ethical decision-making model might be beneficial in addressing dilemmas that require negotiation of the two ethics codes on the matter of roles and relationships with clients, which is directed by the AMHCA (2010) Code Section I.3.b.

## HEALTH AND REHABILITATION

Some types of relationships counselors may have with clients outside of the counselor–client relationship may be detrimental to the well-being of the client with a disability—even if clients are desirous of pursuing them. These extra-counseling relationships are based on a power differential and may risk impairing the objectivity of the rehabilitation counselor (see Chapter 6). Sexual intimacy is strictly prohibited with current clients by the rehabilitation counseling code of ethics because the potential for serious harm to the client in such relationships has been documented as very high. Like the ACA ethics code, the Commission on Rehabilitation Counselor Certification (CRCC) *Code of Professional Ethics for Rehabilitation Counselors* (2010) discourages sexual relationships with former clients. However, the CRCC code does allow the potential for such a relationship after a minimum of 5 years have passed, as does both the AMHCA (2010) and ACA (2014) codes. The CRCC code requires that the relationship occurs only after full examination of its implications and thorough documentation of the evaluation undertaken to ensure it is not exploitative in nature. The counselor is also directed to seek peer consultation prior to entering into the relationship.

In rehabilitation counseling, involvements routinely may be incorporated into vocational, independent living skill, or behavioral interventions that may result in additional tensions around the issue of counselor–client relationships. By necessity, many of these interventions take place in natural social, recreational, residential, or vocational settings. For example, social skills training

**CASE SCENARIO 9.1** Allegations of Sex With a Client

Your colleague, Mary, has been hospitalized quite suddenly to have surgery for a ruptured appendix. She was quite ill and on medical leave, so you were assigned to cover some of her cases. Two of her clients tell you that Mary has been having sexual relations with them. You do not question Mary's intentions because you know her to be a conscientious rehabilitation counselor. On Mary's return, you ask her about these charges, and she replies that she has had a "very close personal relationship" with these individuals. However, she states that it is not a problem because she has only provided these clients limited case management services and purchased some vocationally required adaptive equipment—she is not counseling them. She assures you that she will not continue the relationships because she realizes that other counselors who do not see clients with disabilities in as positive a light might misconstrue these relationships. What should you do?

Mary clearly has engaged in serious, unethical conduct. Sexual contact with current clients is always unethical and is even a felony for licensed professionals in some states. Her position that the ethical standard did not apply because she was not "really" counseling these individuals is seriously inappropriate. The code of ethics makes no such distinction and case management services are counseling services, delivered as one of a potential range of rehabilitation counseling services. You must immediately report Mary's behavior to your supervisor, who will take steps to evaluate the well-being of these two clients, take appropriate action against Mary, and ensure the safety of any future clients of the agency. Mary herself may have emotional or personal issues for which she might be evaluated and for which she might need help herself. This course of action will be difficult for you because of your friendship and because you do not like being cast in the role of a whistle-blower. However, it is essential that you act, or you yourself will be behaving in an unethical manner.

intentionally may simulate some behavioral elements of, but not the emotional content of, relationships such as friend or coworker. For a naive client or an emotionally needy counselor, the climate can create confusion about relationship boundaries. On the other hand, innovative and constructive intervention styles such as mentoring, coaching, and providing a personalized climate for successful achievement, such as that found in a job club, may be beneficial for many of the nontraditional, diverse clients needing vocational and life skills seen by these specialty counselors.

Some ethical relationship issues involve situations in which the rehabilitation counselor may have monetary, business, or personal interests with another party to the client's rehabilitation process. These other professionals may be such parties as attorneys, claims adjusters, or case managers involved in a long-term disability insurance case on which you are the client's rehabilitation counselor. These may be serious conflicts of interest affecting the rehabilitation counselor's judgment. Even if the rehabilitation counselor proceeds ethically, the appearance of such a conflict does exist and should be avoided. An example would be a counselor entering into a sexually intimate relationship with the plaintiff's

attorney in a client's workers' compensation case, or becoming a business partner of this person. Such conflicting relationships may be difficult to avoid since
it seems convenient and natural to hire experts and consultants who are familiar
and well known. However, caution should be taken to fully evaluate the potential for conflicts of interest and the appearance of conflict, even if no direct rehabilitation counseling services are provided.

## COUPLE AND FAMILY THERAPY

The historical issue of "dual" or "multiple" relationships (e.g., a counselor
and client establishing a relationship outside of counseling, whether sexual
or nonsexual) in couple and family counseling has aroused some debate in the
field (e.g., American Association for Marriage and Family Therapy [AAMFT],
1993; Ryder & Hepworth, 1990). The reason for the debate probably centers
on marriage and family counseling's underlying philosophical position that
relationships have great potential in the process of aiding others. Social systems theory posits that relationships are the primary cause of disturbance
in individuals and also can affect a positive change in observed behavior,
as defined within a specified cultural context. In effect, establishing healthy
relationships with clients is basic to the systemic-relational framework. The
question of potentially detrimental relationships, then, is an important one.
Certain relationships outside of the counseling relationship can be viewed as
very helpful to clients.

Obviously, certain types of relationships can be harmful. But should all relationships outside of counseling be considered harmful or potentially harmful? It
has been argued (Ryder & Hepworth, 1990; Tomm, 1993) that a closer examination of the issue is warranted because a blanket ban on relationships outside of
counseling may prevent the development of some healthy interactions between
a counselor and client. For example, Ryder and Hepworth (1990) suggested that
the AAMFT rule to avoid dual relationships (relationships in addition to the
initially contracted therapeutic relationship), which was expanded to nonsexual and apparently nonromantic relationships in 1988, was undesirable. They
argued that such a rule masked a complex issue that should be addressed by
students in marriage and family therapy. They took the position that it is more
important that dual relationship issues be viewed as complex, and they believed
the issues of exploitation and power were the crucial concerns. In effect, they
argued against a blanket ban on all dual relationships while arguing in favor of
a "serious emphasis" in training and supervision programs on the assessment
of complex relationship issues.

As a result of the Ryder and Hepworth (1990) article, and a response by Karl
Tomm (1993), a highly recognized marriage and family therapy theorist, a 1993
AAMFT conference plenary session was held on the topic, entitled "Dual Relationships: Sex, Power, and Exploitation" (AAMFT, 1993). The plenary allowed
for an airing of concerns in a forum where differences of opinion could be and
were expressed in a public way. Participants included Ingeborg Haug, Karl
Tomm, Linda Terry, and Katharine Wexler. Interestingly, several of the presenters described personal experiences in which they were in violation of the

proscription to avoid dual relationships. Tomm described situations wherein he was in violation of the code. He stated:

> When I reviewed the draft of the 1991 code, I realized I was in violation of dual relationship provisions in all three sections—clinical, teaching, and research areas. Clinically, I had colleagues who were in therapy with me—friends I had seen in therapy. In terms of teaching, there were some students and trainees who asked to see me in therapy. I did see them during some important crises they were going through. In the research area, I just completed writing a paper with a couple that I was seeing in therapy and whom I'm still seeing from time-to-time, and part of this paper was to distinguish the therapeutic moments of our work together—this was obviously a dual relationship.[1]

Tomm, after consulting colleagues and even the involved parties, came to the conclusion that he had done nothing harmful, and that perhaps the code proscriptions to avoid such relationships were in error. Likewise, Linda Terry described situations in which she was involved in friendship relationships with her clinical supervisor and a university trainee. She argued that those friendships brought about "desirable possibilities that would not have been happening without the multiple role relationships." She concluded: "Dual relationships can be growth enhancing at times." Katharine Wexler described several cases of accidental dual relationships—one that proved to be beneficial as described by a client. The presenters essentially provided case examples in which relationships other than the initial professional relationship proved to be harmless or even beneficial to the client/trainee.

There were some persuasive arguments made against a blanket ban on counselor–client or counselor–trainee relationships subsequent to the initial contracted relationship. Tomm made the case that exploitation was clearly the issue. He argued against a linear, causal view of dual relationships and in favor of exploration of "what it is, in fact, that does enhance the possibilities of exploitation and injuries." He proposed that the focus should be on generating "a greater sense of inner responsibility and respect," and how counselors can relate to "clients on the basis of that responsibility and respect." Linda Terry, focusing primarily on the circumstances faced by women and minorities, argued that "continuity and loyalty" in counselor–client relationships are critical, and she pointed out cases in which therapists must go out of their way to communicate these messages. She stated:

> Standards should define ethical responsibilities of therapists to manage interpersonal boundaries with respect for multi-contextual influences. Our system underpinnings describe that interpersonal boundaries are managed in terms of the balance of hierarchy and reciprocity, proximity and distance, stability and change, and interpersonal stage.

---

[1]Page numbers are unavailable for the 1993 AAMFT plenary—quotes were transcribed from an audiotape.

She essentially made the case for "culturally responsive care" and posed that dual or multiple roles in such circumstances should be viewed as positive.

On the other side of the argument, Ingeborg Haug, speaking as the chair of the AAMFT ethics committee, made a compelling presentation about problems of potentially detrimental relationships. She stated that "two-thirds of all complaints against our members alleged dual relationships in various forms including sexual." That is a staggering percentage. She argued that "multiple relationships give rise to multiple agendas." Further, she stated that therapists "naively fail to realize there are multiple realities and that our clients' perceptions and experiences can be very different from the therapists'." She described the road from nonsexual, dual relationships to sexual, dual relationships as a "slippery slope," and quoted statistics that showed that "a clear relationship between nonsexual and sexual dual relationships does exist."

The plenary presentations made it clear that counselor–client and counselor–trainee relationships subsequent to the initial contracted relationship are complex. Where there are multiple roles, there are multiple meanings. Some relationships can be entered with ideal intentions; others can be, or can evolve into, detrimental interactions. The question is, "How does a profession, based on a systemic-relational worldview, maximize the beneficial effects of counselor–client and counselor–trainee interactions without risking harm to clients or trainees?"

The issue of dual relationships, which can be viewed as straightforward by many, actually presents a dilemma for those who value relationships as elements in facilitating the emotional health of clients or the professional development of trainees.

The recent revision of the AAMFT *Code of Ethics* (2015) may have actually created less clarity, unfortunately (see Cottone's 2005 critique of the 2001 AAMFT code and its similar standards). Although the new code appropriately bans outright sexual intimacy with clients in a separate standard (Section 1.4), it opts for a statement that bans only multiple roles that "could impair professional judgment or increase the risk of exploitation" (Section 1.3). The new standard appears to put the burden on the client to prove that the counselor's intent was to exploit, or that the counselor was in some way impaired. The new AAMFT standard does not allow for potentially beneficial interactions or relationships with client where clear forethought and written documentation are involved and no harm is done to clients.

Related to training of marriage and family therapists on the issue of sexual attraction and the need to educate future therapists to be ethical in such a situation, Harris (2001) argued that "When it comes to sexual attraction we have a responsibility to educate about and even normalize the process of being attracted to another person. At the same time, we need to promote sound ethical, moral, and clinical practices" (p. 127). Indeed, a dialogue on this matter needs to be reinitiated within the ranks of couple and family counselors.

The Ethical Code for the International Association of Marriage and Family Counselors (IAMFC, Hendricks, Bradley, Southern, Oliver, & Birdsall, 2011) states (Section A.9) that "couple and family counselors avoid, whenever possible, multiple relationships such as business, social, or sexual contacts with any current clients or their family members. Couple and family counselors should refrain generally from non-professional relationships with former clients and their family members. . ." (p. 217). The standards go on to address the issue of harm and exploitation, reminding counselors of their responsibility to avoid exploitation of clients.

## SCHOOL COUNSELING

Whenever a counselor interacts with a client in more than one capacity, potentially detrimental relationships can occur (Fisher & Hennessy, 1994). The ethical standards of the American School Counselor Association (ASCA, 2010) state that counselors must avoid these relationships if possible. Further it states, "If a dual relationship is unavoidable, the school counselor is responsible for taking action to eliminate or reduce the potential for harm to the student through use of safeguards, which might include informed consent, consultation, supervision and documentation" (Standard A.4.a). Corey, Corey, and Callanan (1998) stated that in these situations, incompatible roles have the potential for drastically decreasing the effectiveness of the professional relationship. Potentially detrimental relationships to be avoided include counseling relatives, close friends, or associates. If a counselor finds it impossible to avoid conflicting relationships, he or she must be active in eliminating or reducing the potential for harm in those relationships by using the safeguards described in the standard.

Potentially detrimental relationships vary from those that are potentially very harmful to those with little potential for harm. Counselors in such a relationship are always obligated to reduce the potential for harm. Counselors need to monitor the relationship closely, gauging the benefits of counseling with the risks of impaired judgment or exploitation of the student client. Counselors should also continually evaluate the effectiveness of their counseling and refer the student to another counselor if possible (Froeschle & Crews, 2010). Counselors should seek consultation or supervision, use informed consent, and document carefully to reduce the potential for harm inherent in potentially detrimental relationships (Muro & Kottman, 1995). Sexual relationships with student clients are prohibited in the ethical standards of all mental health organizations and are illegal in many states (Kitchener & Harding, 1990).

In determining what action to take in ethical dilemmas presented by potentially harmful relationships, school counselors should follow these steps:

- Identify the primary client (the student in school).
- Identify the ethical issues or dilemma involved.
- Consult the necessary codes and experts.
- Think carefully before acting.

Using an ethical decision-making model presented in Chapter 4 may also help school counselors make responsible and ethical choices. Herlihy and Corey (2015) noted that the harm to clients is derived from the practitioner who exploits the relationship rather than from the duality itself.

## ADDICTIONS

As in other counseling areas, acting in roles outside the contracted initial treatment relationship with a client may be problematic, since the counselor often holds a substantial amount of power over the client. Some relationships are clearly inappropriate and harmful to clients. For instance, most ethical codes draw firm distinctions between sexual and nonsexual relationships. The ACA and The National Association for Alcoholism and Drug Abuse Counselors (NAADAC, 2012) ethical codes prohibit an addiction counselor from having a sexual relationship with a current client. The NAADAC code goes so far as to ban such relationships into perpetuity (a perpetuity rule) meaning members may never have a sexual relationship with a current or former client: "The addiction professional will not, under any circumstances, engage in sexual behavior with current or former clients" (Standard I.3.4). Most ethical codes and ethical standards contained in licensure statutes prohibit such contacts during active treatment and for up to 5 years after treatment has ceased. The ethical standards also mention other types of relationships, including friendship or social relations, business association, and supervision. As in other specialties, the passage of time may affect the ethical ramifications of entering or avoiding such a relationship (Doyle, 1997). In any case, counselors should not harm current or former clients in any of these relationships.

The unique relationship issues in addiction treatment are highlighted by the dilemmas faced by a professional counselor who is also in recovery from addiction. The ACA ethical standards offer general guidelines but do not include specific references to the potentially difficult situations faced by recovering counselors. Among the dilemmas the counselor will face include issues of confidentiality and anonymity, attending self-help groups with current or former clients, social relationships among self-help members, and employment issues (Doyle, 1997). Within 12-step groups, membership status is protected by **anonymity (clients participate without providing their identity)** as detailed in Tradition 12 of Alcoholics Anonymous (Alcoholics Anonymous, 1976): "Anonymity is the spiritual foundation of all our Traditions, ever reminding us to place principles over personalities" (p. 564). When a counselor acts as a client's therapist but is also a peer in a 12-step group, both the client's right to confidentiality and the counselor's anonymity are at risk. Legally, the counselor may not acknowledge in a 12-step group that a client is in treatment. A recovery counselor may see a client at a social gathering, be invited by a client to be a 12-step "sponsor," or feel unwilling to share personal information in a meeting where a client is present. At these times, the recovering counselor must recognize the treatment needs of the client, consider the counseling relationship, and be aware of his or her own recovery needs.

Although ethical guidelines do not speak directly to these issues, the ACA ethical code offers general information on counselor roles and relationships. The NAADAC code bars counselors from exploiting relationships with current or former clients for personal gain, including social and business relationships. The counselor can take certain steps to minimize the potential and the impact of these conflicts. Counselors should make use of clinical supervision and develop consulting relationships with professional peers. When possible, recovering counselors should take advantage of the wide range of self-help meetings and other recovery-oriented events so that the potential for dual relationships is minimized; in some communities, self-help groups are available specifically for addiction professionals (Doyle, 1997). In rural areas or with a particular population where nonprofessional roles are more difficult to avoid, treatment agencies may wish to inform clients about expectations for client–counselor interactions that occur outside of treatment (Chapman, 1997). The NAADAC *Code of Ethics* (Standard 3.7) states: "The addiction professional recognizes that there are situations in which dual relationships are difficult to avoid. Rural areas, small communities, and other situations necessitate discussion of the counseling relationship and [counselors] take steps to distinguish the counseling relationship from other interactions." So there is sensitivity to the unique circumstances that can arise in counseling individuals with addictions.

## GROUP COUNSELING

When it comes to roles and relationships with clients, group counseling presents some different ethical configurations, however. Although it would be unethical for a counselor to establish a romantic relationship with a group member, can group members establish romantic or other dual relationships among themselves? The counselor must discourage such activity. The Association for Specialists in Group Work (ASGW) "Best Practice Guidelines" (Thomas & Pender, 2008) require only that informed consent statements address "implications of out-of-group contact or involvement among members" (Section A.7.b.). Counselors should discourage outside relationships among group members because of their possible negative effects on the group process and possible negative personal outcomes. Obviously, if a member of a group is privy to outside information about another member or is intimately involved with another member, revelations of information that otherwise would be considered private may be made. There is also the potential for covert coalitions among members of a group, which could result in **scapegoating** another member—**a process wherein one member of a group is placed in an "odd person out" position or is treated by others as a deviant, thereby receiving negative messages from some other members of the group**. Scapegoating has been implicated in producing an unhealthy social context, or a two- (or more) against-one scenario (Clark, 2002; Hoffman, 1981). However, the activities of group members outside of the group cannot be enforced by a group leader, and certainly, a group leader cannot be held responsible for extra-group entanglements. In this regard, counselors can minimize risks by using a contract for treatment that addresses relationships and other issues. Corey et al. (1995) stated:

> One way to minimize psychological risks in groups is to use a contract in which leaders specify what their responsibilities are and members specify their commitment to the group by declaring what they are willing to do. If members and leaders operate under a contract that clarifies expectations, there is less chance for members to be exploited or damaged by a group experience. (p. 172)

There is great potential benefit through group treatment, but there are added risks.

Some authors (e.g., Brittain & Merriam, 1988) caution counselors against leading two related types of groups—for example, one group of clients and another group of "significant others" to the first group. A counselor should not lead a group of survivors of child sexual abuse and also lead a group of significant others to survivors of child sexual abuse. Running a group for victims and a second group for perpetrators may adversely affect the counselor, as personal value issues and personal "blind spots" may inadvertently affect the counseling process. In such cases, the objectivity of the counselor may be jeopardized (Brittain & Merriam, 1988). The ASGW Best Practice Guidelines 2007 Revisions (Thomas & Pender, 2008) Section A.3.a. states, in part, that "Group workers assess their values, beliefs and theoretical orientation and how these impact upon the group, particularly when working with a diverse and multicultural population" (pp. 112–113). Thus, in those instances when a group counselor does lead two related types of groups, the counselor must assess his or her values and beliefs, especially as such are influenced by the two groups.

## CAREER

Counselor roles and relationships with clients are an important and common area of concern for counselors working in all areas of the profession. Career counselors are no exception, and the National Career Development Association (NCDA, 2007) *Code of Ethics* prohibits engaging in potentially detrimental relationships. However, it does allow for potentially beneficial interactions with forethought and clear ethical constraints. Would it be unethical for a career counselor to attend a graduation ceremony for a client following career counseling? Of course not, so long as there are clear boundaries defined before the interaction to address any possible breaches of privacy or confidentiality.

The core issues that make some relationships so potentially dangerous to client and counselor are the power differential between the two parties and a potential loss of objectivity on the part of the counselor. The effects of such relationships may range from harmful to positive or no appreciable effect. However, due to the potential for harm, the counselor should avoid these overlapping roles whenever possible. The NCDA code (Section A.5.c.) strictly prohibits sexual intimacy with current clients because of the strong potential for serious harm to the client in such relationships.

Herlihy and Corey (2015) provided specific safeguards to assist counselors in any specialty practice in managing these potentially detrimental counselor–client relationships, including the following areas:

1. Setting boundaries: Beginning at the outset of the relationship healthy boundaries should be set, and the client should be involved in doing so although the ultimate responsibility to avoid a problematic dual relationship still rests with the professional.
2. Informed consent: The counselor should fully inform the client of all possible risks involved, the limitations of the relationships, and the safeguards in place; the recommendation is to include this information in professional disclosure statements of informed consent documents.

3. Ongoing discussions: The counselor should have periodic discussions with all the parties involved in the relationships to identify and work through any conflicts or concerns that develop.
4. Consultation: If the counselor does proceed with the potentially detrimental relationship, an ongoing consultation with a colleague should be in place so that all aspects of the situation will be evaluated to guard against overlooking a problem.
5. Supervision: If the situation involves a high risk for harm, more continuous supervision may be warranted.
6. Documentation: Counselors should document all aspects of the potentially detrimental relationship and issues that arise within the process, including the techniques used to manage the situation.

A major issue in career counseling concerns the emergence of issues that could be described loosely as contiguous professional or nonprofessional relationships—issues that involve conflicts of interest for the counselor. In these situations, counselors provide services that involve a group or team of professionals affiliated with the same client. If one team member has a monetary or business interest in a certain outcome for the client's case, such as an attorney in litigation or a managed care case manager paid through capitation, there may be potential for danger to the client if the counselor begins a noncollegial type of relationship with the first team member. If there is only a professional relationship between the counselor and the other professional, there is no unusual conflict for the counselor in protecting the client's interests. If, however, the counselor is the other professional's lover or business partner, there could be considerable negative pressure exerted on the counselor. Even the appearance of such undue influence is ethically troublesome. Because career counselors pursue various private practice options, the possibilities for business and personal concerns creating multiple and conflicting loyalties are an increasing danger. Consultants and vocational experts are often well known to the hiring organization or professional. This increases the potential for conflicts of interest. Counselors must evaluate such circumstances carefully before entering into or continuing a professional service relationship (Newman, 1993), even if they do not provide direct counseling services. For example, a career counselor is invited to a former client's graduation party. According to the NCDA (2007) *Code of Ethics*, such attendance would be allowed. Career counselors must apply an appropriate decision-making process when confronted with such ambiguous ethical situations.

## CLINICAL SUPERVISION

Supervision is complicated when supervisors have potentially detrimental roles with their supervisees. These relationships occur when counselors or supervisors take on two or more roles, either professional or personal, simultaneously or sequentially with each other or with the clients served (Herlihy & Corey, 2015). These relationships may be intimate, therapeutic, and/or social in nature. Examples of such relationships include, but are not limited to, familial, social, financial, business, therapeutic, or close personal relationships with clients or supervisees. Borders (2001) noted that potentially detrimental relationships may be a particularly challenging area in supervision because there is a high probability that many supervisors and supervisees will have such relationships. Bernard and Goodyear (2009) noted that these relationships between supervisors and supervisees have proven to be a difficult issue to resolve, as evidenced by much debate in the literature. Such relationships should be anticipated and, when they occur, handled with care (Herlihy & Corey, 1997).

All relevant ethical codes for counseling professionals make some reference to potentially uncomfortable or harmful relationships between supervisors and supervisees. The factors that make such a relationship unethical are: (a) the likelihood that it will impair the supervisor's judgment and (b) the risk of exploitation to the supervisee (Gottlieb, Robinson, & Younggren, 2007; Hall, 1988). The primary risk factor is a power differential; misuse of this power is exploitive and could cause harm. Kitchener and Harding (1990) identified two additional factors that create the risk of harm: (a) incompatible expectations of the counselor or supervisor in different roles and (b) incompatible responsibilities of the counselor or supervisor. Whatever the rationale, it is the consensus of the profession that all potentially detrimental relationships should be avoided if at all possible.

The Association for Counselor Education and Supervision (ACES, 2011) "Best Practices in Clinical Supervision" guidelines provide guidance beyond that of the ACA (2014) *Code of Ethics*. Supervisors who have multiple roles (e.g., teacher, clinical supervisor, administrative supervisor) with supervisees should minimize potential conflicts. Supervisors should convey carefully the expectations and responsibilities associated with each supervisory role. Stoltenberg and McNeill (2010) noted that the supervisor needs to "be alert to possible inappropriate relationships between supervisees and their patients or clients" and "to avoid multiple relationships in supervisory assignments" (p. 226). Specifically, when a potentially detrimental relationship cannot be avoided, counselors and supervisors should take appropriate professional precautions such as informed consent, consultation, supervision, and documentation to ensure that judgment is not impaired and that no exploitation occurs (ACA, 2014).

Bernard and Goodyear (2009) provided a detailed review of potentially detrimental relationship issues related to supervisee–supervisor. The following is drawn from their discussion.

*Sexual Attraction.* Ellis and Douce (1994) identified sexual attraction between the supervisee–supervisor "as one of eight recurring issues in supervision." Ladany, Hill, Corbett, and Nutt (1996) found counselor-client and supervisor-supervisee attractions "among the topics that trainees were unwilling to disclose in supervision" (Bernard & Goodyear, 2009, p. 61). This topic needs to be discussed openly, ethically, and viewed as a relatively normal part of supervision and therapy.

*Sexual Harassment.* "Unlike sexual attraction, sexual harassment is an aberration of the supervision process" (Bernard & Goodyear, 2009, p. 61). It is never acceptable to put the supervisor's own needs and wants in the foreground to the detriment of the professional development needs of the supervisee (Peterson, 1993). The ACA code clearly states that counselors and supervisors do not engage in sexual relationships with students or supervisees and do not subject them to sexual harassment.

*Hidden Consensual Sexual Relationship.* Brodsky (1980) asserted "when one person in a relationship has a position of power over the other, there is no true consent for the acceptance of a personal relationship" (p. 516). Bartell and Rubin (1990) advised "sexual involvement may further a human relationship, but it does so at the expense of the professional relationship" (p. 446). Supervisors should not participate in any form of sexual contact with supervisees nor engage in any form of social contact or interaction that would compromise the supervisor–supervisee relationship.

*Nonsexual Relationships.* "Goodyear and Sinnett (1984) argued that it is inevitable that supervisors and their supervisees will have multiple relationships" (Bernard & Goodyear, 2009, p. 62). Supervisors should not establish a therapeutic relationship as a substitute for supervision. Personal issues should be addressed in supervision only in terms of the impact of these issues on clients and on professional functioning. If students or supervisees request counseling, supervisors or counselor educators should provide them with acceptable referrals. Supervisors or counselor educators should not serve as a counselor to students or supervisees over whom they hold administrative, teaching, or evaluative roles (ACA, 2014, Standard F.6.c.). In addition to personal counseling provided by another professional, a supervisor may recommend participation in activities such as personal growth groups when it has been determined that a supervisee has deficits in the areas of self-understanding and problem resolution that impede his or her professional functioning. Again, supervisors should not be the direct provider of these activities for the supervisee.

*Strategy to Resolve Potentially Detrimental Relationships.* Bernard and Goodyear (1998) proposed the following strategy when a potentially detrimental relationship emerges within the context of supervision: (a) The supervisee should get a new supervisor in a manner that will not negatively affect clients being served or the professional growth of the trainee. If it is not possible to replace the supervisor, an additional supervisor should be involved to monitor the supervisory relationship. (b) If it is not possible to remove the supervisor, both the supervisor and the supervisee should document their work together with audio/video examples of the supervisee's work to enable a second opinion. The topics covered in supervision should be recorded; the supervisor should request consultation with colleagues; and if group supervision is used, personal relationships should be made known to the group.

*Harmful Relationships Exist on a Continuum.* Peterson (1993) cautioned that these "multiple relationship challenges abound in supervisory relationships and cannot be regulated out of existence" (Bernard & Goodyear, 2009, p. 63). The ACA *Code of Ethics* states that counselors must clearly define and maintain ethical, professional, and social relationship boundaries with their students and supervisees. Boundaries in this relationship must be carefully managed because supervisors have considerable power in the relationship (Case Scenario 9.2).

**CASE SCENARIO 9.2** Establishing Boundaries
in Doctoral Education

Brett, a doctoral student in counselor education, is on a graduate student volleyball team
with Jim, a master's student. When Brett sees the list of master's students to supervise,
he immediately asks to supervise Jim, without mentioning the volleyball team. Their
outside activity is not private, so is there any problem with Brett's decision? What are
the ethical issues?

This relationship may not cause any issues for Brett or for Jim. At the same time, because
there was a choice of supervisees, Brett should not have asked to supervise Jim
because of their ongoing athletic team relationship. It is difficult to know a priori what
type of potentially detrimental relationship can become problematic. Furthermore, this
could also be seen as a violation of Jim's informed consent rights in that he was not
consulted before the choice was made.

## FORENSIC PRACTICE

If a counselor becomes involved in a potentially harmful interaction with a client,
the counseling supervisor will likely become involved, if not professionally then
legally. A breach of ethics by a student or supervisee reflects on the supervisor,
and the supervisor may be legally liable for the actions of those under supervision.

Counselors are unlikely to be in a position of supervising other counselors in
specialized forensic practices. More likely, counselor supervisors may be asked
to address a legal concern or to guide a supervisee in courtroom or legal hearing
testimony. Whenever an unlicensed professional under supervision is called to be
a witness, it is most likely that the supervisor will be called instead or in addition
to the unlicensed professional providing services. This may also be true of counseling students, where academic or site supervisors may be required to appear
in a legal hearing on a legal matter. Regardless, counselor supervisors must be
prepared to address legal issues that arise in counseling practice, and when necessary, they may be called to officially address legal concerns in a legal context.

Forensic practitioners must make their roles with clients very clear. Is the role
evaluative or rehabilitative? Is the relationship to be contained by the number of
contacts or circumscribed by some other matter (a court date)? Regardless, it is
wise that the forensic practitioner should have no contact with the client outside
the parameters defined by the formal forensic relationship. To meet with a client
outside circumscribed roles may compromise the forensic practice relationship.
In other words, any boundary extension is potentially problematic in forensic
practice.

## CONCLUSION

This chapter addressed roles and relationships with clients. The matter is complex, as not all roles and relationships with clients are damaging or potentially
problematic. Counselors must show, in any specialty, forethought and ethical
judgment when extending boundaries with clients.

# PROFESSIONAL RESPONSIBILITY

## OBJECTIVES

- To provide a discussion of the ethical standard of "responsibility" across specialties of counseling practice.
- To define the specific professional responsibilities that align with counseling specialties and the obligations of counselors and psychotherapists as they practice within specialties.

As was defined in Chapter 6, professional responsibility, as an ethical standard, relates to the primary obligation of the counselor or psychotherapist. Codes of ethics in the mental health professions clearly agree on the responsibility of the mental health professional to align with the best interests of clients being served—the client receiving counseling or psychotherapy services. This means that the person actually receiving services, the client, is the principal focus of responsibility. However, the concept of professional responsibility gets blurry at times when counseling specialties are addressed. Who is the client in couple counseling? Who is the client when there is a third-party payer? Who is the client when a third party hires a counselor to evaluate a client on some set of criteria, as in forensic practice? These questions will be addressed in this chapter, where the responsibility of counselors is explored across the specialties of mental health practice.

## CLINICAL MENTAL HEALTH COUNSELING

The American Mental Health Counselors Association (AMHCA, 2010) *Code of Ethics* states that the "primary responsibility of mental health counselors is to respect client dignity and promote client welfare" (Principle I.A.1.a).

Professional obligation should always start with the client. This is especially true for the mental health counselor, who may be working with individuals who are vulnerable to the whims of others or to agencies involved in the client's treatment. What should a mental health counselor do if a request for additional services is denied by a managed care organization, when such a denial is to the detriment of the patient or even endangers the patient or other parties? Obviously, the mental health counselor's primary obligation is to the patient. The counselor should make an effort to inform the managed care organization that actions to deny services may, in fact, endanger the client or others and/or it may be to the detriment of a patient. The counselor should inform the managed care organization in an appropriate and professional manner, and, if necessary, provide and seek written documentation of correspondence with the managed care organization. It is imperative that counselors not accede to the insurance company's decisions when serious issues of client survival or welfare are imminent. If unsuccessful in appealing what may appear to be an unwise decision to discontinue treatment by an insurer (managed or not), the counselor must consider treating the client **pro bono publico—for the public good (without a fee or for a minimal fee)**. Standard I.E.2.c of the AMHCA (2010) *Code of Ethics* states: "Mental health counselors contribute to society by providing pro bono services." And the ACA *Code of Ethics* (Section A, Introduction) recognizes such work as an aspirational guideline. Regardless, the counselor must be prepared to take the appeal to higher authorities if it is believed that a client has been treated unjustly.

Mental health counselors must never confuse their primary responsibility to patients with secondary obligations to paying parties or employers. Counselors are working to benefit individuals with mental health conditions, and counselors must never lose sight of their obligation to the person receiving services even when there are pressures from third-party payers or employers. With employers, counselors have an ethical obligation to educate administrators as to the counselor's primary responsibility to clients.

## HEALTH AND REHABILITATION

The *Code of Professional Ethics for Rehabilitation Counselors* (Commission on Rehabilitation Counselor Certification [CRCC], 2010) clearly asserts that the primary responsibility of the counselor is to the client. The code defines clients as "individuals with, or directly affected by, a disability, functional limitation(s), or medical condition and who receive services from rehabilitation counselors. . . . In all instances, the primary obligation of rehabilitation counselors is to promote the welfare of their clients" (CRCC, 2010, Section A.1.a). It is clear rehabilitation counselors have secondary responsibilities to other parties. For example, rehabilitation counselors are told to recognize that families are usually important to clients' rehabilitation and to enlist the understanding of family members and their positive involvement in rehabilitation, with client permission of course when necessary. Another relationship that is acknowledged is the rehabilitation counselor's need to place clients "in available positions that are consistent with the interest, culture, and the welfare of clients and/or employers" (CRCC, 2010, Standard A.1.c.).

It would seem that the imperative need in contemporary rehabilitation counseling is to acknowledge the important moral theme of interdependence as the true human condition rather than the traditional and excessive U.S. emphasis on individualism and independence (Gatens-Robinson & Tarvydas, 1992). This view of interdependence is also more respectful of multiculturally diverse client groups who have a more collectivist worldview emphasizing central importance of family members in ethical decision making (Garcia, Cartwright, Winston, & Borzuchowska, 2003), for example.

Rehabilitation counseling has a long history of practicing primarily within agency or institutional settings. This fact is embodied by standards that enjoin counselors to respect the rights and responsibilities that they owe to their employing agencies and the need to try to resolve disputes with them through constructive, internal processes. However, they also have the responsibility to alert the employer to conditions that may be disruptive to their professional practice or limit their effectiveness (CRCC, 2010, Standard E.1.b; E.1.c).

There has been substantial documentation on disability in the sociological, political science, and anthropological literatures that people with disabilities are often denied basic human rights. Even well-meaning individuals and institutions inadvertently deny these individuals equal opportunities for participation and inclusion. For that well-recognized reason, the rehabilitation counseling *Code of Professional Ethics* contains a section (Section C: Advocacy and Accessibility) on the obligation of counselors to advocate on behalf of their clients and other people with disabilities, and to assist in ensuring accessibility of facilities and services. This provision is unique among professional codes of ethics and has become an important aspect of the definition for this specialty. It requires the rehabilitation counselor to "address attitudinal barriers, including stereotyping and discrimination, toward individuals with disabilities. They increase their own awareness and sensitivity to such individuals with disabilities" (CRCC, 2010, Section C.1.a.). The section goes on to detail the many facets of this advocacy role. The concept is laudatory and was updated at revision of the code from an emphasis on only advocating for clients, to emphasizing the need to encouraging people with disabilities to advocate for themselves through providing appropriate information and supporting their efforts at self-advocacy (Standard C.1.b.). This standard acknowledges the leadership and primary role of people with disabilities in advocating for their own interests, and the responsibilities of rehabilitation counselors to assist and to teach self-advocacy skills as needed (Waldmann & Blackwell, 2010).

While the need to work for the best interests of the rehabilitation client is clear, the exact nature of the balance to be struck between the ethical principles of autonomy and beneficence in actual rehabilitation practice situations is not determined so easily. This tension centers on the temptation of paternalism, which originated within the tradition of medical practice in the treatment of acute problems. This tendency toward paternalism is difficult to resolve. It originated in the observations of caregivers that clients, at some early points in their adjustment to disability, might not be able to discern what they might want or need at some later point in their recovery, when they are better equipped emotionally to make stable judgments regarding their needs and wishes. Unfortunately, the beneficence of the caregiver—wishing to influence the process for the good of the client through controlling information and decision making—clashes with the client's right to autonomous ability to exercise self-discretion on such matters (Gatens-Robinson & Tarvydas, 1992; Purtilo, Jensen, & Brasic Royeen, 2005). Greenspan and Love (1995) provided a perspective on this issue:

> In disability services, the perception has been that a majority of persons with disabilities (particularly those with cognitive limitations) have sufficiently limited access to autonomy as to justify the substituted decision making of weak paternalism. The reality, however, is that the vast majority of people with disabilities (including cognitive limitations) do have access to autonomy (sometimes with assistance, but more often not). This fact suggests that much of the weak paternalism that is perceived as ethically permissible is, in reality, a form of strong paternalism that should be considered much less acceptable than it is. (p. 80)

The importance of work as a meaningful human activity is a central value shared by both career and rehabilitation counselors (typically in a broad discussion of work values). New employment and workforce development initiatives by the federal and state government provide a number of ethical challenges to rehabilitation counselors that are not dissimilar to other challenges faced throughout the years of the profession's evolution. Positive legislative reform driven by changes in disability policy has sought to remove barriers to work for people receiving Social Security Disability Insurance (SSDI) and Supplemental Security Income (SSI) programs through the work incentive policies and in programs that are workforce investments. New pressures have been placed on the abilities of rehabilitation counselors to respond to their primary responsibilities to their own clients while at the same time honoring their responsibility to the welfare of their agencies and the need to serve new populations of clients. Counselors struggle to adapt to new service models and methods that are difficult to reconcile with a primary responsibility to clients, and many issues are far from resolved and await the process of experience-based refinements of policies and procedures. Such periods of change are stressful for counselors, clients, and all agency personnel.

## COUPLE AND FAMILY THERAPY

The issue of responsibility to clients, which seems uncomplicated when only one client is being seen in individual treatment, becomes a concern when more than one person is in the counselor's office. Margolin (1982) stated:

The dilemma with multiple clients is that in some situations an intervention that serves one person's best interests may be counter-therapeutic to another. Indeed, the very reason that families tend to seek therapy is because they have conflicting goals and interests. (p. 789)

Couple and family counselors are in a unique counseling circumstance in which competing interests may enter into therapeutic decision making, if, in fact, the individuals in treatment are viewed as clients to be served. Fortunately, systemic-relational theory (Cottone, 2012b) provides guidance in supporting the contention that the system of relationships is the focus of treatment. This theoretical focus allows the therapist the flexibility to define the system itself, or the relationship of significance, as the target of treatment. Allegiance, therefore, can be given to the system or the relationships. Margolin described this as relationship advocacy. She stated, "The family therapist then becomes an advocate of the family system and avoids becoming an agent of any one family member" (p. 789). Of course, there are circumstances in which advocating for the system or relationships must be abandoned, such as in cases of child abuse or neglect, or situations in which one party is endangered by the threats or actions of another member in the family. In such situations, relationship advocacy must be abandoned to protect the endangered party (Margolin, 1982). For the vast majority of cases, however, relationship advocacy is a legitimate position. Counselors simply define the couple or the family as the unit to which they are responsible and focus their activities on doing what is right for the relationship or the family as a whole. Relationship advocacy is one option of the couple and family counselor that is not available to counselors who provide individual treatment. It is a difference of ethical significance that is theoretically and practically unique to systemic-relational practice.

## SCHOOL COUNSELING

The difficulties of ethical practice often emerge when school counselors try to balance the responsibilities to students with those to parents or guardians. Counselors must determine how to maintain confidentiality for a student and provide information to parents. The American School Counselor Association (ASCA) Ethical Standards for School Counselors (2010) Standard B.1.a. states: "Professional school counselors: Respect the rights and responsibilities of parents/guardians for their children and endeavor to establish, as appropriate, a collaborative relationship with parents/guardians to facilitate students' maximum development." School counselors also "inform parents of the nature of counseling services provided in the school setting" (Section B.1.d.).

In some cases, counselors need a clear understanding of the meaning of custody and the legal issues that affect noncustodial parents and their access to information about their children. Wilcoxon and Magnuson (1999) presented definitions and other considerations for school counselors serving noncustodial parents. For example, these authors encourage school counselors to assist schools in developing guidelines that promote family involvement rather than focusing only on the custodial parent. They recommend that school counselors anticipate difficulties caused by the marital decree and design policies and procedures that are not only sensitive to the family but also prevent difficulties in the school setting.

Balancing the responsibilities to students and to parents presents counselors with ethical dilemmas that often have to be decided case by case. School counselors "have a primary obligation to the students, who are to be treated with dignity and respect as unique individuals" (Section A.1.a). Consultation with another counselor and supervision may be helpful in making those decisions to involve other individuals in any decision process. Welfel (1998) noted that parents are often reassured when they learn that counselors have no intention of working beyond the limits of their competence, that counselors will make reasonable efforts to honor the parents' requests, and that counselors will be respectful of family values. She suggested a brochure or handbook to distribute this information. The ASCA code asks school counselors to "consider the involvement of support networks valued by the individual students" (Standard A.1.f). Stromberg et al. (1993 [as cited in Corey, Corey, Callanan, 1998]) stated the general rule is that a parent is entitled to general information from the counselor about the child's progress in counseling. School counselors may satisfy parents' requests for information with short updates on the child's progress. Corey, Corey, Corey, and Callanan (2014) recognized that school counselors must be discreet in the kind and extent of information revealed to parents or guardians, but they also recognize the responsibility counselors have to parents and other school personnel: "To the degree possible, school counselors aim to establish collaborative relationships with parents and school personnel" (p. 211).

School counselors have an obligation to "establish and maintain professional relationships with colleagues and professional associates" (ASCA, 2010, Standard C), as well as having a responsibility to students and parents/guardians. Those relationships help maximize the potential of the school counseling program. School counselors must carefully define the parameters of their professional roles and responsibilities by informing colleagues about guidelines regarding confidentiality, public and private information, and consultation. Freeman (2000) suggested that ethical counselors maintain open communication lines and provide school personnel with information they need to provide services to students. That exchange of information occurs within the framework of confidentiality and privileged communication guidelines.

Counselors should also be active in co-operating and collaborating with community agencies, organizations, and individuals in the best interests of students and, therefore, establish a network to be used in referring students and their families. Section D of the code addresses responsibilities to school, communities, and families. When school counselors do refer students to other professionals, counselors must provide information that is accurate, objective, and concise in order to assist. Muro and Kottman (1995) suggested providing at least three referral sources. If a counselee is being seen by another mental health professional, the school counselor should ask the counselee and parents where necessary for permission to talk to the other professional. The school counselor and mental health professional should develop agreements to prevent confusion and conflict for the counselee.

School counselors have obligations to the school program and to the community as well as to faculty, staff, and administration.

Huey (1986) stated, "Counselors should adhere to local school policies, whether determined by the principal or the board of education, to the extent possible without compromising their primary responsibility to the client" (p. 321). When conflicts exist between loyalty to the student client and to the employer, Huey suggested a resolution that protects the rights of the student. Counselors may actively try to change existing policies that cause the conflicts.

The dilemma of parents' rights in educational control is an ongoing controversy. Parents may continue to challenge the content and activities of school counseling programs. Kaplan (1997) reviewed the current status of parents' rights and listed ways for counselors to prevent and to respond to parental concerns. Kaplan (1996) also suggested that bringing parents into the program might prevent problems as well as heighten their sensitivity. Including parents on an advisory committee would be one way school counselors could provide an opportunity for this involvement.

School counselors also have obligations to themselves (Standard E: Responsibilities to Self) and to their ability to accomplish their duties, including operating within the boundaries of their individual professional competence and being aware of their personal strengths and limitations. Counselors who monitor their own psychological health, participate in continuing education, and stay current with literature in the profession maintain competence in the school counseling setting. Carroll, Schneider, and Wesley (1985) identified formal education, professional training, and supervised experience as the criteria that define competence.

Varhely and Cowles (1991) discussed the counselor's responsibility to engage in self-examination continually. These authors outlined a process for this self-scrutiny. The first step is recognizing that one's personal beliefs, values, and needs may bias behavior in ways that are beyond one's consciousness. As counselors increase their awareness of the impact of their personal worldviews, their thoughtful, ongoing exploration of self is the next step. These two processes lead the counselor to become more aware of cues that may imply a conflict between personal issues and professional responsibilities. By constantly examining their own values, counselors become sensitive to whether they are unconsciously influencing students.

School counselors should monitor their personal performance and effectiveness, always avoiding any inadequacy in professional services or any potential harm to students. Counselors must be aware of their own biases and personal characteristics and their potential effects on students. School counselors must have specific training to ensure they provide appropriate and effective services to people who have differences related to age, gender, race, religion, sexual orientation, and socioeconomic and ethnic backgrounds. Hobson and Kanitz (1996) considered multicultural counseling as an ethical issue for school counselors and challenged school counselors to assess their level of multicultural competence and seek training opportunities to overcome any deficiencies.

School counselors have obligations to the profession that include maintaining professionally appropriate conduct, participating in advancing knowledge in the field of counseling, and belonging to professional organizations. School counselors should not use their position to recruit or to gain clients or to receive personal gains. The ASCA standards emphasize that school counselors must abide by ethical standards of the profession as well as other official policy statements and relevant legal mandates.

## ADDICTIONS

The responsibility of addiction counselors is first and foremost to their clients. The National Association for Alcoholism and Drug Abuse Counselors (NAADAC) *Code of Ethics* (2012) states: "It is the responsibility of the addiction professional to safeguard the integrity of the counseling relationship and to ensure that the client is provided with services that are most beneficial" (Section I: The Counseling Relationship). Clients hold the highest priority in terms of the actions of the counselor. In addition, counselors are obligated to their employers and their profession.

A counselor may face conflicting or multiple responsibilities, for instance, when clients are mandated to treatment through the legal system. In such a situation, the counselor must address the counseling needs of the clients, maintain confidentiality, and also communicate appropriately with legal representatives, who have a vested interest in a client's progress. If there is a conflict between a counselor's responsibility to a client and to a third party (such as an employer), the counselor must act to rectify the conflict. The NAADAC code states that addiction professionals will "attempt to resolve ethical dilemmas with direct and open communication among all parties involved and seek supervision and/or consultation as appropriate" (Standard VIII). In the end, the counselor should take actions in accordance with a client's welfare (Standard I.1).

A client's welfare is a responsibility of the treating counselor. Counselors must do their best to serve their clients, recognizing that services may not provide the intended purpose. If a counselor recognizes that his or her client is not benefiting from services, it is the counselor's responsibility to cease treatment and, if necessary, to refer the client to appropriate services provided by other professionals or in other treatment contexts.

Even in cases of family treatment, if an individual with addiction problems is the identified patient and has sought treatment primarily for the addiction, the counselor must advocate for the individual with the addiction. The counselor should not compromise the client's treatment progress even with the intent of serving the larger system of relationships in the family. If treatment is undertaken primarily as a means of assisting in the recovery of the addicted individual, that individual's welfare is the focus of counselor responsibility.

## GROUP COUNSELING

The Association for Specialists in Group Work (ASGW) Best Practice Guidelines (Thomas & Pender, 2008) basically defer to the ACA (2014) *Code of Ethics* on matters of professional responsibility. Group leaders have a dual responsibility to individual members of the group and to the group itself. The responsibility to the group does not supersede responsibility to individual members of the group. For example, if a counselor recognizes that one member of a group is being scapegoated and believes that the client's continued participation in the group could be detrimental to his or her mental health, the counselor is obligated to protect the individual participant, even if it means that the group membership and process might be negatively affected. Counselors should be equitable in their treatment to all members, and they are directed by the ACA code to protect the welfare of their clients. Implicit in such directives is recognition that when there are conflicts between the needs of the group and the needs of an individual member who is potentially traumatized by the group, the counselor must protect the individual. The group counselor should not abdicate his responsibility for the group, but must clearly take action to protect the scapegoated or targeted individual (ACA, 2014, A.9.b.).

The counselor's responsibility to the individual group member is critical when the force of the group can have negative consequences. Glass (1998) said:

> Recognizing that powerful forces are generated in groups, and that the leader has only partial control over what occurs, the group therapist faces a complex set of responsibilities. Not only must he or she act ethically, but moreover also create an ethical climate in the group. Some leaders may respond to this challenge by becoming overly controlling and authoritarian in an attempt to insure that the group functions in an appropriate fashion. Unfortunately this undermines the very element which is the group's strength, namely, its collective influence for therapeutic benefit. Conversely, the laissez faire leader who simply encourages the group to "do its own thing" without guidance or direction may be courting disaster. Such leaders often are reluctant to interfere with the functioning of the group out of a belief that groups are inherently wise, offer only good advice, and bring to bear pressures on their members that are ultimately for the individual's own good. Such a leadership approach often results in chaos, where the group never gels into an effective entity, or in harming members through coercive patterns that may emerge in the group. (pp. 99–100)

A group leader must be watchful of serious, personal challenges to a group member that may have detrimental effects (Glass, 1998). Leader responsibility and the ability to intervene at critical moments of potential harm are important aspects of group facilitation.

Sometimes groups are led by more than one therapist, which also adds a complicating element to such practice. Haeseler (1992) stated: "The complex transference/countertransference issues in a group can give rise to jealous and aggressive feelings between cotherapists. Such problems, if unresolved, can hinder the therapeutic effectiveness of the group and create an ethical dilemma" (p. 4). The responsibility to the group supersedes any issues between cotherapists, and it is the responsibility of the cotherapist to be alert to potential conflicts and to address those conflicts in a way that does not negatively affect the group process.

## CASE SCENARIO 10.1    Equalizing Group Interactions

A client in a group has been excessively verbal during group sessions, and has monopolized much of the group sessions. It has become increasingly obvious, as communicated by the nonverbal behavior of other group members, that the client's continual verbalizing interferes with the ability of the other clients to process information in the group and to respond in a way that addresses the concerns of others. Other clients often sigh, give "dirty looks" to other group members, or self-distract when the overtalkative member speaks. The counselor realizes that the benefits of the group are being jeopardized. The counselor speaks out in the group and tells the overtalkative client to hold his thoughts while others speak. The client acts perturbed, and the counselor confronts him in front of the group and expresses a feeling that the client's verbalizations are negatively affecting the other group members. The overtalkative client begins to tear up, but his behavior is not addressed by the counselor or other members of the group. His tears are never acknowledged by the group members.

Has the counselor addressed this concern appropriately?

NO. In such a situation, it is wise for the counselor to meet with the client individually to address the counselor's perceptions of the client's negative effect on the group process. If there are serious personal issues needing attention that cannot be addressed in the group context, the counselor may offer to refer the client for individual counseling. If the counselor can educate the client about the group process and group norms, and the client is willing to try to respond appropriately, then the client can benefit by the individual intervention of the counselor. Regardless, it is unwise for a counselor to confront a client in a group context who is in obvious need of individual counsel about group norms or group etiquette, especially during a time when the client is being scapegoated within the group context or when the client is in distress. In this case, the mental health needs of the individual client outweigh the counselor's responsibility to the group as a whole.

When a client ends affiliation with a group, the counselor should follow the formal "termination" procedures that were established and communicated before the client consented to group treatment. The counselor should make an appropriate referral so that the client can receive continued treatment, if necessary.

There are cases, however, in which the needs of the individual and the needs of the group are not in serious conflict yet still require attention. For example, if a group member in a cancer support group raises concerns over disciplining a misbehaving child, the group leader must weigh the needs of the individual against the needs of the group. To focus on the issue of a misbehaving child, which may be tangential to the group purpose, would be a disservice to other group members. In such a case, the counselor would be wise to refer the member to an appropriate treatment source for the child-rearing concern. In this case, neither the individual client nor the group as a whole is placed in a position of lesser priority. Of course, the counselor must ensure that the focus of the group was clearly stated initially so that referral for such a concern does not seem out of the ordinary.

Ethical codes alone are not enough to ensure responsible group counselors. Kotter (1982) suggested self-monitoring related to personal responsibility as important to group leadership. Gregory and McConnell (1986) stated:

> The notion of equal treatment of all group members is often more myth than reality. Therapists like mere human beings are more attracted to some persons than others. Despite efforts to equalize interactions, therapists are prone to give more time, attention, and to be more responsive to group members whom they find personally reinforcing. (p. 60)

Counselors must recognize their own limits and ensure that they do not inadvertently scapegoat members of the group. Counselors, therefore, have a responsibility to self-monitor throughout the group process and to take appropriate corrective action if serious biases reveal themselves (Case Scenario 10.1).

## CAREER

The National Career Development Association (NCDA) *Code of Ethics* (2015) clearly asserts that the primary responsibility of the counselor is to the client. The code states: "The primary responsibility of career professionals is to respect the dignity and to promote the welfare of the individuals to whom they provide services" (Standard A.1.a.). It is clear, however, that there are secondary responsibilities to other parties in counseling. Career counseling has a long history of practicing primarily within agency or institutional settings. This fact is embodied by standards that enjoin career counselors to respect the rights and responsibilities they owe to their employing agencies and the need to try to resolve disputes with them through constructive, internal processes. NCDA elaborates about the nature of that obligation by stating:

> The acceptance of employment in an agency or institution implies that career professionals are in agreement with its general policies and principles. . . . When such policies are potentially disruptive or damaging to clients or may limit the effectiveness of services provided and change cannot be achieved, career professionals take appropriate further action. Such action may include referral to appropriate certification, accreditation, or state licensure organizations, or voluntary termination of employment. (NCDA, 2015, p. 12)

If the ethical values of the institution are in conflict with a career counselor's professional ethics, the career counselor must seriously consider resigning.

## CLINICAL SUPERVISION

In clinical supervision, the issue of professional responsibility is compounded by the triadic nature of the supervisor–supervisee–client relationship. The supervisor obviously has an obligation to the supervisee, who may be paying for supervision, is a student, or who may be a direct-line employee. The ACES (2011) "Best Practices in Clinical Supervision" document makes it clear, however, that "The supervisor understands that client welfare is his/her first and highest responsibility and acts accordingly" (Standard 7.C.). Supervisors must make judgments to assess the status and welfare of clients being served by a supervisee. If there is any question about the competency or ethical nature of services being provided by the supervisee, the supervisor must intervene and directly address or attempt to remedy any problems.

It may be that supervisees may understate their concerns about conflicts or difficulties with clients, as to minimize the repercussions for them as individuals under supervision. Supervisors must always be alert to not dismiss a trivial concern communicated by the supervisee, as those issues may become more problematic with the passage of time. Supervisors have the prerogative to meet with a client without the supervisee in cases where there is any question as to concerns related to the counselor's competency or ethical behavior.

There are times when counseling supervisees make mistakes that may be minor ethical breaches. In such cases, the supervisor must act to clarify the nature of the ethics breach and assess the consequences, if any. If an issue is correctable, then it should be corrected under the direction and guidance of the supervisor. If there is a major breach of ethics, the supervisor must act quickly and decisively to address the welfare of the client and to ensure no harm has been done.

## FORENSIC PRACTICE

The area of forensic practice poses some serious concerns related to professional responsibility. Forensic specialists may be evaluating a client for a specific legal purpose, and the forensic specialist has an obligation to provide an objective, scientifically based, and unbiased opinion about the status of the client being evaluated. In some cases, the findings of such an evaluation may act to impose additional punishments on a client or may in some way compromise a client's claim to disability or some other desired status (eligibility for some service). In some ways, the forensic practitioner is beholden to the nature of forensics first—the idea that scientific assessment and objectivity are the primary obligation of the practitioner. This obligation must be fully expressed to the client at the time services are contracted. Forensic practice is a major area of specialization for many rehabilitation counselors. Therefore, the rehabilitation counseling specialty has taken additional steps to clarify some of these ethical complexities in Section F, an extensive section on forensic and indirect services (CRCC, 2010). Among other matters, the code Preamble states that "Rehabilitation counselors do not have clients in a forensic setting. The subjects of the objective and unbiased evaluations are evaluees" (CRCC, 2010). The CRCC code further discusses issues of informed consent, dual roles, confidentiality, forensic competency, and conduct including business practices at some length. It must be clearly understood that the forensic practitioner is acting as an independent agent and is not obligated to act in a way that is biased toward the needs or desires of the client. This understanding must be clearly articulated and agreed to prior to the initiation of forensic services. In other words, in forensic practice, the obligation of the counselor is to the process and not to the person. This is a unique circumstance in mental health professional practice.

## CONCLUSION

This chapter has provided a summary of issues of professional responsibility across the counseling specialties. In most counseling specialties, loyalty always goes to the person receiving counseling services—the client or person with a disability or condition seeking treatment. However, there are circumstances where a counselor's responsibility is split across relationships—to employers, payers of services, agencies, school personnel, relatives or family members. Typically in cases of split loyalty, when there is conflict, the counselor is guided to side with the welfare or benefit of the client receiving services. In forensic practice, however, counselors may be primarily obligated to the process and not the person, and such an obligation or loyalty must be clearly defined, and agreed to, at the outset of service provision.

# COUNSELOR COMPETENCY

## OBJECTIVES

- To address the complicated issue of professional counselor competency across counseling specialties.
- To define the skills, knowledge, and training associated with the counseling specialties.

Counselors practicing counseling specialties should have specialized training, education, and supervision in the specialty. As was defined in Chapter 6, the issue of competency relates to: (a) the **scope of professional practice**, that is, **the extent and limits of certain types of professional activities by a counselor, typically defined in licensure statutes or by specialty designation boards;** and (b) the **quality of services** provided by the professional counselor, which is **the level of skill and the capacity of the counselor to provide a minimal level of safe and effective treatment.**

The scope of professional practice includes those areas in which the counselor has the requisite education, training, and experience. However, it does not necessarily exclude those areas in which the counselor does not wish to practice in simply because the counselor's personal values are at odds with the topic of discussion. For example, a highly experienced counselor may not refuse to counsel persons considering abortion simply because the counselor's values are against abortion. As discussed more fully in Chapter 3, this sort of competency requires that the counselor is competent in understanding the values of clients whose cultures differ from that of the counselor. While the American Counseling Association (ACA, 2014) *Code of Ethics* states that, "if counselors lack the competence to be of professional assistance to clients, they avoid entering or continuing counseling relationships" (Section A.11.a.), "Counselors must refrain from referring prospective and current clients based solely on the counselor's personally held values, attitudes, beliefs, and behaviors" (Section A.11.b.). Thus, counselors must be competent in understanding the values, as well as "the diverse cultural backgrounds of the clients they serve" (ACA, 2014, Section A.).

In counseling specialties, skills and practice limits vary. This chapter explores both the skills and limits of specialty practice in counseling and psychotherapy.

## CLINICAL MENTAL HEALTH

Counselor competence involves (a) the quality of the provided service and (b) the boundaries or scope of professional activity. The American Mental Health Counselors Association (AMHCA) *Code of Ethics* (AMHCA, 2010) provides a detailed section outlining the principle of "competence" (Section I.C.1). High standards are to be maintained, according to the code. The "competence" standard reads as follows: "The maintenance of high standards of professional competence is a responsibility shared by all mental health counselors in the best interests of the client, the public, and the profession" (Standard I.C.1.). Mental health counselors recognize the boundaries of their particular competencies and the limitation of their expertise (Standard I.C.1.a.). Mental health counselors "provide only those services and use only those techniques for which they are qualified by education, training or experience" (Standard I.C.1.b.). Mental health counselors "maintain knowledge of relevant scientific and professional information related to the services rendered, and [recognize] the need for on-going education" (Standard I.C.1.c.). Mental health counselors are also responsible to accurately represent their training and experience and to maintain high standards of conduct. Among other directives, they are also held responsible for continuing their education so that they are educated about changes in the field.

Consider the standard of "competence" in light of a news report by *CBS News* (2001) about two Colorado therapists who were convicted of "reckless child abuse resulting in death" of a 10-year-old client. The therapists were using a "rebirthing" technique to treat a "reactive attachment disorder." The client was bound in a sheet and told to fight her way out so that she could be "reborn" to her adoptive mother. *CBS News* (2001) stated, "The girl begged for air and screamed for mercy after she was bound head-to-toe in a flannel sheet during a discredited psychotherapy procedure called rebirthing." Further, the article stated, "the girl begged for air and screamed that she was dying only to have her pleas met with sarcasm from the therapists." She lost consciousness during the procedure and died the next day. The state of Colorado has now banned this sort of treatment. The two therapists were convicted and each was sentenced to 16 years in prison. Obviously, clients should not be physically endangered by a therapeutic technique. Counselors must ensure that the techniques they use have sound empirical and theoretical foundations (based on theory that has stood the test of refereed review in the best counseling journals). The procedure in the Colorado case was dangerous, and it also raised the issue of competency:

Was this procedure a sound technique and was application of this technique within the scope of the therapists' practice?

Use of new, untested, or controversial techniques is always unwise. It is best to delay use of untested techniques until research supports the technique. The use of "paradoxical technique" is a good example. In this procedure, the counselor directs a client to do something illogical, such as "prescribing the symptom," to produce a resistance reaction wherein the client resists being symptomatic. Sexton, Montgomery, Goff, and Nugent (1993) stated:

> The use of paradox is a complicated matter and the debate concerning its use is likely to continue. However, consideration of the ethical treatment and the legal issues associated with paradox can help guide the mental health counselor. For example, given the current status of the research, the current enthusiasm for paradoxical therapeutic procedures is not altogether justified. Although there is strong anecdotal evidence, and some controlled experimental evidence of treatment effectiveness, additional well-controlled research is needed to substantiate proponents' claims. At this time, it seems that results of empirical research most clearly support the use of paradox with sleep-onset insomnia and some anxiety disorders. The effects of paradox with other types of concerns, such as family problems, appear to be [sic] less clearly documented empirical support. Furthermore, there appears to be little knowledge of either possible inadvertent effects or of issues such as treatment acceptability. (pp. 271–272)

When counselors are put in the position of having to defend the choice of a professional technique or procedure, they are wise to have chosen techniques that are based on sound empirical or traditional theoretical grounds.

On more general issues related to the scope of professional practice, there are continual "turf battles" over the extent of services to be provided by counselors and other mental health providers. Such a battle raged in Ohio in 1996, when the state attorney general offered a legal opinion allowing licensed professional or clinical counselors to use the term psychological to "describe their work of testing and evaluating people for mental and emotional disorders" ("Ohio," 1996, p. 9). The opinion was opposed by the Ohio Board of Psychology and the Ohio Psychological and School Psychologist associations. In essence, counselors, by the opinion of the leading law enforcement agency of the state, were told they could use a term that had been associated historically only with the practice of psychology. Some viewed this opinion as a major challenge to psychology in Ohio. Typically, battles over scope of practice of mental health counselors involve the issues of testing, diagnosis, and the use of the term "psychotherapy." Counselors are required by licensure laws to practice within the limits of their defined competence and training and consistent with definitions of practice within licensure statutes.

Counselors must also know that they should not act in a way that pushes the limits of the defined scope of practice of their profession. For example, a counselor should not say to a client "You should take Saint John's wort [an herbal preparation] as an antidepressant—it's better and more natural than your prescribed antidepressant, which I wouldn't recommend you continue taking." Such a statement is dangerous on several counts. First, counselors are not trained as pharmacologists and herbal medicine prescription is not in the scope of practice of professional counseling. Second, telling someone to not take a prescribed medication is practicing medicine without a license. You must have a medical license to both prescribe and to discontinue medication. Third, certain herbal treatments may be unsafe as they are not necessarily regulated substances, so there are issues of purity and toxicity. So counselors, in general, should not mix their counseling practices with herbal medication prescription, massage or other touch-based therapies, or even sales of goods that do not directly relate to counseling practices. If sales of goods related to counseling practice are offered (meditation guides, relaxation tapes, books related to the treatment being provided, etc.), there must be a legal sales license in the jurisdiction where the sales take place, and the counselor should not exert undo pressure on clients to purchase such goods.

## HEALTH AND REHABILITATION

The work of rehabilitation counselors is extremely diverse, presenting counselors with many challenges to stay competent in the range of skills practiced, and add new skills in areas of evolving practice. It is an ethical requirement of rehabilitation counselors that they continuously monitor their levels of competency and practice only within the limits of their own individual scopes of practice. One new challenge to evaluating one's individual scope of practice is presented by the increasing involvement of rehabilitation counselors in psychiatric rehabilitation, mental health, and substance abuse counseling areas where diagnosis of mental disorders is a prominent responsibility (see Case Scenario 11.1). The *Code of Professional Ethics for Rehabilitation Counselors* (Commission on Rehabilitation Counselor Certification [CRCC], 2010) has a section that establishes ethical standards for rehabilitation counselors to provide "proper diagnosis of mental disorders" (Section G.3). In addition, extensive standards address evaluation, assessment, and interpretation of various tests and psychometric instruments.

For some rehabilitation counselors, the issue of adopting a medically based diagnostic paradigm has profound, troubling implications for the long-valued, "asset-focused," person before disability, nonstigmatizing rehabilitation model. The "asset-focused" model centered on functional assessment and not diagnosis of medical problems or pathologies as a basis for treatment. Other rehabilitation counselors do not find the task of reconciling a medical diagnostic framework as a background to functionally based treatment strategies to be problematic. The psychiatric rehabilitation model developed by Anthony, Cohen, Farkas, and Gagne (2002) is an example of such a model. The model builds from a medical rehabilitation model used with physical disabilities, and allows for medical diagnosis; yet, it emphasizes rehabilitation intervention using a behaviorally oriented, highly supportive, client-directed, and positive model. Recently, a Clinical Rehabilitation Counseling specialty accreditation through the affiliation agreement between the Council on Rehabilitation Education (CORE) and the Council for Accreditation of Counseling and Related Educational Programs (CACREP) has been added for rehabilitation counselor education programs.

## CASE SCENARIO 11.1  Can I Diagnose?

Sophie is a rehabilitation counselor who graduated 2 years ago from an excellent rehabilitation counselor education program that allowed her to specialize in psychiatric rehabilitation. Since graduation, she has been working in a psychiatric rehabilitation agency that provides a wide range of mental health and rehabilitation services for people with severe and long-term psychiatric disabilities; she finds it to be a fine environment in which to practice. Recently, the agency was purchased by a larger institution and Sophie was assigned to a new supervisor, Mike. Mike tells her that she will have to begin assessing and diagnosing the new clients who come to the agency, rather than referring clients out for evaluations to establish a diagnosis. The clients' records are reviewed once every 3 months by the consulting psychiatrist, but Sophie is very concerned that this cursory review will not provide sufficient oversight to her fledgling diagnostic attempts. She is worried that this might be unethical, and is also concerned about rumors that indicate those who are not "on board" with the new requirements will be fired. Is it unethical for Sophie to begin doing diagnostic evaluations?

PROBABLY. Given the limited information provided, Sophie is not likely to be capable of independently determining psychiatric diagnoses. She may, however, have a reasonable start in learning this skill. The CRCC (2010) *Code of Ethics* does allow for properly prepared individuals to do so with proper care. However, the difficulty is determining what is proper preparation in this area—very little consensus exists. First, counselors need to determine if mental health counselors are licensed in their particular state and the basic requirements for that license, and then actually work toward achieving those requirements. Generally, in addition to a strong basic preparation as a counselor, such credentials require specific courses in psychopathology and specialized assessment, and diagnosis and treatment planning at a minimum. Beyond that coursework, supervised practice under a properly credentialed, experienced diagnostician is critical. In most states, that is the equivalent of at least 2, if not 3, years of supervised practice. Obviously, supervised practice in diagnostics with diverse types of client conditions is essential. Sophie should contact the state licensure board to gather this basic information and form a professional development plan in consultation with Mike, her supervisor, to permit her to gain this expertise in an appropriate manner. Sophie is delighted to discover that she had the required courses during her master's education, but lacks the supervised experience needed for licensure and to do diagnoses. Mike may be willing to provide her with some access to proper supervision, but states that the agency cannot afford to provide the extensive supervision required. Sophie agrees to contract with a consulting supervisor, an appropriately credentialed psychologist, who is acceptable to her and to the agency to provide the remaining necessary supervision hours. Mike agrees to allow Sophie to see this supervisor on agency time. While Sophie will have to pay this consultant and ensure that her clients give proper release of information for this consultation, she thinks this investment is well worthwhile to allow her to grow in her professional skills and to learn how to properly assess and diagnose her clients. If some type of satisfactory arrangement had not been reached, and Sophie had still been pressured to diagnose her new clients, she would have to have considered leaving that position in the agency, or even leave the agency altogether.

These curriculum standards may further support the development of clinical diagnostic capabilities for rehabilitation counselors. Case Scenario 11.1 focuses on the question of when a rehabilitation counselor is competent to provide a diagnosis.

The professional development plan of individual rehabilitation counselors wishing to gain or to increase diagnostic competencies must carefully address the ethical and complete preparation through such added experiences as coursework, continuing education workshops, and expertly supervised practice.

The 2010 ethics code for rehabilitation counselors also emphasizes standards for evaluation, assessment, and interpretation of various psychometric instruments. Counselors should review and seek to conform to these qualification requirements for any and all tests they utilize in their practices. The CRCC (2010) *Code of Ethics* has specific and detailed requirements concerning the ethical obligations of its members in observing the competence standards for the use of these instruments and techniques. In addition, rehabilitation counselors must be knowledgeable of guidelines for the use and release of test data and be aware of relevant federal and state statutes and rules and regulations that relate to release of test data (Blackwell, Autry, & Guglielmo, 2001).

## COUPLE AND FAMILY THERAPY

Given that the specialty of couple and family counseling is founded on a theoretical framework that is philosophically quite distinct from the foundations of individual psychotherapy (Cottone, 2012b), it is imperative that couple and family counselors have special training and supervision in systemic-relational treatment. Both the American Association for Marriage and Family Therapy (AAMFT) and the National Credentialing Academy for Certified Family Therapists have set standards for professional marriage and family counselors. The standards are specific in defining the need for a thorough understanding of relationship theory. The standards are also quite demanding regarding adequate supervision: Those who aspire to become specialists in couple and family counseling must obtain supervision under the direction of qualified supervisors. In fact, the AAMFT certifies individuals as "approved supervisors" for the oversight of clinicians in training. It is not enough for a counselor to receive a general counseling degree and then to begin seeing couples or families in practice; practitioners must complete adequate coursework or supervision specifically in couple or family counseling. A counselor providing couple or family counseling without adequate training and competence in this area is vulnerable ethically and legally. How could an untrained counselor defend himself or herself, for example, if sued subsequent to a couple's divorce for incompetent practice if the counselor had no training or supervised experience in marriage or couple counseling? Specialty designation as a trained specialist demonstrates the counselor's commitment to advanced specialty training, which will serve the counselor well if his or her competence is ever challenged.

Because procedures and techniques in couple and family counseling vary dramatically from procedures and techniques in individual counseling, practitioners should have more than a cursory understanding of specialty approaches.

There is a unique literature in the field of couple and family counseling that may be complementary to, or even incompatible with, good clinical practice in individual counseling. For example, a counselor who treats an individual might be trained to be empathic and acknowledging of the client's perspective. A couple's counselor might be viewed as taking sides if the counselor is overly empathic or acknowledging of one person's perspective, unless the counselor conveys an attitude of neutrality. Family counseling techniques are also designed to facilitate interaction between participants and require an active style of counseling to prevent the counselor from losing control of the process, which can occur easily when there are several active counseling participants. All in all, the practice of couple and family counseling is different to the degree that some practices of individual counseling do not easily or competently apply.

Competency also requires that counselors use up-to-date theory and technique. The practice of couple counseling is being affected significantly by the works of Gottman (e.g., Gottman, 1994), who has done well-controlled empirical research related to marriage success and failure. Some classic myths of marriage have been uncovered by his work. For example, for years it has been believed that similarity of opinions is beneficial to a marriage. Gottman's response is as follows:

> In my research, where I actually observed couples hashing out disagreements and then tracked them down years later to check on how stable their marriages were, I found that couples who initially had complaints about each other's attitudes were among the most stable marriages as the years went on. My research shows that much more important than having compatible views is how couples work out their differences. In fact, occasional discontent, especially during a marriage's early years, seems to be good for the union in the long run. (pp. 23–24)

Teaching couples in their early years to communicate in a way that prevents complaining may actually be counterproductive to the relationship; following Gottman's ideas, they need to learn to work through their differences, not to avoid them. Couple and family counselors, like all counselors, must ensure that they are current on the literature and applying valid theory and technique.

## SCHOOL COUNSELING

The American School Counselor Association (ASCA, 2010) "Ethical Standards for School Counselors" has a section that directly addresses "professional competence" (Section E.1.). The standard requires school counselors to "function within the boundaries of individual professional competence and accept responsibility for the consequences of their actions" (Standard E.1.a.). Further, it requires counselors to "monitor personal responsibility and recognize the high standard of care a professional in this critical position of trust must maintain on and off the job" (Standard E.1.c.). Thereby both the scope of practice of school counselors and the individual school counselor's capability to provide quality services are addressed.

While an ASCA (2015) position statement states that "although school counselors do not provide long-term mental health therapy in schools, they provide a comprehensive school counseling program designed to meet the developmental needs of all students" (p. 58). Accordingly, school counselors "provide school-based prevention and universal interventions and targeted interventions for students with mental health and behavioral health concerns" (p. 57) and "direct students and parents to school and/or community resources for additional assistance through referrals that treat mental health issues (suicidal ideation, violence, abuse and depression)" (p. 58). Thus, school counselors should have some level of competency in identifying and treating mental health issues that typically arise in their student population.

Another ASCA (2011) position statement states that school counselors must focus on activities to prevent bullying and harassment, though intervention strategies are important, as well. Thus, school counselors must ensure that they are competent to intervene when bullying occurs and to provide short-term counseling when such bullying affects the mental health of a student (and to help the student to find additional assistance if long-term treatment is necessary).

The "Ethical Standards for School Counselors" (ASCA, 2010) also directs counselors to monitor their emotional and physical health and to enhance their personal self-awareness and effectiveness. Counselors are required to "stay abreast" of current research on school counseling practice. They are encouraged to participate in self-development to ensure quality services. They must "maintain current membership in professional associations to ensure ethical and best practices" (Standard E.1.g.).

## ADDICTIONS

It is not enough for a counselor to receive a general or community counseling degree and then to practice primarily as an addiction counselor without receiving additional training and specialized supervision. The intricacies of addiction treatment, especially related to alcohol and drug effects, the process of addiction and recovery, specialized treatment approaches, and adjunctive involvement with 12-step or other self-help groups, require in-depth knowledge best gained through a combination of academic preparation, an internship or practicum focused on addiction competencies, and supervision under the direction of a counselor well versed in treating addictions. In the addiction field, core competencies have been established in screening, assessment, treatment planning, referral, service coordination, individual and group counseling, psychoeducation, and documentation (Center for Substance Abuse Treatment, 1998; National Association for Alcoholism and Drug Abuse Counselors [NAADAC], 2012).

Other aspects of counselor competence should be considered. Counselors should maintain effective working relationships with other professionals (including physicians, lawyers, judges, probation officers, and other mental health professionals) who are almost always involved in cases in which clients receive treatment for addictions. In this way, competence relates to the boundaries of professional practice: Counselors must be cautious not to overstep their professional bounds because other professionals have integral and important roles in the treatment of individuals with complex addictive disorders.

Given the potential for burnout among professionals who serve clients with addiction problems, counselors must be alert to their own limitations. If counselors recognize they are becoming impatient or uncompromising with clients, they should consider methods for professional rejuvenation, including the use of appropriate supervision, linkage to a professional organization, continuing education, or even a sabbatical from addiction treatment. This is especially true of counselors who are in recovery themselves. The counseling role should not be so stressful as to produce undue distress in the treating professional. This becomes a competency issue when the quality of services is compromised.

## GROUP COUNSELING

To reiterate, the ethical standard of competence relates to two issues: (a) the quality of provided services and (b) the boundaries or scope of professional activity. This text takes the position that individual counselors must be trained and appropriately credentialed (e.g., licensed) professionals—a somewhat controversial position in the area of group counseling. A number of self-help groups are led by peers, nonprofessionals, or paraprofessionals (individuals trained usually to the level of a bachelor's degree). Some of the best examples of these are 12-step groups such as Alcoholics Anonymous, Narcotics Anonymous, and Overeaters Anonymous, where peers lead themselves, and no mental health professional may be involved. Some facilities also have paraprofessionals (not a licensed mental health professional) leading groups; this is common in the field of rehabilitation wherein individuals with bachelor's degrees serve as group educators/counselors for individuals needing guidance on various psychosocial skills areas such as job procurement, social skills, money management, or grooming. It can be argued that there is no need to have a highly trained counselor directing such groups when nonprofessionals and paraprofessionals are able to provide quality services. However, such a response does not take into account issues of ethics other than the obligation to provide quality services. When a mental health professional is involved, the client is guaranteed some legal protection (depending on the laws and statutes in the legal jurisdiction). In states where there are licensure statutes with ethical standards, an unlicensed provider or paraprofessional does not afford the group member legal or professional confidentiality (or in some cases, privileged communication). Clients have no recourse if they suspect a breach of privacy or malpractice, unless they sue the agency that directs the nonlicensed provider. Having a professional lead a group is some protection to group members. Attending a group with a nonprofessional group leader puts clients at added risk if there is dissatisfaction with the group or the group leader. When clients seek any service for a fee, they are always wise to learn the credentials of the provider and to address protection or limits under the law.

Is licensure as a mental health professional an acceptable standard for group counseling practice? Licensure in and of itself is no guarantee that a counselor has been adequately trained and experienced in leading groups. Even though group counseling has been defined as a "mode of treatment" (not meeting other criteria for a specialty designation), group counseling still qualifies as a technically sophisticated mode of treatment requiring special training. General credentials are not enough to provide the group leader adequate background in group processes and ethical standards. This is the position of the Association for Specialists in Group Work (ASGW; Thomas & Pender, 2008). The ASGW standard is that group counselors are "mental health professionals who use a group modality as an intervention" (Thomas & Pender, 2008, p. 111). This position is consistent with the position of CACREP (2015), which requires accredited graduate programs in counseling to include training in "group work." CACREP (2015) requires study of group topics such as (a) group dynamics; (b) group leadership; (c) theories of group counseling; (d) methods of group counseling; (e) approaches used in such group types as task, psychoeducational, and therapy groups; (f) professional preparation standards for group leaders; and (g) ethical considerations. Additionally, the CACREP clinical training standards (e.g., practicum and internship training as part of the degree program) require development of individual counseling and group work skills under supervision. Subsequent to receipt of the degree, an ethical counselor who plans to provide group services must seek supervision of his or her group work activity.

## CAREER

Competence issues occur in the work of all counselors on an ongoing basis. Counselors must develop and practice an approach to quality control in their work that ensures quality and the safety of services they provide to their clients. Counselors must also work within the legal and ethical boundaries of their scopes of practice. Career counselors monitor competence in at least two specific areas of contemporary practice: (a) the integration of a mental health counseling or diagnostic focus with their usual practices and (b) competence around assessment services (Case Scenario 11.2).

The managed care treatment paradigm has grown tremendously through health care reform efforts and the forceful advocacy of the AMHCA for mental health specialization as the core clinical counseling specialization. Both of these forces require all counselors to reevaluate the role of diagnosis and clinical models of practice in their work.

The career counseling tradition is significant in that it is a counseling model that is highly focused on developmental counseling traditions and interventions. Thus, it is at odds with any model based on psychopathological interpretations. Niles and Pate (1989) described the distinction between career counseling and mental health counseling as artificial. They saw the fields as needing to be integrated because mental health and work concerns are inextricably linked in the human experiences brought to counseling. As a result of this reasoning, they made a case for examining how the competence and educational standards of both groups need to be enhanced. They viewed the lack of past career counseling competence standards (knowledge and skill) in standards related to

## CASE SCENARIO 11.2  The Case of Ms. Diagnosis

Shelby Diagnosis was the daughter of a prominent banker in a small town in the Midwest. She was referred by her family physician to Carerra Decisiones, MEd, LPC, MCC, for career counseling. Counselor Decisiones did a diagnostic interview with Ms. Diagnosis and reported to the family physician that Ms. Diagnosis was very "clinically depressed" and "had to be treated for that before career counseling would be effective." Ms. Diagnosis stated that she would only go to Counselor Decisiones for treatment of her depression. Counselor Decisiones has a degree that is regionally accredited by the Western Association of Schools and Colleges and CACREP in both community counseling and career counseling. Counselor Decisiones proceeded to treat Ms. Diagnosis for depression and, when those symptoms were under control, she commenced counseling for the career problems for which Ms. Diagnosis had originally been referred. Did Counselor Decisiones do anything that might be considered unethical?

NO. As a licensed professional counselor, Counselor Decisiones was operating well within her scope of practice. Her university and her program were also both appropriately accredited. It might appear as if the counselor had competence only in career counseling, but she has the appropriate training and licenses to address general mental health issues. Further, the fact that she graduated from a CACREP-accredited program means she met competencies in counseling individuals for personal concerns. Finally, assessment is also a core competency of all CACREP-accredited programs.

treatment of mental and emotional disorders as distressing. If adding diagnostic and treatment planning competencies will be required of career counselors in the future, this will occasion a redesign of training standards in the field to ensure that practitioners meet minimum levels of knowledge and skill in this complex area. Of course, individual practitioners may reach these levels of capability through their individualized programs of specialized professional experience and preparation.

The second area of specialized emphasis on counselor competence is assessment and testing. Career counselors spend substantial portions of their time in performing these functions. The use of various vocational assessment devices has been integral to the development of the trait and factor model of career counseling that is at the core of this specialized area. Assessment and testing are primary tools to gain information to be used by client and counselor alike in the career counseling processes (Hood & Johnson, 2007). As such, these tools have tremendous potential for both assistance and harm to clients. Hays (2013) explained tests and assessments:

> A test is a systematic and often standardized process for sampling and describing a behavior of interest for individuals or groups. . . . Tests are only one aspect of assessment. Assessment is a more comprehensive activity than testing by itself because it includes the integration and interpretation of test results and other evaluation methods. (p. 5)

Career counselors are often involved in using career assessment inventories with clients. Career counselors use inventories developed to measure career interest patterns, personality, values, career beliefs, work environment, aptitude, achievement, salience, career maturity, and career obstacles. Career counselors who have been trained to use such inventories for personnel selection must always ensure that the examinee's welfare, explicit prior understanding, and agreement determine who will receive the test results. Further, if such results are to be used in research and publication, each of the elements of informed consent must be met.

The issue of who has sufficient knowledge and training to administer the different types and levels of tests properly is a critical counselor competence issue. Tests vary greatly in the complexity of administration and interpretation required for appropriate usage. At one extreme are tests such as the individually administered intelligence tests, for example, the Wechsler intelligence tests. At the other extreme are simple tests of vocational skills, including typing or language skills such as spelling. Copious work has been done to develop competence standards for the qualifications required of test users and other standards for educational and psychological tests. These standards primarily have exerted an influence in controlling the qualifications of test users. Many of the major test distributors require a statement of qualifications by the purchasers of tests. This statement embodies qualifications developed by the Test User Qualifications Group in consultation with test developers (Hood & Johnson, 2007). The Test User Qualifications Group is composed of a number of professional associations, whose members perform assessment and testing services, including ACA and American Psychological Association (APA). Counselors should review and seek to conform to these qualification requirements for any and all tests that they utilize in their practices. The National Career Development Association (NCDA, 2015) *Code of Ethics* (Section E) has specific and detailed requirements concerning the ethical obligations of their members in observing the competence standards set for use of these instruments and techniques.

Controversies continue to rage around the attempts of psychology to restrict the ability of nonpsychologists to administer various testing instruments, and they demonstrate the tremendously important role of user competence standards. Several psychology boards have taken a variety of legal actions to restrict other helping professionals from using various tests. States where actions have been taken include California, Georgia, Indiana, Louisiana, and Ohio (Marino, 1996). In 2004, the governor of Indiana refused to approve new guidelines that restricted the use by nonpsychologists of hundreds of inventories, including several inventories used regularly by career counselors. Various concerned professional groups formed a coalition to develop strategies to deal with this threat to professional autonomy and scope of practice. The group, the Fair Access Coalition on Testing (FACT), is said to represent more than 500,000 professionals (Marino, 1996). The concerns of career counselors have been represented by the leaders of NCDA in the activities of FACT. While the issues may be resolved in the future, the importance of preserving this essential function of the counselor's role in practice is clear. Career counselors always have worked closely with vocational testing and other types of assessment. The ethical obligations of career counselors should be affirmed by all counselors as they work to preserve this aspect of their services to clients.

Career counseling has a broad area of practice and a diverse practitioner base, yet has clearly identified standards for what constitutes appropriate professional practice. NCDA, a division of ACA, is the organization most closely aligned with career counseling. NCDA has strongly promulgated training standards for the Master Career Counselor credential, a credential offered directly by the NCDA.

NCDA has developed specific standards for competent computer delivery of career guidance and information systems along with guidelines for the evaluation of printed career information, videos, and software. The Career Information Review Service (CIRS), an NCDA committee, uses these guidelines to annually evaluate career materials. Reviews are also published in various ways by NCDA, including in the *Career Development Quarterly* (NCDA journal), in *Career Developments* (NCDA newsletter), and on the Internet at the NCDA website (www.ncda.org). These guidelines can be found at www.ncda.org. NCDA is currently developing its own "seal of approval" for materials judged by CIRS reviewers to meet the guidelines. NCDA has also adopted Career Counselor Assessment and Evaluation Competencies (NCDA, 2010), which is also available on their website.

The use of various computer-based career guidance and information systems to deliver career counseling services as well as the use of the Internet in such delivery are some of the most important issues confronting professional career counseling. NCDA has been a leader in the development of standards for such delivery and published the *NCDA Guidelines for the Use of the Internet for Provision of Career Information and Planning Services* in October 1997. These guidelines can be found at www.ncda.org. These guidelines were developed by the NCDA Ethics Committee—David Caulum, Don Doerr, Pat Howland, Spencer Niles, Ray Palmer, Richard Pyle (Chair), David Reile, James Sampson, and Don Schutt. Issues raised by the NCDA Ethics Committee included standards by which such systems and services are evaluated; ways in which to use computer-based systems and Internet services to assist individuals with career planning that are consistent with ethical standards; characteristics of clients that make them profit more or less from the use of technology-driven systems; and methods to evaluate and select a system to meet local needs.

## CLINICAL SUPERVISION

The ACA (2014) *Code of Ethics* states that counselors must practice only within the boundaries of their competence. The Association for Counselor Education and Supervision (ACES, 2011) "Best Practices in Clinical Supervision" document indicates: "The supervisor provides supervision only for those supervisees and clients for whom the supervisor has adequate training and experiences" (7.b.i.). Supervisors should teach courses and/or supervise clinical work only in areas in which they are fully competent and experienced. Thus, the capacity of the supervisor to perform the essential functions of both counselor and supervisor is fundamental to the ethical practice of supervision. Professional competence refers to the "ability to carry out certain tasks appropriately and effectively" (Johnson et al., 2011, p. 95), which means having the ability to perform a task at an acceptable level.

The essential competencies for the counselor supervisor have been established by ACES in its "Best Practices for Clinical Supervision." A detailed description of these competencies can be found in the source document and include the following.

The supervisor is (a) "competent in providing clinical supervision" (11.a.), (b) "a competent and experienced practitioner who has knowledge of a range of theoretical orientations and techniques and experience with diverse client populations, relevant to their counseling setting" (11.a.i.), (c) "highly competent, morally sensitive, and ethical in the practice of counseling and supervision" (11.a.ii.), (d) "competent in multicultural counseling and supervision" (11.a.vi.), (e) "competent in implementing advocacy competencies in counseling and supervision" (11.a.vii.), and (f) "competent in the use of the technology employed in supervision" (4.f.iv.). Additionally, "the supervisor ensures that the supervisee chooses goals that fit within the supervisor's area of competence" (11.b.iii.) and "continually monitors his/her own level of competence in providing supervision and acts accordingly" (7.b.).

Thus, ACES standards require that the supervisor first be an effective counselor. Importantly, the supervisor must be more advanced than the supervisee in all areas of counseling practice. Counselors must assess their counseling competencies and then determine the kinds of clients they would not supervise, the settings that are out of their scopes of expertise, and the kinds of clients they would supervise only working under supervision or in conjunction with a consultant.

Being a competent counselor does not necessarily mean an individual is also a competent supervisor. The ACES guidelines state that supervisors should have training in supervision prior to initiating their role as supervisors. The guidelines go on to state that supervisors should be knowledgeable regarding the ethical, legal, and regulatory aspects of the profession. They also must be skilled in applying that knowledge and in making students and supervisees aware of their responsibilities. Again, as supervisors, professionals must assess their competencies.

Supervisors have the oversight responsibility for supervisees' work in relation to their competence. Supervisors should therefore assess their supervisees' skills and experience to establish the level of their supervisees' competence. Supervisors should then restrict their supervisees' activities to those that are commensurate with their current level of skills and experiences. The only way for supervisors to have confidence in their assessment is to use direct forms of supervision, at least on an intermittent basis. The task for supervisors and supervisees is to recognize when they are and are not qualified to serve prospective clients and to accept clients who will challenge them to stretch the boundaries of their competence with consultation.

Stoltenberg and McNeill (2010) spoke to the ethical mandate to permit supervisees to provide only those services within their competence. They noted that supervisors must select the type and number of clients to match the supervisee's level of competence. Supervisors then need to be vigilant to monitor client welfare and base their level of monitoring on the level of education and experience of the supervisee. In addition, the amount of time supervisors have available to supervise and their competency relative to pertinent issues must be factored into ethical supervisory decisions.

The ACES (2011) "Best Practices" document speaks directly to the issue of supervisee impairment by stating that supervisors, through ongoing supervisee assessment and evaluation, should be aware of any personal or professional limitations of supervisees that are likely to impede future professional performance. Standard 7.b.vi. states: "The supervisor appropriately engages in and models self-care." Lamb, Cochran, and Jackson (1991) defined the impairment of competence as an inability or unwillingness (a) to acquire and integrate one's repertoire of professional standards into one's repertoire of professional behavior; (b) to acquire professional skills and reach an accepted level of competency; and/or (c) to control personal stress, psychological dysfunction, or emotional reactions that may affect professional functioning. Any one or combination of these factors requires responsible action on the part of the supervisor. Case Scenario 11.3 addresses a situation that is complex but requires the supervisor to consider issues of supervisee impairment and competence.

Supervisors have the responsibility of recommending remedial assistance to the supervisee and of screening from the training program, applied counseling setting, or state licensure those supervisees who are unable to provide competent

---

## CASE SCENARIO 11.3 Practicum

Alice is the faculty member assigned to Teresa's practicum class. Teresa conceptualizes her cases adequately and seems to have good technical skills, but she is not available emotionally to her clients. In fact, she appears "shut down" in all of her interactions with her clients, with Alice, and with her peers. During one particular supervision session, Alice challenges Teresa more than usual about her affective unavailability. Teresa cries and shares that she was emotionally and sexually abused as a child. She shares that she is in counseling, but, obviously, she still has difficulty trusting others and allowing herself to feel emotions during counseling. She asks Alice to keep her background in confidence. What are the ethical issues?

This example is laden with ethical issues. First, there is the issue of informed consent. Was there a supervision contract that made it clear that Alice would not keep in confidence information that was relevant to Teresa's standing in the program? If not, and Alice feels obliged to share this information, she has denied Teresa informed consent. Second, if Alice keeps the confidence, she is in danger of forming an inappropriate, potentially detrimental relationship with Teresa by treating her more like a client than a student. Finally, the issue of competence must be addressed. If Teresa is not able to assess her own feelings or to deal with the feelings of clients, Alice must question her competence at this time. To ignore this limitation in evaluation would be an ethical concern.

professional services. These recommendations should be clearly and professionally explained in writing to the supervisees who are so evaluated (ACA, 2014, Standard F.4.a.). Stoltenberg and Delworth (1988) described the reciprocal ethical responsibility on the part of supervisees to recognize personal problems that may interfere with their practice, to let the supervisor know of them, and to seek appropriate assistance.

Ultimately, supervisors should not endorse a supervisee for certification, licensure, completion of an academic training program, or continued employment if the supervisor believes the supervisee is impaired in any way that would interfere with the performance of counseling duties (see Case Scenario 11.4). The presence of any such impairment should begin a process of feedback and remediation wherever possible, so that the supervisee understands the nature of the impairment and has the opportunity to remedy the problem and continue with his or her professional development.

Competence is not a static concept; counselors and supervisors need to participate in continuing education activities to maintain their competence (ACA, 2014). In addition, a supervisor must remain competent as both counselor and supervisor. The issue of competence for both the supervisor and the supervisee is central to the most pressing ethical responsibility—that of protecting client welfare (ACES, 2011). The ACES code speaks directly to this issue, stating that supervisors should pursue professional and personal continuing education activities such as advanced courses, seminars, and professional conferences on a regular and ongoing basis. These activities should include both counseling and supervision topics and skills. Supervisors are also expected to be active participants in peer review and peer supervision procedures (ACES, 2011).

---

### CASE SCENARIO 11.4    Endorsement Ethics

Alex has been Jaime's post-master's supervisor as part of the requirements for seeking licensure in her state. Alex has been both supportive and challenging in his supervision. Now that Jaime has completed her required hours, she gives Alex an endorsement form for him to fill out and file with the state. A week later, Jaime receives an e-mail from Alex that he has studied the form and he does not feel comfortable endorsing her at this time. Alex recommends that Jaime seek additional supervision from another supervisor. What are the ethical issues?

Alex might actually believe (and it could be argued) that he is behaving in an ethical manner by withholding endorsement from a supervisee for whom he has marginal confidence. At the same time, Jaime has due process rights that Alex has violated. Because Alex knew that Jaime was interested in seeking licensure, he needed to share his reservations earlier in the supervisory relationship and to stipulate exactly what those reservations were. By doing so, Jaime would have had an opportunity to work on her deficits and perhaps ultimately receive Alex's endorsement. It is also possible that Alex's expectations are higher than reasonable. By informing Jaime sooner about his evaluation, Jaime would have had an opportunity to seek another supervisor with whom to work.

Supervisors must be committed to continuing education. They need to keep current in their own specialty areas and be aware of advances in the area of clinical supervision. Many professionals become complacent with their degree of competence and wean themselves from professional literature and/or attendance at professional meetings or workshops (Campbell, 1994). In addition to continuing education, liberal use of consultation with peers is important to prevent the kind of isolation that diminishes competence (Sherry, 1991).

## FORENSIC PRACTICE

Special skills are necessary for forensic practice. There has to be, first of all, a commitment to "produce objective findings that can be substantiated based on information and techniques appropriate to the evaluation" (CRCC, 2010, F.1.a.). Forensic practice in counseling typically will involve assessment of the client— meaning that a formal examination will be performed, likely with a mental status examination (an examination designed to objectively facilitate the manifestations of symptoms of mental disorder). Also, forensic examiners are often asked to do intelligence, personality, and other testing to assess the capacity of the client and any mental predispositions. Importantly, forensic practitioners must have well-developed testing and examination skills. They must be keen to predispositions of clients to present themselves for their primary interests, which may bias results. For example, a client seeking disability benefits may present himself or herself in a bad light in order to demonstrate incapacity and the need for assistance. Examiners are often faced with addressing the client's potential for malingering (consciously faking in a way that has purpose). Offenders may also seek to present in a certain light—as mentally ill, for example, in order to avoid standard punishment. So forensic practitioners must be adept at addressing these issues as examiners and as communicators to those who are the legal arbiters.

Forensic practitioners typically do not evaluate clients with whom they have established practices. They also do not typically serve examined clients subsequently as clients for nonforensic services. These limits help to ensure that the forensic specialist's obligation is to objective assessment and unbiased opinion.

Forensic practitioners also must be comfortable with, or skilled at, testimony. A good part of forensic work may lead to testimony on findings and opinions in legal proceedings. The abilities to remain calm under pressure (cross-examination) and to be objective in communicating findings and conclusions are important in legal proceedings.

Forensic practitioners must carefully avoid becoming biased in their opinions. They must avoid tailoring conclusions to the needs of the attorney or organization purchasing forensic services. It is too easy for practitioners to become "hired guns," that is, forensic experts known to side with either plaintiffs or defendants and not providing objective evaluations that may even go against the need of the purchaser of services.

## CONCLUSION

This chapter has provided a summary of the ethical issue of "competency" across counseling specialties. Specialty practice requires special training. Competency, as defined, requires counselors to be able to demonstrate knowledge, education, and supervised experience in specialty areas of practice, or otherwise the counselor may be vulnerable to a challenge of competency. Counselors also must practice within the scope of their practice. They should clearly know their profession's defined limitations of specialty practice, limits defined by licensure and other laws, and limits defined by specialty guidelines addressed by organizations that represent specialists. A well-trained and ethical specialist will likely benefit from the additional training and supervision that is often necessary to establish credentials in the specialty.

# ORGANIZATIONAL, ADMINISTRATIVE, AND TECHNOLOGY ISSUES

# ETHICAL CLIMATE

## OBJECTIVES

■ To outline the concepts and elements of organizational culture and to explain their effects on the ethical climate of an organization.

■ To define "impaired professional" and to describe the effects of impairment on professional practice.

■ To explain counselor burnout, to relate it to job stress, and to describe the factors that may increase its incidence or assist in alleviating its detrimental effects.

■ To describe professional boundary problems, specifically related to sexual harassment on the job, as defined in codes of ethics.

■ To discuss the problems that accompany substance abuse problems among counselors.

■ To explain mobbing behavior in the workplace and its effects on workers, its relationship to organizational characteristics, and ways to reduce its incidence.

■ To discuss whistle-blowing and its consequences for the whistle-blower and all others involved.

Whether counselors realize it or not, they are profoundly influenced by the environments and work cultures in which they practice. If they are unaware of these influences, they are powerless to develop appropriate responses or strategies to respond intentionally to these work culture challenges—or to draw upon the work culture's strengths. Work environments are cultures that create particular ethical climates that influence the quality of service provided to clients. Unethical individuals in the workplace have the ability to influence others to behave unethically, and vice versa.

Ivey and Ivey (2003) asserted, "Intentionality is a core goal . . . [of effective counseling]" (p. 14). They stated the following:

> Intentionality is acting with a sense of capability and deciding from among a range of alternative actions. The intentional individual has more than one action, thought, or behavior to choose from in responding to changing life situations. The intentional individual can generate alternatives in a given situation and approach a problem from different vantage points, using a variety of skills and personal qualities, adapting styles to suit different individuals and cultures. (p. 14)

Building on Ivey and Ivey's concept of intentional, theory-based counseling to include ethical decision making or applied ethics, it is important to understand that an ethical perspective and process must also be skill-based and intentional. Further, issues of morality and ethical decision making are ever-present in everyday counseling practice. Every counseling decision contains an ethical or moral aspect, and each of these decisions is embedded in an influencing context. To achieve a more complete approach to intentional counseling, counselors must be equally aware of, and proactive about, work environment factors that may influence decisions.

Research continues to explore significant factors that may influence effectiveness in ethical decision making. Factors that have been examined include variables related to the individual counselor, such as moral orientation (Liddell, Halpin, & Halpin, 1992), the number and type of consulted relationships (Cottone, Tarvydas, & House, 1994), or level of ethics education (Lambie, Hagedorn, & Ieva, 2010; Tarvydas, 1994). Additionally, the effect of context-related factors on ethical decision making has been examined. Factors such as the effect of working in a certain type of environment, such as within a school-based or health care team; or with particular people, such as individuals from numerous disciplines, may influence the ethics of practice. The need is great for ongoing research that will continue to identify, to clarify, and to define factors as they relate to sound, ethical decision making in counseling practice.

Applied ethics in counseling occurs within organizational or institutional settings; for example (a) hospitals, (b) community mental health centers, (c) small mental health private practice groups, (d) schools, (e) military settings, and (f) rehabilitation settings. An ethical or unethical climate has effects on the intentional ethical decision-making process of counselors. Counselors may face a significant environmental challenge by sharing a work environment with one or more unethical colleagues.

## ORGANIZATIONAL CULTURE

More and more, counseling occurs within the context of an organization or institution. To understand more clearly how ethical decision making can be affected by participation in an organizational setting, think of an organization as a type of culture. The use of a cultural perspective can help counselors realize the organization's complexity and the interactive nature of variables within a setting as they influence decision making. This includes a need to understand the unique aspects of group or team experiences. The social, political, and cultural dynamics that occur in a larger organization, such as a hospital, also occur within smaller group settings such as a classroom within a school.

## Culture

Conceptual models used to develop an understanding of multicultural and cross-cultural counseling suggest that counselors must fully examine the potential influence of their worldview upon their counseling practice (Ivey, Ivey, & Zalaquett, 2014). **A worldview is made up of the observable artifacts, values, and underlying assumptions held by an individual.** Counselors must strive to understand how a developed worldview may influence (a) the decision making of members of any culture, (b) any individual who interacts with members of the culture, and (c) the effects of the interaction between an insider (a member of the culture) and an outsider. Multicultural models typically assume that the counselor is the outsider; however, the converse may also be true. If clients take an active decision-making role regarding their care within a health care team, or if students and their parents construct an education plan, the clients are working to gain acceptance within the team that is providing services. The team is a cultural group with its own language and style of communicating. The client is the outsider and may feel very uncomfortable about this difference. Counselors' worldviews are shaped partially by their participation in a specific organizational culture. These worldviews may affect their decision making, including the ethical components of those decisions.

Schein (2010), an organizational psychologist, implied that **a specified group of people who have had stability over time and a shared history of working together forms a culture. The culture is what the group learns over a period of time in regard to problem solving. This type of learning is manifested as observable behaviors—ways of thinking about the world and ways of feeling.** More specifically, Schein stated:

> The culture of a group can now be defined as a pattern of shared basic assumptions learned by a group as it solved its problems of external adaptation and internal integration, which has worked well enough to be considered valid and, therefore, to be taught to new members as the correct way to perceive, think, and feel in relation to those problems. (p. 18)

This description of culture clearly reflects experiences reported by counselors who have been part of a working group, whether on a school team with one or two members or on a larger team of health care workers. For example, a group of counselors assumes, based on recent complaints about services provided by one member of the group, that discussing appeal procedures with clients sets a tone that encourages client complaints. Consequently, the group falls into the practice of merely giving clients a brochure on client rights without further discussion with the client. This practice becomes so routine that new staff members are told not to spend valuable time discussing appeal rights with clients. Such procedures become crystallized over time and any divergence from the procedure is viewed as problematic within the organization. Change is necessary to best serve the interests of clients, but change is hard to initiate in such a crystallized framework. The question becomes, "Over time, what effects will a change in the agency culture have on the atmosphere in the agency, on the counselor–client relationship, and on the rights of clients?"

Any definable group with a shared history can have a culture within an organization. Therefore, an organization can have many subcultures. Specific units within an agency, or disciplines within the same organization, can have fully functioning subcultures complete with their own language and practices—and degrees of respect for ethical practice standards. They may also have their own set of ethical practice ideals and standards due to different ethical traditions, degrees of education, and exposure to ethical standards.

## Ethics and Organizational Culture

Hospital-based practice is a specific type of organizational culture that generally manifests a model of practice reflected by a definable paradigm. The hospital practice model, typically known as the medical model, represents the organic-medical paradigm (Cottone, 2012b). This model is becoming increasingly prevalent in the behavioral health practices of counselors due to the influence of managed care on all mental health disciplines. The medical culture is characterized as one in which the physician diagnoses and treats the disease of the client, and the client is relieved of blame. The role of the physician (expert) is often defined as autocratic. The role of both the client and the ancillary staff (including the counselor) is to trust and to co-operate with the physician (expert). The historical shaping of this model was developed from the values and procedures of its religious and military roots. Historically, this model contains a deference and deeply rooted respect for chain-of-command orders over and above individual beliefs. Therefore, this approach represents a parental and hierarchically based framework that has potential for creating ethical tension. The tension inherent in this culture is encountered when the "order" from the physician (expert) conflicts with the needs of the client or other caregivers.

Professional roles are constructed in response to institutional expectations and professional practices. Beauchamp and Childress (2012) stated that such roles also incorporate virtues and obligations. Roles encompass social expectations as well as standards and ideals. The hospital culture is an example of an environment or context with definitive ideas about how the helping process should occur (Case Scenario 12.1).

Political and moral or ethical problems will arise and persist as long as some professionals make the decisions and order their implementation by others who have not participated in the decision making. Beauchamp and Childress (2012) pointed out that these conflicts are avoidable but must be anticipated and prevented by establishing practices that honor open and collaborative decision making. Obligations of fidelity must be made clear; open routes to collegial dialogue must be valued. If this is not the case, Beauchamp and Childress warned,

## CASE SCENARIO 12.1  A Cultural Setting

A rehabilitation counselor is asked by a client to represent her at a rehabilitation residential care treatment center's interdisciplinary team meeting. The client's desire is to remain in the center until she feels more able to manage her own care. After careful assessment, the counselor concurs with the client that a delayed discharge would be in her best interest. The client's psychiatrist orders that the client be prepared for discharge immediately. The implicit rule of the organization is that clients belong to the doctors and that the center and its staff are only assisting the physicians in the care of their clients. Dissenting opinions at team meetings are discouraged strongly due to their historically fruitless outcomes and the time they take from the staff. Should the counselor persist in forwarding the desire of the client? How?

YES. Ethical standards in counseling clearly define counselors' obligation to their clients, and the rehabilitation counselor's code of ethics also requires that the counselor assist clients in advocating for their needs and rights (CRCC, 2010, Section C.1.c.). Further, collaboration is considered a necessary condition for ethical decision making.

compassion, while cherished as a core virtue, can also cloud judgment and work against rational and effective decision making. Based on the levels of organizational practice discussed in Tarvydas and Cottone (1991), a useful, ethical decision-making model for use in the larger organizational context is provided in Chapter 4—the Tarvydas model. Given guidelines such as those provided in this model, decision making that involves complexity and conflict can be broken down into manageable tasks that help facilitate collaborative discussion among all rightful parties.

The setting, including the people with whom counselors work, significantly influences ethical decision making. Doherty (1995) summarized this point well:

> Unsupportive and alienating work settings inevitably affect therapists' ability to care, especially for difficult clients at the end of a long workday or workweek. Having our work undermined by other professionals in positions of greater institutional power erodes motivation and investment in clinical care. Seeing too many clients during a workweek does the same, as does having to fit the client's needs to the rigidly enforced restrictions of managed care contracts. Therapists start to go through the motions, it shows, and we know it. We become negative about our clients, we hope for no-shows and cancellations, our natural caring declines, and our ethical caring begins to feel like martyrdom. When such conditions arise, it is time to change the context or get out, in my view, because we cannot sustain the fundamental virtue of caring. (p. 13)

Clearly, the work setting, whether it is an informal group or a more formal organizational structure, influences counselors' decision-making processes significantly.

## ORGANIZATIONAL CLIMATE

Several authors have suggested that an organizational climate is the outward manifestation of its culture (Mohan, 1993; Schein, 2010). **Climate is a metaphor that suggests an image wherein the environment, as the sum total of energy, presents atmospheric conditions as a type of aura. These conditions hold, support, create, and sustain the type of ethical decision making that occurs.** An awareness of these conditions is particularly important when counselors confront a decision with an emotional component, such as one that presents an ethical dilemma. Using the atmospheric conditions of our weather example, the climate may be fair or stormy. Bellah, Madsen, Sullivan, Swidler, and Tipton (1996) described this phenomenon as our moral ecology.

**Organizational climate is how people characterize a system's practices and procedures, such as the sense of safety or fear of retribution that a counselor may feel when faced with big or small decisions within this context.** Therefore, the concept of organizational climate—more specifically, the ethical climate—is one level of analysis that can help us understand and explain moral behavior as it is observed. **An ethical climate, one facet of an organizational climate, describes the shared perceptions that colleagues hold concerning ethical procedures and practices within an organization.** It upholds or erodes virtues such as compassion, discernment, truthfulness, and integrity.

The individual and organizational variables that contribute to the ethicality of the climate are complex and multilayered (Tarvydas & Cottone, 1991). The decision maker is faced with individual, client, team, and organizationally factors that must be considered. For example, decisions within an organization are often made by teams or groups rather than by individuals. Such decisions affect the workings of a team or group within the organization significantly. A growing body of literature is examining the dynamics inherent in team-based, ethical decision making (Agich, 1982; Klebe-Trevino, 1986; O'Rourke, 1996; Shapira-Lishchinsky, 2013). A basic understanding of some of the identified variables, both for the individual and for the team, is essential to intentional ethical counseling within an organizational setting.

Two basic individual skills have been identified as essential to the collaborative process: (a) the ability to assert one's thoughts and ideas and (b) the ability to clarify the content of others' contributions to the decision-making process (Maylone, Ranieri, Griffin, McNulty, & Fitzpatrick, 2011; Weiss & Davis, 1985). These basic skills are useful in any decision-making process involving two or more individuals and are particularly important in a hierarchically structured context wherein one person has more power than others.

Given the potential inequities and complexities inherent in making team-based decisions, it is essential that a working team should establish a process in a particular form for its decision-making practices. The mechanism of such a process must be sensitive to multiple disciplinary perspectives and cultural gender differences, and must be able to facilitate the production of a group decision. Constructing a useful process that is both efficient and equitable is a complex task. For example, the following questions may arise: How do we proceed if a particular professional disagrees with a team decision? Is team consensus necessary to adopt a decision? How do we provide client confidentiality when decisions made about the client occur within a larger organization that has nonprofessional support staff and reporting or billing requirements? What is an appropriate appeal process that is truly accessible to clients? Like the construction of a group culture in group counseling that has established normative behavior, the working relationship of a team develops over time and must be shaped proactively from its beginning (Case Scenario 12.2).

## CASE SCENARIO 12.2 Confidentiality and the Implications of Setting

A school counselor is working with a young woman who has had numerous behavioral problems, including shoplifting. The student has demonstrated significant improvement during the last semester in both her motivation toward school and in her social behavior. Trust was difficult to establish between the girl and her counselor, but they have developed a working relationship. During the annual Individual Education Plan (IEP) meeting, one of the girl's teachers suggested that the student might benefit from having a job. There is an opening in the lost-and-found department of the school office. Should the counselor tell the team, which includes the student's mother, that she has concerns about the student's current ability to handle other people's property? What could this disclosure do to the trust that has been built with the client? Should the counselor voice her concerns?

PROBABLY YES. The counselor has a responsibility to support the young woman and help her achieve her counseling goal of avoiding behavioral problems such as stealing. Allowing her to be placed prematurely in a setting that exposes her to overwhelming triggers for stealing behavior would present considerable therapeutic risk. Another concern involves the degree to which the team understands the critical importance of confidentiality and the team's shared responsibility for assisting the student's progress toward dealing with her behavioral problems. The counselor must be an active participant in setting the climate for these team responsibilities and may have to engage in tactful, active teaching or reminders. This sets the stage for any appropriate client disclosures. If the team is truly to function as a treatment team, important observations should be shared—but with the shared responsibility to ensure that the student's trust and confidentiality are not violated.

Finally, but most importantly, the integrity of the student must be respected. The counselor must gain the student's permission (and even direct participation) in bringing this concern to the team and her mother. Her ability to directly evaluate the risk to herself and bring the issue to the team might have significant therapeutic benefits. At the outset of counseling, the student should have been informed that information and counselor judgments integral to her case would be shared with the treatment team, thus setting the stage for this discussion. If the student is reluctant and the counselor still thinks the opinion must be shared, the counselor should at least discuss the reasons for the disclosure and its perceived benefits and risks with the student before the team meeting.

## ACCOUNTABILITY TO THE ORGANIZATION

The nature of the counseling environment plays a significant role in counselors' decision-making processes. Ethical standards mandate that counselors are accountable to both their clients and to the organizations in which they work. As a result, it is ethically sound practice for counselors to explore fully and to commit to the mission and standards of practice of any organizations for which they work. Conversely, it is the organization's ethical obligation to fully disclose all relevant information about its mission and practices, including its provision of **due process (fair and just procedures) for resolution of conflicts** with employees. Counselors who accept a position with an organization enter into a tacit agreement with that organization to honor its values and standards of practice. At the same time, counselors have an obligation to honor their professional code of ethics. Intentional practice is served by having a preexisting plan to resolve any conflicts between organizational and professional obligations. Institutions have attempted to be more intentional by constructing mechanisms to provide due process through working ethics committees and the use of case consultation meetings. Again, the Tarvydas decision-making model described in Chapter 6, which fully embraces an analysis of contextual factors, is useful for any individual counselor seeking to reconcile professional and institutional aspects of ethical dilemmas.

Consider the effect of a specific, overarching philosophy that creates a hospital's climate, such as a religious affiliation. Clinical decisions concerning use of client service options such as provision of pregnancy termination and birth control, or withdrawal of nutrition and hydration from a client in a persistent vegetative state, become enmeshed in the ethical value climate of that particular institution. Extend this consideration to a school environment, such as a gender controversy in providing a support group for gay, lesbian, and bisexual students in a high school. An institution's values and moral orientation are often the overriding aspect of the concerns involved in these situations.

Organizational values and morality subsequently influence the ethical decision-making processes of members. This is particularly evident when moral obligations and religious standards are in conflict with an institution's espoused ethical practices (Case Scenario 12.3).

### CASE SCENARIO 12.3 Accountability

A counselor is working with a client who has been treated for depression at a local Catholic mental health outpatient clinic. During the course of her treatment, the client disclosed that she had been raped several weeks earlier but is otherwise not sexually active. A pregnancy test reveals that she is pregnant. She is requesting information from the counselor about obtaining a therapeutic abortion. Should the counselor engage in a dialogue about this issue with the client, given that it is strictly forbidden by institutional values?

YES. As part of informed consent, the counselor must inform the client about the limits of their relationship and offer to help her identify her alternatives.

## CLIMATE FACTORS AND ETHICAL DECISIONS

Factors in the work environment that influence the ethical decision-making climate of service organizations include socialization practices, interpersonal relationships with significant others in the workplace (peers and superiors), role perceptions, and individual levels of development of the service providers. Research has examined specific elements of an organizational environment that have shown influence on the ethical behavior of employees. These factors include (a) structure (centralized versus participatory management), (b) ethical climate (reinforceable values; e.g., beneficence), (c) task dimensions, (d) influence of significant others in the environment, (e) role perceptions, and (f) levels of personal development of the individual service provider (Wiles, 1993). These elements include the influence of significant others such as peers and superiors, the opportunity to behave ethically as guided by a code of ethics, and the application of rewards and punishments for both ethical and unethical behavior.

Clearly, an ethical climate is constructed as a product of the interaction among the institution, the individual counselor, and numerous contributing influences from both sources. The codes of ethics of the mental health professions generally recognize these influences and clearly define standards of practice regarding personnel administration. It is the responsibility of the individual counselor to address some of these influences before making a working covenant with the institution.

The remainder of this chapter examines factors related to the influence of significant individuals within the work environment who may have been unethical in their behavior or impaired in their ability to practice.

## IMPAIRED PROFESSIONALS

The impairment of ability to function in professional roles is a growing concern in U.S. society. Impairment should not be seen as being judgmental. Rather, it is a relative term that describes function and is distinct from a disability. **A disability is an identifiable condition that may be more stable and whose functional limitations, when manifested, are recognized and often overcome with appropriate changes, assistance, or accommodations.** In contrast, **an impairment is often a gradually recognized condition that manifests when an individual attempts to perform some activity. It is not immediately obvious and involves a level of diminished function (obtained by documented evidence).** Impairments may be manifested on a continuum by varying degrees of loss of optimal function and can have many causes. A person with a disability may also become impaired, given this perspective. In fact, all counselors are impaired to some degree at some time in their practice. Impairment may be the result of having a headache or the flu. The more dysfunctional and pervasive impairments that can disrupt professional performance typically include unrecognized or untreated chronic physical illness, substance abuse, and emotional or psychological factors such as burnout and sexual acting-out behaviors. Lamb, Cochran, and Jackson (1991) defined impairment broadly as it is applied to psychology interns in the following way:

> An interference in professional functioning that is reflected in one or more of the following ways: (a) an inability or unwillingness to acquire and integrate professional standards into one's repertoire of professional behavior; (b) an inability to acquire professional skills and reach an accepted level. (p. 293)

Falender, Collins, and Shafranske (2009) noted that the word impairment in such situations can be problematic, as it may conflict with the term impairment, as used by the Americans with Disabilities Act (ADA); they suggest that traditional considerations of impairment may actually be referring to competency problems. Ethically, **professional impairment is a matter of decreased level of professional competence.** The term can be applied to people in various professional roles, including those of student, counselor, and supervisor. Three of the more common issues related to professional impairment are (a) burnout and job stress, (b) violation of professional boundaries, and (c) substance abuse.

Counselors who continue to provide professional services while impaired may be in violation of their ethical code. A counselor who is aware that a colleague or student is providing unethical services but fails to intervene may also be behaving unethically due to failure to address this issue. This failure to act may detract from the quality of client care or actually result in harm to a client.

Awareness that includes a working knowledge of practice standards and sensitivity to violation of these standards is key to ethical behavior. The impaired professional often provides clues over time that a pattern of problem behavior exists. Typically, the unethical behavior of an impaired colleague is not an isolated occurrence. For example, it is not difficult to imagine a colleague who comes in late frequently, is irritable with other staff members, and often cuts client sessions short. After some time, you and your colleagues are shocked, but not surprised, to discover that the supervisor has found this colleague has not been staying current with his or her charting and has even falsified some of these documents. Worse yet, there is speculation that the colleague has been seeing one of his or her clients socially after work.

## BURNOUT AND JOB STRESS

According to Skorupa and Agresti (1993), **burnout is an emotional exhaustion in which the professional no longer has any positive feelings, sympathy, or respect for clients.** It is often associated with fatigue, frustration, and apathy that result from prolonged stress and overwork. Burnout is thought to have three distinct factors: (a) emotional exhaustion, including feeling emotionally overextended with work; (b) depersonalization, including having unfeeling or impersonal reactions to clients; and (c) a lack of personal accomplishment or feeling incompetent at your work (Maslach, Jackson, & Leiter, 1986; Thompson, Amatea, & Thompson, 2014).

Counseling and the work done in the helping and mental health professions are very stressful by their very nature. Counselors work to help clients in very intimate and personal ways, but work with clients whom they cannot and should not control, and within institutions and financial and practical constraints over which they have little control. This uncertainty and lack of control are often coupled with witnessing the emotional ups and downs of clients' lives and working within crisis or traumatic situations. All counselors at some time experience some degree of the signs of burnout. Studies reviewed by Welfel (2002) have shown that about "1 to 5% of those sampled suffer from a full syndrome of burnout, but approximately one-third of the counselors scored high in emotional exhaustion in a number of these studies" (p. 59).

Burnout should be differentiated from job stress. Stadler (1990) noted that "impaired counselors have lost the ability to transcend stressful events" (p. 178). Not all stress is negative or rises to the level that it seriously affects the function of the individuals experiencing it. In fact, stress can be positive and, in its most basic sense, is the individual's reaction to challenges and changes. It can mobilize, focus, and energize the individual's work and responses, hopefully leading to the satisfaction of a job well done or a difficult challenge resolved positively. There are quite a number of resources that counselors can use to enhance their personal and professional well-being in dealing with job stress and preventing burnout. Research has shown that some personal characteristics cast a protective influence over distress. For example, research has shown that for some individuals, the quality of personality hardiness can interrupt the stress-exhaustion process (Maddi, Kahn, & Maddi, 1998; Maddi & Kobasa, 1984). Nevertheless, preventive steps are important for the well-being of all helping professionals, either to increase their quality of life or to prevent some serious, negative reaction. Brems (2000) has provided a personal and professional self-care plan for counselors, whether they are novices or seasoned professionals. She provides detailed information about self-care skills. See Box 12.1.

## BOX 12.1 Self-Care Plan by Brems (2000)

### Professional Self-Care Skills
Continuing education
Consultation and supervision
Networking
Stress management strategies

### Personal Self-Care Skills
Healthy personal habits
Attention to relationships
Recreational activities
Relaxation and centeredness
Self-exploration and awareness

**CASE SCENARIO 12.4  Burnout?**

A social worker with many years of experience is working as your colleague and mentor. You notice that she has become increasingly judgmental. She becomes anxious and rejects her clients when they start to place demands on her or when they "don't do what is good for them." You understand her job-related stresses: All of you are expected to take more and more clients, do more documentation of services, and are no longer offered overtime pay. What strategies can you offer your colleague to help her deal with this situation? Is her behavior severe enough to constitute burnout? Impairment?

YES AND NO. Yes, certainly these are signs of counselor fatigue and high levels of job stress. However, impairment is present only if your colleague's judgmental attitudes influence her actual practice. Approach her as a concerned colleague and remind her of the importance of managing her job-related stress. Support her in identifying and practicing strategies to increase her levels of personal and professional wellness. Since you discover she wants to learn some stress management techniques, you invite her to join your evening meditation class at the yoga center.

Studies suggest that certain client factors may contribute to therapist burnout. Among these are the number of contact hours with clients and the number of clients in a caseload that present with pervasive stressful behavior, such as aggression or limit testing (Hellman, 1986). These factors are of concern in the increasingly dominant environment of managed care. Interestingly, therapists who work in agency settings were more prone to burnout than those working in private settings (Hellman, 1986; Thompson, Amatea, & Thompson, 2014). These data indicate the importance of climate conditions on an individual. Implications for ethical practice may include (a) setting limits on the size of a caseload, (b) acknowledging a duty to understand the process of burnout and prevention techniques, (c) conducting research to determine how work settings can affect counselors, and (d) mediating untoward effects of workplace stress on the work of counselors (Case Scenario 12.4).

## BOUNDARY AND HARASSMENT ISSUES IN EMPLOYMENT AND SUPERVISION

Professionals who transgress boundaries with employees, students, or participants in research violate clearly stated ethical standards related to detriment of the professional relationships. Employers, supervisors, and educators have responsibilities to avoid conflicting relationships (see Chapter 9). Schoener (1995) described the types of individuals who may become boundary violators in clinical practice. These types describe the predictive traits of professionals who are reported violators. The six traits are: (a) psychotic and severe borderline disorders, (b) manic disorders, (c) impulse control disorders, (d) chronic neurosis and isolation, (e) situational offenders, and (f) deficits due to naivete. The same may hold true in regard to employers, supervisors, and educators. *Being an employer, supervisor, or educator does not insulate one from having problems, or even mental disorders or disturbances.* So it is critically important for colleagues of impaired professionals to address behaviors that signal the likelihood of boundary crossing or behaviors that may actually represent a breach of roles and relationship standards in the professions (Case Scenario 12.5).

There has been a good deal of research on the factors that appear to be related to increased risk of boundary violations. Counselors should be mindful of these characteristics. The professional who seems to be at most risk is a male who is experiencing personal burnout. He may also be professionally isolated and in the midst of a serious life crisis or experiencing distress in his private life (Borys & Pope, 1989; Smith & Fitzpatrick, 1995). A sufficiently impaired individual may meet his or her personal needs by entering into an inappropriate relationship with an employee, student, or supervisee.

Sexual harassment also is another salient matter for employees, supervisees, and students of counseling. Across the board, the codes of the mental health professions ban sexual harassment. The American Psychological Association (APA, 2010) code states:

> Psychologists do not engage in sexual harassment. Sexual harassment is sexual solicitation, physical advances, or verbal or nonverbal conduct that is sexual in nature, that occurs in connection with the psychologist's activities or roles as a psychologist, and that either (1) is unwelcome, is offensive, or creates a hostile workplace or educational environment, and the psychologist knows or is told this or (2) is sufficiently severe or intense to be abusive to a reasonable person in the context. (Section 3.02)

The ACA (2014) has a similar prohibition: "Counselors do not engage in or condone sexual harassment. Sexual harassment can consist of a single intense or severe act, or multiple persistent or pervasive acts" (Section C.6.a). The American Association for Marriage and Family Therapy (AAMFT, 2015) code reads as follows: "Marriage and family therapists do not engage in sexual or other forms

---

### CASE SCENARIO 12.5  Boundary Issues

Last semester, as a graduate assistant, you were supervising a student on a project that reflects your own interests. You met outside of your scheduled supervisory hour on several occasions and began to know more about each other's personal lives. You really like this student and want to see him succeed. You have just received your class list for the course you are teaching next semester. This student's name is on the list. Do you have any ethical concerns? What actions can you take to ensure that you and the student remain ethical?

Yes. Your friendship with this student has the potential either to make objective judgment difficult or to create the appearance of unfairness in the minds of other students. Raise this issue with both the student and the supervising faculty member so that alternate arrangements might be discussed, such as transfer of yourself or the student to another section. It might be possible for the student to continue in your class if you end your social relationship and arrange for more intense faculty review of your grading.

of harassment of clients, students, trainees, supervisees, employees, colleagues, or research subjects" (Standard 3.7). The National Association of Social Workers (NASW, 2008) code, too, bans sexual harassment: "Social workers should not sexually harass supervisees, students, trainees, or colleagues. Sexual harassment includes sexual advances, sexual solicitation, requests for sexual favors, and other verbal or physical conduct of a sexual nature" (Standard 2.07). Clearly these standards are consistent and send a clear message about the need for employers, supervisors, and educators to treat their charges with respect and professionalism.

## SUBSTANCE ABUSE

While the etiology of substance dependence and abuse is varied, preexisting faulty coping mechanisms and certain predictive behaviors seem to precede professional impairment. Knowledge of risk factors related to chemical dependency can aid in early recognition and intervention. The following etiologic factors have been consistently cited in the literature: (a) genetic predisposition, (b) poor coping skills, (c) lack of education about impairment, (d) absence of effective prevention strategies, (e) drug and alcohol availability, (f) the context of a permissive environment, and (g) denial.

Ironically, as with any lethal malady, early diagnosis and intervention are critical, but the hallmark of chemical dependency continues to be denial. Waiting for spontaneous insight from an affected colleague is unconscionable—and unethical. While the workplace is traditionally the last area to be affected, professional competence is affected adversely. Barriers to early recognition of the chemical dependency of a colleague include (a) lack of training in recognition of early signs of abuse, (b) the insidious and confusing effect of the disease's progression on daily function that lends to signs that are easily rationalized away, and (c) the subsequent denial of both the impaired professional and the individual's colleagues.

The task of differentiating impairment from problematic behaviors is difficult. Acting on the conclusion that impairment is imminent is even more difficult. Relatively few counselors have received training in this area. The literature (Skorina, DeSoto, & Bissell, 1990; Smith & Moss, 2009) suggests that counselors tend to underestimate or fail to recognize impairment in colleagues. Therefore, intervention, and the colleague's recovery, may be delayed.

Suggestions for dealing intentionally with potential impairment among one's peers include primary, secondary, and tertiary levels of intervention based on the timing and need of the situation. Primary interventions include involvement in educational programs (e.g., graduate education or in-service programs). These educational programs provide (a) values clarification regarding impairment and the individual conditions that often cause the impairment (e.g., adopting an attitude of assistance and compassion versus one of blame); (b) knowledge of potential signs of impending impairment for each condition; and (c) enactment of prevention strategies that address each area of potential impairment (both individually and institutionally). Secondary interventions include the establishment

CASE SCENARIO 12.6  Substance Abuse

The medical director of the treatment center where you work as a chemical dependency counselor has started to miss the morning staff meetings fairly regularly. He always has a rational explanation. Two weeks ago, an evening nurse confided in you that she thought she smelled alcohol on the doctor's breath as he attended to a client. Is this enough evidence to initiate an intervention with the physician?

NO. Impairment requires the documentation of significantly impaired function. However, there is enough evidence to discuss your concerns with the physician.

and knowledge of sound practice standards. These standards include steps to obtain due process for the individual who may be impaired as well as the individual's colleagues. Tertiary intervention involves understanding and involving the necessary resources to make a direct intervention with an impaired colleague (Case Scenario 12.6).

## MOBBING

Lately, the concept of emotional abuse in the workplace began to be recognized, discussed, and treated in the United States. Increased numbers of high-profile, shocking incidents of violence in schools and the workplace caused scholars to consider factors that create negative, and sometimes unbearable, forces acting on individuals. Counselors and the settings in which they work are not immune to these forces. A recent text by Davenport, Distler Schwartz, and Pursell Elliott (1999) described **mobbing as "workplace expulsion through emotional abuse"** (p. 20). These authors noted that the term was derived from its root word, **mob, meaning a disorderly crowd engaged in lawless violence.** This term was first used, as applied to human behavior, in the 1960s by an Austrian ethnologist, Konrad Lorenz. Lorenz described human behavior as being similar to the behavior that animals show in scaring away an enemy.

Later, Heinesmann, a Swedish physician, researched similar behavior among children that has subsequently been labeled bullying. His early work, "Mobbing: Group Violence Among Children," was published in Sweden in 1972. Until 1982, this concept was used exclusively in the study of children. Leymann (1996) then used the term "mobbing" to describe similar violence among adults in the workplace. He found that work cultures created circumstances wherein marked individuals were labeled as difficult and pushed to the margins of the workgroup culture. Leymann's work has generated much interest in Europe.

According to Davenport et al. (1999), mobbing is an emotional assault that targets an individual via two types of hurtful conduct from work colleagues. One type of misconduct is overt and is considered to be active aggression. The other involves passive tactics that are more covert and often disguised between acts of occasional kindness. Mobbing is a process that happens insidiously over time. Leymann (1996) distinguished five phases in this process: conflict, aggressive acts, management involvement, branding (as "difficult" or "mentally ill"), and expulsion. Other terms have been used for these phenomena: bullying, workplace trauma, harassment, and emotional abuse in the workplace (Keashly, 1998).

**Mobbing** is the process of an emotional assault (Davenport et al., 1999) that often begins with passive, insidious marking of an individual as a threat to the norms of the organizational culture. The mobbing process is like the process of marking among people with disabilities that has been so well described by Jones et al. (1984) in their classic text, *Social Stigma: The Psychology of Marked Relationships*. This stigmatizing process is always relational. In the classic case, the process begins when an individual's flaw or mark of deviance initiates a pronounced attribution process. The process of attributing certain negative characteristics to the person results in an attack on the person's basic integrity and often results in hostile rejection. The outcome is not necessarily based on who the person actually is, but whom the person may represent to the organizational culture. For example, a counseling intern frequently asks pointed questions about the billing practices of the supervisor and the other counselors in the agency. This intern may eventually be ostracized by all of the counselors as someone who is "holier than thou" and has no potential for the "real" work of counseling.

A distinguishable characteristic of mobbing is the organizational collusion that typically supports this insidious process. Davenport et al. (1999) identified organizational elements that make a working environment vulnerable to participation in mobbing: bad management (e.g., excessive bottom-line orientation at the expense of human resources), stress-intensive workplace, monotony, disbelief or denial by managers, unethical activities, flat organizations, and downsizing/restructuring/merging. These authors asserted that it is the culture of the organization that determines whether mobbing will be allowed to develop or will be extinguished, particularly the organization's ability to handle differences and conflict. Davenport et al. (1999) offer a number of suggested actions to reduce mobbing behavior, including clarifying structure and reporting levels in the organization, selecting new employees on emotional intelligence as well as on technical skills, providing training that includes human relations topics, and providing conflict resolution or mediation mechanisms with clear follow-up procedures until conflicts are successfully resolved.

Within this vulnerable organizational context, Davenport et al. (1999) suggested that the complex dynamics that result in mobbing is the outcome of an interaction among five elements: (a) the psychology and the circumstances of the mobbers; (b) the organizational culture and structure; (c) the psychology of the mobbee's personality; (d) the circumstances of the mobbee; and (e) a triggering event, a conflict, and factors outside the organization (i.e., values and norms in U.S. culture).

## WHISTLE-BLOWING

Counselors are mandated by their codes of ethics and by state licensure guidelines to report questionable or unethical behavior, yet many are hesitant to become whistle-blowers. **Whistle-blowing is the ethical reporting of unethical**

**behavior**, and it has often been used in a pejorative sense. Collegial support may be mixed when a colleague reports the suspected behavior of a peer.

Mixed support may be particularly evident in hierarchical organizations, such as large bureaucracies or hospitals, if the accused is an administrator, supervisor, or physician who also occupies a place on the upper level of the hierarchy, or if the whistle-blowing disrupts the immediate work team in any setting. On the other hand, whistle-blowing can be beneficial and override the negative risks by (a) providing a climate that supports the protection of current and future clients as well as coworkers, (b) facilitating communication among colleagues, and (c) encouraging constructive problem solving. Several laws have been designed to safeguard employees who suspect the unethical behavior of their colleagues. However, court actions suggest that legal protection for whistle-blowers is tentative. For example, a 1981 Michigan state law protects employees who expose illegal or dangerous employee activity from wrongful discharge from any government or private-sector organization. However, as stated in Chapter 3, counselors are obligated to their employers as well as to their clients, making the decisions concerning disclosure ethically complex. The actual experience of becoming a whistle-blower can be a life-changing event if the situation is serious enough. At times, the counselor may receive sufficient support and the process may be difficult, but gratifying. In other instances, the experience can be harrowing even though the counselor may eventually be vindicated. Box 12.2 relates the story of two counselors who "did the right thing" and are proud of it, yet they paid a serious price. Note the characteristic mobbing behaviors that were directed against them in the process.

Ethical codes for the mental health professions do provide codified standards of behavior for addressing concerns regarding unethical behavior of a colleague. The APA, the ACA, the AAMFT, and the NASW codes of ethics provide standards for reporting unethical conduct. The ACA, APA, and NASW codes all provide mechanisms for an informal resolution of ethical violations and for reporting ethical violations. Ideally, the professional should first attempt to resolve the situation by discussing it directly and informally with the other individual, providing that confidentiality rights of the client are not violated in the process. If the violation is too serious, or is not resolved after this informal discussion, the professional will take further action including possible referral to licensure boards and/or professional organizations' ethics committees for adjudication. This last course of action would not be possible if there are violations of the client's confidentiality rights that cannot be resolved.

In a more general sense, Felie (1983) suggested several guidelines for whether, when, and how to blow the whistle on a colleague if informal routes prove to be ineffective and if the colleague is not of one's own discipline but works as a peer within an organizational setting. She has outlined six steps for addressing the problem (see Box 12.3).

The act of taking a colleague to task for ethically inappropriate behavior is daunting. Nevertheless, counselors have an important obligation to their clients and society at large to protect them and to uphold the trust placed in the profession.

## BOX 12.2  Two Colleagues Make the Ultimate Ethical Decision

We live in an interdependent world where work and ethics are inextricably linked. Knowing that we are providing a useful service to others lets us routinely deal with difficulties and problems that are part of any job. In our place of work, routine circumstances led to a chain of events that uncovered fraudulent billing practices. We attempted to correct this by working within the corporation. Our attempts to correct unethical and fraudulent activities were "spun" by corporate managers as "politics," described as "trying to get workers" (those who were responsible for the fraudulent activities). We experienced firsthand how a system that had lost its moral compass protects itself through attacks on our professional credibility. We were threatened and isolated. One of us was fired, the other was forced out. Later we found ourselves unemployable. We worried that we had been blacklisted. We can attest that "whistle-blowers suffer certain and severe retaliation from management especially if their information proves to be significant, reveals systematic misconduct, and the practices exposed are part of the regular profit accumulation of the organization" (Rothschild & Miethe, 1999).

We are not experts, but when we found ourselves in a whistle-blower situation, we experienced firsthand the connection between work and ethical expression. We were dumbfounded when the corporation ignored the bad billing practices we had discovered. Instead of backing our efforts, the corporation criticized us for not getting along with subordinates. Overnight everything changed. We went from the model team to troublemakers.

We were disappointed by the behavior of some coworkers. Professional colleagues whom we had once respected became overwhelmed by concerns for job security. We found silence where we had expected support from the organization and other members of the helping professions. We experienced the effects of extreme trauma, shame, fear, loss of confidence, and depression that impacted all of our relationships and family. Despite our own fear of what the future could bring, we summoned our courage and proceeded with integrity. We could do the right thing by having our case heard and decided in a court of law. We took the initiative with energy and conviction, persevering and being willing to hang in there, no matter what.

Having our case heard in a court of law made a big difference. Even if the case had not been won, having a trial was the right thing. The trial was based on evidence and we had the documentation that made the difference. The procedures of the trial were daunting; however, the trial was our only opportunity to make our case to the public. By taking a stand we were effectively cut off from the support systems one traditionally turns to in times of great stress.

Our former boss apparently forgot that he had nominated one of us for Employee of the Year when he testified that that person was always a problem. The chief executive officer (CEO) was angry and embarrassed when confronted by the evidence. One of our frustrations with the discovery process was that the only documentary evidence of the billing problem came from us. Despite our requests

(continued)

## BOX 12.2 Two Colleagues Make the Ultimate Ethical Decision (*continued*)

for documentation, the corporation seemed not to have any of the many memos we had generated on the subject. We were appalled to learn that one of the employees we had tried to correct had searched our offices and thrown many papers away. Realizing that our concerns about the organization practices needed to be supported by evidence, we carefully documented them in a report to the clinical supervisor as we sought for the identified issues to be addressed by appropriate supervisors in the organization. This report and retention of records of our repeated attempts to seek the support of organization officers in correcting these practices provided the evidence that made the difference. The money won in the lawsuit is a representation of some justice for the individuals involved.

Being a whistle-blower was a life-altering experience. In its entirety, the experience was painful. We had acted in good faith to seek remedies to fraudulent practices and the system did not recognize or honor that effort. The experience also was an opportunity. It gave us a window in time to evaluate our ethics and our values. When work and life are rooted in ethical practice, you have the energy and the vision to do whatever is necessary. We all want to contribute and make a positive difference with our work. We are all drawn to what is good and right and each one of us is capable of making this difference. We found that in our materialistic society, ethical and value-based action is not to be taken for granted and is the only thing that gives authenticity and substance to living and working.

A decision to step forward should not be taken without serious consideration. Sound legal advice and documentation are crucial as well. The role of whistle-blower was forced upon us. After the fact, we realized that even though we could not predict what the outcome of our actions might be, our response of finding justice through the legal system was the right and good thing to do. We did not know that it would work out to a positive conclusion. We only knew that it was the right action to take and did so without regrets. We could not turn a blind eye to our professional ethics or the rights of our clients to honest and ethical services. When life and work are guided by ethical values, we are empowered to act responsibly and compassionately, even in the midst of challenging circumstances. Each one of us has the ability to make this difference. Never forget what the priorities are.

---

The Civil Rights Act of 1967, Title VII, made it unlawful for an employer to discriminate or to fire an individual based on race, color, religion, sex, or national origin. Subsequently, federal and state legislation extended this protection; for example, The Age Discrimination in Employment Act of 1967; The Vocational Rehabilitation Act of 1973; and The Americans with Disabilities Act of 1990. The Supreme Court ruled that Title VII is not limited to tangible discrimination but is also intended to be applied to people who may be subjected to a hostile work environment. For example, the claim of "hostile environment" has been used in litigation involving sexual harassment.

**BOX 12.3  Steps for Blowing the Whistle**

1. Confirm the issue. Conduct an objective assessment of the situation. Make certain that you are competent to make this determination and that your desire to make this report is not based on personal motives.
2. Check your perceptions with peers. Examine them against the norms of your institution and your discipline. Compare the activity against your state's practice guidelines and those of your institution. Does the situation truly exceed acceptable standards? Maintain a nonjudgmental attitude throughout the process.
3. Involve others in an action plan. Develop a plan of action for voicing your concerns. Respect your institution's chain of command. Multiple participants are more effective in providing a successful intervention. Have intervention goals established in advance. Anticipate possible reactions.
4. Set deadlines. They demonstrate that you are serious. Implement your plan after conferring with your immediate supervisor.
5. Document details of your discussion. Include time, date, and the basic content of the conversation. Timing of any intervention is crucial—soon after a precipitant crisis is optimal.
6. If needed, take the problem upstairs. If your supervisor dismisses or fails to address the situation, be prepared to move up the organizational ladder.

*Source:* Felie (1983). Reprinted by permission of Lippincott-Raven Publishers, Philadelphia, PA.

Recent U.S. legislation has attempted to extend compensatory relief to individuals who have suffered significant mental injury as a result of a hostile working environment. Arizona, California, Iowa, Wisconsin, and Wyoming legally acknowledge that mental injury can result from excessive stress on the job—calling it mental-health injury.

Mental health, rehabilitation, and other helping organizations that employ professionals who work directly with clients should take seriously the need to establish a nonthreatening, positive environment.

Mobbing and whistle-blowing often begin with the presence of an unresolved conflict and the admirable attempt of an individual to resolve the situation. One result of an unresolved situation of conflict may be the act of whistle-blowing. The conflict may actually provide a potentially explosive atmosphere with the fuel it needs to ignite. In turn, the whistle-blower can serve as a target for unresolved hostility, or mobbing.

## CONCLUSION

Counselors are profoundly influenced by the environments and work cultures in which they practice. Work environments are cultures that create a particular ethical climate that influences the quality of services provided to clients.

Ethical and unethical colleagues influence their coworkers to behave ethically and unethically.

Organizational climate is how people characterize a system's practices and procedures, such as the sense of safety or fear of retribution that a counselor may feel. Ethical climate describes the shared perceptions that colleagues hold concerning ethical procedures and practices within an organization.

A disability is an identifiable condition that may be stable and is often overcome with appropriate changes, assistance, or accommodations. An impairment is a gradually recognized condition that manifests when an individual attempts to perform some activity. Chronic physical illness, substance abuse, burnout, and sexual acting-out behaviors are pervasive impairments that can disrupt professional performance. Substance abuse adversely affects professional competence. Early diagnosis and intervention are essential. Burnout is an emotional exhaustion in which the professional no longer has any positive feelings, sympathy, or respect for clients.

Boundary violations occur when professionals' ethical standards are loose with clients, students, or research participants. Those most likely to violate professional boundaries are those who have psychotic disorders, manic disorders, impulse control disorders, chronic neurosis and isolation, and naivete, and those who are situational offenders.

Mobbing is an emotional assault that targets a work colleague. Organizational elements that contribute to mobbing include bad management, a stress-intensive workplace, monotony, disbelief or denial by managers, unethical activities, flat organizations, and downsizing/restructuring. Whistle-blowing is the ethical reporting of unethical behavior. Whistle-blowing receives mixed support, particularly in hierarchical organizations. It can be beneficial and override the negative risks by providing a protective environment for clients and coworkers, and facilitating communication. The experience of becoming a whistle-blower can be a life-changing event.

# OFFICE AND
# ADMINISTRATIVE PRACTICES

One of the most overlooked areas of study in the ethics literature relates to business practices. Yet, business practice is one of the most challenging areas of ethical practice—and one of the areas most challenged by clients and other individuals served by professional counselors and psychotherapists. Many of the complaints before licensure boards and certification bodies are about business, administrative, or office practices, such as inadequate record-keeping or fraudulent acts (e.g., false billing; Association of State and Provincial Psychology Boards, 2001). Nothing will raise the ire of a client (or third-party payer) more than a bill for unsatisfactory services, a bill that does not reflect the actual services requested or provided, a bill that breaches confidentiality, or a bill that reflects financial irregularities. Generally, mental health professionals are ill-prepared to address these issues and to set standards and office procedures to prevent problems. Classic examples of problematic office practices include: (a) waiting rooms that do not provide any privacy (e.g., secretaries discuss issues with clients in the open or there is no discreet entry or exit); (b) use of electronic equipment without adequate encryption (e.g., fax machines, cell phones, intercoms, video conferencing); (c) advertising (misrepresentation through advertising, for example); (d) fee setting and collection of unpaid bills; (e) maintenance of records and disposal of confidential records (e.g., shredding of records); (f) referral and termination procedures; (g) poor sound insulation in offices; (h) misrepresentation of credentials to the public (e.g., licensure status); and (i) fraudulent billing practices.

## THE LAYOUT OF THE OFFICE

Privacy issues should be of the utmost importance in the design of a professional office. A professional supervisor recently visited a student intern at a reputable sex therapy clinic. While waiting in the lobby area, he was able to overhear a secretary asking detailed, intimate questions of a prospective client over the phone. The secretary repeated the prospective client's name, phone number, and address as she recorded them, and everyone in the waiting area could hear. The secretary, in this case, was acting unethically as an extension of the agency and the provider, putting both at risk for a claim of a breach of confidentiality; in these situations, staff members must be trained to understand the full ethical obligation of the mental health practitioners they represent. Soundproofing or screening in such a situation is absolutely necessary. Waiting areas should be designed so that people entering or leaving the counseling suites can do so without passing other waiting clients. A separate exit door is ideal, or if space restrictions prevent a separate exit door, scheduling should take place so that a minimal number of people are in the waiting area at one time. Files should not be left out in the open so that visitors in the waiting area can see them, and computer monitors should be turned so that confidential information is not easily viewed by the waiting public. Sign-in sheets at the reception area are a blatant breach of confidentiality, as subsequent clients can see the names of individuals who signed in earlier. These are basic issues of privacy. Nothing is more disturbing than waiting in a physician's office and having one's medical problems broadcast to everyone present. Counseling clients may have issues even more sensitive than those of patients in a physician's office. Counselors and administrators must be very sensitive to these common breaches of privacy, which can be prevented by careful planning. Mental health professionals are guided by the American Counseling Association (ACA), American Psychological Association (APA), National Association of Social Workers (NASW), and American Association for Marriage and Family Therapy (AAMFT) ethics codes, which make it clear that counselors must respect the privacy of their clients.

Offices should also be organized to provide for the safety of clients and staff. If safety concerns arise from the nature of the clientele that is served by the agency, staff should be prepared to deal with emergency situations. Some professionals provide counsel to ex-offenders, individuals with anger or impulse control problems, or individuals with poor or impaired judgment. A rehabilitation counselor in a nonprofit agency was punched in the face by a client diagnosed as having paranoid schizophrenia. The client reported that he overheard the counselor make a racial slur while the counselor was on the phone trying to assist in job placement of the client. The client had a record of assaulting other individuals for racial slurs, even when no such slurs were heard by bystanders. The client was apparently hallucinating and became violent in response to the hallucinations. Given the client's record, precautions should have been taken in this case. When working with potentially dangerous or violent clients, counselors should establish safety and contingency plans. Procedures for warning or alerting others of potential, imminent, or active crises should be in place. Equipment might be purchased to help to ensure safety (door key pads, warning systems), or offices can be designed to allow visual access (counselor offices with windows to another secure office) so that other professional staff can monitor activities. Counselors, staff, and clients should feel safe in the counseling setting, and administrative and professional staff should be alert to potential concerns and methods for preventing problems.

The common practice of sharing office space is another area of concern. Some counselors, by choice or by necessity, share office space. They may see clients at different times during the same day or on different days. In most cases, this arrangement is a matter of economics. Private practitioners in part-time, private practices may be unable to afford an individual office on their own; they may enter into an agreement with a colleague to share costs and space. Some agencies and schools are pressed for space and are unable to provide individual offices for professional staff. Whatever the arrangement, counselors who share space should have a clear agreement about the boundaries related to client information. Unless the counselors are employed by the same agency or school and have their clients' understanding of the organization's right to share information, they must make efforts to secure files and other case-relevant information. Separate storage areas (e.g., file cabinets; computer electronic folders; access to cloud storage) should be secured even from colleagues who share space; licenses should be displayed according to law for all of the people who use the office; and procedures for taking calls and messages must be established to provide for maximum security. A formal, written ethics agreement between parties sharing space is also recommended. Extra precautions should be taken to ensure that a client's rights are not compromised because of financial exigency and a shortage of space.

Counselors also must be sensitive to accessibility issues—individuals with disabilities often have impairments that affect their mobility. Special parking spaces for those with mobility problems must be provided. Offices and buildings should be designed to maximize the accessibility of individuals with problems negotiating spaces. Elevators (and back-up elevators) should be available in storied buildings, facilities should be wheelchair accessible, and bathrooms must be made accessible. Special accommodations for the hearing or visually impaired should be in place. Sensitivity to disability-related concerns is important when serving individuals in need. In most states, the state department that provides rehabilitation services addresses accessibility issues in establishing and maintaining an office. Offices that receive federal funds must be in compliance with accessibility standards, but all counseling offices should strive for accessibility to comply with best practices for cultural and diversity competency.

> **Question for Reflection:** You are a counselor in an agency with paper-thin walls. You are counseling a client, and both you and your client are able to overhear a very private counseling session from an adjoining room. What should you do?

## FEE SETTING, BILLING, AND COLLECTIONS

Fee issues are among those that appear to produce the most variability of confidence when practitioners are asked to rate ethical acceptability (Gibson & Pope, 1993; Neukrug & Milliken, 2011). Gibson and Pope (1993), citing their own findings and the work of Pope and Vasquez (1991), concluded, "The topic of fee is one that often evokes feelings of discomfort and may therefore be relatively neglected in training programs" (p. 334). Counselors should follow some simple advice in establishing their billing and collection policies—be cautious and be fair. If clients or third-party payers feel cheated or slighted, there is potential for conflict.

The professional associations all have sections of their codes of ethics that address fee issues (the AAMFT, 2015, code Standard VIII; the APA, 2010, Section 6.04; the ACA, 2014, Section A.10.c.; and the NASW, 2008, Standard 1.13). These standards generally agree that fee setting should be fair and any issues around fees (collections, modifications, etc.) should be discussed in advance of initiation of the counseling relationship.

A classic area of debate related to fee setting among practicing professionals is the issue of **"sliding fee scales." In this system, individuals are required to pay a certain amount for a service based on their income** (see Lien, 1993). A person with a very low income may be required to pay an amount less than a person with a high income for an hour of counseling or psychotherapy. There are benefits and problems with this sort of fee setting (Lien, 1993). Some argue that it provides people with low incomes an opportunity to receive services they otherwise could not afford. Others argue that it is inherently unfair and prejudicial of the wealthy client or the client with insurance or other benefits. It also appears to be in conflict with the ethical code of the ACA, which requires that there be no discrimination against individuals on the basis of socioeconomic status. Some agencies have compromised by charging lower fees for the services of student counselors (predegree) or counselors-in-training (degreed, but unlicensed or provisionally licensed professionals working to meet licensure standards). Some still argue that this may provide an inferior (or at least a less clinically savvy) product to the poorer client. It is also possible that if a practitioner receives a lower fee, he or she might be less conscientious.

Hartsell and Bernstein (2013) warn therapists that "flexible fee policies represent a dangerous legal trap" (p. 152). They stated that "all states prohibit a health care provider from charging a higher fee to a client who has insurance coverage than to one without insurance, when insurance (or the lack of it) is the only differentiating criterion applied" (p. 152). And therapists who have waived copays (the client's share of the fee) while providing services under a managed care or other insurance contract have been sued for fraud. Hartsell and Bernstein stated: "Never waive a copay" (p. 153). To avoid legal traps, and to avoid appearing unfair, it is wise to avoid any variable or sliding fee policy.

The flat fee, variable collection procedure is another option. In this system, one fee is charged for all clients, say $100 per hour. All clients are required to pay at least 50% of the fee before they leave the office ($50). The remainder is billed to the client. Some clients may choose to pay the total amount at the time of the service. Other clients may have insurance that may cover the balance, or even more than the balance (in which case the client would be due a refund). The procedure is invariable in collection of at least a certain percentage of the fee at the time of service. However, the agency can use discretion in collection of the unpaid balance. Clients who have fewer resources may not be billed on the remainder as often, or may not be required to pay as much on the balance of their bill at each billing cycle. Some of these bills will go uncollected, so the agency has some flexibility in attempting to collect the balance. The unpaid balance is a private matter, and not one that is prejudicial of certain groups at the time of the service agreement. On the negative side, this approach may scare away clients who may not be able to afford the full fee; they may be hesitant to commit to services even with knowledge of the nonaggressive collection procedures. They may seek services from an agency with a lower or sliding scale.

Some counselors are willing to charge lower fees but require full payment at the time of service. They may serve only a clientele that has ready access to funds to pay for services. This method avoids all of the work and expense of billing. Others use credit or debit card payments. Although a small fee is charged to the counselor for use of credit or debit cards, this method allows immediate guaranteed payment for services. However, counselors should be careful how their credit card billing appears on statements or in electronic records. Using a credit card to bill for services for a mental health agency transmits and stores that information in electronic forms, and having that record of service from a mental health agency may be a concern to clients who want to keep their privacy (especially in electronic media). Having a company name like "Jones and Associates" is better than something like "The Sexual Trauma Recovery Center." Which business would you prefer on a billing statement and in the hands of the credit card company (and potential hackers)?

Regardless of the fee and billing procedure, it is important that counselors have a clearly articulated fee schedule and stick to the schedule. Varying fees and billing practices may be viewed as prejudicial and could be grounds for legitimate complaints against an agency or a professional.

Raising fees during counseling may prove uncomfortable for both the counselor and the client. Some counselors have a set fee for a particular client. If the client's case is terminated and then reopened, it is reopened at the current rate, even if that rate constitutes an increase over the previous rate. Once opened, the fee remains the same, no matter what changes occur in the fee schedule. Some professionals never raise a fee on a case once the client has initiated treatment—the fee always remains the same. This kind of policy helps to encourage future client contact with the professional. Other agencies or private practitioners raise fees regularly, even in the course of treatment of a client. Clients are (and should be) informed that rates are not permanent and may be increased during their treatment. No one fee-raising method is more ethical than another, but, certainly, clients should know the rules from the very beginning of counseling.

If arrangements are made about collections, such as hiring a collection agency or attorney to secure unpaid balances, these arrangements should be explained to clients when they initially agree to services (see the ACA, AAMFT, NASW, and APA codes). Clients should agree to services with full knowledge of potential collection procedures by signing a written statement of the agreement. If collections or payments are made through a credit or debit card, it is wise to use an agency name that does not imply mental health services to avoid a potential breach of privacy. As in the earlier example of "The Sexual Trauma Recovery Center," the credit card company or bank receives a debit from "Anita's Counseling and Psychotherapy Service," the credit world knows that the client received such services. If the name of the agency is abbreviated in some way to disguise the service (e.g., Anita's Services, or Anita, Inc.), it is less likely that individuals will be able to identify the service provided.

Counselors can take some simple actions to prevent breach of client privacy. Mailed envelopes should list only the return address, without the agency name so that people picking up a client's mail (e.g., roommates or family members) do not know that there has been contact with a mental health service provider. Likewise, counselors should not leave detailed phone messages that imply counseling services on answering machines or with anyone other than the client. Leaving a name and return phone number is sufficient.

Fraudulent billing is another major issue. In many cases, medical insurance programs will not pay for certain types of counseling services unless they can be clearly defined as psychotherapy for a person diagnosed with a mental disorder. Counselors often provide services that technically do not meet the definition of psychotherapy in treatment of mental disorders. For example, marriage or family counseling is not technically medical psychotherapy. It is fraudulent billing practice to provide a service outside of the realm of medical psychotherapy and then to bill it as such. Clients may want services billed in a way that meets medical insurance standards to avoid paying out-of-pocket costs, but their consent in no way protects the counselor in cases of fraudulent billing. If marriage counseling is provided, marriage counseling should be billed, regardless of reimbursement issues. Clients should also know that when medical insurance is billed, it requires a medical (psychiatric) diagnosis. Counselors should not diagnose mental disorders unless they "are qualified and competent to render them under state licensing statutes" (Wheeler & Bertram, 2015, p. 97). Some clients prefer to avoid communicating such diagnoses to third-party payers, and they may request to make other payment arrangements.

Billing for services that were not provided or justified is another fraudulent practice. A psychologist was sued for, and found guilty of, Medicare fraud when it was learned he was billing for the intelligence testing of nursing home residents who suffered from diagnosed dementia (loss of intelligence). In most cases, the tests were never given, or only cursory procedures were used to document attempts to test the patients. The testing was found to be unnecessary and, in most cases, there was no record of actual test administration. This was a clear case of fraudulent practice. A physician at the nursing home reported him to Medicare.

Some mental health professionals have been found guilty of double billing—for example, billing a government agency and then billing a client or client's family in full for services already reimbursed by a third party.

Also there are instances of (a) billing for an individual session when the client is seen in group and (b) billing at a full credentialed rate for services rendered by students, counselors-in-training, or a paraprofessional assistant. These are charges of fraud that are fairly common in the current managed care marketplace. Playing "get-rich schemes" at the expense of a third-party payer is a very dangerous game—such violations can result in felony convictions for insurance fraud, a loss of a license to practice, and/or censure from a professional organization.

Another issue of concern is submitting forms to a third-party provider (such as a managed care company) requesting therapy for a client and purposefully **"overdiagnosing" the client to ensure payment or permission to treat the patient for an extended period of time**. This practice is called **upcoding**, and it is fraudulent practice. The counselor purposefully uses a diagnosis that is more severe than diagnostically justified to ensure adequate insurance coverage for the anticipated treatments (Cummings, 1998). Cummings (1998) stated:

> With indemnity insurance and in times past, providers characteristically underdiagnosed ostensibly for the protection of their patients. The most innocuous reimbursable diagnosis was overly used, whereas schizophrenia was seldom evoked as in many states the patient could suffer such consequences as loss of a driver's license or ineligibility for life insurance. In contrast, the era of managed care has seen the mushrooming of the use of severe diagnoses. Forced on many occasions to demonstrate concepts of "medical necessity" or "life threatening," practitioners' exaggeration of findings on evaluation has become widespread. (p. 61)

Obviously, this is unacceptable activity. In the past, **underdiagnosing (downcoding)** was a standard way to protect clients. Now upcoding is a serious concern. In addition to constituting insurance fraud, overdiagnosing can do harm to clients. Diagnoses may follow clients for a lifetime, and a false diagnosis may affect the client's future insurability and future relations with mental health professionals.

Missed sessions are another issue. Should clients be billed when they miss appointments without giving adequate notice to allow rescheduling? Woody (1989) stated: "Missed sessions are troubling for both the client and the practitioner. If a client fails to show up for an appointment, the client suffers from lack of treatment, and the practitioner suffers from lack of income" (p. 150). Most practitioners have a general rule about billing missed appointments, and whatever policy is established, it should be communicated clearly (on informed consent forms) and implemented consistently. Missed appointments are usually not upsetting to the practitioner who has other work to fill the time, but if the missed appointment is inconvenient and represents wasted time, it becomes problematic for the counselor. Legitimate emergencies that prevent attendance should be excused without penalty, and a policy about adequate advanced notice to cancel appointments should be clearly communicated to clients initiating treatment. Note that insurance companies do not pay for missed appointments—they pay only for services rendered, so bills for missed appointments go directly to the client.

Should counselors charge clients for phone contacts? Some charge one-tenth of an hour for every 6 minutes on the phone. Others do not charge for phone contacts unless they represent an extended therapeutic interaction. As with other billing issues, clients should know how they are being charged well in advance. A surprise on a bill is likely to incite already fragile clients and create a conflict situation. Phone contacts are typically not reimbursed by insurance carriers.

Counselors have at least two options in dealing with clients who do not pay their fees. First, the counselor has the right to terminate the counseling relationship. Ethics codes generally allow that termination is appropriate when clients do not pay charged fees. If, however, it is clear that clients cannot pay fees, the counselor has the option of serving the client **"pro bono publico," for the public good, at no fee**. Ethics codes generally encourage such work. Counselors should know how much of their work is "pro bono" and if such an arrangement is acceptable to administrators and supervisors.

**Questions for Reflection:** You learn that one of your colleagues in a private agency is billing medical insurance for "medical psychotherapy" when, in fact, the counselor is providing career counseling services, including resume writing guidance. It is obvious that the individuals receiving the counselor's services are not seeking treatment for a mental disorder. What are your obligations in this situation as a professional counselor? Why is this conduct unethical? What specific course of action should you take?

## AGREEMENTS WITH NONPROFESSIONAL STAFF MEMBERS

Most agencies and schools employ nonprofessional staff members, such as clerical and janitorial staff. All nonprofessional staff members (as well as other professional and paraprofessional staff) must be fully aware of the ethical obligations of professional counselors and must be fully informed of their specific obligations to ensure the ethical rights of clients. Counselors are ethically and legally responsible to guarantee that there is no breach of ethics by staff members under their direction. In-service (in agency or within school) ethics training with staff members is highly recommended. A formal written agreement between counselors and their staff members is also recommended; this assigns a formality and importance to matters of ethical sensitivity. A breach of ethics could, and in some cases should, lead to termination of an employee who knowingly breaks the rules. Staff members should be especially sensitive to the client's right to privacy and confidentiality. Use of temporary staff or temporary agency workers should be avoided—such workers may work at the counseling site for short periods and may be replaced prior to adequate ethics training.

## ADVERTISING

It was once considered unprofessional for highly educated professionals to advertise or solicit for clients. Professional codes of ethics banned lawyers and doctors from advertising. Legal challenges to these ethics code edicts were successful, and today radio and TV advertisements for doctors, lawyers, health service providers, and mental health professionals are common. A 1987 survey of psychologists found that about one fourth of the respondents advertised in newspapers and similar media (Pope, Tabachnick, & Keith-Spiegel, 1987). Today it is very common for professionals to have websites and to use electronic means of advertising (e.g., Google ads, Facebook ads).

Deception is the major issue related to advertising and soliciting clients. The ethics codes caution practitioners and define deceptive advertising as unethical. In fact, ACA (2014) Section C.3.a. states: "When advertising or otherwise representing their services to the public, counselors identify their credentials in an accurate manner that is not false, misleading, deceptive, or fraudulent." Examples of deception include: (a) A master's-level, licensed professional counselor who earns a doctoral degree from a bogus degree program (or a degree in a field unrelated to counseling) and lists the doctorate as a professional qualification (Dattilio, 1989). A counselor who lists himself as a PhD candidate or claims to have completed "PhD studies," although not technically a misrepresentation, certainly is being deceptive—such status does not necessarily lead to attainment of the degree and may mislead the public. In fact, ACA (2014) Section C.4.d. specifically states: "Counselors do not imply doctoral-level competence when possessing a master's degree in counseling or a related field by referring to themselves as 'Dr.' in a counseling context when their doctorate is not in counseling or a related field. Counselors do not use 'ABD' (all but dissertation) or other such terms to imply competency." (b) A counselor who lists bogus, unrelated, or unfinished degrees as credentials is deceptive and is misrepresenting his or her legitimate (acceptable), professional counseling training. This is specifically codified in ACA (2014) Section C.4.a., which states, in part, "Counselors claim or imply only professional qualifications actually completed and correct any known misrepresentations of their qualifications by others."

Additionally, client testimonials should be solicited only from clients who are not vulnerable in any way related to consent. As per ACA (2014) Section C.3.b., "Counselors who use testimonials do not solicit them from current clients, former clients, or any other persons who may be vulnerable to undue influence. Counselors discuss with clients the implications of and obtain permission for the use of any testimonial." Counselors should avoid making global statements related to the nature or success of treatment, such as "loving care," "your way to health and happiness"—counselors cannot guarantee that they will care in a loving way for all of their clients, nor should they guarantee that all clients will be "happy" once services are provided (happiness may not be the acceptable outcome!). Trying to defend oneself against a client's claims that he or she did not feel happier after services, for example, could be a nightmare.

Caution aside, and given the competitive nature of the health enterprise today, it may serve a counselor well to advertise. However, advertising should be prudent, tasteful, and free from global statements or guarantees that cannot be substantiated by professional literature or objective data.

If a counselor sells products in addition to providing services, such products should be advertised in a way that accurately depicts the product or service (ACA, 2014, Section C.3.e.). It is quite legitimate for a counselor to sell relaxation audiotapes or videotapes or electronic files to clients for use in the privacy of their homes. However, in many places a formal retail sales license is needed to sell products, and local laws must be examined to ensure there is nothing illegal with selling such products. Counselors should sell only products within the purview of their professional and sales license. Selling herbs or herbal cures is risky, for example, because counselors do not hold licenses that are related to pharmaceuticals. Also, selling health aids for matters unrelated to mental health might be easily challenged by a client who is disenchanted by the product; such sales may constitute a potentially detrimental relationship. If a counselor sells vitamins or cleaning products as a sideline, selling such products to clients may infringe on the professional relationship. But a counselor might legitimately sell self-help books that meet a high professional standard, or training tapes related to specific goals of treatment. The general rule is to sell only products that can be clearly linked to the goals of treatment and clearly related to the professional license scope of practice. It is important to keep the role of the mental health professional clearly delineated.

Counselors employed in two or more settings should also avoid soliciting clients from one agency or setting of employment to another—for example, a counselor employed by a school should avoid soliciting clients for a private practice while in the role of a school counselor.

## CREDENTIALS

For the professionally motivated individual, there is nothing more rewarding than earning a degree and being able to list degree initials after one's name. Once licensure status is earned, professionals can add additional letters after their names, such as LPC for the licensed professional counselor, LCSW for the licensed clinical social worker, the LMFT for the licensed marriage and family therapist, and the LP for the licensed psychologist. Professional certification by legitimate, professional certifying bodies offers a counselor another way of distinguishing himself or herself. The National Board for Certified Counselors (NBCC) and the Commission on Rehabilitation Counselor Certification (CRCC), two highly recognized and valued certifying bodies in professional counseling, allow individuals to list NCC or CRC after their names to signify certification. It is common to see the initials MA, LPC, NCC after a counselor's name on correspondence, in case files, on letterhead, and on professional business cards. In social work, the NASW has two valuable clinical credentials—the Academy of Certified Social Workers (ACSW) credential and the Diplomate in Clinical Social Work (DCSW), both requiring the Master's in Social Work degree and demonstration of knowledge in social work, with the DCSW being the highest credential for mature and accomplished social work clinicians. In marriage and family therapy, there are no specialty boards to certify designated specialty practice, but the LMFT serves as a recognized license and credential in the field. Psychologists may seek specialty certification through the respected American Board of Professional Psychology (ABPP), which offers specialty certifications in a number of recognized specialties (see Chapter 2 for a more thorough discussion). These licenses and specialty designations for the mental health professions offer clinicians a way of designating their specialty and knowledge base in a way that provides recognition and signifies accomplishment.

Mental health professionals are proud to list such credentials. It is wise to list credentials in case file information to distinguish the provider as a professional counselor, a clinical psychologist, social worker, or family therapist. In some cases, it is unnecessary to list all credentials—one does not have to present a resume with every letter of correspondence. A listing of basic credentials is sufficient. And in case files, it may be sufficient and prudent to list initials or titles associated with the professional license, for example "LPC," "LCSW," "LMFT," or "Licensed Psychologist." Counselors must not misrepresent their credentials. Also, it is unacceptable for a counselor to state that one is licensed without providing information on what kind of license he or she holds. There should be no question as to whether a person is a licensed counselor, psychologist, social worker, family therapist, a nurse, or a physician.

Although professional memberships can be announced in correspondence, membership itself should not be held out as a credential, unless the association has a special designated membership level. For example, the AAMFT has a "clinical member" category, which requires the member to have intense, approved supervision after receiving a degree. AAMFT "clinical membership" is a sought-after status and is a well-recognized credential.

Credentials in the mental health field are a dime a dozen. Literally anyone can set up a certification body and charge a fee for a fancy diploma. The use of such credentials to mislead the public about the competence or qualifications is highly dubious and reflects badly on the counselor and the profession (see Chapter 2). Such credentials may not stand the test of a court challenge in defense against incompetent practice or malpractice as a specialist. Generally, only credentials with linkages to legitimate professional organizations are valued in the mental health field. Beyond the NBCC and the CRCC, two examples of acceptable counseling credentials are those offered by (a) the National Academy of Certified Family Therapists (which has linkage to the ACA through its affiliate, the International Association for Marriage and Family Counseling), and (b) the "Certificate in Clinical Hypnosis" sponsored by the American Society of

Clinical Hypnosis. In social work, the ACSW and DCSW credentials are well respected. In psychology, the ABPP credential is well established. Agency and school administrators should communicate which credentials are acceptable or valued and how, when, and where acceptable professional credentials are to be displayed or listed.

**Questions for Reflection:** A counselor lists on his business card that he is a certified hypnotherapist, but provides no further information. Is this unethical? If so, why?

## MAINTENANCE OF RECORDS AND FILES

Offices sometimes become sloppy. It is not unusual to visit a professional counselor's office and to feel that it is "lived in" (to put it nicely). Although a professional office may feel like home to many, there are serious differences between professional and nonprofessional offices. Client records, unlike personal records, need to be protected. They should be filed in a safe place and locked away when not in use. Files should not be left out in the open, especially after work hours or when other clients are in close, visual contact. Electronic files must be safeguarded, password protected, and stored in inaccessible storage places (a safe "cloud" storage site or a removable external flash or hard drive on a computer).

It is standard procedure to destroy records a certain number of years after services have been terminated. Most licensure boards require that records be kept a certain period of time after services have been terminated for legal reasons (e.g., in case there is an ethics complaint). Records are generally kept for 5 to 7 years after services have been terminated; Wheeler and Bertram (2015) recommend 7 years in the absence of a state requirement. Attorneys typically recommend holding records until the **statute of limitations (the date before which a suit must be filed subsequent to an illegal act)** has expired; some attorneys will argue records should never be destroyed until a practitioner retires, as the records are a best defense against any claim made against the professional (see Hartsell & Bernstein, 2013). Disposal of records is not as simple as just throwing them in the trash—records should be destroyed in a way that removes identification or by shredding or by burning. Old bills, office notes, and calendars should also be destroyed in a way that ensures privacy.

Wheeler and Bertram (2015) recommend that counselors draft a records retention policy, which conforms to all state and federal laws, and which specifies the procedures for maintenance, storage, and destruction of such records, as well as keeping a record of which documents were destroyed and when.

Counselors should also have policies about removing files from the office. Some agencies have strict policies that forbid removal of files (paper or electronic) from the office, since removing a file from a safe place can be a dangerous practice. A file in a briefcase can be stolen, files may be left in an unlocked automobile, and a counselor's family members may have access to files in the home setting. Flash drives should be password protected and kept in the office. Obviously, removing files from the office is not good ethical practice. Counselors should have a compelling reason to remove a file to an unsecured environment.

## COMMUNICATIONS WITH OTHER PROFESSIONALS

Communication with other professionals can take several forms. Communication occurs among the professionals within an agency and with professionals outside of the agency. Schools also have internal and external means of communications, primarily between counselors and teachers or administrators.

Clear agency or school guidelines should be established for intra- (within) agency/school communications, with the client's best interests at heart. Most agencies have general statements of confidentiality that allow for internal communications among professionals, such as counselors, psychologists, psychiatrists, and social workers, and/or marriage/family therapists on staff. Schools, however, may have policies that prevent the communication of sensitive counseling material to teachers or administrators without compelling educational or safety-related reasons. The prudent course of action is to keep confidential information as confidential as possible within a school or agency setting. Clients should never be the brunt of gossip in a teachers' lounge, nor should agency personnel know more than they need to know in regard to interactions with clients. However, there are cases that require cross-professional involvement— for example, between a psychiatrist and a counselor who are both involved with a client. Generally, clients should know when such interaction is necessary and the reasons for consultation. In most cases, special consent is not necessary for within-agency or school consultation; however, local and federal laws should be examined to assess if special obligations exist.

Communications with professionals outside of an agency or school are governed by rules of confidentiality and privacy. Formal consent should be obtained—confidentiality and privacy statements signed by the client at the outset of treatment should describe circumstances under which a counselor can communicate to other professionals in the best interests of the client (as in emergency situations). If ongoing formal consultation is requested, the counselor should have a formal agreement with the consultant allowing for such interaction—for example, a private practitioner might have an agreement with another private practitioner to discuss difficult cases. To ensure that professional feedback can occur without a breach of client rights, counselors can develop a consultant agreement that allows for detailed discussion of cases, perhaps without identifying information. Such agreements are in no way reflective of a supervisory or controlling relationship and simply allow for professional communication on challenging cases.

When a counselor makes a referral, he or she cannot receive remuneration for the referral (ACA, 2014, Section A.10.b.). Such payment could compromise professional judgment, leading to referral to the remunerating professional for less than professional reasons. Counselors should refer to a list of qualified professionals rather than to one professional and allow clients to choose from the list on their own after researching their options. Counselors must consider the legal ramifications of referrals. Attorneys sometimes "shot-gun" lawsuits—broadly "shooting at" (suing) any involved professional. If a professional to whom a counselor referred a client does something wrong, the client's lawyer might sue the counselor as the referring agent.

> **Question for Reflection:** You are a professional school counselor employed in a secondary school. At lunch in the teachers' lounge, you overhear one of your counseling colleagues and a teacher discussing the family problems of a student. There is some laughter involved. What should you do?

## DISAGREEMENTS WITH EMPLOYERS OR SUPERVISORS

Professional counselors sometimes have disagreements with employers, administrators, or supervisors. It is important to have a clear understanding of the role of the supervisor and the role of the supervised counselor. If the supervision is for professional licensure or certification, both parties should sign a formal supervision agreement (Remley & Herlihy, 2014). Such an agreement should spell out the responsibilities of both parties, the amount of time and the place where supervision is to take place, the nature of job duties covered by the supervision, the ethical obligations of the supervisor and supervised counselor, the nature of legal responsibility for work that is accomplished, the requirement of malpractice insurance and coverage on the supervisor's policy, an agreement on how the supervision can end (e.g., the circumstances and actions that can lead to a negative recommendation by the supervisor regarding licensure or certification), and the length of the proposed supervision. Failure to clarify details on such matters can lead to difficulties if there are disagreements. Supervised counselors should also have some understanding about what to do if they question the ethical judgment of their supervisors. An arbitration arrangement to address disagreement is one way to avoid conflicts—that is, if there is disagreement, an arbitrator acceptable to both parties is consulted to make a judgment on the acceptable course of action. Remley and Herlihy (2014) offer a "Clinical Supervision Model Agreement" that serves as an excellent example of licensure supervision.

Conflicts with administrators sometimes are more problematic. If a non-counselor administrator establishes policy that conflicts with the conventional ethical wisdom of the profession, counselors have an obligation to educate the administrator. Administrative policies are sometimes crucial to the effectiveness of counseling—for example, an administrator may require that a number of clients too large to accomplish effective group counseling should be scheduled for group sessions. Counselors may be assigned a caseload that is too large to provide competent services; equipment and supplies may be out of date; facilities may be inadequate. A number of administrative issues can become problematic; counselors are obligated to address the problems with the people in charge. If changes are not made to ensure adequate, competent, and ethical services, a counselor should examine other employment options. (This may be hard to do if one's retirement benefits are an issue.) However, the counselor's primary responsibility is to try to inspire changes within the organization, which would be the ethical course of action.

Counselors also have an obligation to prevent discrimination. If it appears that administrative policies are such that certain constituents are singled out, denied services, or treated unfairly, it is the counselor's obligation to address concerns with the administration. The mental health professional ethical codes have stipulations about nondiscrimination.

## CONCLUSION

Privacy issues should be of the utmost importance in the design of a professional office. Soundproofing, separate entry/exit doors, and maintaining privacy of client files are issues of importance. Offices should be organized to provide for the safety of clients and staff. In space-sharing arrangements, counselors must ensure the privacy of all client files and other case-relevant information. Formal, written ethics agreements between parties are recommended. Counselors must make provisions for individuals with disabilities: elevators in storied buildings, wheelchair accessible bathrooms, and accommodations for hearing or visually impaired clients. Offices that receive federal funds must be in compliance with accessibility standards.

Several systems are available for fee setting: (a) sliding fee scales; (b) flat fee, variable collection procedures; (c) low fee cash-only service, and (d) credit/debit card payments. Regardless of the fee and billing procedures, counselors must have a clearly articulated fee schedule and stick to the schedule. Clients must understand the procedures at initiation of treatment. Fraudulent billing is a major concern related to billing. Billing for services that were not provided or justified is fraudulent practice. Double billing can result in felony convictions for insurance fraud, a loss of license to practice, and censure from a professional organization. Overdiagnosing also constitutes insurance fraud and can do harm to clients.

All nonprofessional staff must be fully aware of their ethical obligations. Counselors are ethically responsible to guarantee no breach of ethics by staff members under their direction.

Counselors must avoid deception in advertising. Client testimonials should be solicited only from clients who are not vulnerable in any way related to consent. Counselors should avoid global statements they cannot guarantee. Counselors must not misrepresent their credentials. Use of credentials to mislead the public about competence or qualifications is highly dubious.

It is standard practice to destroy case records a certain number of years after services have been terminated, generally 5 to 7 years. Records should be destroyed in a way that removes identification or by shredding or burning.

Communication with other professionals can occur among the professionals within an agency and with professionals outside the agency. Clear guidelines should be established with the client's best interests at heart. Most agencies have general statements of confidentiality that allow for internal communications. Communications outside an agency or school are governed by rules of confidentiality and privacy.

It is important to have a clear understanding of the roles of the supervisor and the supervised counselor in case of disagreements. Agreements should spell out the responsibilities of both parties.

# TECHNOLOGY IN THE PRACTICE OF COUNSELING AND PSYCHOTHERAPY

*David B. Peterson and*
*Robert Rocco Cottone*

## OBJECTIVES

- To provide an overview of technology as it is applied to counseling practice.
- To relate such technology to the ethical practice of counseling professionals in:
    - maintaining confidential records,
    - conducting confidential communication,
    - using technology to enhance counseling services,
    - using technology in place of direct counseling services,
    - using the Internet as a counseling service modality, and
    - conducting assessments to enhance counseling practice.
- To review ethical standards of practice relevant to the use of technology in the mental health professions.
- To explore the use of technology in counselor education.

## "TECHNOCENTERED" AND "TECHNOANXIOUS"

Harris-Bowlsbey (2000), an early pioneer in the development of computer-based, career planning systems, suggested that many warm and caring counselors with enterprising and artistic proclivities may find embracing **cybertechnology (computer technology, especially involving the Internet or electronic communication at a distance)** as foreign and uncomfortable. The reactions of mental health professionals to technology span a continuum from acceptance to anxiety. Brod (1984) dichotomized people's reactions to technology as **technocentered (comfortable with computer technology)** and **technoanxious (fearful and avoiding computerization of the profession)**.

The resistance of counselors and psychotherapists to computerization of various work-relevant tasks could be explained in part by technoanxiety (Ford, 1993). The benefits of technological advances are numerous and substantial. Technology has broad application to the mental health enterprise, as technological means of service provision and therapist education are already having a significant effect on the provision of mental health services. Provision of mental health services through electronic means is in sync with the development of **telehealth** services in general **(the provision of health advice and treatments at a distance by means of technological communications)**.

Technoanxiety aside, there are many ethical concerns associated with the implementation of new technology, so the use of computers and related technology in mental health services must be carried out carefully, thoughtfully, and in a way that ensures competent and ethical service provision. Counselors and psychotherapists must be aware of limitations before embarking on their own professional electronic practices.

## ELECTRONIC CAPABILITY—A HISTORICAL PERSPECTIVE

During the past 50 years, computer capabilities have dramatically increased while costs to implement such technology have decreased significantly (Ford, 1993; Sampson, 2000; Simons, 1985). Personal computers (PCs), laptops, electronic tablets, digitized watches, and mobile and smartphones have increased in sophistication. These changes have increased the use of such technology in the counseling profession (Bloom & Walz, 2000; Colby, 1980; Ford, 1993; Levitan, Willis, & Vogelgesang, 1985; Sampson, 2000).

Computer-based applications for clinical situations in counseling-related professions began as early as the 1960s, with computer-based test interpretation (Butcher, 1987; Fowler, 1985). During the 1970s, researchers expanded computer-assisted testing capabilities to include administration, scoring, and interpretation of psychological tests (Butcher, 1987). Computer-assisted assessments increased in number throughout the 1980s and into the 21st century; and the use, assets, and limitations of such technologies were quickly explored in the counseling literature (Bloom & Walz, 2000; Butcher, 1985, 1987; Eyde, 1987; Ford, 1993; Fowler, 1985; French, 1986; Matarazzo, 1985, 1986; Merrell, 1986; Sampson, 1990, 2000).

Computer-assisted therapy also originated in the 1960s, with much less success than computerized assessment applications (Colby, Gould, & Aronson, 1989; Colby, Watt, & Gilbert, 1966; Ford, 1993). Therapeutic applications received little further attention until the 1980s (Ford, 1993). Since then, various types of computer-assisted therapies have been used, including professional consultation programs, client therapeutic learning programs, and online therapy. Unlike computer-assisted assessment, little was written on the ethical issues related to the use of computer-assisted therapy until the 1990s (Bloom & Walz, 2000; Peterson, Murray, & Chan, 1998; Sampson, Kolodinski, & Greeno, 1997).

As computer technology has become more affordable and desk and laptop computers, electronic tablets, mobile and smartphones, and digitized watches have grown in number, tasks once dedicated to paper, typewriter, or pen have been transferred to more convenient computerized technologies. The advent of **facsimile machines (faxes, which transmit exact copies of documents over phone lines or the Internet)**, computer networks (e.g., the Internet), wireless satellite networks, and the **cloud (an Internet-accessed remote storage system)** has resulted in new forms of electronic media that mental health professionals use with increasing frequency.

The ethical codes of practice and the literature associated with counseling and the mental health professions have been hard-pressed to keep pace with the dramatic changes in technology (Granello, 2000). In fact, one of the major reasons for the motivation to update the 2014 American Counseling Association (ACA) *Code of Ethics* was the need to address emerging technology issues, specifically social media. Some ethical issues related to recent technological developments have been of concern to mental health professionals for many years. Other issues are unique to more recent technological developments. Several mental health professional organizations have addressed new standards of practice related to technology.

## STANDARDS ACROSS THE MENTAL HEALTH PROFESSIONS

The American Psychological Association (APA) has developed "Guidelines for the Practice of Telepsychology" (APA, 2013) which defines telepsychology as:

> Telepsychology is defined, for the purpose of these guidelines, as the provision of psychological services using telecommunication technologies. Telecommunications is the preparation, transmission, communication, or related processing of information by electrical, electromagnetic, electromechanical, electro-optical, or electronic means (Committee on National Security Systems, 2010). Telecommunication technologies include but are not limited to telephone, mobile devices, interactive videoconferencing, e-mail, chat, text, and Internet (e.g., self-help websites, blogs, and social media). The information that is transmitted may be in writing, or include images, sounds or other data. These communications may be synchronous with multiple parties communicating in real time (e.g., interactive videoconferencing, telephone) or asynchronous (e.g., e-mail,

online bulletin boards, storing and forwarding information). Technologies may augment traditional in-person services (e.g., psychoeducational materials online after an in-person therapy session), or be used as stand-alone services (e.g., therapy or leadership development provided over videoconferencing). Different technologies may be used in various combinations and for different purposes during the provision of telepsychology services. For example, videoconferencing and telephone may also be utilized for direct service while e-mail and text is used for non-direct services (e.g., scheduling). Regardless of the purpose, psychologists strive to be aware of the potential benefits and limitations in their choices of technologies for particular clients in particular situations. (APA, 2013)

As the APA definition implies, telepsychology is complex and may involve many methods of electronic communication individually or in combination. The APA "guidelines" provide a number of technical definitions that may be helpful to beginning therapists; for example, terms like "remote," "information systems," and "security" are defined and explained in the context of telepsychology work. The guidelines then address ethical standards and the specific concerns that arise as those standards apply. For example, the standard of "competence" is addressed at the level of both clinical competence and technical competence working within the electronic medium. Informed consent is addressed, specifically related to the laws that apply to provision of services in the locale of the client, and also addressing the need to define the unique circumstances involved in counseling through electronic means (e.g., counseling at a distance). Confidentiality and data storage is covered in the guidelines, as the nature of electronically produced information makes it easy to store as digital data. Data storage should be addressed in a presentation on matters of confidentiality. How data will be stored and destroyed need to be addressed. Any special application of testing or assessment must be clearly outlined and facts on how information will be scored, interpreted, and communicated are important to provide. Practice across jurisdictions (across state lines, for example) must be addressed and the laws of the state where the client is housed must be followed. In effect, the APA document is thorough, and it provides excellent guidance on the ethical application of telepsychology practice.

The American Counseling Association (ACA, 2014) also has addressed electronic methods of counseling and education in a section of the *Code of Ethics*. Section H, titled "Distance Counseling, Technology, and Social Media," specifically addresses legal considerations, competency, informed consent and disclosure, confidentiality, security, and the need to acknowledge the limitations of services provided by electronic means. The standards also describe the need to verify the identity of the client. Ethical professional boundary standards apply, as the counselor's role should be clearly demarcated as a helper role. Records and maintenance of records issues are defined, including the need for security and encryption. Clients should be aware of their rights from the beginning of the electronic relationship. Business media or other professional websites may be shared with clients, but personal social media pages or personal webpages should not be shared with clients. Counselors should not view the social media of clients without the consent of clients.

The American Association for Marriage and Family Therapy (AAMFT, 2015) standards address technology in Standard VI, which is about technology-assisted professional services. Before entering into such a professional relationship with a client, the client must be informed of the potential risks and benefits. Consent issues are addressed in the standard, as are the issues of confidentiality and documentation. Practitioners are not to practice outside the jurisdictional limits of their credentials. They must be well trained and competent in both the delivery of clinical services and the technological means of service provision.

The National Association of Social Workers (NASW) together with the Association of Social Work Boards published "Standards for Technology and Social Work Practice" in 2005 (NASW, 2005). The standards define technology and social work practice as: "'any electronic mediated activity used in the conduct of competent and ethical delivery of social work services" (p. 3). Importantly, the standards require that social workers advocate for their clients to ensure access to technology. The standards require social workers to be clinically and technically competent at providing services through electronic means, making sure to follow regulations that apply in jurisdictions of practice. Verification of client identity is required. Privacy, confidentiality, documentation, and security issues are addressed. Risks must be addressed.

Both the NASW and the APA have developed separate standard documents related to technology. The ACA and the AAMFT have addressed technology issues directly in their codes of ethics. It is essential for mental health professionals to remain current with efforts to develop and to establish ethical standards and codes of conduct to protect and benefit their clients. Technology is developing rapidly, and technological applications to the practice of counseling and psychotherapy will likely change accordingly. In fact, Cottone (2015) raised the issue of technological singularity, that moment in time when artificial intelligence (computer-based) reaches or surpasses human intellectual capacity; he predicted that the mental health enterprise would change dramatically, even to the degree surrogates are employed as counselors, or counselors or clients may be genetically or structurally modified. The possibilities are both exciting and perturbing, as service delivery may be radically reformed.

## ETHICAL MANAGEMENT OF ELECTRONIC MEDIA

Ethical codes addressing the maintenance of client records, such as those established by the APA, mandate that psychologists maintain appropriate confidentiality in creating, storing, accessing, transferring, and disposing of all manner of records in their care. The ACA, AAMFT, and NASW have similar requirements—the ethical professional must protect the client's right to confidentiality regardless of the type of electronic media.

All forms of electronic media used in counseling may contain sensitive material protected by client–therapist confidentiality and privileged communication. It is important that ethical counselors are aware of how the use of electronic media influences professional practice. Protocols need to be in place to ensure that electronic media will be accessible only to ethically appropriate parties. Electronic media storage systems may not be immediately understandable or visible to the counseling professional, and therefore ethical management of such data may be easily overlooked. Counseling professionals use a variety of types of electronic media, including PCs, laptop computers, tablets, faxes, e-mail, and mobile or smartphones.

## ELECTRONIC MEDIA, INFORMATION, AND STORAGE

PC systems commonly used by counseling professionals are composed of hardware and software. **Hardware consists of the electrical and mechanical devices of the computer system, including the central processing unit (CPU) of the computer (or the "brains" in the computer), the monitor, the printer, and various peripheral (outside of the CPU) devices, such as a scanner.** Hardware that stores electronic information includes (a) a hard disk drive, which is a sealed memory system located either within the chassis of the CPU or in a portable peripheral unit; (b) flash drives or external hard drives that store the information loaded to a program and the CPU; (c) an in-house (local) server that has a large data storage drive for a network of computers; and (d) the **cloud, which is an Internet-accessed central storage system with massive storage capability.** At the time of writing, the cloud is the newest storage model being used by mental health professionals. **A "cloud" actually is a structure including computer infrastructure and a physical space—usually a temperature-controlled secured building with back-up electric generators that houses massive computers that act as servers to those that access the cloud through devices connected to the Internet or other means of access.** Users may access the cloud through a cloud storage gateway or web-based content management systems. Hosting companies typically own and provide access to data storage, usually for a fee (e.g., Adobe, AT&T, Google, and Apple all host clouds). Several organizations now provide **cloud-based practice management systems** (sometimes called suites) specifically designed for mental health providers; for a monthly fee, the practitioner or the agency/organization can use the clinical services, applications, and data storage provided by the systems.

Electronic information can be safeguarded at the hardware level with a mechanical lock and key that prevents power from reaching the computer, thus maintaining confidentiality of the information within. Once turned on, such systems should not be left unattended and they should only be accessed by a secure password.

Software includes the programs written for the CPU to perform various functions, or applications. Common computer applications used by counseling professionals include document production using word processing applications, financial and records management using spreadsheets, and record filing on databases. Word processors generate media formerly produced by typewriters and handwriting, such as case notes, letters, and test reports. Spreadsheets are used for numerical record-keeping tasks like client billing and miscellaneous records. Databases are electronic "file cabinets" used to store and control large amounts of information, such as client mailing lists and community referral sources.

Most recently, the development of software "suites" provides multiple functions in one software package. **A suite (also called a practice management system) is software that helps to manage lists of clients and referral resources, diagnostic codes, insurance billing transactions, reporting capabilities, managed care authorizations, and progress notes.** Software suites may be cloud-connected or designed for local computers and servers only.

Documents created by a word processor, spreadsheet, or database application can be printed to create a hard copy and stored as files on memory systems. In addition to the need to control access to printed matter generated from computers, the data stored electronically must be carefully controlled. Personnel with access to such data must be well trained regarding ethical management of electronic media. A **flash drive (a removable portable storage device inserted into a computer's universal serial bus [USB] port to access the computer; a flash drive is sometimes called a "thumb drive" due to its size)** containing confidential information may be less obvious than a notebook-size chart containing paper copies of the same information. A password-protected flash drive can store information equivalent to many client charts and is much easier to remove from an office than a rack full of confidential records. Regardless, paper records and electronically stored information must be secured in ways that are tamper-proof. Information storage devices must be password protected or **encrypted (meaning the data are converted or encoded into a language that can only be read by approved recipients).**

The storage of confidential material on a hard drive may be even less obvious to the counselor. All staff members within a counseling organization must be oriented to the appropriate ethical procedures for storage of client records and the related access protocols. For hard drives on PCs, security software is available that will allow access to certain files only if a person has an access code or password. People who are issued access codes must protect their codes from misuse. If a PC in a counseling organization does not require a security code to access confidential information, large amounts of data are at risk of being viewed by people who should not have access to such information.

Organizations that use a server for a **network of computers**, sometimes called a **local area network (LAN)**, need to establish protocols that limit access only to ethically relevant parties. Servers can be accessed by PCs or wirelessly (using wireless devices like smartphones or tablets), which greatly increases the probability of unauthorized persons having access to the secured data. Computer systems management specialists who set up systems for business organizations must be made aware of the location of sensitive confidential material. They can design the system with the appropriate safeguards and security protocols to maintain confidentiality through security software that requires pass codes and the requisite employee training. LAN administrators routinely back up or duplicate LAN files as archives in the event of a hardware or software malfunction that results in the loss of data. If a PC user on the network has stored files on the server (e.g., word processor documents, spreadsheet files, database files, e-mail), the archived files may contain confidential material. Even though a given file may be deleted locally by a network user, there may be an archived copy stored somewhere, accessible to potentially inappropriate parties. Protocols must be established with LAN administrators regarding the archiving of potentially confidential information.

Unfortunately, counseling professionals may not be motivated to purchase adequate systems of protection due to ignorance or the presumed unlikelihood of unethical file disclosure. Establishing a secure computer system can be time-consuming and costly; nevertheless, confidential client information needs to be protected.

## FAXES AND E-MAIL

**Facsimile (fax) machines (machines used for copying and transmitting electronic versions of documents)** allow the transmission of information either from paper or directly from a computer file. Generally, faxes are composed of printed matter, which can include any type of client information protected by client–therapist confidentiality. Counselors need to use caution when sending confidential information by fax. Many businesses have centrally located, public fax machines that are inappropriate for receiving confidential information. It is the counselor's responsibility to ensure that confidential fax transmissions arrive in a secured environment. Faxes can be sent directly to a PC by fax. The security precautions mentioned for electronic media storage apply to fax transmissions sent to PCs. A quick phone call to assess the situation before sending a confidential fax is appropriate to ensure safe arrival of sensitive information. In the event that a destination PC or fax machine is not secure, the counselor should phone before transmitting documents to alert appropriate parties to intercept confidential information. Disclaimers placed on fax cover sheets are not sufficient protection against unscrupulous interception of confidential data.

**Electronic mail, or e-mail, uses the Internet to send and receive messages among individuals or groups, simulating the sending and receiving of letters through paper "mail."** Confidential information on e-mail is vulnerable to interception by people other than the designated recipient; therefore, counselors must use caution when sending counseling-related information. Because of frequent use of e-mail by counselors, it is important to emphasize the ethical vulnerability of such communication. Today it is possible to attach scanned documents or **portable document format (PDF)** by means of e-mail, which is even more convenient than faxing. Scanned or PDF files are easily attached to e-mails and can be accessed directly on a recipient's computer or electronic device.

## MOBILE OR SMARTPHONES

**While mobile (wireless) or smartphones (wireless phones with computer and Internet capacities beyond communication)** are a tremendous convenience in today's frenetically paced society, they are neither secure nor private forms of communication. Discussion of confidential material should not occur over mobile or smartphone networks.

## COMPUTER-ASSISTED COUNSELING

Computer-assisted counseling exists in a variety of forms. Some programs function as therapeutic consultants (Goodman, Gingerich, & Shazer, 1989). The advent of the Internet and chat rooms has created the opportunity for direct, online communication between counselor and client (online counseling). Therapeutic software that is marketed to operate without therapist assistance is also available (Lawrence, 1986; Sampson, 1986). Cottone (2015) predicted the day when surrogate counselors will be doing the work of live counselors, as artificial intelligence begins to surpass the capacity of humans—the moment known as the "singularity." It's not hard to predict that major changes are on the way related to the delivery of counseling services—all based on the development of smart machines.

## History

Computer-assisted therapy was first developed in the 1960s (Colby et al., 1966), but was relatively unsuccessful. Attempts to computerize psychotherapy were rejuvenated in the 1980s with the popularization of behavioral modes of therapy and the emphasis of bringing about change through education (Ford, 1993; Wagman, 1988). Early versions of counseling software that did not require counselor assistance included MORTON, which was based on cognitive behavior therapy and was designed primarily to treat mild forms of depression (Selmi, Klein, Greist, Johnson, & Harris, 1982). MORTON began with an educational component that addressed a cognitive model of depression with subsequent testing of the client's comprehension of the theory, feedback on a test of depression (Beck Depression Inventory), review of homework, and exercises to combat thoughts that perpetuate depression. The program offered response choices to the client, with limited free responding. One experimental program, GURU, attempted to expand interactive conversation capabilities with the goal of increasing self-awareness (Colby, Colby, & Stoller, 1990).

Virtual psychotherapy programs began to be developed, such as Avatars (Duncan, 1997). This software depicts characterizations of the client via a computer image or graphic, with bubbles overhead to indicate ongoing dialogue. Another application, Palace, develops an **"Intranet," or closed Internet system**, allowing for virtual psychotherapy with a controlled audience (Duncan, 1997). Today, a number of websites offer counseling services for a fee; some appear sophisticated and professionally and ethically designed, while others appear fly-by-night and potentially exploitive of the uneducated public.

## Career and Rehabilitation Counseling

Computerized career counseling has been evaluated by Kilvingham, Johnston, Hogan, and Mauer (1994). They concluded that clients who were highly motivated and goal directed benefited from the System for Interactive Guidance and Information-Plus (SIGI-PLUS). However, they determined that clients with less clear goals and less motivation for independence did not benefit as much from the use of this program. Group or individual counseling was proposed as more appropriate in the latter case. In such a case, using computer career counseling software as an adjunct to individual and group counseling would be exemplary of good, ethical counseling practice.

Career counseling often involves a psychoeducational approach (information provision), which lends itself well to delivery through computer-assisted venues. A comprehensive review of research evaluating one of the most popular career guidance systems, DISCOVER, suggested that the computer-assisted format helped to increase self-efficacy and decision-making skills, increased planfulness, increased knowledge about specific occupations, and resulted in more targeted career goals (Taber & Luzzo, 1999).

In rehabilitation, as early as 1978, video games were used in the later phases of cognitive retraining for persons with a head injury. Cognitive retraining falls under the domain of therapy in a rehabilitation hospital setting. The novelty of the games made the monotonous, repetitive exercises that enhanced cognitive functioning more enjoyable (Caplan, 1987). A more sophisticated computerized testing application, the Computer-Assisted Cognitive Retraining (CACR) system, was developed in 1987 by the Brain Injury Rehabilitation Unit in Palo Alto, California. The CACR used various computer-driven exercises to enhance the individual's alertness, attention, concentration, fine-motor skills, memory, and certain language abilities (e.g., spelling, reading, and word finding). Performance scores were recorded by the computer and a graph indicated the client's progress.

## Programs Associated With Specific Theoretical Orientations

A variety of theoretical orientations were adapted to computer-assisted counseling, including behavioral, cognitive, educational, and psychodynamic approaches (Ford, 1993). Software was developed to target AIDS education (Schinke & Orlandi, 1990; Schinke et al., 1989), the treatment of drug and alcohol abuse (Moncher et al., 1985), obesity (Burnett, Magel, Harrington, & Taylor, 1989; Burnett, Taylor, & Agras, 1985; Taylor, Agras, Losch, Plante, & Burnett, 1991), personal distress (Wagman, 1980, 1988; Wagman & Kerber, 1980), sexual dysfunction (Binik, Servan-Schreiber, Freiwald, & Hall, 1988; Servan-Schreiber & Binik, 1989), smoking (Burling et al., 1989; Schneider, 1986; Schneider, Walter, & O'Donnell, 1990), and stress (Smith, 1987). Various clinical populations have benefited from computer-assisted counseling, including persons with depression (Selmi, Klein, Greist, Sorell, & Erdman, 1990), persons with phobia (Carr, Ghosh, & Marks, 1988; Salyer, 1997), people who are violent offenders (Ford & Vitelli, 1992), patients with burn pain (Salyer, 1997), and head trauma patients who need cognitive retraining (Niemann, Ruff, & Baser, 1990).

As computer technology continues to improve, so will the capabilities of computer-assisted therapy. The ethical implications of widespread use of such technology have not been adequately explored (Ford, 1993; Peterson, Murray, & Chan, 1998; Sampson et al., 1997).

## Computer-Assisted Counseling: Real Therapy?

Many counselors wonder—is computer-assisted counseling "real therapy?" The concepts of counseling and psychotherapy are so inclusive that further clarification of computer-assisted counseling is necessary before the point can be argued successfully. Grencavage and Norcross (1990) suggested that psychotherapies do have commonalities: (a) development of a therapeutic alliance, (b) opportunity for catharsis, (c) acquisition and practice of new behaviors, and (d) clients' positive expectations. The literature supports the contention that computer-assisted counseling can be used to practice new behaviors, to test simulated situations, to express feelings and emotions, to receive feedback, to develop insight, and to learn how to better interact with others (Ford, 1993). Ford (1993) contended that if sharing a number of commonalities with recognized psychotherapy techniques is the criterion for determining the viability of computer-assisted psychotherapy, it can be argued strongly that such technology is, in fact, a form of psychotherapy.

## Independent Use

The use of computer-assisted therapy independent from a therapist presents another ethical quandary. Many counselors are opposed to using such technology as a replacement for human therapists (Bloom & Walz, 2000; Colby et al., 1989; Davidson, 1985; Ford, 1988, 1993; Ford & Vitelli, 1992; Hartman, 1986; Selmi et al., 1990). Cottone (2015) also raised the possibility of surrogate counselors—computer programs that take the place of live counselors. One fact is clear: Counselors are necessary for the development and evaluation of effective computer-assisted counseling programs (Ford, 1993). But individual counselors alone may not have the skills to do all that is necessary to produce and to implement computer programs sufficient to do the full realm of practice-related functions of a living therapist. Cottone (2015) argued that individual therapists may be replaced by **counseling technological conglomerates—organizations that employ counselors, website builders, billing specialists, programmers, and monitors to address the delivery of competent and ethical services over electronic media**. It will be unlikely that a single counselor, even one who is technologically savvy, could do all that is necessary to produce and to oversee the competent and ethical provision of counseling services delivered electronically.

The criteria for determining whether a program should be used by a consumer who requires professional intervention remain a question. Due to the cost-effectiveness of computer-assisted therapy, help can be made available to people who otherwise could not afford therapy provided by a counselor (Colby, 1980, 1986; Davidson, 1985; Ford, 1993; Ford & Vitelli, 1992; Sampson & Krumboltz, 1991). However, making such technology available for those who may benefit from it also presents the potential for some to be harmed through its use.

Legal and ethical ramifications exist for improper use of computer-assisted therapy. Three probable malpractice complaints against counselors that may result from improper use of such technology are (a) negligent rendering of services, (b) negligence that leads to suicide, and (c) improper supervision of a disturbed client (Ford, 1993). As malpractice suits unfold, perhaps the necessary laws, codes, and standards will evolve. Some might believe that it is best that computer-assisted counseling should be an adjunct to the relationship between a live counselor and client, so that harm to the client will be avoided through careful supervision.

## ETHICAL DILEMMAS IN COMPUTER-ASSISTED COUNSELING

There are at least four parties involved in computer-assisted counseling: (a) the client, (b) the counselor, (c) the software manufacturer, and (d) professional bodies such as the ACA, the APA, the NASW, and the AAMFT. Responsibility for the ethical provision of electronic mental health services according to a specified set of standards is borne by the latter four parties at some level, and that responsibility must be given consideration by all participants involved.

The ACA *Code of Ethics* (ACA, 2014) established a standard that addresses the use of computer technology in counseling. In summary, counselors have an obligation to ensure that "clients are intellectually, emotionally, physically, linguistically, and functionally capable of using the application and that the application is appropriate for the needs of the client" (Standard H.4.c).

Likewise, the APA "Guidelines for the Practice of Telepsychology" (APA, 2013) describe controls to ensure provision of ethical and competent services. The NASW (2005) also has defined some control over the way technology is utilized in social work practice.

Ford (1993) discussed the independent use of computer-assisted counseling services, specifically the legal issues that may arise out of litigation and legislation related to the electronic provision of counseling services. The lack of face-to-face monitoring of clients in computer-assisted telepsychology and cybercounseling sessions and issues related to *Tarasoff* liability (VandeCreek & Knapp, 1993) may result in malpractice lawsuits that shape legislative policy and ethical code development. Due to the nature of a fiduciary relationship established via electronic media, it is critical that counseling professionals using such technology remain aware of case law developments that affect practice. Legal issues ultimately may involve federal, state, and local legislation—and litigation. The literature that likely will be developed as a result of this new and technological enterprise will be of great importance to mental health professionals.

## ONLINE COUNSELING FORUMS
### The Internet

The **Internet** is a product of computer networks originally used by the military to communicate with academics, government workers, and business people working on military projects (Sampson et al., 1997). **This international network of computer networks (a network of networks) allows for the interchange of messages, files, software, and communication among computer systems.** The **World Wide Web (WWW) is just one of the services found on the Internet,** allowing for transfer of information in a specific format known as hyperlink transfer protocol (http), which is the language used for the transfer of data. The Internet can also be used for transfer of other data using other languages. The government, for example, uses the Internet for any number of administrative and service activities (e.g., processing disability claims) that are not on the WWW.

E-mail uses the Internet to send and receive messages. List servers are e-mail type software that provide easy, international dissemination of discussion lists and electronic journals (Sampson et al., 1997). Mental health professionals who use e-mail should recognize the ethical vulnerability of such communication—e-mail is vulnerable to interception by people other than the designated recipient.

Internet relay chat (IRC), or chat mode of Internet communication, allows two people to correspond in real time on monitors (Duncan, 1997; Sampson et al., 1997). Computer conferencing allows groups of individuals to converse simultaneously through text, with one person potentially serving as moderator. In addition to the group counseling dynamics of such communication, the same limitations exist on the e-mail level of confidentiality. Chat rooms, a version of IRC with a little more privacy, are in frequent use. Although the audience is more limited in a chat room, the same ethical questions arise.

The WWW is composed of computer servers and graphical interfaces that are connected to the Internet. Together they provide an avenue of information exchange, including audio and visual material and text-based information. Individuals and organizations can establish and maintain a home page on the WWW, which is accessed on the Internet, to convey information about a specific person or organization. A website on the WWW comprises a home page with links, which are indicated by various graphical means. When activated (or "clicked" with a mouse), these links open up related home pages, websites, and multimedia files. The colloquialism **"surfing the Net" implies searching for information on the WWW**, which is connected via the Internet. Various software packages facilitate connection with the WWW and the associated home pages, websites, and links (e.g., Google Chrome, Mozilla Firefox, Internet Explorer).

## Counseling Electronic Applications

Sampson et al. (1997) predicted that the future information highway will be an integration of the Internet, multimedia-based PCs, cable TV networks, and wired and wireless telephone networks. The application potential of such an information highway is tremendous—enhancing existing technologies and creating uses not yet conceived. The information highway has become a reality for many citizens in the United States (Bloom & Walz, 2000; Gates, Myhrvold, & Rinearson, 1995). Many cable service satellite carriers have combined efforts with telephone services, allowing access to the information highway through cable, optical networks, or satellite networks.

Actual counseling sessions can occur in real time, using online computer technology on the information highway. The information highway allows "counselors to overcome problems of distance and time to offer opportunities for networking and interacting not otherwise available" (Walz, 1996, p. 417;

see also Hufford, Glueckauf, & Webb, 1999). Orientation to counseling services can occur using computer-assisted instruction (Sampson, 1986), freeing up online and counselor time and, subsequently, lessening client expense. The protocols necessary to protect such communication over the Internet, such as data encryption and video signal scrambling, need to be in place to guarantee confidential communication. Otherwise, such practice could be considered unethical.

## Ethical Concerns With Online Counseling

Direct, online counseling services are increasingly prevalent on the Internet. A quick informal survey of the Internet will reveal a broad range of charges per hour for a 60-minute "session." Services range from single-treatment interventions to multiple specialty services. Credentials of practitioners vary, including PhD, MD, MA, and LPC. Some individuals who indicated degree credentials after their names did not indicate the disciplines in which they received their degrees, and many "professionals" do not indicate any credentials or training. The 2014 ACA *Code of Ethics*, for example, requires that counselors identify their credentials in a manner that is not false, misleading, deceptive, or fraudulent. As codes and ethical standards are revised, specific guidelines for electronic counseling activities are being addressed.

Psychotherapy in cyberspace brings with it a number of ethical concerns, including (a) licensing criteria for such practice, (b) confidentiality issues, and (c) client safety issues (Stricker, 1996). People who offer mental health services over the Internet should use technological safeguards to protect confidentiality. Such assurances should be sought out before using such services. If the providers are not using appropriate security measures, such practice should be deemed unethical. A fully functional information highway needs a solid data security system, including means of safely transferring money (Duncan, 1997; Gates et al., 1995). Data encryption must become more sophisticated to keep pace with the increasing sophistication of people who illegally break such codes. As biometric technology (e.g., voiceprints or thumbprints) becomes more reliable and cost-effective, it will likely be used to control users at the receiving end of the information highway (Sampson et al., 1997).

## ETHICS AND POLICY DEVELOPMENTS IN ONLINE MENTAL HEALTH SERVICES
### The Emergence of Telehealth

One of the greatest potentials in using the Internet to deliver mental health services is the ability to reach remote areas that were formerly without access to such services (Harris-Bowlsbey, 2000). **Telehealth services, or remote, electronic consultation between consumers and providers in the health care professions (e.g., via videoconferencing),** have received increasing attention throughout the helping professions over the past decade.

Health care providers that participate in telehealth services are eligible for Medicare reimbursement in rural areas determined by the federal government to have a shortage of health professionals (e.g., North Dakota and Montana), with fee schedules remaining the same as those for regular office visits. In 1997, the states of California and Louisiana passed laws requiring private insurance carriers to provide reimbursement for such services. The Federal Communications Commission (FCC) provided grants for public, nonprofit entities wishing to develop their potential in these areas.

In addition to the federal and state support for telehealth, a number of professional organizations have responded to the presence of Internet-based counseling services by developing policies and standards that can help guide counseling professionals through this new frontier. The APA (2013) has developed a guidebook for the provision of telepsychology services.

## COMPUTER-ASSISTED ASSESSMENT

The application of computers to the area of assessment includes the ability to administer, score, and interpret most of the psychological assessment instruments and procedures that are used by clinicians—such as personality tests, cognitive tests, and structured interviews. Intelligence test scoring and interpretation applications were among the first commercially available programs for PCs and have been the primary focus of software developers (Honaker & Fowler, 1990). Past development of the application of computerized cognitive and aptitude assessment includes (a) subtests of the Wechsler Adult Intelligence Scale (French & Beaumont, 1992; Psychological Corporation, 1997), (b) Air Force flight performance tests (Park & Lee, 1992), (c) the Wonderlic Personnel Test (Kennedy, Baltzley, Turnage, & Jones, 1989), (d) memory subtests from the Wechsler Memory Scale-III and the Benton Tests (Youngjohn, Larrabee, & Crook, 1991), and (e) multidimensional assessment of elderly people (Stones & Kozma, 1989). At the beginning of the 1990s, computer programs involving personality assessment accounted for the largest single number of assessment software applications available—45% of all computerized assessment products (Honaker & Fowler, 1990). Such tests included the Minnesota Multiphasic Personality Inventory-2 (MMPI-2), the California Psychological Inventory (CPI), the Millon Clinical Multiaxial Inventory (MCMI), the 16 Personality Factor Test (16PF), the NEO Personality Inventory-Revised (NEO PI-R), and the Rorschach inkblot test.

### Benefits of Computer-Assisted Test Administration

One benefit of computerized test administration is rapid presentation of reliable and repetitive information, which can be taxing on both the client and the test administrator if administered orally (Argentero, 1989; Caplan, 1987). The storing and retrieval of test data can be simplified with computer applications, which allow the professional to attend to other important dynamics in the assessment and training process (Honaker & Fowler, 1990). Human error during data collection also can be minimized. Additionally, there is evidence of increased reliability in the scoring of intelligence tests administered in a computer format, which further increases the veracity of test results (Honaker & Fowler, 1990). However, the reliability of computer-assisted assessment depends on the competency of the administrator of the software. The administrator must understand the non-computerized administration procedures of a given test and how these are influenced by computer technology (Drummond, 1996). A thorough understanding of an assessment tool (i.e., its development, validity, reliability, and theoretical framework) is essential before administration. Unfortunately, the ease of computer-assisted assessment is deceptive—this perception may encourage use by people who are not trained adequately in measurement and statistics or are operating outside a given area of competency, thereby practicing unethically.

Another benefit of the use of computer-administered assessment is the development of adaptive or tailored testing (Weiss, 1985; Wise & Plake, 1990). Computer technology allows the examinee's responses to determine which subsequent items are to be administered. The resultant number of items required generally is reduced by 50%, therefore reducing test time. For higher ability examinees, boredom is avoided by offering more challenging items. Lower ability examinees may avoid discouragement that can occur secondary to item difficulty. This provides for more equal and ethical test administration to examinees, regardless of ability level, thus optimizing a given person's performance (Wise & Plake, 1990).

The ethical administration of tests requires precision and consistency. Computerized administration of testing has the potential to improve precision and consistency, thus enhancing the ethical administration of tests. It is important that the test developers and users continue to demonstrate the validity and reliability of computerized assessment tools and compare their performance with comparable and better established, paper-and-pencil tests.

## Limitations of Computerized Administration

The benefits of this reported ease of administration and data collection can be misleading. Accurate interpretation of test performance also requires careful observation of the examinee during the administration of any test. Computerized test administration may encourage less vigilance on the administrator's part, possibly resulting in the absence of important clinical data. Specifically, situational factors related to the individual during the testing process may be overlooked. Interpreting a test without taking into account those factors (e.g., environmental stimuli, distracters, arousal level of the client during the assessment process, and fluctuations in performance related to such factors) may result in the unethical use of test data. Thus, the data gathered are essentially incomplete and may not present a holistic view of the person (Maki, 1986).

While computerized assessment has its place in the assessment process, it cannot, nor should it, replace the involvement of the professional. It can, however, serve as a useful adjunct to the assessment process (Binder & Thompson, 1994). Thus, the ethical use of computerized technology must be considered within the context of the discipline using such technology and the comprehensive provision of services by the involved professional.

A social issue associated with computerized assessment is the limited access to such technology for people with socioeconomic limitations. In a publication addressing the ethical treatment of patients with brain injury, Ackerman and Banks (1990) highlighted the limitations that socioeconomic status of a consumer or providing institution can impose upon the availability of such technology. It is important that technology that improves outcomes in patient treatment is made available to all who need it, regardless of their ability to pay.

The use of computers to administer assessment instruments is not a replacement for the competent professional who is a testing specialist. Testing is essentially a human-to-human encounter. The use of technology in assessment may facilitate tester–testee relations; however, implementation of technology in the testing process also requires careful monitoring and supervision by experienced and appropriately licensed/credentialed professionals to promote sound ethical practice (see also Wall, 2000).

## Computer-Generated Assessment and Interpretation

The use of PCs to assist in interpreting psychological test results is increasing and is known as computer-based test interpretation (CBTI). A great deal of controversy surrounds this area of technology. Programs have been developed to meet the demands of the mental health professional, including systems that schedule appointments, administer a battery of tests, perform statistical and data management functions, and produce results in the form of computer-generated reports. However, reliability and validity information for these integrated systems is limited. While the sophistication of modular-integrated systems of assessment is increasing, some serious ethical considerations remain.

When a mental health professional has access to computer-generated test results from given test data, there is potential for overreliance on the computer to interpret the protocol. The computer is unable to incorporate qualitative data that are accessible to the counselor. Qualitative data can take exception to direct interpretation of the quantitative test data. Computer-generated test reports must be interpreted carefully to avoid unethical assessment practice. The mental health professional must review the entire report for accuracy and the validity of the test administration (some tests have validity indices that indicate the likelihood that the results are invalid).

Organizational pressures in today's mental health care settings from managed care and third-party payment sources may force many organizations to do more with less. Such pressure encourages the use of less qualified technicians who are paid less to perform assessment procedures. Overreliance on the ease of computer technology is of even greater concern when less qualified examiners are used in the assessment process. The temptation to take any information that a computer generates and accept it at face value has potentially serious consequences. Technology can help make test administration, interpretation, and report generation a more efficient process. However, computerized assessment must be viewed in light of its assets and limitations.

## Research Issues in Computerized Assessment

The ethical appropriateness of using PCs or other devices to administer tests is being examined in research today. The ethical codes of ACA and APA address the importance of ethical behavior regarding the application of any technology in the assessment of, and subsequent treatment of, clients.

Equivalence is a major issue addressed by the APA. The interchange of information between computer-based and conventional (paper-and-pencil) tests has been deemed allowable if (a) the rank orders of scores tested in alternative modes closely approximate each other and (b) the means, dispersions, and shapes of the score distributions are approximately the same, or have been made approximately the same by rescaling the scores from the computer mode. The computerized version must be psychometrically similar to the paper-and-pencil version; hence, the term equivalence.

Scholars also are exploring the possibility that the exchange of people, paper, and pencil for computer technology changes how the examinee responds to evaluation. For example, personally sensitive issues appear to be easier to divulge to a computer program than to an actual therapist, which may increase the amount of data available to the counselor (Honaker & Fowler, 1990; Sampson, 2000). The psychological constructs tapped by clinical interviews and the traditional methods of testing may be different from those tapped when a computer is used for these same purposes. Because of these potential differences, norms generated by noncomputerized assessment tools may not generalize to the computer format.

To use a computer for ease of administration and then interpret the test by paper-and-pencil norms may not be ethical due to the potential error that can be introduced. More time is needed to establish appropriate norms for computerized test interpretation. Many computerized assessment instruments must be treated as experimental until further research clarifies the effect of the computer medium on the overall assessment process. Manuals that accompany any tests must be reviewed carefully to determine the appropriateness of the use of the instrument.

## COMPUTER-ASSISTED COUNSELOR EDUCATION

### Distance Learning

**Distance learning** may be conceptualized as **education through the use of technology in nonlocal or remote locations, providing educational material by means other than live local interaction.** New technologies are being used to deliver **preservice (before employment)** and **in-service (in-house during employment)** training to counselors from various specialty areas (Davis & Yazak, 1995). Since the development of the British Open University in 1969, distance-learning programs have expanded worldwide. Distance learning is useful for persons in remote and rural areas, for learners who have limited mobility, and for professionals with busy schedules or economic limitations who wish to further their professional development through licensure and certification (Steele, 1993).

Advancement in technology is one factor that influences educators to consider distance learning (Davis & Yazak, 1995). Another compelling factor is the potential cost-effectiveness of distance education in an era of increased college costs and student debt. The Internet connects millions of computers worldwide, allowing access to databases and library materials, and facilitating communication between instructors and students. Multimedia presentation of written material, and high-quality graphics have made learning through computer software a viable alternative or supplement to the traditional classroom experience (Bloom & Walz, 2000; Scriven, 1991; Sirkin, 1994).

## Current Mental Health Professional Standards for Online Education

As of this writing, the APA does not accredit fully online programs in professional psychology (Clay, 2012). In 2010, the APA Commission on Accreditation (CoA) implemented a rule that prohibits the accreditation of programs that are fully online. But the CoA did not rule out the use of distance education coursework as part of a doctoral program. Rather it took a stand that there must be a component of face-to-face education, between faculty and students, in a clinical health training program.

The 2016 Council for Accreditation of Counseling and Related Educational Programs (CACREP, 2015) standards for accreditation do not address distance education. Technology is addressed only in the sense of programs offering technologies as part of the instructional environment. Supervision is in person, so practica or field experiences must be supervised by employed faculty members. Individual or triadic supervision may be provided by site supervisors, but group supervision must be under the direct control of program faculty members. These standards give programs broad leeway in delivery systems, including distance education. Regardless, clinical courses require the direct accessible presence of supervisors. Two master's programs are defined as online on the CACREP website, and a number of doctoral programs are so defined, although the program information appears to present the programs more as **hybrid** than fully online formats **("hybrid" programs provide traditional coursework on campus apart from online coursework or distance education).**

The Council on Social Work Education (CSWE) Committee on Accreditation allows for delivery of courses by different means. The CSWE website indicates that all accredited programs are subject to the same accreditation standards and review criteria by the Commission on Accreditation, regardless of the curriculum delivery methods used. A number of programs offer a significant number of courses online (sometimes calling themselves "hybrid" programs), but on-campus or on-site practica are typically required by the programs listed by the CSWE. There are a few programs that identify themselves as fully online (e.g., Arizona State University), but even these programs require practica with supervision on site. Both bachelor's and master's online or hybrid programs have been accredited, and the CSWE lists those programs on their website.

The 2016 Accreditation Standards of the Commission on the Accreditation of Marriage and Family Therapy Education (COAMFTE) do not address the delivery of degree programs by online methods. Regardless, there are a number of online master's degree programs and one doctoral degree program (at the time of writing) accredited by COAMFTE. The first accredited doctoral program was at North Central University, the first PhD degree program that received COAMFTE accreditation according to university documents. Doctoral practica and internships are completed at the students' locale, but all other courses are online. Two distance-based master's programs were listed on the COAMFTE website, Capella University and North Central University.

## Synchronous and Asynchronous Learning Paradigms

Two popular, web-based distance-learning paradigms include synchronous and asynchronous modalities. **Asynchronous** curriculum delivery can occur over the web using software programs (like Blackboard); curricula are delivered through online files that are available continuously. **Asynchronous technological models allow students to interact with the system on their own schedule.** By contrast, **synchronous delivery systems have a set time for online interaction, sometimes using streaming video to deliver online lectures to a prescheduled audience. There is an opportunity for immediate multidirectional interaction by students and faculty in the program.** There are also combinations of the two modalities that create a multimodal interactive curriculum.

The U.S. Department of Education has supported efforts to further distance-learning initiatives. Many institutions are developing "online" programs. The APA and CACREP now will accredit programs with some online coursework at the master's and doctoral levels. The CSWE and COAMFTE accredit programs that are largely online.

## Ethical Concerns With Distance Learning

Distance learning brings several ethical concerns for counselor educators. Program integrity, continuity, and sophistication affect the quality of education that a given counselor receives. The available resources that facilitate a program's capacity to accomplish its objectives through distance learning must be considered case by case. It is erroneous to assume that an in vivo course of study will readily translate to a distance-learning format. An outcome research base is necessary to compare the difference between distance-learning programs and exemplary, traditional, university-based programs, and to examine the effectiveness of distance learning.

In traditional university settings, courses can be evaluated through peer review. Course activity between teacher and student can be observed and evaluated by fellow professionals to provide developmental suggestions that enhance an instructor's pedagogy and, ultimately, the quality of the student's education. In a distance-learning setting, the interpersonal dynamics between instructor and student are different from a face-to-face experience. It is clear these dynamics cannot be observed for distance learning in the same way it is in the traditional classroom setting. The dynamic difference between in vivo and remote education may also influence the student learning process. Preliminary data suggest that modalities overall do not impact grades (Stocks & Freddolino, 1998). Students reported that the distance-education format provided a flexibility that was desirable, but it lacked the personal contact of in vivo formats (Keating & Hargitai, 1999).

Taped presentations of a distance-learning curriculum (asynchronous) do not provide students the opportunity to ask questions and interact contemporaneously with instructors. It is unclear how this may affect the learning process. If a student is having difficulty grasping a concept in a real-time distance-learning presentation, the opportunity for one-to-one interaction for clarification would be highly valuable (synchronous learning). The logistics of interacting with a classroom or an instructor remotely may inherently be more time-consuming than in a traditional classroom setting (e.g., timing of questions, coordinating multiple inquiries, and keeping the course moving in a timely manner). The difficulty associated with cueing an instructor in a remote setting may discourage active and lively class participation. Student-to-student interaction (e.g., breaking into small groups) is limited, although technologically possible. However, these situations introduce a number of factors that affect time, interpersonal interaction, and possibly the willingness to engage others.

If follow-up communication is available between students, faculty, and other students, their ability to graphically clarify a concept is less limited. People who are uncomfortable with electronic communication are at a distinct disadvantage, although video interaction may alleviate some of this concern. Some courses may more readily lend themselves to remote presentation than others, again necessitating a case-by-case approach to the development of distance-learning curricula.

Some literature suggests that students and faculty generally prefer face-to-face interaction over distance learning (Bland, Morrison, & Ross, 1992). Most importantly, the personal development of students in counselor education is arguably as important as their professional and academic development. It is difficult for faculty to provide mentoring and role modeling of professional behavior without in-person live contact with students. This is likely the reason that the professional associations have avoided accrediting fully online or distance education courses, keeping some degree of face-to-face interaction in accreditation standards. There are obviously differences between traditional and online formats that will need to be vetted, researched, and assessed as these programs gain credibility, accreditation approval, licensure board approval, and student enrollments.

## ETHICAL USE OF SOFTWARE

**Software pirating, or the illegal copying and use of software,** is a blatant breach of ethics. The sharing of software between professionals can be considered doing a coworker a favor. Clearly, the motivation is to save several hundred dollars in acquiring a piece of software. However, the unethical reproduction and transfer of computer software results in both increased cost to the consumer and loss of revenue for the author of the product. Because unauthorized reproduction of software is illegal, the ethical integrity of counselors who engage in this behavior is called into question. Software pirating can easily go undetected, increasing the responsibility of counselors to practice the ethical use of electronic media autonomously.

## CONCLUSION

Technology plays an important role in mental health service provision and in training mental health professionals. All forms of electronic media used in counseling may contain sensitive material protected by client–therapist confidentiality and privileged communication. Ethical codes that address maintenance of client records mandate that counselors maintain appropriate confidentiality in creating, storing, accessing, transferring, and disposing of all client records.

Counseling professionals use a variety of types of electronic media. Protocols must be in place to ensure that all types of media are accessible and used by ethically appropriate parties.

Computer-assisted counseling exists in a variety of forms, including therapeutic software, online counseling, career counseling, rehabilitation software, and behavioral, cognitive, educational, and psychodynamic approaches. Software has been developed to target AIDS education, drug and alcohol abuse, obesity, personal distress, sexual dysfunction, smoking, and stress.

Online counseling forums represent a recent technological development in computer applications. These forums use the Internet primarily for the public exchange of information. Search engines and information databases assist counselors in accessing diverse information quickly. Ethical concerns with online counseling include security, access to services, and cost.

Telehealth services are remote electronic consultations between consumers and the health care provider, often in remote or rural areas that have a shortage of health professionals.

The application of computers to the area of assessment includes the ability to administer, score, and interpret psychological assessment instruments. Computer-assisted assessment has the benefits of rapid presentation of information and increased reliability in test scoring. However, test administrators may have less vigilance and may overlook situational factors during testing. Some domains of assessment do not transfer well to computerized assessment.

Computer-assisted counselor education includes online supervision and virtual practica, distance learning, and synchronous and asynchronous curriculum delivery. Computer-assisted instruction uses tutorials to present concepts and instructional tasks.

## ACKNOWLEDGMENTS

The authors wish to express thanks to and acknowledge the conceptual and editorial contributions of Fong Chan, University of Wisconsin–Madison, and the editorial contributions of Gerry Murray, The University of Iowa, to the first edition of this chapter, as they continue to influence this iteration.

# CONCLUSION

# THE ETHICAL PROFESSIONAL COUNSELOR AND PSYCHOTHERAPIST

## OBJECTIVES

- To describe ethical practice in counseling and psychotherapy.
- To provide current statistics on ethical complaint adjudication.
- To explain what a counselor should do when confronted with an allegation of ethical misconduct.
- To describe the counselor's response to an ethical challenge in the context of potential legal and professional scrutiny.
- To explain the consequences for clients who are victims of unethical professional conduct.

The study of ethics is like a journey. After an individual first reads a code of ethics, he or she may feel confident about his or her knowledge and have a sense that nothing can create a serious ethical crisis in his or her professional life. However, as the journey progresses, it becomes clearer that the practice of counseling is complex. Often when challenged, no easy answers emerge. At the end of the journey, there is the realization that ethical dilemmas do arise, and they challenge even the most sophisticated and ethically sensitive practitioner.

No professional is immune to ethical dilemmas—no matter how ethically sensitive counselors may be, circumstances will always arise that place them in

**BOX 15.1  Organizational Guidance on Resolving and Reporting Ethical Violations**

What sections of the American Counseling Association (ACA), American Psychological Association (APA), National Association of Social Workers (NASW), and American Association for Marriage and Family Therapy (AAMFT) codes address how to resolve ethical dilemmas?

What sections of the ACA, APA, NASW, and AAMFT ethical codes specifically address how to report ethical violations?

a quandary. It is important, however, that counselors recognize when they are facing a serious ethical challenge. With such recognition, wise counselors protect themselves from a naive decision and a possible breach of ethical standards (see Box 15.1).

No professional is immune from being accused of ethical misconduct. Complaints against mental health professionals increased dramatically in the 1990s. Bass et al. (1996) reported a 500% increase in disciplinary actions by state and provincial licensing boards in psychology over a 10-year period. They stated:

> A wide range of behaviors and practices may lead to disciplinary or legal action before a regulatory board, professional association, or court of law. . . . Common problem areas include (a) competence, (b) informed consent and confidentiality, (c) dual relationships, and (d) financial arrangements. (p. 71)

Even counselor educators are concerned about the ethics of educating counselors (Hill, 2004; Schwab & Neukrug, 1994). Clients and students of counseling are becoming more sophisticated about their rights. Licensure and regulatory boards are more experienced at addressing complaints, and there may be a tendency among licensure board members to assume guilt rather than innocence when a licensed professional is accused (Peterson, 2001). American society is also a litigious culture. It can be expected that a good percentage of mental health professionals will be accused formally of unethical or illegal practice during their careers. Innocent or not, the consequences can be serious. Professional careers can be ruined by poor decisions made in the moments of an ethical dilemma or in the face of an ethical complaint.

## CONSEQUENCES OF A BREACH OF ETHICS FOR THE MENTAL HEALTH PROFESSIONAL

The professional consequences of a breach of an ethical standard can range from no formal repercussions to serious repercussions, such as professional and personal censure and the loss of a license to practice. Once confronted with an allegation of unethical conduct, it is wise for counselors to not discuss the complaint openly with family or friends, to contact their malpractice insurance carrier, and to retain the services of an attorney (Chauvin & Remley, 1996; Remley & Herlihy, 2014). Chauvin and Remley stated:

> The immediate reaction of most counselors would be shock and disbelief accompanied by deep sorrow, embarrassment, or extreme anger, or very likely a combination of all three. A first inclination of most counselors would be to call a best friend or family member and describe the details of the accusation and lament the injustice of what has been alleged. A lawyer most likely would advise against such a response. (p. 565)

To consult other individuals (for personal rather than professional reasons) with details of a client's allegation of impropriety is, in effect, a breach of the client's confidentiality and/or privacy; such action essentially compounds an already tenuous professional situation. Personal needs must be dealt with in a way that will not complicate the situation. Counselors suffering serious emotional pain over an allegation of unethical behavior should seek confidential treatment by mental health professionals (Chauvin & Remley, 1996; Remley & Herlihy, 2014). Even then, what is said should be said carefully, because the mental health professional may not be able to guarantee privileged communications in certain cases (especially those of a criminal nature).

Revelation of serious unethical practice can be devastating to the professional—guilt may prevent an unfettered return to practice. Remorseful counselors will be faced with guilt over possible damage done to any victims involved in the ethical breach. They may feel anxiety over the professional consequences related to licensure board or other certifying board actions. Legal problems may arise, such as malpractice. Malpractice insurance companies, valued by counselors as shields against financial ruin, may be untrusting and unwilling participants in defense of charges of unethical conduct.

There are always cases of professional counselors who are accused falsely of serious ethical misconduct, adding the issue of anger. If cleared of all allegations of misconduct, the exonerated counselors may have done themselves serious professional damage by having communicated to others about the complaint. Trusted colleagues from the past may view them with suspicion or disdain. For their own benefit, counselors are well advised to maintain the secrecy of an ethical complaint against them or be willing to suffer the consequence of professional stigmatization, even in cases of total innocence. In many cases, licensure or certifying bodies will keep the complaint confidential, unless legal standards exist that require public knowledge or public hearing of such complaints (Chauvin & Remley, 1996). It is possible that the complaint will be dismissed by the licensure board as unfounded, without merit, or poorly supported. In cases in which a certifying or licensing authority dismisses a case, the dismissal may signify the end of the charge, unless the client brings legal action (e.g., malpractice charges). According to a 2004 report of the American Counseling Association (ACA) Ethics Committee (Hubert & Freeman, 2004), 33 complaints were received, but only 12 complaints were made against ACA members (therefore the committee only had jurisdiction over these 12 complaints). Of the 12, only three were found to have substance. Of the three processed cases, two were dismissed of charges and one was upheld and the member was sanctioned. The chances of being sanctioned on a formal charge of unethical conduct, therefore, are very slight. In fact, there has been a decrease in ethical complaints received by the ACA, which received nine complaints in 2010 to 2011, six complaints in 2011 to 2012, and just four complaints in 2012 to 2013 (Johnston, Tarvydas, & Butler, 2016). In effect, counselors should not panic when faced with a charge of unethical conduct; they should address complaints as a professional faced with a matter of professional business. If personal stress somehow affects the practitioner's judgment, professional counsel should be sought from an attorney and a mental health professional.

## CONSEQUENCES OF A BREACH OF ETHICAL STANDARDS FOR THE CLIENT

Unethical situations are even more difficult for a client who suffers an injustice. Victimized clients have to deal with the unacceptable actions of the counselor, but they must also deal with a professional system that may be reluctant to discipline one of its own. The legal system may also become involved, and once the legal wheels begin to roll, it is difficult to steer a new direction. Financial and personal commitments may place a strain on the victim of unethical practice. In some cases, there may be degrees of embarrassment or public humiliation. Just the revelation of treatment by a mental health professional may be embarrassing to some individuals. The conduct of the professional also may be embarrassing to the client or may inadvertently or inappropriately reflect on the morals or judgment of the client. Friendships may be strained or destroyed. In the end, the brave victims of serious unethical practice who file formal complaints may place themselves in positions of double or multiple victimization.

### Filing a Complaint to a Licensure Authority

Procedures for filing complaints about unethical practitioners in the mental health field are fairly standard. Licensed professionals practicing in a particular state are bound legally to the ethical and administrative standards of practice as adopted by statute and regulation in that state. These standards and disciplinary procedures are usually available to the public through the state's department of regulation or licensure (Johnston, Tarvydas, & Butler, 2016). Related to psychology licensure, Reaves (1996) stated:

> Virtually all jurisdictions require that complaints concerning psychologists' behavior be in writing. Unless a complaint is determined to be frivolous or made in bad faith, an investigation ensues. In some jurisdictions, trained investigators are employed to perform this task. In smaller jurisdictions, a board member may be assigned as an investigating officer. The method used to investigate a complaint varies with the type or substance of the complaint. For example, an allegation that a licensee has been convicted of a felony would involve obtaining documentation from the court where

the conviction occurred, whereas an allegation of sexual intimacies with a client would likely involve interviews and possible collection of other evidence. (p. 102)

Reaves further noted that a license to practice a profession is considered a "property" and, therefore, a license cannot be taken away without due process of law.

If a professional is accused of unethical conduct and simply admits to the conduct, the case is uncontested. Settlement on such cases may be a matter of the regulatory board's disposition—in such cases the board may make a decision as to the consequences of the unethical conduct. **Contested cases, wherein the professional essentially pleads innocent to some or all of the charges,** typically lead to a civil court (versus criminal court) hearing or legal proceeding. In such cases, a hearing officer is present and attorneys may be involved. In some jurisdictions, hearings may be open to the public (Chauvin & Remley, 1996). Chauvin and Remley (1996) stated, "If a hearing is held, the complainant, the witnesses, and the accused counselor would be given an opportunity to present their positions and would be questioned by the board members" (p. 565). After a hearing, the board most typically makes a decision, which could include the following consequences: reprimand, probation, suspension of a certificate or license, or revocation of a certificate or a license (Remley & Herlihy, 2014). The counselor or psychologist is allowed to appeal. According to Chauvin and Remley (1996), "After an appeal, if the counselor still disagrees with the board's findings, he or she could sue the board in court in an effort to have the board's decision overturned" (p. 565).

Clients or involved laypersons who desire to file complaints should be provided adequate information to file such complaints. Responsible counselors who are knowledgeable about the questionable or unethical practices of colleagues are obligated by law (in most cases) and by mandatory professional ethical standards to file complaints. Filing of a complaint is required if direct, informal attempts to resolve the issue with the offending professional fail or if the conduct is either serious or repetitive.

It is standard procedure for a complaint to be filed in writing. Any member of the public or the profession may file a complaint, regardless of residence (inside or outside of the state of the alleged ethical violation). Complaints can be based on personal knowledge, public record, or information received from third-party sources. The complainant and the individual filing the complaint (often the same person) must be identified fully in the complaint by name and address and in writing. Complaints typically are logged by the date and nature of the complaint. Each complaint will be acknowledged by the board in writing and the complainant will be notified of the ultimate disposition of the complaint. Complaints may be dismissed on several grounds, including insufficient evidence or information, non–cooperation of the complainant, or inability to prove or to refute charges due to lack of probable corroboration (e.g., hearsay evidence only).

Complainants to licensure boards may file complaints against a suspected unethical practitioner simultaneously with the professional associations to which the practitioner belongs (e.g., the ACA, American Psychological Association [APA], National Association of Social Workers [NASW], or American Association for Marriage and Family Therapy [AAMFT]). See for example, *ACA Policies and Procedures for Processing Complaints of Ethical Violations* (2005). Counselors are obligated to disclose information about their professional qualifications and affiliations to interested parties. Withholding such information, especially to clients, may be considered a breach of ethics in and of itself, depending on state statute or professional ethical standards. The important issue is the availability of information so that complainants can make informed complaints to appropriate authorities; concerned individuals should not be impeded in their attempts to file complaints.

Counselors who are guilty of unethical conduct and who have the intention of practicing again have a responsibility to "rehabilitate" themselves and to seek guidance so that they never repeat their actions (Chauvin & Remley, 1996). There is nothing more repulsive to the public or to professional colleagues than a repeat offender, especially in cases of serious ethical misconduct. In fact, Walden, Herlihy, and Ashton (2003), in a survey of former chairs of the ACA Ethics Committee, found that "Former chairs . . . wrote about learning lessons that were, for some, rather disappointing or disillusioning" related to the actions of some professional counselors who harmed their clients. In cases of repeat offenders, it becomes obvious that the unethical practitioner has become a predator, is incompetent, or is simply interested in personal gain. Such activity reflects badly on the profession of counseling, and all professionals have an obligation to prevent such activity.

## THE DEVELOPMENT OF THE ETHICAL MENTAL HEALTH PROFESSIONAL

Professional associations such as the ACA, APA, NASW, and AAMFT have a special role in helping to develop ethical behavior in practitioners. In a survey of certified counselors who were asked to rate 16 sources of ethical information (Gibson & Pope, 1993), the ACA ethical code, the ACA Ethics Committee, and the ACA *Journal of Counseling and Development* were given the highest ratings. This is characteristic of all of the mental health professions—they all appear to clearly communicate the importance of ethical behavior and they attempt to create an ethical climate in and around the profession. However, accessing good information may not be enough. The development of the ethically sensitive counselor is a complex process. It is not simply a matter of information, education, supervision, and training. As Pettifor (1996) stated:

> Psychologists who maintain high levels of professional conduct are encouraged by aspirational ethics to practice appropriately and . . . the measures they take to maintain competence are voluntary and targeted to specific professional needs. Aspirational ethics are based on moral principles that always place the well-being of the other, the consumer, above self-interest, as opposed to codes of conduct that define minimal levels of acceptable behavior. (pp. 91–92)

Professional training may not be enough. The works of Kohlberg (1964, 1971, 1981) demonstrated that the application of moral thinking stems from a developmental process. It may be that training, no matter how targeted to moral development, may not adequately inspire ethical decision making in certain counselors. In the end, even the most trained mental health professional may choose to act unethically. Therefore, it is as important to study what prevents unethical conduct as it is to study the correlates of unethical conduct (see Lamb, Catanzaro, & Moorman, 2004). It may be that what prevents unethical conduct, as Pettifor implied, is a moral standard and moral directives that supersede even the most powerful motivations to breach an accepted ethical standard. Counselors must have the constitution to make moral choices when other needs enter into decisions. And it is known that willingness and resoluteness are factors in making an ethical decision (see Chapter 4).

One approach, deriving from the "positive psychology" movement (Seligman & Csikszentmihalyi, 2000) is to address ethical issues in a positive light—focusing on building strengths against ethical breaches rather than approaching ethics as a crisis and remedial concern. Handelsman, Knapp, and Gottlieb (2002) make a compelling argument for positive ethics:

> Our view of positive ethics encompasses a broad context of ethical behavior—including aspirational elements that range from the personal to the societal in nature—which goes beyond a focus on rules and risk. We propose that the morality of professional actions can be explored without emphasizing the prohibitions or potential sanctions found within psychology's disciplinary codes. At the same time, we are not advocating the abandonment of ethical rules and prohibitions; they do have a basis in morality that psychologists need to understand. Likewise, psychologists should know the laws that govern the practice of psychology and the ways to reduce legal risk. We are suggesting that whereas rules and good risk management strategies are not antithetical to positive ethics, they are not sufficient to ensure optimal ethical practice. What is necessary is an awareness of several interacting perspectives. (p. 734)

Handelsman et al. (2002) recommended "seven themes of positive ethics," which are: (a) values and virtues; (b) sensitivity and integration; (c) ethics as ongoing self-care; (d) ethical reasoning and decision making; (e) appreciation of the moral traditions underlying ethical principles; (f) prevention of misconduct and promotion of positive behaviors; and (g) sensitivity to larger professional contexts. With the positive psychology movement, there is an opportunity to redefine professional ethics around a positive developmental process rather than a remedial postcrisis event. Palmiter (2012) stated "positive ethics is less about 'don't do this because that bad thing could happen' and more about 'do this so that your mission is more fully realized'" (p. 399).

Handelsman, Gottlieb, and Knapp (2005) have gone a step farther in exploring an "acculturation model" of ethics training. In a groundbreaking work, they conceptualized the process of ethics education of psychologists-in-training as akin to the process of acculturation, a developmental process requiring adaptation strategies. Using Berry's (1980) model of acculturation strategies,

Handelsman et al. (2005) outlined the process of ethics training. They concluded: "An acculturation model may help improve the socialization of students, especially in the acquisition of their ethical identity" (p. 64).

On the other hand, some might argue that no matter how ethically focused or sophisticated the profession becomes at ethics training, there always will be practitioners who consciously breach or challenge the limits of ethical behavior. Also, if a profession is struggling—that is, if trained professionals are having difficulty making a living—temptations to sell clients short of ethical services may become more common. In this light, it is important for the leaders of the profession to ensure that ethical professionals are rewarded adequately in their professional practices; otherwise, the fringe ethical behaviors of desperate practitioners may erode the reputation of the profession as a whole.

Ideally, counselors should make the best of their education to take ethics to heart and develop a moral stance. A profession devoted to helping others should facilitate a personal, as well as academic, interest in defining what is right and wrong in the treatment of individuals in need. The clients of these mental health professionals deserve no less.

## DECISION MAKING IN CONTEXT

As the popular adage goes: "An ounce of prevention is worth a pound of cure." In fact, related to preventing unethical conduct, counselors are well advised to consider decision making an ongoing process of everyday practice, rather than an isolated event when confronted with a dilemma. By being cognizant of the subtleties of ethical practice, a wise counselor builds procedures into his or her daily practice that will act as safeguards against ethical compromises. By being alert to the nuance of ethical practice in the daily decisions that occur in the practice of counseling, big mistakes may be avoided. Counselors can take pride in their practices when they consider the ethical consequences of their policies and procedures as a standard way of operating. Ethics is not an event, it is a way of practice, and decision making should not be viewed as "after-the-fact" of an ethical challenge.

## CONCLUSION

This text has been organized to provide the developing mental health professional with a clear and concise overview of ethical issues in counseling and psychotherapy. The intent of the book is to provide a thorough and scholarly foundation, defining ethical concepts and practice, legal issues, methods for clarifying values, decision-making models, and contemporaneous and emerging issues. Additionally, the book addresses issues related to some of the largest specialties in the mental health profession. It is hoped that this text will inspire ethically sensitive counselors and psychotherapists who will reflect before acting and who will consult with educated colleagues at those moments when ethical dilemmas arise. In the end, ethical counselors and psychotherapists are those who have the best interests of their clients at heart, and who also respect the rights that derive from being professionals.

# REFERENCES

Ackerman, R. J., & Banks, M. E. (1990). Computers and the ethical treatment of brain-injured patients. *Social Science Computer Review, 8*(1), 83–95.

Agich, G. J. (Ed.). (1982). *Responsibility in health care.* Boston, MA: D. Reidel.

Alcoholics Anonymous. (1976). *Alcoholics Anonymous.* New York, NY: Author.

Altekruse, M. K. (2001). *Counselor portability.* Presentation made to the American Association of State Counseling Boards. Available from Dr. Altekruse at NTU, P. O. Box 311337, Denton, TX 76203-1337.

American Association for Marriage and Family Therapy. (1991). *AAMFT code of ethics.* Washington, DC: Author.

American Association for Marriage and Family Therapy. (1993). *Dual relationships: Sex, power, and exploitation.* [Audiotape cassette recording]. AAMFT luncheon plenary (Call: 1-800-241-7785). AAMFT Resource Link, Norcross, GA.

American Association for Marriage and Family Therapy. (2015). *AAMFT code of ethics.* Washington, DC: Author.

American Association of Suicidology. (2013a). *Recommendations for reporting on suicide.* Retrieved from http://www.suicidology.org/Resources/Recommendations-for-Reporting-on-Suicide

American Association of Suicidology. (2013b). *U.S. suicide: 2013 official final data.* Retrieved from http://www.suicidology.org

American Counseling Association. (1995, June). Code of ethics and standards of practice. *Counseling Today, 37*(12), 33–40.

American Counseling Association. (1996, July). Supreme Court extends confidentiality privilege. *Counseling Today, 39*(1), 1, 6, 10.

American Counseling Association. (1998a). *Code of ethics and standards of practice.* Alexandria, VA: Author.

American Counseling Association. (1998b). *Professional counselor's guide to federal law on student records.* Alexandria, VA: Author.

American Counseling Association. (2005a). *ACA policies and procedures for processing complaints of ethical violations.* Alexandria, VA: Author. Retrieved from http://www.counseling.org/docs/ethics/policies_procedures.pdf?sfvrsn=2

American Counseling Association. (2005b). *Code of ethics.* Alexandria, VA: Author.

American Counseling Association. (2014). *Code of ethics.* Alexandria, VA: Author.

American Mental Health Counselors Association. (2010). *AMHCA code of ethics.* Alexandria, VA: Author.

American Psychiatric Association. (2013). *Diagnostic and statistical manual of mental disorders* (5th ed.). Washington, DC: Author.

American Psychological Association. (2010). *Ethical principles of psychologists and code of conduct*. Washington, DC: Author.

American Psychological Association. (2013). *Guidelines for the practice of telepsychology*. Washington, DC: Author.

American School Counselor Association. (1999a). *ASCA position statement: The professional school counselor and acquired immune deficiency syndrome (AIDS)* (Rev. ed.). Alexandria, VA: Author.

American School Counselor Association. (1999b). *ASCA position statement: The professional school counselor and censorship* (Rev. ed.). Alexandria, VA: Author.

American School Counselor Association. (1999c). *ASCA position statement: The professional school counselor and child abuse and neglect prevention* (Rev. ed.). Alexandria, VA: Author.

American School Counselor Association. (1999d). *ASCA position statement: The professional school counselor and confidentiality* (Rev. ed.). Alexandria, VA: Author.

American School Counselor Association. (2010). *Ethical standards for school counselors*. Alexandria, VA: Author.

American School Counselor Association. (2011). *The school counselor and the promotion of safe schools through conflict resolution and bullying/harassment prevention*. Retrieved from http://schoolcounselor.org/asca/media/asca/PositionStatements/PS_Bullying.pdf

American School Counselor Association. (2015). *ASCA position statements*. Alexandria, VA: Author. Retrieved from http://schoolcounselor.org/asca/media/asca/Position-Statements/PositionStatements.pdf

Anderson, B. S. (1996). *The counselor and the law* (4th ed.). Alexandria, VA: American Counseling Association.

Anderson, J. R., & Barrett, R. L. (2001). *Ethics in HIV-related psychotherapy: Clinical decision making in complex cases*. Washington, DC: American Psychological Association.

Anderson, S. K., & Kitchener, K. S. (1998). Nonsexual posttherapy relationships: A conceptual framework to assess ethical risks. *Professional Psychology: Research and Practice, 29*, 91–99.

Anthony, W. A., Cohen, M. R., Farkas, M. D., & Gagne, C. (2002). *Psychiatric rehabilitation* (2nd ed.). Boston, MA: Boston University, Center for Psychiatric Rehabilitation.

Argentero, P. (1989). Computerized psychological testing: An annotated bibliography. *Bollettino di Psicologia Applicata, 190*, 21–38.

Arrendondo, P. (1998). Integrating multicultural counseling competencies and universal helping conditions in culture-specific contexts. *The Counseling Psychologist, 26*, 592–602.

Association for Counselor Education and Supervision. (1993). ACES ethical guidelines for counseling supervisors. *ACES Spectrum, 53*, 5–8.

Association for Counselor Education and Supervision. (1999). *Technical competencies for counselor education students: Recommended guidelines for program development*. Alexandria, VA: Author.

Association for Counselor Education and Supervision. (2011). *Best practices in clinical supervision*. Alexandria, VA: Author.

Association for Specialists in Group Work. (1998a). *Best practice guidelines*. Alexandria, VA: Author.

Association for Specialists in Group Work. (1998b). *Principles for diversity-competent group workers*. Alexandria, VA: Author.

Association of State and Provincial Psychology Boards. (2001). *Ethics, law and avoiding liability in the practice of psychology.* Montgomery, AL: Author.

Bartell, P. A., & Rubin, L. J. (1990). Dangerous liaisons: Sexual intimacies in supervision. *Professional Psychology: Research and Practice, 21,* 442–450.

Bass, L. J., DeMers, S. T., Ogloff, J. R., Peterson, C., Pettifor, J. L., Reaves, R. P., . . . Tipton, R. M. (1996). *Professional conduct and discipline in psychology.* Washington, DC: American Psychological Association.

Beauchamp, T. L., & Childress, J. F. (1979). *Principles of biomedical ethics.* New York, NY: Oxford University Press.

Beauchamp, T. L., & Childress, J. F. (1983). *Principles of biomedical ethics.* Oxford, England: Oxford University Press.

Beauchamp, T. L., & Childress, J. F. (1994). *Principles of biomedical ethics* (4th ed.). New York, NY: Oxford University Press.

Beauchamp, T. L., & Childress, J. F. (2012). *Principles of biomedical ethics* (7th ed.). New York, NY: Oxford University Press.

Beauchamp, T. L., & Walters, L. (1994). *Contemporary issues in bioethics* (4th ed.). Belmont, CA: Wadsworth.

Bellah, R. N., Madsen, R., Sullivan, W. M., Swidler, A., & Tipton, S. M. (1996). *Habits of the heart: Individualism and commitment in American life.* Retrieved from http://www .amazon.com/Habits-Heart-Individualism-Commitment-American-ebook/dp/ B003EV5PNE/ref=sr_1_3?s=digital-text&ie=UTF8&qid=1439995695&sr=1-3

Bergin, A. E. (1985). Proposed values for guiding and evaluating psychotherapy. *Counseling and Values, 29,* 99–116.

Bernard, J. L., & Jara, C. S. (1986). The failure of clinical psychology graduate students to apply understood ethical principles. *Professional Psychology: Research and Practice, 17,* 313–315.

Bernard, J. M., & Goodyear, R. K. (1998). *Fundamentals of clinical supervision* (2nd ed.). Boston, MA: Allyn & Bacon.

Bernard, J. M., & Goodyear, R. K. (2009). *Fundamentals of clinical supervision* (4th ed.). Upper Saddle River, NJ: Pearson.

Bernstein, B. E., & Hartsell, T. L. (2004). *The portable lawyer for mental health professionals.* Hoboken, NJ: Wiley.

Berry, J. W. (1980). Acculturation as varieties of adaptation. In A. M. Padilla (Ed.), *Acculturation: Theory, models, and some new findings* (pp. 9–25). Boulder, CO: Westview Press.

Betan, E. J. (1997). Toward a hermeneutic model of ethical decision-making in clinical practice. *Ethics and Behavior, 7,* 347–365.

Betan, E. J., & Stanton, A. L. (1999). Fostering ethical willingness: Integrating emotional and contextual awareness with rational analysis. *Professional Psychology: Research and Practice, 30,* 295–301.

Beutler, L. E., Pollack, S., & Jobe, A. (1978). Acceptance, values, and therapeutic change. *Journal of Consulting and Clinical Psychology, 46,* 198–199.

Binder, L. M., & Thompson, L. L. (1994). The ethics code and neuropsychological assessment practices. *Archives of Clinical Neuropsychology, 10,* 27–46.

Binik, Y. M., Servan-Schreiber, D., Freiwald, S., & Hall, K. S. (1988). Intelligent computer-based assessment and psychotherapy: An expert system for sexual dysfunction. *Journal of Nervous and Mental Disease, 176,* 387–400.

Blackwell, T. L., Autry, T. L., & Guglielmo, D. E. (2001). Ethical issues in disclosure of test data. *Rehabilitation Counseling Bulletin, 44,* 161–169.

Blackwell, T. L., Martin, W. E., & Scalia, V. A. (1994). *Ethics in rehabilitation: A guide for rehabilitation professionals.* Athens, GA: Elliot & Fitzpatrick.

Bland, K., Morrison, G. R., & Ross, S. M. (1992). *Student attitudes toward learning link: A distance education project.* Paper presented at the annual meeting of the Mid-South Educational Research Association, Knoxville, TN.

Bloom, J. W., & Walz, G. R. (Eds.). (2000). *Cybercounseling and cyberlearning: Strategies and resources for the millennium.* Alexandria, VA: American Counseling Association.

Borders, L. D. (2001). Counseling supervision: A deliberate educational process. In D. Locke, J. Myers, & E. Herr (Eds.), *Handbook of counseling* (pp. 417–432). Thousand Oaks, CA: Sage.

Borys, D. S., & Pope, K. S. (1989). Dual relationships between therapist and client: A national study of psychologists, psychiatrists, and social workers. *Professional Psychology: Research and Practice, 20*(5), 283–293.

Bouhoutsos, J., Holroyd, J., Lerman, H., Forer, B. R., & Greenberg, M. (1983). Sexual intimacy between psychotherapists and patients. *Professional Psychology: Research and Practice, 14*, 185–196.

Brandt, R. (1959). *Ethical theory.* Upper Saddle River, NJ: Prentice Hall.

Brems, C. (2000). The challenge of preventing burnout and assuring growth: Self-care. In *Dealing with challenges in psychotherapy and counseling.* Pacific Grove, CA: Brooks/Cole.

Bridge, P., & Bascue, L. O. (1990). Documentation of psychotherapy supervision. *Psychotherapy in Private Practice, 8*, 79–86.

Brittain, D. E., & Merriam, K. (1988). Groups for significant others of survivors of child sexual abuse. *Journal of Interpersonal Violence, 3*, 90–101.

Brod, C. (1984). *Technostress: The human cost of the computer revolution.* Canada: Addison-Wesley.

Brodsky, A. (1980). Sex role issues in the supervision of therapy. In A. K. Hess (Ed.), *Psychotherapy supervision: Theory, research, and practice* (pp. 509–524). New York, NY: Wiley.

Burling, T. A., Marotta, J., Gonzalez, R., Moltzen, J. O., Eng, A. M., Schmidt, G. A., . . . Reilly, P. M. (1989). Computerized smoking cessation program for the worksite: Treatment outcome and feasibility. *Journal of Consulting and Clinical Psychology, 57*, 619–622.

Burnett, K. F., Magel, P. M., Harrington, S., & Taylor, C. B. (1989). Computer-assisted behavioral health counseling for high school students. *Journal of Counseling Psychology, 36*, 63–67.

Burnett, K. F., Taylor, C. B., & Agras, W. S. (1985). Ambulatory computer-assisted therapy for obesity: A new frontier for behavior therapy. *Journal of Consulting and Clinical Psychology, 53*, 698–703.

Butcher, J. N. (Ed.). (1985). Perspectives on computerized psychological assessment [Special issue]. *Journal of Consulting and Clinical Psychology, 53*, 745–838.

Butcher, J. N. (1987). The use of computers in psychological assessment: An overview of practices and issues. In J. N. Butcher (Ed.), *Computerized psychological assessment: A practitioner's guide* (pp. 3–14). New York, NY: Basic Books.

Butler, M. H., Brimhall, A. S., & Harper, J. M. (2011). A primer on the evolution of therapeutic engagement in MFT: Understanding and resolving the dialectic tension of alliance and neutrality. Part 2—Recommendations: Dynamic neutrality through multiparty and enactments. *American Journal of Family Therapy, 39*(3), 193–213. doi: 10.1080/01926187.2010.493112

Cain, H. I., Harkness, J. L., Smith, A. L., & Markowski, E. M. (2003). Protecting persons in family therapy research: An overview of ethical and regulatory standards. *Journal of Marital and Family Therapy, 29*, 47–57.

Campbell, T. W. (1994). Psychotherapy and malpractice exposure. *American Journal of Forensic Psychology, 12,* 5–41.

Caplan, B. (1987). *Rehabilitation psychology desk reference.* Rockville, MD: Aspen.

Carr, A. C., Ghosh, A., & Marks, I. M. (1988). Computer-supervised exposure treatment for phobias. *Canadian Journal of Psychiatry, 33,* 112–117.

Carrier, J. W. (2004). Assessing suicidal risk. In D. Capuzzi (Ed.), *Suicide across the life span: Implications for counselors* (pp. 139–162). Alexandria, VA: American Counseling Association.

Carroll, M. A., Schneider, H. G., & Wesley, G. R. (1985). *Ethics in the practice of psychology.* Upper Saddle River, NJ: Prentice Hall.

Caudill, O. B. (1998, February/March). The hidden issue of informed consent. *Family Therapy News,* p. 7.

CBS News. (2001, June 18). *Rebirthing therapist sentenced.* Retrieved from http://www.cbsnews.com/news/rebirthing-therapist-sentenced

Center for Substance Abuse Treatment. (1998). *Addiction counseling competencies: The knowledge, skills and attitudes of professional practice* (Technical Assistance Publication [TAP] Series 21. DHHS Publication No. [SMA] 98-3171). Rockville, MD: Substance Abuse and Mental Health Services Administration.

Chapman, C. (1997). Dual relationships in substance abuse treatment: Ethical implications. *Alcoholism Treatment Quarterly, 15,* 73–79.

Chauvin, J. C., & Remley, T. P. (1996). Responding to allegations of unethical conduct. *Journal of Counseling & Development, 74,* 563–568.

Clark, A. J. (2002). Scapegoating: Dynamics and interventions in group counseling. *Journal of Counseling & Development, 80*(3), 271–276. doi:10.1002/j.1556-6678.2002.tb00191.x

Clay, R. A. (2012, June). What you should know about on-line education. *APA Monitor, 43*(6), 42.

Cohen, E. D. (1990). Confidentiality, counseling, and clients who have AIDS: Ethical foundations of a model rule. *Journal of Counseling & Development, 68,* 282–286.

Colby, K. M. (1980). Computer psychotherapists. In J. B. Sidorski, J. H. Johnson, & T. A. Williams (Eds.), *Technology in mental health care delivery systems* (pp. 109–117). Norwood, NJ: Ablex.

Colby, K. M. (1986). Ethics of computer-assisted psychotherapy. *Psychiatric Annals, 16,* 414–415.

Colby, K. M., Colby, P. M., & Stoller, R. J. (1990). Dialogues in natural language with GURU, a psychological inference engine. *Philosophical Psychology, 3,* 171–186.

Colby, K. M., Gould, R. L., & Aronson, G. (1989). Some pros and cons of computer-assisted psychotherapy. *Journal of Nervous and Mental Disease, 177,* 105–108.

Colby, K. M., Watt, J. B., & Gilbert, J. P. (1966). A computer method of psychotherapy: Preliminary communication. *Journal of Nervous and Mental Disease, 142,* 148–152.

Coll, K. M. (1995). Legal challenges in secondary prevention programming for students with substance abuse problems. *The School Counselor, 43,* 35–41.

Commission on Rehabilitation Counselor Certification. (2001). *Code of ethics for rehabilitation counselors.* Rolling Meadows, IL: Author.

Commission on Rehabilitation Counselor Certification. (2010). *Code of professional ethics for rehabilitation counselors.* Schaumburg, IL: Author.

Committee on National Security Systems. (2010). *National information assurance glossary.* Washington, DC: Author.

Constantine, M. G., & Sue, D. W. (Eds.). (2005). *Strategies for building multicultural competence in mental health and educational settings.* Hoboken, NJ: Wiley. Retrieved from http://www.ebrary.com

Corey, G., Corey, M. S., & Callanan, P. (1998). *Issues and ethics in the helping professions* (5th ed.). Pacific Grove, CA: Brooks/Cole.

Corey, G., Corey, M. S., & Callanan, P. (2003). *Issues and ethics in the helping professions* (6th ed.). Pacific Grove, CA: Brooks/Cole.

Corey, G., Corey, M. S., & Callanan, P. (2007). *Issues and ethics in the helping professions* (7th ed.). Pacific Grove, CA: Brooks/Cole.

Corey, G., Corey, M. S., Corey, C., & Callanan, P. (2014). *Issues and ethics in the helping professions* (9th ed.). Pacific Grove, CA: Brooks/Cole.

Corey, G., Williams, G. T., & Moline, M. E. (1995). Ethical and legal issues in group counseling. *Ethics and Behavior, 5,* 161–183.

Corr, C. A., & Balk, D. E. (2010). *Children's encounters with death, bereavement, and coping.* New York, NY: Springer Publishing Company.

Costa, L., & Altekruse, M. (1994). Duty-to-warn guidelines for mental health counselors. *Journal of Counseling & Development, 72,* 346–350.

Cottone, R. R. (1982). Ethical issues in private-for-profit rehabilitation. *Journal of Applied Rehabilitation Counseling, 13*(3), 14–17, 24.

Cottone, R. R. (1989a). Defining the psychomedical and systemic paradigms in marital and family therapy. *Journal of Marital and Family Therapy, 15,* 225–235.

Cottone, R. R. (1989b). On ethical and contextual research in marital and family therapy: A reply to Taggart. *Journal of Marital and Family Therapy, 15,* 243–248.

Cottone, R. R. (1992). *Theories and paradigms of counseling and psychotherapy.* Needham Heights, MA: Allyn & Bacon.

Cottone, R. R. (2001). A social constructivism model of ethical decision-making in counseling. *Journal of Counseling & Development, 79,* 39–45.

Cottone, R. R. (2004). Displacing the psychology of the individual in ethical decision-making: The social constructivism model. *Canadian Journal of Counselling, 38,* 5–13.

Cottone, R. R. (2005). Detrimental therapist-client relationships—Beyond thinking of "dual" or "multiple" roles: Reflections on the 2001 AAMFT Code of Ethics. *American Journal of Family Therapy, 33,* 1–17.

Cottone, R. R. (2011). *Toward a positive psychology of religion: Belief science in the postmodern era.* Winchester, UK: John Hunt Publishing.

Cottone, R. R. (2012a). Ethical decision making in mental health contexts: Representative models and an organizational framework. In S. J. Knapp, M. C. Gottlieb, M. M. Handelsman, & L. D. VandeCreek (Eds.), *APA handbook of ethics in psychology: Vol. 1. Moral foundations and common themes* (pp. 99–121). Washington, DC: American Psychological Association.

Cottone, R. R. (2012b). *Paradigms of counseling and psychotherapy.* Retrieved from www.smashwords.com/books/view/165398

Cottone, R. R. (2014). On replacing the ethical principle of autonomy with an ethical principle of accordance. *Counseling and Values, 59,* 238–248.

Cottone, R. R. (2015, April). The end of counseling as we know it. *Counseling Today, 57*(10), 48–53.

Cottone, R. R., & Claus, R. E. (2000). Ethical decision-making models: A review of the literature. *Journal of Counseling & Development, 78,* 275–283.

Cottone, R. R., Glosoff, H., & Kocet, M. (2005). *Building a foundation for ethical practice in counseling—An online course* [Online course]. Alexandria, VA: American Counseling Association.

Cottone, R. R., Tarvydas, V., & House, G. (1994). The effect of number and type of consulted relationships on the ethical decision-making of graduate students in counseling. *Counseling and Values, 39,* 56–68.

Cottone, R. R., & Tarvydas, V. M. (2003). *Ethical and professional issues in counseling* (2nd ed.). Columbus, OH: Pearson/Prentice Hall.

Council for Accreditation of Counseling and Related Educational Programs. (2015). *CACREP accreditation standards and procedures manual* (Rev. ed.). Alexandria, VA: Author.

Cummings, N. A. (1998). Moral issues in managed mental health care. In R. F. Small & L. R. Barnhill (Eds.), *Practicing in the new mental health marketplace: Ethical, legal and moral issues.* Washington, DC: American Psychological Association.

Dattilio, F. M. (1989). Fraudulent degrees: A threat to the mental health counseling field. *Journal of Mental Health Counseling, 11,* 151–154.

Davenport, N., Schwartz, R. D., & Elliott, G. P. (1999). *Mobbing: Emotional abuse in the American workplace.* Ames, IA: Civil Society of Publishing.

Davidson, R. S. (1985). Applications of computer technology to learning therapy. *Journal of Organizational Behavior Management, 6,* 155–168.

Davis, A., & Yazak, D. (1995). Implementation and accreditation issues in the development of distance learning programs. *Rehabilitation Education, 9,* 293–307.

Davis, T., & Ritchie, M. (1993). Confidentiality and the school counselor: A challenge for the 1990s. *The School Counselor, 41,* 23–30.

Dell, P. (1983). From pathology to ethics. *The Family Therapy Networker, 7*(6), 29–31, 64.

Dinger, T. J. (1997, April). *Do ethical decision-making models really work? An empirical study.* Paper presented at the American Counseling Association world conference, Orlando, FL.

Disney, M. J., & Stephens, A. M. (1994). *Legal issues in clinical supervision.* Alexandria, VA: ACA Press.

Doherty, W., & Boss, P. (1991). Values and ethics in family therapy. In A. S. Gurman & D. P. Kniskern (Eds.), *Handbook of family therapy* (Vol. 2). New York, NY: Brunner/Mazel.

Doherty, W. J. (1995). *Soul searching: Why psychotherapy must promote moral responsibility.* New York, NY: Basic Books.

Dorken, H. (1976). *The professional psychologist.* San Francisco, CA: Jossey-Bass.

Doyle, K. (1997). Substance abuse counselors in recovery: Implications for the ethical issue of dual relationships. *Journal of Counseling & Development, 75,* 428–432.

Drug Abuse Office and Treatment Act. 42 U.S.C. 290 S3 & 42 C.F.R (1976).

Drummond, R. J. (1996). *Appraisal procedures for counselors and helping professionals.* Upper Saddle River, NJ: Prentice Hall.

Duncan, D. M. (1997). *Counseling over the internet: Ethical and legal considerations.* Presentation at the American Counseling Association's 1997 World Conference, Orlando, FL.

Ellis, M. V., & Douce, L. A. (1994). Group supervision of novice clinical supervisors: Eight recurring issues. *Journal of Counseling & Development, 72,* 520–525.

Eyde, L. D. (Ed.). (1987). Computerized psychological testing [Special issue]. *Applied Psychology: An International Review, 36,* 223–235.

Falender, C. A., Collins, C. J., & Shafranske, E. P. (2009). "Impairment" and performance issues in clinical supervision: After the 2008 ADA Amendments Act. *Training and Education in Professional Psychology, 3*(4), 240–249. Retrieved from http://doi.org/10.1037/a0017153

Family Educational Rights and Privacy Act of 1974, 20 U.S.C. § 1232g (1974).

Felie, A. G. (1983). The risks of blowing the whistle. *American Journal of Nursing, 83,* 1387–1388, 1390.

Fischer, L., & Sorenson, G. P. (1996). *School law for counselors, psychologists, and social workers* (3rd ed.). White Plains, NY: Longman.

Fisher, C. B., & Hennessy, J. (1994). Ethical issues. In J. L. Ronch, W. Van Ornum, & N. C. Stilwel (Eds.), *The counseling sourcebook: A practical reference on contemporary issues* (pp. 175–185). New York, NY: Crossroad.

Fisher, M. A. (2012). Confidentiality and record keeping. In S. J. Knapp, M. M. Handelsman, & L. D. VandeCreek (Eds.), *APA handbook of ethics in psychology: Vol. 1. Moral foundations and common themes* (pp. 333–375). Washington, DC: American Psychological Association.

Ford, B. D. (1988). *An ongoing computerized adjunct to psychotherapy program: Two years plus in a two years minus correctional center.* Paper presented at Counseling as Education Conference, Lakehead University, Ontario, Canada.

Ford, B. D. (1993). Ethical and professional issues in computer-assisted therapy. *Computers in Human Behavior, 9,* 387–400.

Ford, B. D., & Vitelli, R. (1992). Inmate attitudes towards computerized clinical interventions. *Computers in Human Behavior, 8,* 223–230.

Forester-Miller, H., & Davis, T. E. (1996). *A practitioner's guide to ethical decision making.* Alexandria, VA: American Counseling Association.

Fowler, R. D. (1985). Landmarks in computer-assisted psychological assessment. *Journal of Consulting and Clinical Psychology, 53,* 748–759.

Fowler, R. D. (1996, June). Clinical psychology celebrates its 100th. *The APA Monitor, 27*(6), 3.

Francouer, R. T. (1983). Teaching decision-making in biomedical ethics for the allied health student. *Journal of Allied Health, 12,* 202–209.

Frank-Stromborg, M. (2004). They're real and they're here: The new federally regulated privacy rules under HIPAA. *Dermatology Nursing, 16,* 13–24.

Freeman, S. J. (2000). *Ethics: An introduction to philosophy and practice.* Boston, MA: Wadsworth.

French, C., & Beaumont, J. G. (1992). Microcomputer version of a digit span test in clinical use. *Interacting with Computers, 4,* 163–178.

French, C. F. (1986). Microcomputers and psychometric assessment. *British Journal of Guidance and Counseling, 14,* 33–45.

Fretz, B. R., & Simon, N. P. (1992). Professional issues in counseling psychology: Continuity, change, and challenge. In S. D. Brown & R. W. Lent (Eds.), *Handbook of counseling psychology* (2nd ed.). New York, NY: John Wiley & Sons.

Froeschle, J. G., & Crews, C. (2010). An ethics challenge for school counselors. In M. A. Hermann, T. P. Remley, & W. C. Huey (Eds.), *Ethical and legal issues in school counseling* (3rd ed., pp. 27–40). Alexandria, VA: American School Counselor Association.

Garcia, J., Cartwright, B., Winston, S. M., & Borzuchowska, B. (2003). A transcultural integrative ethical decision-making model in counseling. *Journal of Counseling & Development, 81,* 268–277.

Gatens-Robinson, E., & Rubin, S. E. (1995). Societal values and ethical commitments that influence rehabilitation service delivery behavior. In S. E. Rubin & R. T. Roessler (Eds.), *Foundations of the vocational rehabilitation process* (pp. 157–174). Austin, TX: Pro-Ed.

Gatens-Robinson, E., & Tarvydas, V. M. (1992). Ethics of care, women's perspectives and the status of the mainstream rehabilitation ethical analysis. *Journal of Applied Rehabilitation Counseling, 23,* 26–33.

Gates, W., Myhrvold, N., & Rinearson, P. (1995). *The road ahead.* New York, NY: Viking.

Gehring, D. D. (1982). The counselor's "duty to warn." *Personnel and Guidance Journal, 61,* 208–210.

Gelso, C. J., & Fretz, B. R. (1992). *Counseling psychology.* Fort Worth, TX: Harcourt Brace Jovanovich.

Gergen, K. J. (1985). The social constructionist movement in modern psychology. *American Psychologist, 40,* 266–275.

Gergen, K. J. (1991). *The saturated self*. New York, NY: Basic Books.

Gergen, K. J. (1994). *Toward transformation in social knowledge* (2nd ed.). London: Sage.

Gergen, K. J. (2001). Psychological science in a postmodern context. *American Psychologist, 56*, 803–813. doi:10.1037//0003-066X.56.10.803

Gibson, W. T., & Pope, K. S. (1993). The ethics of counseling: A national survey of certified counselors. *Journal of Counseling & Development, 71*, 330–336.

Ginsberg, S. W., & Herma, J. L. (1953). Values and their relationship to psychiatric principles and practice. *American Journal of Psychotherapy, 7*, 536–573.

Ginter, E. J. (chair), Ellis, A., Guterman, J. T., Ivey, A. E., Lock, D. C., & Rigazio-Digilio, S. A. (1996, April). *Ethical issues in the postmodern era*. Panel discussion conducted at the 1996 world conference of the American Counseling Association, Pittsburgh, PA.

Glass, T. A. (1998). Ethical issues in group work. In R. M. Anderson, T. L. Needels, & H. V. Hall (Eds.), *Avoiding ethical misconduct in psychology specialty areas*. Springfield, IL: Charles C Thomas.

Glosoff, H. L., Herlihy, B., & Spence, E. B. (2000). Privileged communication in the counselor-client relationship. *Journal of Counseling & Development, 78*(4), 454–462. doi:10.1002/j.1556-6676.2000.tb01929.x

Goodman, H., Gingerich, W. J., & Shazer, S. (1989). Briefer: An expert system for clinical practice. *Computers in Human Services, 5*, 53–68.

Goodyear, R. K., & Sinnett, E. D. (1984). Current and emerging ethical issues for counseling psychologists. *Counseling Psychologist, 12*, 87–98.

Gordon, L. V. (1976). *Survey of interpersonal values: Revised manual*. Chicago, IL: Science Research Associates.

Gottlieb, M. C., & Coleman, A. (2012). Ethical challenges in forensic psychology practice. In S. J. Knapp, M. M. Handelsman, & L. D. VandeCreek (Eds.), *APA handbook of ethics in psychology: Vol. 2. Practice, teaching, and research* (pp. 91–123). Washington, DC: American Psychological Association.

Gottlieb, M. C., Robinson, K., & Younggren, J. N. (2007). Multiple relations in supervision: Guidance for administrators, supervisors, and students. *Professional Psychology: Research and Practice, 38*(3), 241–247. doi:10.1037/0735-7028.38.3.241

Gottman, J. (1994). *Why marriages succeed or fail*. New York, NY: Fireside.

Granello, P. F. (2000). Historical context: The relationship of computer technologies and counseling. In J. W. Bloom & G. R. Walz (Eds.), *Cybercounseling and cyberlearning: Strategies and resources for the millennium* (pp. 3–15). Alexandria, VA: American Counseling Association.

Greenspan, S., & Love, P. (1995). Ethical challenges in supporting persons with disabilities. In O. C. Karan & S. Greenspan (Eds.), *Community rehabilitation services for people with disabilities* (pp. 71–89). Boston, MA: Butterworth-Heineman.

Gregory, J. C., & McConnell, S. C. (1986). Ethical issues with psychotherapy in group contexts. *Psychotherapy in Private Practice, 4*, 51–62.

Grencavage, L. M., & Norcross, J. C. (1990). Where are the commonalities among the therapeutic common factors? *Professional Psychology: Research and Practice, 21*, 372–378.

Gross, D. R., & Robinson, S. E. (1987). Ethics, violence, and counseling: Hear no evil, see no evil, speak no evil? *Journal of Counseling & Development, 65*, 340–344.

Gustafson, K. E., & McNamara, J. R. (1987). Confidentiality with minor clients: Issues and guidelines for therapists. *Professional Psychology: Research and Practice, 18*, 503–508.

Gutheil, T. G., Bursztajn, H. J., Brodsky, A., & Alexander, V. (1991). *Decision-making in psychiatry and the law*. Baltimore, MD: Williams & Wilkins.

Haas, L. J., & Malouf, J. L. (Eds.). (2005). *Keeping up the good work: A practitioner's guide to mental health ethics* (4th ed.). Sarasota, FL: Professional Resource Press.

Haeseler, M. P. (1992). Ethical considerations for the group therapist. *American Journal of Art Therapy, 31,* 2–9.

Haffey, W. J. (1989). The assessment of clinical competency to consent to medical rehabilitation interventions. *Journal of Head Trauma Rehabilitation, 4,* 43–56.

Hall, J. E. (1988). Dual relationships in supervision. *Register Report, 15,* 5–6.

Handelsman, M. M. (2001). Accurate and effective informed consent. In E. Welfel & E. Ingersoll (Eds.), *The mental health desk reference: A sourcebook for counselors and therapists* (pp. 453–458). New York, NY: Wiley.

Handelsman, M. M., & Galvin, M. D. (1988). Facilitating informed consent for outpatient psychotherapy: A suggested written format. *Professional Psychology: Research and Practice, 19,* 223–225.

Handelsman, M. M., Gottlieb, M. C., & Knapp, S. (2005). Training ethical psychologists: An acculturation model. *Professional Psychology: Research and Practice, 36,* 59–65.

Handelsman, M. M., Kemper, M. B., Kesson-Craig, P., McLain, J., & Johnsrud, C. (1986). Use, content, and readability of written informed consent forms for treatment. *Professional Psychology: Research and Practice, 17,* 514–518.

Handelsman, M. M., Knapp, S., & Gottlieb, M. C. (2002). Positive ethics. In C. R. Snyder & S. J. Lopez (Eds.), *Handbook of positive psychology* (pp. 731–744). New York, NY: Oxford University Press.

Hansen, N. D., Pepitone-Arreola-Rockwell, F., & Green, A. F. (2000). Multicultural competence: Criteria and case examples. *Professional Psychology: Research and Practice, 31,* 652–660.

Harding, A. K., Gray, L. A., & Neal, M. (1993). Confidentiality limits with clients who have HIV: A review of ethical and legal guidelines and professional policies. *Journal of Counseling & Development, 71,* 297–305.

Hare, R. (1981). The philosophical basis of psychiatric ethics. In S. Bloch & P. Chodoff (Eds.), *Psychiatric ethics* (pp. 31–45). Oxford, England: Oxford University Press.

Hare, R. (1991). The philosophical basis of psychiatric ethics. In S. Bloch & P. Chodoff (Eds.), *Psychiatric ethics* (2nd ed., pp. 31–45). Oxford, England: Oxford University Press.

Harris, S. M. (2001). Teaching family therapists about sexual attraction in therapy. *Journal of Marital and Family Therapy, 27,* 123–128.

Harris-Bowlsbey, J. (2000). The Internet: Blessing or bane for the counseling profession? In J. W. Bloom & G. R. Walz (Eds.), *Cybercounseling and cyberlearning: Strategies and resources for the millennium* (pp. 39–49). Alexandria, VA: American Counseling Association.

Hartman, D. E. (1986). Artificial intelligence or artificial psychologist? Conceptual issues in clinical microcomputer use. *Professional Psychology: Research and Practice, 17,* 528–534.

Hartsell, T. L., & Bernstein, B. E. (2013). *The portable lawyer for mental health professionals* (3rd ed.). Hoboken, NJ: John Wiley & Sons.

Haug, I. (1993). *Dual Relationships: Sex, power, and exploitation* [Audiotape cassette recording]. AAMFT luncheon plenary (Call: 1-800-241-7785). AAMFT Resource Link, Norcross, GA.

Havranek, J. E. (1997). Ethical issues in forensic rehabilitation. *Journal of Applied Rehabilitation Counseling, 28,* 11–16.

Hays, D. G. (2013). *Assessment in counseling: A guide to the use of psychological assessment procedures* (5th ed.). Alexandria, VA: American Counseling Association.

Health Insurance Portability and Accountability Act. Pub. L., 104-191, 11- Stat. 136 (1996).

Health Insurance Reform Security Standards; Final Rule, 68, Fed. Reg. 8334 (February 20, 2003) (to be codified at 45 C.F.R. pts. 160, 162 & 164).

Hellman, I. D., Morrison, T. L., & Abramowitz, S. I. (1986). The stresses of psychotherapeutic work: A replication and extension. *Journal of Clinical Psychology, 42*(1), 197–205.

Henderson, K. (2001, March). *An overview of ADA, IDEA, and Section 504: Update 2001.* Retrieved from http://ericec.org/digests/e606.html

Hendricks, B., Bradley, L. J., Southern, S., Oliver, M., & Birdsall, B. (2011). Ethical code for the International Association of Marriage and Family Counselors. *Family Journal: Counseling and Therapy for Couples and Families, 19*, 217–224.

Heppner, P. P., Casas, J. M., Carter, J., & Stone, G. L. (2000). The maturation of counseling psychology: Multifaceted perspectives, 1978–1998. In S. D. Brown & R. W. Lent (Eds.), *Handbook of counseling psychology* (3rd ed.). New York, NY: John Wiley & Sons.

Herlihy, B., & Corey, G. (1997). Codes of ethics as catalysts for improving practice. In B. Herlihy & G. Corey (Eds.), *Ethics in therapy* (pp. 37–56). New York, NY: Hatherleigh.

Herlihy, B., & Corey, G. (2015). *Boundary issues in counseling: Multiples roles and responsibilities* (3rd ed.). Alexandria, VA: American Counseling Association.

Herlihy, B., & Sheeley, V. L. (1987). Privileged communication in selected helping professions: A comparison among statutes. *Journal of Counseling & Development, 65*, 479–483.

Herr, E. L., & Niles, S. (1988). The values of counseling: Three domains. *Counseling and Values, 33*, 4–17.

Hill, A. L. (2004). Ethics education: Recommendations for an evolving discipline. *Counseling and Values, 48*(3), 183–203. Retrieved from http://doi.org/10.1002/j.2161-007x.2004.tb00245.x

Hill, M., Glaser, K., & Harden, J. (1995). A feminist model for ethical decision-making. In E. J. Rave & C. C. Larsen (Eds.), *Ethical decision-making in therapy: Feminist perspectives* (pp. 18–37). New York, NY: Guilford Press.

Hinkeldey, N. S., & Spokane, A. R. (1985). Effects of pressure and legal guideline clarity on counselor decision-making in legal and ethical conflict situations. *Journal of Counseling & Development, 64*, 240–245.

Hobson, S. M., & Kanitz, H. M. (1996). Multicultural counseling: An ethical issue for school counselors. *The School Counselor, 43*, 245–255.

Hoffman, L. (1981). *Foundations of family therapy.* New York, NY: Basic Books.

Hofstede, G. (1980). *Culture's consequences: International differences in work values.* Beverly Hills, CA: Sage.

Honaker, L. M., & Fowler, R. D. (1990). Computer-assisted psychological assessment. In G. Goldstein & M. Hersen (Eds.), *Handbook of psychological assessment* (2nd ed., pp. 521–546). Elmsford, NY: Pergamon Press.

Hood, A. B., & Johnson, R. W. (2007). *Assessment in counseling: A guide to the use of psychological assessment procedures* (4th ed.). Alexandria, VA: National Career Development Association.

Hopkins, B. R., & Anderson, B. S. (1990). *The counselor and the law.* Alexandria, VA: American Association for Counseling and Development.

Hopkins, W. E. (1997). *Ethical dimensions of diversity.* Thousand Oaks, CA: Sage.

Howell-Nigrelli, J. (1988). Shared responsibility for reporting child abuse cases: A reaction to Spiegel. *Elementary School Guidance and Counseling, 22*, 289–290.

Howie, J., Gatens-Robinson, E., & Rubin, S. E. (1992). Applying ethical principles in rehabilitation counseling. *Rehabilitation Education, 6*, 41–55.

Huber, C. H. (1994). *Ethical, legal, and professional issues in the practice of marriage and family therapy* (2nd ed.). Upper Saddle River, NJ: Merrill/Prentice Hall.

Hubert, R. M., & Freeman, L. T. (2004). Report of the ACA Ethics Committee: 2002–2003. *Journal of Counseling & Development, 82*, 248–251.

Huey, W. C. (1986). Ethical concerns in school counseling. *Journal of Counseling & Development, 64*, 321–322.

Huey, W. C. (1996). Counseling minor clients. In B. Herlihy & G. Corey (Eds.), *ACA ethical standards casebook* (5th ed.). Alexandria, VA: American Counseling Association.

Hufford, B. J., Glueckauf, R. L., & Webb, P. M. (1999). Home-based, interactive videoconferencing for adolescents with epilepsy and their families. *Rehabilitation Psychology, 44*, 176–193.

Hummel, D. L., Talbutt, L. C., & Alexander, M. D. (1985). *Law and ethics in counseling.* New York, NY: Van Nostrand Reinhold.

Illinois Mental Health and Developmental Disabilities Confidentiality Act, 740 ILCS 110 (1978).

Isaacs, M. L. (1997). The duty to warn and protect: Tarasoff and the elementary school counselor. *Elementary School Guidance and Counseling, 31*, 326–342.

Isaacs, M. L. (1999). School counselors and confidentiality: Factors affecting professional choices. *Professional School Counseling, 99*, 258–267.

Isaacs, M. L., & Stone, C. (1999). School counselors and confidentiality: Factors affecting professional choices. *Professional School Counseling, 2*, 258–266.

Ivey, A. E., & Ivey, M. B. (2003). *Intentional interviewing and counseling: Facilitating client change in a multicultural society.* Pacific Grove, CA: Brooks/Cole.

Ivey, A. E., Ivey, M. B., & Zalaquett, C. P. (2014). *Intentional interviewing and counseling: Facilitating client development in a multicultural society* (8th ed.). Belmont, CA: Brooks/Cole.

Jaffee v. Redmond et al. 1996 WL 315841 (U.S. June 13, 1996).

Janis, I. L., & Mann, L. (1977). *Decision-making: A psychological analysis of conflict, choice, and commitment.* New York, NY: The Free Press.

Jensen, J. P., & Bergin, A. E. (1988). Mental health values of professional therapists: A national interdisciplinary study. *Professional Psychology: Research and Practice, 19*, 290–297.

Johnson, O. A. (1999). *Ethics: Selections from classical and contemporary writers.* Fort Worth, TX: Harcourt Brace.

Johnston, S. P., Tarvydas, V. M., & Butler, M. (2016). Managing risk in ethical and legal situations. In I. Marini & M. Stebnicki (Eds.), *The professional counselor's desk reference* (2nd ed.). New York, NY: Springer Publishing Company.

Jones, E. E., Farina, A., Hestrof, A. H., Markus, H., Miller, D. T., & Scott, R. A. (1984). *Social stigma: The psychology of marked relationships.* New York, NY: W. H. Freeman.

Kant, I. (1949). *Critique of practical reason and other writings in moral philosophy* (L. W. Beck, Trans.). Chicago, IL: University of Chicago Press.

Kaplan, L. S. (1996). Outrageous or legitimate concerns: What some parents are saying about school counseling. *The School Counselor, 43*, 165–170.

Kaplan, L. S. (1997). Parents' rights: Are school counselors at risk? *The School Counselor, 44*, 334–343.

Keashly, L. (1998). Emotional abuse in the workplace: Conceptual and empirical issues. *Journal of Emotional Abuse, 1*(1), 85–117.

Keating, A. B., & Hargitai, J. (1999). *The wired professor.* New York, NY: New York University Press.

Keith-Spiegel, P., & Koocher, G. P. (1985). *Ethics in psychology.* New York, NY: Random House.

Kennedy, R., Baltzley, D., Turnage, J., & Jones, M. (1989). Factor analysis and predictive validity of microcomputer-based tests. *Perceptual and Motor Skills, 69*, 1059–1074.

Kilvingham, Jr., F. M., Johnston, J. A., Hogan, R. S., & Mauer, E. (1994). Who benefits from computerized career counseling? *Journal of Counseling & Development, 72,* 289–292.

King, M. L., Jr. (1968, February 4). *Drum Major Instinct sermon: A sermon by Dr. Martin Luther King, Jr.* Atlanta, GA: Ebenezer Baptist Church.

Kinnier, R. T. (1995). A reconceptualization of values clarification: Values conflict resolution. *Journal of Counseling & Development, 74,* 18–24.

Kinnier, R. T., Dixon, A. L., Barratt, T. M., & Moyer, E. L. (2008). Should universalism trump cultural relativism in counseling? *Counseling and Values, 52*(2), 113–124. doi:10.1002/j.2161-007X.2008.tb00095.x

Kinnier, R. T., Kernes, J. L., & Dautheribes, T. M. (2000). A short list of universal moral values. *Counseling and Values, 45,* 4–16.

Kirschenbaum, H. (2000). From values clarification to character education: A personal journey. *Journal of Humanistic Counseling, Education and Development, 39,* 4–20.

Kitchener, K. S. (1984). Intuition, critical evaluation and ethical principles: The foundation for ethical decisions in counseling psychology. *The Counseling Psychologist, 12,* 43–55.

Kitchener, K. S. (1988). Dual role relationships: What makes them so problematic? *Journal of Counseling & Development, 67,* 217–221.

Kitchener, K. S., & Anderson, S. K. (Eds.). (2011). *Foundations of ethical practice, research, and teaching in psychology and counseling* (2nd ed.). New York, NY: Routledge.

Kitchener, K. S., & Harding, S. S. (1990). Dual role relationships. In B. Herlihy & L. Golden (Eds.), *Ethical standards casebook* (4th ed., pp. 145–148). Alexandria, VA: American Association for Counseling and Development.

Klebe-Trevino, L. (1986). Ethical decision making in organizations: A person-situation interactionist model. *Academy of Management Review, 11*(3), 601–617.

Kluckhorn, C. (1951). Values and value-orientations in the theory of action: An exploration in definition and clarification. In T. Parsons & E. A. Shils (Eds.), *Toward a general theory of action* (pp. 338–433). Cambridge, MA: Harvard University Press.

Knauss, L. K., & Knauss, J. W. (2012). Ethical issues in multiperson therapy. In S. J. Knapp, M. M. Handelsman, & L. D. VandeCreek (Eds.), *APA handbook of ethics in psychology: Vol. 2. Practice, teaching, and research* (pp. 29–43). Washington, DC: American Psychological Association.

Kocet, M. M., & Herlihy, B. J. (2014). Addressing value-based conflicts within the counseling relationship: A decision-making model. *Journal of Counseling & Development, 92*(2), 180–186. doi:10.1002/j.1556-6676.2014.00146.x

Kohlberg, L. (1964). Development of moral character and moral ecology. In M. L. Hoffman & L. W. Hoffman (Eds.), *Review of child development research* (Vol. 1). New York, NY: Russell Sage Foundation.

Kohlberg, L. (1969). Stage and sequence: The cognitive-developmental approach to socialization. In D. Soslin (Ed.), *Handbook of socialization theory and research* (pp. 347–480). Chicago, IL: Rand McNally.

Kohlberg, L. (1971). Moral development and the education of adolescents. In R. Purnell (Ed.), *Adolescents and the American high school.* New York, NY: Holt, Rinehart & Winston.

Kohlberg, L. (1980). High school democracy and educating a just society. In R. L. Mosher (Ed.), *Moral education: A generation of research and development* (pp. 20–57). New York, NY: Praeger.

Kohlberg, L. (1981). *Philosophy of moral development.* San Francisco, CA: Harper & Row.

Koocher, G. P., & Daniel, J. H. (2012). Treating children and adolescents. In S. J. Knapp, M. M. Handelsman, & L. D. VandeCreek (Eds.), *APA handbook of ethics in psychology: Vol. 2. Practice, teaching, and research* (pp. 3–14). Washington, DC: American Psychological Association.

Koocher, G. P., & Keith-Spiegel, P. (1998). *Ethics in psychology* (2nd ed.). New York, NY: Oxford University Press.

Kotter, J. A. (1982). Ethics comes of age: Introduction to the special issue. *Journal for Specialists in Group Work, 7,* 138–139.

Ladany, N., Hill, C. E., Corbett, M., & Nutt, E. A. (1996). Nature, extent, and importance of what psychotherapy trainees do not disclose to their supervisors. *Journal of Counseling Psychology, 43,* 10–24.

Lamb, D. H., Catanzaro, S. J., & Moorman, A. S. (2004). A preliminary look at how psychologists identify, evaluate, and proceed when faced with possible multiple relationship dilemmas. *Professional Psychology: Research and Practice, 35,* 248–254.

Lamb, D. H., Cochran, D. J., & Jackson, V. R. (1991). Training and organizational issues associated with identifying and responding to intern impairment. *Professional Psychology: Research and Practice, 22,* 291–296.

Lambie, G. W., Hagedorn, W. B., & Ieva, K. P. (2010). Social-cognitive development, ethical and legal knowledge, and ethical decision making of counselor education students. *Counselor Education and Supervision, 49*(4), 228–246. doi:10.1002/j.1556-6978.2010.tb00100.x

Landfield, A. W., & Nawas, M. M. (1964). Psychotherapeutic improvement as a function of communication and adoption of therapist's values. *Journal of Counseling Psychology, 11,* 336–341.

Lawrence, G. H. (1986). Using computers for the treatment of psychological problems. *Computers in Human Behavior, 2,* 43–62.

Lazarus, A. A. (2001, January/February). Not all "dual relationships" are taboo: Some tend to enhance treatment outcomes. *The National Psychologist, 10*(1), 16.

Lazarus, A. A., & Zur, O. (Eds.). (2002). *Dual relationships and psychotherapy.* New York, NY: Springer Publishing Company.

Levitan, K. B., Willis, E. A., & Vogelgesang, J. (1985). Microcomputers and the individual practitioner: A review of the literature in psychology and psychiatry. *Computers in Human Services, 1,* 65–84.

Lewis, M. M., & Hardin, S. I. (2002). Relations among and between career values and Christian religious values. *Counseling and Values, 46*(2), 96–107. doi:10.1002/j.2161-007X.2002.tb00280.x

Leymann, H. (1996). The content and development of mobbing at work. *European Journal of Work and Organizational Psychology, 5*(2), 10–22.

Liddell, D. L., Halpin, G., & Halpin, W. G. (1992). The Measure of Moral Orientation: Measuring the ethics of care and justice. *Journal of College Student Development, 33,* 325–330.

Lien, C. (1993). The ethics of the sliding fee scale. *Journal of Mental Health Counseling, 15,* 334–341.

London, P. (1986). *Modes and morals of psychotherapy* (2nd ed.). New York, NY: Holt, Rinehart & Winston.

Lyddon, W. J. (1995). Forms and facets of constructivist psychology. In R. A. Neimeyer & M. J. Mahoney (Eds.), *Constructivism in psychotherapy* (pp. 69–92). Washington, DC: American Psychological Association.

Lynch, S. K. (1993). AIDS: Balancing confidentiality and the duty to protect. *Journal of College Student Development, 34,* 148–153.

Mabe, A. R., & Rollin, S. A. (1986). The role of a code of ethical standards in counseling. *Journal of Counseling & Development, 64,* 294–297.

Maddi, S. R., Kahn, S., & Maddi, K. L. (1998). The effectiveness of hardiness training. *Consulting Psychology Journal: Practice and Research, 50*(2), 78–86. doi:10.1037/1061-4087.50.2.78

Maddi, S. R., & Kobasa, S. C. (1984). *The hardy executive: Health under stress.* Homewood, IL: Dow Jones-Irwin.

Maki, D. (1986). Foundations of applied rehabilitation counseling. In T. Riggar, D. Maki, & A. Wolf (Eds.), *Applied rehabilitation counseling* (pp. 3–11). New York, NY: Springer Publishing Company.

Margolin, G. (1982). Ethical and legal considerations in marital and family therapy. *American Psychologist, 37*, 788–801.

Marino, T. W. (1996, November). Fair Access Coalition on Testing holds meeting in Washington, D.C. *Counseling Today, 13*, 19.

Martz, E., & Kaplan, D. (2014, October). New responsibilities when making referrals. *Counseling Today, 57*(4), 24–25. Retrieved from https://www.counseling.org

Maslach, C., Jackson, S. E., & Leiter, M. P. (1986). *Maslach burnout inventory: Manual* (2nd ed.). Palo Alto, CA: Consulting Psychologists Press.

Matarazzo, J. D. (1985). Clinical psychological test interpretations by computer: Hardware outpaces software. *Computers in Human Behavior, 1*, 235–253.

Matarazzo, J. D. (1986). Computerized clinical psychological test interpretation: Unvalidated plus all mean and no sigma. *American Psychologist, 41*, 14–25.

Maturana, H. R. (1970). Biology of cognition. In H. R. Maturana & F. J. Varela (Eds.), *Autopoiesis and cognition: The realization of the living* (pp. 112–114). Boston, MA: D. Reidel.

Maturana, H. R. (1978). Biology of language: The epistemology of reality. In G. A. Miller & E. Lenneberg (Eds.), *Psychology and biology of language and thought* (pp. 27–63). New York, NY: Academic Press.

Maturana, H. R. (1988). Reality: The search for objectivity or the quest for a compelling argument. *Irish Journal of Psychology, 9*(1), 25–82.

Maturana, H. R., & Varela, F. J. (1980). *Autopoiesis and cognition: The realization of the living.* Boston: D. Reidel.

Maylone, M. M., Ranieri, L., Griffin, M. T. Q., McNulty, R., & Fitzpatrick, J. J. (2011). Collaboration and autonomy: Perceptions among nurse practitioners. *Journal of the American Academy of Nurse Practitioners, 23*, 51–57. doi:10.1111/j.1745-7599.2010.00576.x; Retrieved from http://onlinelibrary.wiley.com.proxy.lib.uiowa.edu/doi/10.1111/j.1745-7599.2010.00576.x/abstract;jsessionid=F7A6F203631E592CE47595EEDBAD6561.f01t01

McCarthy, P., Sugden, S., Koker, M., Lamendola, F., Maurer, S., & Renninger, S. (1995). A practical guide to informed consent in clinical supervision. *Counselor Education and Supervision, 35*, 130–138.

McCrady, B. S., & Bux, D. A. (1999). Ethical issues in informed consent with substance abusers. *Journal of Consulting and Clinical Psychology, 67*, 186–193.

McWhirter, J. J., McWhirter, B. T., McWhirter, A. M., & McWhirter, E. H. (1998). *At-risk youth: A comprehensive response* (2nd ed.). Pacific Grove, CA: Brooks/Cole.

Meara, N. M., Schmidt, L. D., & Day, J. D. (1996). Principles and virtue: A foundation for ethical decisions, policies, and character. *The Counseling Psychologist, 24*(1), 4–77.

Merrell, K. W. (1986). Computer use in psychometric assessment: Evaluating benefits and potential problems. *Computers in Human Services, 1*(3), 59–67.

Minard, S. M. (1993). The school counselor's role in confronting child sexual abuse. *The School Counselor, 41*, 9–15.

Mohan, J. (1993). The business of medicine. *Sociology, 22*, 648–649.

Moncher, M. S., Parms, C. A., Orlandi, M. A., Schinke, S. P., Miller, S. O., Palleja, J., & Schinke, M. B. (1985). Microcomputer-based approaches for preventing drug and alcohol abuse among adolescents from ethnic-racial minority backgrounds. *Computers in Human Behavior, 5*, 79–93.

Moyer, M., & Sullivan, J. (2008). Student risk-taking behaviors: When do school counselors break confidentiality? *Professional School Counseling, 11*(4), 236–245. doi:10.5330/PSC.n.2010-11.236

Muro, J. J., & Kottman, T. (1995). *Guidance and counseling in the elementary and middle schools: A practical approach.* Madison, WI: Brown & Benchmark.

National Association for Alcoholism and Drug Abuse Counselors. (2012). *NAADAC/ NCC AP code of ethics.* Alexandria, VA: Author.

National Association of Social Workers. (2008). *Code of ethics.* Washington, DC: Author.

National Association of Social Workers and Association of Social Work Boards. (2005). *NASW and ASWB standards for technology and social work practice.* Washington, DC: National Association of Social Workers.

National Board for Certified Counselors. (2015). *Understanding national certification and state licensure* [web page]. Retrieved from http://www.nbcc.org/Certification/ CertificationOrLicensure

National Career Development Association. (2007). *Code of ethics.* Alexandria, VA: Author.

National Career Development Association. (2015). *Code of ethics.* Alexandria, VA: Author.

Neese, L. A. (1989). Psychological maltreatment in schools: Emerging issues for counselors. *Elementary School Guidance and Counseling, 23,* 194–200.

Nelson, H. L. (1992). Against caring. *Journal of Clinical Ethics, 3*(1), 8–14.

Neukrug, E. S., & Milliken, T. (2011). Counselors' perceptions of ethical behaviors. *Journal of Counseling & Development, 89*(2), 206–216. Retrieved from http://doi.org/ 10.1002/j.1556-6678.2011.tb00079.x

New patient records privacy rule takes effect. (2001, Spring). *Practitioner Update, 9*(1), 1, 4.

Newman, J. L. (1993). Ethical issues in consultation. *Journal of Counseling & Development, 72,* 148–156.

Niemann, H., Ruff, R. M., & Baser, C. A. (1990). Computer-assisted attention retraining in head-injured individuals: A controlled efficacy study of an outpatient program. *Journal of Consulting and Clinical Psychology, 58,* 811–817.

Nietzsche, F. (1968a). The Antichrist. In W. Kaufmann (Ed. & Trans.), *The portable Nietzsche* (pp. 565–656). New York, NY: Penguin. (Original work published 1888)

Nietzsche, F. (1968b). Thus spake Zarathustra. In W. Kaufmann (Ed. & Trans.), *The portable Nietzsche* (pp. 565–656). New York, NY: Penguin. (Original work published 1891)

Niles, S. G., & Pate, R. H. Jr. (1989). Competency and training issues related to the integration of career counseling and mental health counseling. *Journal of Career Development, 16*(1), 63–71.

Noddings, N. (1992). In defense of caring. *Journal of Clinical Ethics, 3*(1), 14–17.

Nowinski, J., & Baker, S. (1992). *The twelve-step facilitation handbook: A systematic approach to early recovery from alcoholism and addiction.* San Francisco, CA: Jossey-Bass.

O'Connell, W. P. (2012). Secondary school administrators' attitudes toward confidentiality in school counseling. *NASSP Bulletin, 96*(4), 350–363. doi:10.1177/019263651 2466936

Ohio, A.-G. (1996, July–August). Legal opinion allows counselors to call testing and evaluations 'psychological.' *The National Psychologist,* p. 9.

O'Rourke, B. L. W. (1996). *Individual interdisciplinary team members' perception of ethics decision-making context: A descriptive study* (Unpublished doctoral dissertation). University of Iowa, Iowa City, IA.

Office of Applied Studies, Substance Abuse and Mental Health Services Administration. (2004). *Results from the 2003 National Survey on Drug Use and Health: National findings* (DHHS Publication No. [SMA] 04-3964, NSDUH Series H-25). Rockville, MD: Substance Abuse and Mental Health Services Administration.

Osheroff v. Chestnut Lodge, Inc. (1985). 490 A. 2d. 720 (Md. App. 1985)

Palmiter, D. J. (2012). Positive ethics applied to public education through traditional media and the Internet. In S. J. Knapp, M. M. Handelsman, & L. D. VandeCreek (Eds.), *APA handbook of ethics in psychology: Vol. 2. Practice, teaching, and research* (pp. 199–215). Washington, DC: American Psychological Association.

Park, K., & Lee, S. (1992). A computer aided aptitude test for predicting flight performance of trainees. *Human Factors, 34*, 189–204.

Patterson, J. B. (1992). Ethics and ethical decision-making in rehabilitation counseling. In R. M. Parker & E. M. Szymanski (Eds.), *Rehabilitation counseling: Basics and beyond* (pp. 165–193). Austin, TX: Pro-Ed.

Patterson, J. B., Patrick, A., & Parker, R. M. (2000). Choice ethical and legal rehabilitation challenges. *Rehabilitation Counseling Bulletin, 43*(4), 203–208.

Patterson, J. B, & Settles, R. (1992). The ethics education of certified rehabilitation counselors. *Rehabilitation Education, 6*, 179–184.

Pederson, P. (Ed.). (1985). *Handbook of cross-cultural counseling and therapy.* Westport, CT: Greenwood.

Pepper-Smith, R., Harvey, W. R., Silberfeld, M., Stein, E., & Rutman, D. (1992). Consent to a competency assessment. *International Journal of Law and Psychiatry, 15*, 13–23.

Peterson, D. B., Murray, G., & Chan, F. (1998). Ethics and technology. In R. R. Cottone & V. M. Tarvydas (Eds.), *Ethical and professional issues in counseling* (pp. 196–235). New York, NY: Prentice Hall.

Peterson, M. (1993). Covert agendas in supervision. *Supervision Bulletin, 6*, 7–8.

Peterson, M. B. (2001). Recognizing concerns about how some licensing boards are treating psychologists. *Professional Psychology: Research and Practice, 32*, 339–340.

Pettifor, J. L. (1996). Maintaining professional conduct in daily practice. In L. J. Bass, S. T. DeMers, J. R. P. Ogloff, C. Peterson, J. L. Pettifor, R. P. Reaves . . . R. M. Tipton (Eds.), *Professional conduct and discipline in psychology* (pp. 91–100). Washington, DC: American Psychological Association.

Pietrofesa, J. J., Hoffman, A., Splete, H., & Pinto, D. (1978). *Counseling: Theory, research, and practice.* Chicago, IL: Rand McNally.

Pietrofesa, J. J., Pietrofesa, C. J., & Pietrofesa, J. D. (1990). The mental health counselor and "duty to warn." *Journal of Mental Health Counseling, 12*, 129–137.

Pomerantz, A. M. (2012). Informed consent to psychotherapy (empowered collaboration). In S. J. Knapp, M. M. Handelsman, & L. D. VandeCreek (Eds.), *APA handbook of ethics in psychology: Vol. 1. Moral foundations and common themes* (pp. 311–332). Washington, DC: American Psychological Association.

Pope, K. S. (1988). How clients are harmed by sexual contact with mental health professionals: The syndrome and its prevalence. *Journal of Counseling & Development, 67*, 222–226.

Pope, K. S., Keith-Spiegel, P., & Tabachnick, B. G. (1986). Sexual attraction to clients: The human therapist and the (sometimes) inhuman training system. *American Psychologist, 41*, 147–158.

Pope, K. S., Tabachnick, B. G., & Keith-Spiegel, P. (1987). Ethics of practice: The beliefs and behaviors of psychologists as therapists. *American Psychologist, 42*, 993–1006.

Pope, K. S., & Vasquez, M. J. T. (1991). *Ethics in psychotherapy and counseling.* San Francisco, CA: Jossey-Bass.

Posey, E. C. (1988). Confidentiality in an AIDS support group. *Journal of Counseling & Development, 66*, 226–227.

Psychological Corporation. (1997). *Scoring assistant for the Weschler Scales–adult (SAWS-A)* [Computer software]. San Antonio, TX: Author.

Purtilo, R., Jensen, G. M., & Brasic Royeen, C. (2005). *Educating for moral action: A sourcebook in health and rehabilitation ethics.* Philadelphia, PA: F. A. Davis.

Raths, L., Harmin, M., & Simon, S. (1966). *Values and teaching: Working with values in the classroom.* Upper Saddle River, NJ: Merrill/Prentice Hall.

Raths, L., Harmin, M., & Simon, S. (1978). *Values and teaching: Working with values in the classroom* (2nd ed.). Upper Saddle River, NJ: Merrill/Prentice Hall.

Reaves, R. P. (1996). Enforcement of codes of conduct by regulatory boards and professional associations. In L. J. Bass, S. T. DeMers, J. R. P. Ogloff, C. Peterson, J. L. Pettifor, R. P. Reaves . . . R. M. Tipton (Eds.), *Professional conduct and discipline in psychology* (pp. 101–108). Washington, DC: American Psychological Association.

Reaves, R. P. (1999). *Avoiding liability in mental health practice*. Montgomery, AL: Association of State and Provincial Psychology Boards.

Reimer, J., Paolitto, D. P., & Hersch, R. H. (1983). *Promoting moral growth: From Piaget to Kohlberg*. New York, NY: Longman.

Remley, T. P., Jr. (1985). The law and ethical practices in elementary and middle schools. *Elementary School Guidance and Counseling, 19*, 181–189.

Remley, T. P., Jr. (1990). Counseling records: Legal and ethical issues. In B. Herlihy & L. Golden (Eds.), *AACD ethical standards casebook* (4th ed., pp. 162–169). Alexandria, VA: American Association for Counseling and Development.

Remley, T. P., Jr., & Fry, L. J. (1993). Reporting suspected child abuse: Conflicting roles for the counselor. *The School Counselor, 40*, 253–259.

Remley, T. P., & Herlihy, B. (2010). *Ethical, legal, and professional issues in counseling* (3rd ed.). Upper Saddle River, NJ: Merrill.

Remley, T. P., & Herlihy, B. (2014). *Ethical, legal, and professional issues in counseling* (4th ed.). Upper Saddle River, NJ: Merrill.

Remley, T. P., Jr., Herlihy, B., & Herlihy, S. B. (1997). The U.S. Supreme Court decision in *Jaffee v. Redmond:* Implications for counselors. *Journal of Counseling & Development, 75*, 213–218.

Remley, T. P., Jr., & Sparkman, L. B. (1993). Student suicides: The counselor's limited legal liability. *The School Counselor, 40*, 164–169.

Rest, J. R. (1984). Research on moral development: Implications for training psychologists. *The Counseling Psychologist, 12*(3), 19–29.

Rest, J. R. (1994). Background: Theory and research. In J. R. Rest & D. Narvaez (Eds.), *Moral development in the professions: Psychology and applied ethics* (pp. 1–26). Hillsdale, NJ: Lawrence Erlbaum.

Rest, J. R., Cooper, D., Coder, R., Maganz, J., & Anderson, D. (1974). Judging the important issues in moral dilemmas—An objective test of development. *Developmental Psychology, 10*(4), 491–501.

Rest, J. R., Davison, M. L., & Robbins, S. (1978). Age trends in judging moral issues: A review of cross-sectional, longitudinal, and sequential studies of the Defining Issues Test. *Child Development, 49*(2), 263–279.

Roback, H. B., & Purdon, S. E. (1992). Confidentiality dilemmas in group psycho-therapy. *Small Group Research, 23*, 169–185. (Accessed through the MasterFILE Elite database, pp. 1–10)

Rogers, C. (1951). *Client-centered therapy*. Boston, MA: Houghton Mifflin.

Rokeach, M., & Regan, J. (1980). The role of values in the counseling situation. *Personnel and Guidance Journal, 58*, 576–583.

Rubin, S. E., & Roessler, R. T. (2015). *Foundations of the vocational rehabilitation process* (6th ed.). Austin, TX: Pro-Ed.

Ryder, R., & Hepworth, J. (1990). AAMFT ethical code: "Dual relationships." *Journal of Marital and Family Therapy, 16*, 127–132.

Salyer, S. (1997, July 18–20). The dawn of "virtual therapy." *USA Weekend*, p. 10.

Sampson, J. P., Jr. (1986). The use of computer-assisted instruction in support of psychotherapeutic processes. *Computers in Human Behavior, 2*, 1–19.

Sampson, J. P., Jr. (1990). Computer-assisted testing and the goals of counseling psychology. *The Counseling Psychologist, 18*, 227–239.

Sampson, J. P., Jr. (2000). Computer applications. In C. E. Watkins, Jr. & V. L. Campbell (Eds.), *Testing and assessment in counseling practice* (2nd ed., pp. 517–544). Hillside, NJ: Lawrence Erlbaum.

Sampson, J. P., Jr., Kolodinski, R. W., & Greeno, B. P. (1997). Counseling on the information highway: Future possibilities and potential problems. *Journal of Counseling & Development, 75,* 203–212.

Sampson, J. P., Jr., & Krumboltz, J. D. (1991). Computer-assisted instruction: A missing link in counseling. *Journal of Counseling & Development, 69,* 395–397.

Sandberg, D. N., Crabbs, S. K., & Crabbs, M. A. (1988). Legal issues in child abuse: Questions and answers for counselors. *Elementary School Guidance and Counseling, 22,* 268–274.

Santa Rosa Health Care Corporation v. Garcia, 964 S.W.2nd 940 (Texas, 1998).

Schaffner, A. D., & Dixon, D. N. (2003). Religiosity, gender, and preferences for religious interventions in counseling: A preliminary study. *Counseling and Values, 48*(1), 24–33. doi:10.1002/j.2161-007X.2003.tb00272.x

Schein, E. H. (2010). *Organizational culture and leadership* (4th ed.). San Francisco, CA: Jossey-Bass.

Schinke, S. P., & Orlandi, M. A. (1990). Skills-based, interactive computer interventions to prevent HIV infection among African-American and Hispanic adolescents. *Computers in Human Behavior, 6,* 235–246.

Schinke, S. P., Orlandi, M. A., Gordon, A. N., Weston, R. E., Moncher, M. S., & Parms, C. A. (1989). AIDS prevention via computer-based intervention. *Computers in Human Services, 5,* 147–156.

Schneider, S. J. (1986). Trial of an on-line behavioral smoking cessation program. *Computers in Human Behavior, 2,* 277–286.

Schneider, S. J., Walter, R., & O'Donnell, R. (1990). Computerized communication as a medium for behavioral smoking cessation treatment: Controlled evaluation. *Computers in Human Behavior, 6,* 141–151.

Schoener, R. (1995). Assessment of professionals who have engaged in boundary violations. *Psychiatric Annals, 525,* 95–98.

Schlossberger, E., & Hecker, L. (1996). HIV and family therapists' duty to warn: A legal and ethical analysis. *Journal of Marital and Family Therapy, 22,* 27–40.

Schwab, R., & Neukrug, E. (1994). A survey of counselor educators' ethical concerns. *Counseling and Values, 39,* 42–54.

Schwartz, S. H. (1977). Normative influences on altruism. In L. Berkowitz (Ed.), *Advances in experimental social psychology* (Vol. 10, pp. 221–279). New York, NY: Academic Press.

Scriven, B. (1991). Distance education and open learning: Implications for professional development and retraining. *Distance Education, 12,* 297–305.

Sealander, K. A., Schwiebert, V. L., Oren, T. A., & Weekley, J. L. (1999). Confidentiality and the law. *Professional School Counseling, 3,* 122–127.

Seligman, M. E. P., & Csikszentmihalyi, M. (2000). Positive psychology: An introduction. *American Psychologist, 55,* 5–14.

Selmi, P. M., Klein, M. H., Greist, J. H., Johnson, J. H., & Harris, W. G. (1982). An investigation of computer-assisted cognitive-behavior therapy in the treatment of depression. *Behavior Research Methods and Instrumentation, 14,* 181–185.

Selmi, P. M., Klein, M. H., Greist, J. H., Sorell, S. P., & Erdman, H. P. (1990). Computer-administered cognitive-behavioral therapy for depression. *American Journal of Psychiatry, 147,* 51–56.

Servan-Schreiber, C., & Binik, Y. M. (1989). Extending the intelligent tutoring system paradigm: Sex therapy as intelligent tutoring. *Computers in Human Behavior, 5,* 241–259.

Sexton, T. L., Montgomery, D., Goff, K., & Nugent, W. (1993). Ethical, therapeutic, and legal considerations in the use of paradoxical techniques: The emerging debate. *Journal of Mental Health Counseling, 15,* 260–277.

Shapira-Lishchinsky, O. (2013). Team-based simulations: Learning ethical conduct in teacher trainee programs. *Teaching and Teacher Education, 33,* 1–12. Retrieved from http://dx.doi.org/10.1016/j.tate.2013.02.001

Sheeley, V. L., & Herlihy, B. (1987). Privileged communication in school counseling: Status update. *The School Counselor, 34,* 268–272.

Sheeley, V. L., & Herlihy, B. (1989). Counseling suicidal teens: A duty to warn and protect. *The School Counselor, 37,* 89–97.

Sherry, P. (1991). Ethical issues in the conduct of supervision. *The Counseling Psychologist, 19,* 566–585.

Shulman, L. S., Golde, C. M., Bueschel, A. C., Garabedian, K. J. (2006). Reclaiming education's doctorates: A critique and a proposal. *Educational Researcher, 35,* 25–32. doi:10.3102/0013189X035003025

Sileo, F. J., & Kopala, M. (1993). An A-B-C-D-E worksheet for promoting beneficence when considering ethical issues. *Counseling and Values, 37,* 89–95.

Simons, G. (1985). *Silicon shock.* New York, NY: Basil Blackwell.

Sinclair, C. (2004). *Code comparisons: The Canadian code of ethics for psychologists compared with the APA and ASPPB codes.* Canadian Psychological Association. Retrieved from http://www.cpa.ca/documents/Code_Comparison.pdf

Sirkin, J. (1994). Learning at a distance. *On Campus, 14*(3), 7–10.

Skorina, J. K., Bissell, L., & De Soto, C. B. (1990). Alcoholic psychologists: Routes to recovery. *Professional Psychology: Research and Practice, 21*(4), 248–251.

Skorupa, J., & Agresti, A. A. (1993). Ethical beliefs about burnout and continued professional practice. *Professional Psychology: Research and Practice, 24*(3), 281.

Smith, D., & Fitzpatrick, M. (1995). Patient-therapist boundary issues: An integrative review of theory and research. *Professional Psychology: Research and Practice, 26*(5), 499–506.

Smith, J. J. (1987). The effectiveness of computerized self-help stress coping program with adult males. *Computers in Human Services, 2,* 37–49.

Smith, P. L., & Moss, S. B. (2009). Psychologist impairment: What is it, how can it be prevented, and what can be done to address it? *Clinical Psychology: Science and Practice, 16*(1), 1–15. Retrieved from http://doi.org/10.1111/j.1468-2850.2009.01137.x

Sommers-Flanagan, R. (2012). Boundaries, multiple roles, and the professional relationship. In S. J. Knapp, M. M. Handelsman, & L. D. VandeCreek (Eds.), *APA handbook of ethics in psychology: Vol. 1. Moral foundations and common themes* (pp. 241–277). Washington, DC: American Psychological Association.

Sonne, J. L. (2012). Sexualized relationships. In S. J. Knapp, M. M. Handelsman, & L. D. VandeCreek (Eds.), *APA handbook of ethics in psychology: Vol. 1. Moral foundations and common themes* (pp. 295–310). Washington, DC: American Psychological Association.

Sperry, L. (2007). *The ethical and professional practice of counseling and psychotherapy.* Boston, MA: Pearson/Allyn & Bacon.

Stadler, H. A. (1989). Balancing ethical responsibilities: Reporting child abuse and neglect. *The Counseling Psychologist, 17,* 102–110.

Stadler, H. A. (1990). Counselor impairment. In B. Herlihy & L. Golden (Eds.), *Ethical standards casebook.* Alexandria, VA: American Association for Counseling and Development.

Stanard, R., & Hazler, R. (1995). Legal and ethical implications of HIV and duty to warn for counselors: Does Tarasoff apply? *Journal of Counseling & Development, 73,* 397–400.

Stebnicki, M. A. (1997, October/November/December). Conceptual framework for utilizing a functional assessment approach for determining mental capacity: A new look at informed consent in rehabilitation. *Journal of Rehabilitation, 63*, 32–37.

Steele, R. L. (1993). Distance learning delivery systems: Instructional options. *Media and Methods, 29*(4), 12, 14.

Stocks, T. J., & Freddolino, P. P. (1998). Evaluation of a World-Wide Web: Overview and basic design principles. *Educational Technology, 37*(3), 7–15.

Stoltenberg, C. D., McNeill, B., & Delworth, U. (1998). *IDM supervision: An integrated developmental model for supervising counselors and therapists.* San Francisco, CA: Jossey-Bass.

Stoltenberg, C. D., & McNeill, B. W. (2010). *IDM supervision: An integrative developmental model for supervising counselors and therapists* (3rd ed.). New York, NY: Routledge. Retrieved from http://www.routledge.com/books/details/9780805858259

Stone, C. (2002). Negligence in academic advising and abortion counseling: Courts rulings and implications. *Professional School Counseling, 6*(1), 28–35.

Stone, C. B. (2000). Advocacy for sexual harassment victims: Legal support and ethical aspects. *Professional School Counseling, 4*, 23–30.

Stones, M., & Kozma, A. (1989). Multidimensional assessment of the elderly via a microcomputer: The SENOTS program and battery. *Psychology and Aging, 4*, 113–118.

Strein, W., & Hershenson, D. B. (1991). Confidentiality in nondyadic counseling situations. *Journal of Counseling & Development, 69*, 312–316.

Stricker, G. (1996). Psychotherapy in cyberspace. *Ethics and Behavior, 6*(2), 169, 175–177.

Stromberg, C., & his colleagues in the law firm of Hogan & Harson of Washington, DC (1993, April). *Privacy, confidentiality and privilege. The Psychologist's Legal Update.* Washington, DC: National Register of Health Service Providers in Psychology. As cited in Corey, G., Corey, M. S., & Callanan, P. (1998). *Issues and ethics in the helping professions* (5th ed.). Pacific Grove, CA: Brooks/Cole.

Strupp, H. H. (1980). Humanism and psychotherapy: A personal statement of the therapist's essential values. *Psychotherapy: Theory, Research and Practice, 17*, 396–400.

Substance Abuse and Mental Health Services Administration. (2004, June). *The confidentiality of alcohol and drug abuse patient records regulation and the HIPAA Privacy Rule: Implications for alcohol and substance abuse programs.* Rockville, MD: U.S. Department of Health and Human Services.

Sue, D. W. (1996). Ethical issues in multicultural counseling. In B. Herlihy & G. Corey (Eds.), *ACA ethical standards casebook* (5th ed.). Alexandria, VA: American Counseling Association.

Sue, D. W., Arrendondo, P., & McDavis, R. J. (1992). Multicultural counseling competencies and standards: A call to the profession. *Journal of Counseling & Development, 70*, 477–486.

Taber, B. J., & Luzzo, D. A. (1999). *A comprehensive review of research evaluating the effectiveness of DISCOVER in promoting career development* (ACT Research Report 99.3). Iowa City, IA: ACT.

Talbutt, L. C. (1983). Current legal trends regarding abortions for minors: A dilemma for counselors. *The School Counselor, 31*, 120–124.

Tarvydas, V. M. (1987). Decision-making models in ethics: Models for increased clarity and wisdom. *Journal of Applied Rehabilitation Counseling, 18*(4), 50–52.

Tarvydas, V. M. (1994). Ethical orientations of master's rehabilitation counseling students. *Rehabilitation Counseling Bulletin, 37*, 202–214.

Tarvydas, V. M. (2012). Ethics and ethical decision making. In D. R. Maki & V. M. Tarvydas (Eds.), *The professional practice of rehabilitation counseling* (pp. 339–370). New York, NY: Springer Publishing Company.

Tarvydas, V. M., & Cottone, R. R. (1991). Ethical responses to legislative, organizational, and economic dynamics: A four-level model of ethical practice. *Journal of Applied Rehabilitation Counseling, 22*(4), 11–18.

Tarvydas, V., Vazquez-Ramos, R., & Estrada-Hernandez, N. (2015). Applied participatory ethics: Bridging the social justice chasm between counselor and client. *Counseling & Values, 60*(2), 218–233.

Taylor, C. B., Agras, W. S., Losch, M., Plante, T. G., & Burnett, K. (1991). Improving the effectiveness of computer-assisted weight loss. *Behavior Therapy, 22*(2), 229–236.

Taylor, L., & Adelman, H. (1989). Reframing the confidentiality dilemma to work in children's best interests. *Professional Psychology: Research and Practice, 20*, 79–83.

Thomas, V. (1994). Value analysis: A model of personal and professional ethics in marriage and family counseling. *Counseling and Values, 38*, 193–202.

Thomas, R. V., & Pender, D. A. (2008). Association of specialists in group work: Best practices guidelines 2007 revisions. *Journal for Specialist in Group Work, 33*, 111–117. doi:10.1080/01933920801971184

Thompson, A. (1990). *Guide to ethical practice in psychotherapy*. New York, NY: Wiley.

Thompson, C. L., & Rudolph, L. B. (2000). *Counseling children* (5th ed.). Pacific Grove, CA: Brooks/Cole.

Thompson, I. A., Amatea, E. S., & Thompson, E. S. (2014). Personal and contextual predictors of mental health counselors' compassion fatigue and burnout. *Journal of Mental Health Counseling, 36*(1), 58–77.

Thoreson, R. W., Shaughnessy, P., & Frazier, P. A. (1995). Sexual contact during and after professional relationships: Practices and attitudes of female counselors. *Journal of Counseling & Development, 74*, 84–89.

Thoreson, R. W., Shaughnessy, P., Heppner, P. P., & Cook, S. W. (1993). Sexual contact during and after the professional relationship: Attitudes and practices of male counselors. *Journal of Counseling & Development, 71*, 429–434.

Tjelveit, A. C. (1986). The ethics of value conversion in psychotherapy: Appropriate and inappropriate therapist influence on client values. *Clinical Psychology Review, 6*, 515–537.

Tomm, K. (1993). *Dual relationships: Sex, power, and exploitation* [Audiotape cassette recording]. AAMFT luncheon plenary (Call: 1-800-241-7785). AAMFT Resource Link, Norcross, GA.

Tompkins, L., & Mehring, T. (1993). Client privacy and the school counselor: Privilege, ethics, and employer policies. *The School Counselor, 40*, 335–342.

U.S. Department of Health and Human Services. (1994). *Confidentiality of patient records for alcohol and other drug treatment* (Technical Assistance Publication [TAP] Series 13). Rockville, MD: Author.

U.S. Department of Health and Human Services. (1996). *Checklist for monitoring alcohol and other drug confidentiality compliance* (Technical Assistance Publication [TAP] Series 18). Rockville, MD: Author.

Van Hoose, W. H., & Kottler, J. A. (1985). *Ethical and legal issues in counseling and psychotherapy* (2nd ed.). San Francisco, CA: Jossey-Bass.

VandeCreek, L., & Knapp, S. (1993). *Tarasoff and beyond: Legal and clinical considerations in the treatment of life-endangering patients* (2nd ed.). Sarasota, FL: Professional Resource Press.

Varhely, S. C., & Cowles, J. (1991). Counselor self-awareness and client confidentiality: A relationship revisited. *Elementary School Guidance and Counseling, 25*, 269–276.

Vasquez, M. J. T. (1988). Counselor-client sexual contact: Implications for ethics training. *Journal of Counseling & Development, 67*, 238–241.

Vasquez, M. J. T. (1996). Will virtue ethics improve ethical conduct in multicultural settings and interactions? *The Counseling Psychologist, 24*, 98–104.

Vesper, J. H., & Brock, G. (1991). *Ethics, legalities, and professional practice issues in marriage and family therapy.* Needham Heights, MA: Allyn & Bacon.

von Foerster, H. (1984). On constructing a reality. In P. Watzlawick (Ed.), *The invented reality* (pp. 41–61). New York, NY: W. W. Norton.

von Glasersfeld, E. (1984). An introduction to radical constructivism. In P. Watzlawick (Ed.), *The invented reality* (pp. 17–40). New York, NY: W. W. Norton.

Wagman, M. (1980). PLATO DCS: An interactive computer system for personal counseling. *Journal of Counseling Psychology, 27*, 16–30.

Wagman, M. (1988). *Computer psychotherapy systems.* New York, NY: Gordon and Breach Science.

Wagman, M., & Kerber, K. W. (1980). PLATO DCS, an interactive computer system for personal counseling: Further development and evaluation. *Journal of Counseling Psychology, 27*, 31–39.

Walden, S. L., Herlihy, B., & Ashton, L. (2003). The evolution of ethics: Personal Perspectives of ACA Ethics Committee chairs. *Journal of Counseling & Development, 81*, 106–110.

Waldmann, A. K., & Blackwell T. L. (2010). Advocacy and accessibility standards in the new "Code of Professional Ethics for Rehabilitation Counselors." *Rehabilitation Counseling Bulletin, 53*, 232–236. doi:10.1177/0034355210368866

Waldo, S. L., & Malley, P. (1992). Tarasoff and its progeny: Implications for the school counselor. *The School Counselor, 40*, 46–54.

Walker, M. M., & Larrabee, M. J. (1985). Ethics and school records. *Elementary School Guidance and Counseling, 19*, 210–216.

Wall, J. E. (2000). Technology-delivered assessment: Power, problems, and promise. In J. W. Bloom & G. R. Walz (Eds.), *Cybercounseling and cyberlearning: Strategies and resources for the millennium* (pp. 237–251). Alexandria, VA: American Counseling Association.

Walters, O. S. (1958). Metaphysics, religion, and psychotherapy. *Journal of Counseling Psychology, 5*, 243–252.

Walz, G. R. (1996). Using the I-Way for career development. In R. Feller & G. Walz (Eds.), *Optimizing life transitions in turbulent times: Exploring work, learning and careers* (pp. 415–427). Greensboro, NC: University of North Carolina, ERIC Clearinghouse on Counseling and Student Services.

Weiss, D. J. (1985). Adaptive testing by computer. *Journal of Consulting and Clinical Psychology, 53*, 774–789.

Weiss, S. J. & Davis, H. P. (1985). Validity and reliability of the collaborative practice scale. *Nursing Research, 34*, 299–305.

Welfel, E. R. (1998). *Ethics in counseling and psychotherapy: Standards, research, and emerging issues.* Pacific Grove, CA: Brooks/Cole.

Welfel, E. R. (2002). *Ethics in counseling and psychotherapy: Standards, research, and emerging issues* (2nd ed.). Pacific Grove, CA: Brooks/Cole.

Welfel, E. R. (2006). *Ethics in counseling and psychotherapy: Standards, research, and emerging issues* (3rd ed.). Belmont, CA: Thomson Brooks/Cole.

Welkowitz, J., Cohen, J., & Ortmeyer, D. (1967). Value system similarities: Investigation of patient/therapist dyads. *Journal of Consulting Psychology, 31*(1), 48–55.

Wheeler, A. M. N., & Bertram, B. (2015). *The counselor and the law: A guide to legal and ethical practice* (7th ed.). Alexandria, VA: American Counseling Association.

Whitson, S. C., & Sexton, T. L. (1998). A review of school counseling outcome research: Implications for practice. *Journal of Counseling & Development, 76*, 412–426.

Wilcoxon, S. A., & Magnuson, S. (1999). Considerations for school counselors serving noncustodial parents: Premises and suggestions. *Professional School Counseling, 2,* 275–280.

Wilcoxon, S. A., Remley, T. P., & Gladding, S. T. (2012). *Ethical, legal, and professional issues in the practice of family therapy.* Upper Saddle River, NJ: Pearson.

Wiles, J. (1993). *Socialization and interpersonal influence on the ethical decision-making climate in service organizations* (Unpublished dissertation). University of Memphis, Memphis, TN.

Wilson, C. A., Rubin, S. E., & Millard, R. P. (1991). Preparing rehabilitation educators to deal with ethical dilemmas. *Journal of Applied Rehabilitation Counseling, 22*(1), 30–33.

Wise, S., & Plake, B. S. (1990). Computerized testing in higher education. *Measurement and Evaluation in Counseling and Development, 23,* 3–10.

Wittgenstein, L. (1958). *Philosophical investigations.* New York, NY: Macmillan. (Original work published 1953)

Woody, R. H. (1989). *Business success in mental health practice.* San Francisco, CA: Jossey-Bass.

Younggren, J. N., & Gottlieb, M. C. (2004). Managing risks when contemplating multiple relationships. *Professional Psychology: Research and Practice, 35,* 255–260.

Youngjohn, J. R., Larrabee, G. J., & Crook, T. H. (1991). First-last names and the grocery list selective reminding test: Two computerized measures of everyday verbal learning. *Archives of Clinical Neuropsychology, 6,* 287–300.

Zambo, R., Zambo, D., Buss, R. R., Perry, J. A., & Williams, T. R. (2014). Seven years after the call: Students' and graduates' perceptions of the re-envisioned Ed.D. *Innovative Higher Education, 39*(2), 123–137. doi:10.1007/s10755-013-9262-3

Zingaro, J. C. (1983). Confidentiality: To tell or not to tell. *Elementary School Guidance and Counseling, 17,* 261–267.

# INDEX

CPSIA information can be obtained
at www.ICGtesting.com
Printed in the USA
LVHW010210181218
600779LV00008B/142